THE KING WHO HAD TO GO

THE KING WHO HAD TO GO

*Edward VIII, Mrs Simpson and the
Hidden Politics of the Abdication Crisis*

ADRIAN PHILLIPS

Biteback Publishing

First published in Great Britain in 2016 by
Biteback Publishing Ltd
Westminster Tower
3 Albert Embankment
London SE1 7SP
Copyright © Adrian Phillips 2016

ISBN 978-1-78590-025-9

10 9 8 7 6 5 4 3 2 1

A CIP catalogue record for this book is available from the British Library.

Set in Bulmer by Adrian McLaughlin

Printed and bound in Great Britain by
CPI Group (UK) Ltd, Croydon CR0 4YY

To the memory of my parents: Alice and Julius

CONTENTS

ACKNOWLEDGEMENTS

THIS BOOK HAS taken an unusually long time to write as it gradually evolved from one focused on the top-level machinery of British government in the 1930s to one that examines a single episode, so I owe my thanks to a correspondingly long list of individuals and organisations who have helped me on the way.

Professor Nick Crowson of Birmingham University took me on as graduate student and shared his immense knowledge of the period as well as introducing me properly to the study of history. The late Sir Martin Gilbert provided limitless inspiration and encouragement when I pursued my research into Sir Horace Wilson. Professor Eunan O'Halpin of Trinity College, Dublin and Professor George Peden of Stirling University guided me through the higher reaches of the British Civil Service. Michael Jago steered me through the intricacies of Labour Party politics. John Campbell shared his huge knowledge of David Lloyd George as well as his generous support and hospitality. Julian Hardinge (Lord Hardinge of Penshurst) very helpfully challenged some of my early preconceptions. My former colleague Bernard (Lord) Donoughue explained clearly the importance of power geography at 10 Downing Street. The opinions and judgements expressed in the book are, of course, entirely my own.

I am especially grateful to a number of individuals who have allowed me access to papers still in their personal possession: Lord and the late

Lady Crathorne, who received me most hospitably at Yarm; the Honourable Lady Murray, her son Alex and her nephew Lord Hardinge for the diary of Helen, Lady Hardinge; and Mrs Annie Pollock, who very kindly showed me the papers of her grandfather, Sir Warren Fisher.

My thanks go to everyone at the following archives who assisted me in my research: the Churchill Archives Centre, most especially Andrew Riley, who has been unstinting with his time, efforts and advice; the BBC Written Archives Centre, with special thanks to Jeff Walden; the Cadbury Research Library: Special Collections at the University of Birmingham, in particular Sue Worrall and Ivana Frlan; the Reuters archive, practically synonymous with John Entwistle; the Bank of England Archives with special thanks to Rachael Muir; Balliol College, Oxford, in particular Anna Sander; the Local Studies Library at Aberdeen in the person of David Oswald; the National Archives at Kew; Bundesarchiv, Koblenz; The House of Lords Record Office: Special Collections at the University Library, Cambridge; and the RAF Museum, Hendon. Terry Mace's help was invaluable for the photo of the King's aeroplane.

The following individuals and institutions have kindly granted me permission to use material under their control: Lord Norwich for his father's diary; Lord Crathorne for his parents' papers; the Honourable Lady Murray and Lord Hardinge for the papers of Helen, Lady Hardinge and her *Loyal to Three Kings*; the BBC Written Archives Centre for Sir John Reith's diaries; the Cadbury Research Library: Special Collections, the University of Birmingham for Neville Chamberlain's papers; and the Parliamentary Archives for material from the Beaverbrook papers. The quotations from the writings of Sir Winston Churchill are reproduced with the permission of Curtis Brown, London on behalf of the Estate of Winston S. Churchill. © The Estate of Winston S. Churchill. Every effort has been made to trace copyright holders and to obtain their permission for the use of copyright material. The author apologises for any errors or omissions in the above list and would be grateful if notified of any corrections that should be incorporated in future reprints or editions of this book.

Mrs Jackie Holland sang to me most beautifully the snatch of playground doggerel about Mrs Simpson that she remembered from 1936, and her daughter, Jane Holland, very kindly transcribed it. Mrs Vanessa Donegan made good my ignorance of tactics in contract bridge. Mme Gautier of the Domaine de Candé provided me with the programme of music played at the Duke of Windsor's wedding to Wallis Warfield (as she had very briefly become again) and M. Proust of Tours Cathedral introduced me to the splendours of the Skinner organ at Candé and explained the intricacies of playing it.

Laurie De Decker, my editor at Biteback, whipped my manuscript into shape and introduced me to the previously unfamiliar world of the comma. She and everyone else at Biteback gently guided me through the process of bringing my first book from outline to publication.

Lastly, this book would not have been possible without the help of my wife Sheila, whom I wish to thank for her advice, patience and support.

PROLOGUE

ON THURSDAY 10 December 1936, the British Prime Minister Stanley Baldwin was hurrying to prepare for one of the most important speeches of his political life and one of the most vital speeches ever delivered to the House of Commons. He had to explain how and why King Edward VIII was abdicating after a reign of only eleven months. In January, Edward had become King in the midst of hopes that this glamorous, charming and handsome figure would usher in a new style of monarchy in Britain. After the Victorian-era austerity of his father, George V, he had appeared open and modern. Instead, there had been a worldwide scandal and finally an agonising crisis that had played out in semi-privacy for months before the British press had broken its self-imposed silence the previous Wednesday, catapulting the affair into the full glare of public knowledge and concern. For a week, the whole country had stared into the abyss of a constitutional crisis.

Time was short for Baldwin because the King's final and irrevocable decision had only been taken late the evening before. More for the sake of form than anything, the Cabinet had sent the King a message imploring him to reconsider his intention, but he had not and had signed the Instrument of Abdication that morning at his private house, Fort Belvedere, in the grounds of Windsor Castle. Now Baldwin had to give final confirmation to Parliament and the world beyond, that what had been rumoured and feared for months, weeks and days had finally occurred. Even that morning the newspaper headlines in London had only spoken of the possibility of abdication. Baldwin had to find a way of presenting the bitter reality in a way that minimised the damage and somehow overcame the hurt of those traumatic days. The monarchy was the sacred institution that bound the people of Britain and cemented an Empire that spanned the globe, but its sovereign had decided that he could not carry on because he was not permitted to marry the woman he loved. If Baldwin were to say the wrong thing, the results might be catastrophic. Few had questioned his handling of the crisis whilst it was in progress, but now that it had culminated in the terrible conclusion of abdication, there might be deep and savage recriminations and aftershocks. The leader of the opposition Labour Party had had to fight down the temptation elsewhere in his party to make tactical capital out of the crisis, and Oswald Mosley's British Union of Fascists had campaigned to keep Edward on the throne.

Baldwin worked on his speech entirely alone. The one thing he had to guide him was a log of the day-to-day events of the crisis prepared for him by his civil service right-hand man, Sir Horace Wilson.[1] A modern Prime Minister would have an army of expert advisers analysing every syllable of such a speech, and modern technology would prepare an immaculate text that could be disseminated around the globe at the push of a button. Baldwin relied solely on his own judgement for the words to achieve the near impossible, and scribbled his thoughts on untidy slips of paper. Even by the standards of the day, they did not look impressive; Harold Nicolson, a fastidious and aristocratic government MP, thought they were like pieces of toilet paper '…more squalid than a young Labour candidate would dare produce at a Wapping by-election'.[2] It was not just the appearance of the notes that betrayed the stress of the moment. As Baldwin moved around 10 Downing Street in distracted concentration, he dropped some of the slips in the passageways. When he finally set off for the House of Commons, he completely forgot to bring the notes with him, and his parliamentary private secretary, Tommy Dugdale, had to dash back to retrieve them.

Beneath the bluff exterior of a member of the traditional, unreflecting

Tory squirearchy that he cultivated assiduously, Baldwin was a highly strung and nervous man, and this was all too obvious to the people around him and who knew him well. It was especially acute before he had to make a major speech. At the other end of the scale, one of his Cabinet ministers told the story of a French woman, who did not know who Baldwin was or what he did, and who had instantly assumed from his demeanour that he was an actor.[3] He had an actor's focus on the upcoming performance and the same irrational dread of actually delivering it. Baldwin had operated at the top level of politics for a decade and a half, and he was an accomplished speaker, who cloaked his art in apparent simplicity. He knew that it was a great gift and that he would need it for his speech that afternoon. It would help him accomplish one last act of public service, with which he could draw the curtain on his career in politics. Baldwin had a strong but usually well-hidden tendency towards self-dramatisation, but it was very much in evidence that day. 'This is making history, and I'm the only man who can do it,' he told Dugdale, who observed him switching on his oratorical power as the crucial moment arrived: 'All his power surges to the surface, his retiring humility leaves him.'[4]

The House of Commons was still working its way through an ordinary day's business when Baldwin arrived. The loss of its monarch was not going to be allowed to disrupt the day-to-day work of running the country. This had even provided some grim light relief for MPs with an eye for life's ironies when the order paper for the day included the first reading of 'The Edinburgh Maternity and Simpson Charity Bill' and 'The Family Inheritance Bill. Mr. Windsor'.[5] The chamber was packed to capacity for what would otherwise have been a routine, weekly Question Time. It would now witness an event that no one wanted to miss. One MP observed pedantically that this was the first abdication in Britain for 537 years.[6] Even on this momentous day, there were no concessions for the Prime Minister in the democratic discomfort of the overcrowded chamber. He had to squeeze past the knees of his colleagues to get to his seat.[7] The mood amongst the MPs had been one of subdued tension as they waited for this moment, and they cheered Baldwin as he made his way to his place.

There were final moments of comedy and scene-setting to come. Baldwin had to fumble for the keys to his briefcase before he could extract his scruffy notes and, in dramatic contrast, immaculate sheets of the highest-quality paper marked with the unmistakable red, royal crest, which bore the sombre message from the King. Baldwin had barely time to spread the notes on the Despatch Box in front of him – 'rather proudly', Nicolson thought – when normality reasserted itself. There was one final mundane question left for a minister to answer; it was a mind-numbingly dull and trivial enquiry as to how many of the personnel of the Royal Navy had been punished by civilian courts, but it had to be answered.[8] The First Lord of the Admiralty, the unpopular and widely distrusted Sir Samuel Hoare, strode 'pompously' to the Despatch Box, on which he in turn spread the papers he needed to deliver an appropriately dull reply. He finished and lifted the Admiralty papers, scattering Baldwin's notes to the floor. The Prime Minister had to scrabble to retrieve them. His daughter Lorna whispered to Dugdale's wife, who had secured one of the visitor's tickets that had become as valuable as gold-dust and was sitting next to her in the gallery, 'Poor father, that's just like him. He's so clumsy, he's dropped things all his life.'[9]

From then on, the mood was one of deep seriousness. Baldwin walked to the end of the chamber where the Speaker of the House sat, and handed to him on his high dais the message from the King. As the Speaker read out the few paragraphs in which Edward renounced a task which he felt he could not perform efficiently or to his own satisfaction, emotion welled up in the packed chamber. The Speaker himself could not conceal his own emotion, and his voice quavered. Even hardened parliamentarians had to stifle their sobs. Nicolson reflected, 'I have never known in any assembly such accumulation of pity and terror.'[10]

The moment had arrived for Baldwin to explain how things had ended this way and to start the process of bringing the nation back to an even keel. The performance he delivered was a masterpiece, but like so many masterpieces, it disguised its supreme artistry under a cloak of the utmost simplicity. He admitted that he had had little time to compose his speech,

'...so I must tell what I have to tell truthfully, sincerely and plainly with no attempt to dress up or to adorn'.[11] The members of one of London's gentlemen's clubs were reading the words as they came over the news ticker and contrived to snigger at the idea that truthfulness was a by-product of time pressure, but this did not strike the MPs, who were already in the palm of Baldwin's hand.[12] As he had promised, he delivered a plain account of the events in an even tone with no trace of drama or rhetorical flourish. He even made a capital from the disorder that Hoare had wrought on his notes by pausing every now and again to make sure that the dates he was quoting were correct, occasionally asking the Home Secretary sitting next to him for advice. These asides were so effective that Nicolson mused whether they could have been scripted. The speech was delivered with 'artless but consummate skill' and the whole House listened spellbound to the 'tragic force of its simplicity'.[13] By the time he got to the last few paragraphs many were near tears, but he was heard in perfect, rapt attention until the cheers that greeted his call to rally behind the new King at the very end of his speech.

In reality, there was far more to Baldwin's speech than a mechanical recital of dates and events. His linear narrative provided the framework for a careful and astute choice of deeper content. Above all, Baldwin had seen the simple but vital need to be as kind about the King as possible. It was not the moment for criticism of any sort. Throughout the speech, Baldwin paid 'tribute after tribute' to the King. At every turn, Edward had done what was best for the country and the Empire. There was only the supremely delicate matter of explaining why the King was abdicating. The previous Sunday had been one of the most fraught and darkest moments of the crisis, and Baldwin had been turning over in his mind what he should say if the worst came to the worst. It had come to him in a blinding flash:

> I have got the speech I mean to make and I am certain I can get it across.
> I shall begin this is not a story of conflict between the King & the Cabinet or between crown & the people that I have to unfold; it is the story of conflicting loyalties in a human heart.[14]

The King had had to struggle between two conflicting loyalties and that was all he needed to say about the forces taking him from the throne. It did not need to be spelled out that the loyalties were irreconcilable because the King could not be allowed to marry a woman with two living husbands. Mixed in with the flood of compliments about the King, Baldwin added a couple of rapier thrusts at the handful of men who were thought to have tried to exploit the crisis to their own ends. The criticism was neatly placed in the King's own mouth: 'Any idea to him of what might be called a King's Party, was abhorrent.' The King was alert to the danger 'that there might be sides taken and factions grow up in a matter where no faction ought to exist'. These were, of course, views to which Baldwin and his government fully subscribed.

Baldwin emphasised over and over again that there had been no conflict, that the matter had been settled in friendly and open conversations between the King and him as Prime Minister without a trace of disagreement or conflict. Once again, Baldwin was able to find the vital words in what the King had said to him: 'You and I must settle this together. I will not have anyone interfering.' Throughout the crisis, Baldwin had stuck to the crucial principle that, whatever happened, it would have to be the King's decision. Six days previously, he had faced a Cabinet meeting riven by fears of a dark conspiracy to engineer a full-blown constitutional crisis, but he had insisted that '[h]e did not want to put a Pistol at the head of the King'.[15] Baldwin could – and did – state that he had only asked to see the King on a single occasion during the crisis. Even that admission was wrapped up in a humdrum tale of finding a mutually convenient date for the conversation. Otherwise, it had been the King who took the initiative. In the final stages of the crisis, the accusation had lurked a little beneath the surface that the government was putting pressure on the King. This had to be deflected, whatever truth might lie behind it. The one aspect of the speech that was widely criticised was Baldwin's frequent mentions of his own role in the crisis. This might have been egotism, but it was also accurate. Not only did Baldwin feel that he himself was making history, but he had also made certain that it was only he who had handled the government's end of the affair – above all, the dialogue with the King.

The speech succeeded magnificently, 'the most impressive and persuasive that Baldwin ever made', in the words of one Cabinet minister, and 'a supreme example of his artistry'.[16] Tributes streamed in from every side, but to Baldwin they were only the confirmation of something that his actor's instinct had told him already. He knew that he had crowned his entire political career. Nicolson detected 'that intoxication that comes to a man, even a tired man, after a triumphant success' when Baldwin told him: '"Yes, it was a success I know it. It was almost wholly unprepared. I had a success, my dear Nicolson, at the moment I most needed it. *Now is the time to go*."'[17] He had not just steered the country though an existential crisis, but he had found the right words and the right tone to set out what had happened to put the whole episode behind it. Within months, if not weeks, Edward was fading from people's memories. Many, if not most, people close to the action wrote accounts of something they sensed would be the most dramatic event in their lives, but this is a mark of how rapidly the crisis was being swallowed into history. The debate itself was closed. It shows the effectiveness of Baldwin's performance in the House of Commons that his narrative has stood the test of time and has never seriously been questioned. The lines that he drew under the events of the crisis have held. Over the years since, further, sometimes very important, details have emerged, but if anything, they have been felt to confirm the basic truth of what Baldwin said that day.

Baldwin's speech was not merely a triumph in itself, it was a stunning turnaround in his own fortunes. In the year before the crisis, Baldwin's premiership had been in deep trouble. He was widely criticised for the poor handling of a series of diplomatic episodes beginning with the Hoare–Laval affair, in which the Foreign Secretary had resigned as a scapegoat for a clumsy and cynical attempt to do a deal with France condoning Fascist Italy's invasion of Abyssinia. The government's temporising responses to Nazi remilitarisation of the Rhineland and the outbreak of civil war in Spain were equally unimpressive. Baldwin had contrived to appear both dishonest and uncommitted over Britain's modest rearmament programme. The economy's recovery from the Great Slump was still painfully slow.

A popular minister had been forced to resign over a leak of Budget secrets. By the previous summer, Baldwin had been on the verge of a nervous breakdown and had taken a rest-cure of two months, almost completely cut off from his duties.

One man who would have been delighted to know that Baldwin had told Nicolson that it was time for him to go was Neville Chamberlain, the Chancellor of the Exchequer and de facto Baldwin's deputy. Like so many politicians in his position, he spent his days fuming at what he disliked in the way the Prime Minister did the job, and yearning for the day when he could take over and do it properly. He acknowledged grudgingly that Baldwin 'had reaped a rich harvest of credit which has carried him to the pinnacle of his career'.[18] Chamberlain was vain and resented praise of Baldwin. He had peevishly predicted that Baldwin would 'acquire great kudos, some of which he will have earned'.[19] It was a telling qualification; Chamberlain would not have been happy that Baldwin appeared to take the whole credit for bringing the crisis safely to its conclusion. He felt that he had been instrumental in prodding Baldwin into action and he had certainly been the consistent champion of vigorous action inside government.

Another of the MPs listening to Baldwin was in deep misery, not just at the loss of the King but at the wreckage of his own prospects. The week before Baldwin's speech, Winston Churchill had appeared to be poised, finally, to bring his political career back on track after the long miserable years of the early 1930s, when his successive misjudgements had taken him out of government and to the fringes of mainstream politics. The previous Thursday, he had been the dominant figure at a huge public meeting in the Albert Hall, which launched a campaign under the name of 'The Arms and the Covenant', embracing the whole political spectrum in a call for determined rearmament by Britain to give teeth to the League of Nations' feeble resistance to the fascist dictators. Had all gone well, it would have finally alerted the British people to the danger of these dictators and the need to draw back from the anti-war instincts that had ruled their hearts since the slaughter of the First World War, and for which Baldwin had been so effective a spokesman. But Churchill had ruined his moment. Driven by a combination of genuine sympathetic loyalty to the King and unreflecting opportunism, he had been the only political heavyweight to break with the government's line on handling the crisis. It had been a disaster. The King had sought his help the previous Friday evening, but had completely ignored the trenchant advice which Churchill had given. Even worse, when Churchill had spoken in the House of Commons on the Tuesday evening, pleading for the King to be given more time to consider his position, he had been shouted down and unable to finish his speech. He had 'undone in five minutes the patient reconstruction work of two years'.[20] Afterwards, he was so depressed that he told a friend that his political career was over.

By Thursday, Churchill knew that he was fighting for his political survival. He sat hunched through Baldwin's speech, anxious that the Prime Minister might hammer the final nail into his coffin.[21] After the leaders of the other major parties had delivered their pieces, endorsing Baldwin's words, Churchill rose to speak to a House still seething with indignation and hostility for what some in government saw as outright gangsterish behaviour during the crisis. To many MPs, Baldwin's reference to an abhorrent King's Party was aimed squarely at Churchill and his associates. This time, Churchill judged the mood of his fellow MPs correctly and, in the words of one of them who had criticised him savagely a few days before, '…in an admirably phrased little speech executed a strategical retreat'.[22] It was just enough, and another MP, who was better disposed towards Churchill, thought he had '…regained a good deal of the sympathy he had lost'.[23] But the strategic damage had been done. Any hopes that he would soon lead a movement that brought Britain round to robust opposition to Hitler were fading. The French Embassy in London, ever alert for its national security, confessed it was 'worried at his loss of ground'.[24]

Churchill's unintended act of political suicide had not helped the King in any way, but it had sparked the only noticeable wobble in the government's handling of the crisis. Before speaking to Churchill on the Friday evening, the King had asked the Prime Minister's permission to do so, or at least told him that he was going to do so in a way that, just, gave Baldwin an opportunity to protest. Baldwin did nothing and let the meeting take place, but the following morning he seemed to have had second thoughts. He said to Sir Horace Wilson, 'I have made my first blunder', and when he went into a Cabinet meeting soon afterwards, he said the same thing to his colleagues.[25] Wilson and the assembled ministers successively hastened to assure Baldwin that he was wrong to say so and had done the right thing, doubtless as Baldwin had wanted them to say. This episode stayed in people's minds even though the fear that seemed to have taken hold of Baldwin proved to have been unjustified; Churchill's intervention never for a moment threatened to derail the government's handling and, in fact, diminished him as a political opponent. However insincere it might have been, Baldwin's confession that he had made a mistake gave a glimpse of the self-doubt that anyone carrying his level of responsibility could not help feeling, operating as he was in a situation where a false move could have had calamitous consequences. Duff Cooper, the War Minister, had probably been more deeply involved in the crisis as a personal friend of the King. He joined the throng offering his congratulations to Baldwin on his speech, but also felt that he should assure him personally '…how right you were to agree to the King seeing Winston'. Baldwin was so swept away in the ecstasy of triumph that he let the mask of pretence slip and he hinted to Duff Cooper at the internal battles he had had to fight. He laughed 'very knowingly' and told Duff Cooper, 'I never doubted that I was right for a minute. I am only a simple lad, you know, Duff, but there were reasons why I thought it best to put it to the Cabinet in the way I did.'[26] Not only had Baldwin had to juggle with all the King's problems, but he had also had to manage ministers and his civil service entourage. This gentle confession had barely left his lips when Baldwin realised that he had overstepped a line: 'But suddenly he felt that he had gone too far, the laugh faded, and he hurried on down the corridor in solemn silence.'[27] As far as Baldwin was concerned, the internal battles that he had had to fight during the crisis were now to be consigned to the dustbin of history; they were wounds that should be left to heal themselves. And so they were for a long time afterwards.

HIDDEN
SCANDAL

CHAPTER 1

THE BOY WILL RUIN HIMSELF

After I am dead the boy will ruin himself in twelve months
GEORGE V TO STANLEY BALDWIN[1]

T O THE OUTSIDE world Edward, Prince of Wales and future King Edward VIII, had the air of a golden boy. He was youthful, good-looking and glamorous, a keen sportsman and pilot. He had devastating charm, which melted even hardened observers. He appeared open and engaged. He was the first member of the royal family to have extensive direct contact with the public in Britain and abroad; he became the first celebrity royal. There was no trace of social consciousness in his contacts with people across the whole class spectrum and he had obvious and genuine sympathy for the many people still suffering from the deep economic problems of interwar Britain. He felt a special affinity with the huge number of men who had fought in the First World War. He embraced all things American – then even more than today the benchmark for the modern society. As an eligible bachelor, he exercised a powerful fascination at a human level. He talked freely, easily and without any apparent condescension. He was a clear contrast to the stern and conservative image of his father, King George V. He seemed like a breath of fresh air.

Edward's shining public image masked a far less happy picture in his family. His father clung firmly to the norms of the Victorian era into which he had been born – stern, formal and conservative – and this coloured his ideas of education. His oft-quoted dictum 'My father was afraid of his mother; I was afraid of my father and I am damned well going to make sure that my children are afraid of me' is probably apocryphal, but he treated his sons with the same strict discipline that he had applied to his crew when he was a Royal Navy officer. This was fairly common for the period, but it left him with no serious adult relationship with any of them. The failure was most conspicuous with Edward, who chafed against his father's attempts to impose his will. The question of dress was a particular bone of contention, outwardly trivial but symbolic of two widely different world views. George V was obsessed with a dress code of great complexity and formality that he himself followed as though it were Holy Writ and which he wanted Edward to follow with the same devotion. He never tired of criticising Edward – often publicly – for breaking the rules, even in inconspicuous details. He also objected to his son's choice of friends and courtiers, notably the Irish cavalryman 'Fruity' Metcalfe, whom he held responsible for Edward's dangerously aggressive horse riding.[2]

At the heart of their disagreement lay a very fundamental point. Edward could not accept that his royal status demanded a full-time vocation. Like a reluctant salaried worker, he divided his life into his job, where he was subject to some constraints, and his private life, where he was subject to none. He aspired to be a royal during the week, but an entirely private individual at the weekend. Whilst other members of the royal family were driven by a strong sense of duty to perform their work, he often seemed to do it grudgingly and under complaint. Again his father was at least partly to blame for giving Edward practically no choice but to undertake gruelling tours of the Empire, notably one to India which he disliked greatly.

Edward's touring programme was something of a double-edged weapon. He was widely received with mass, near-hysterical adulation. It was a personal triumph especially when he responded well, but like many celebrities he failed to understand the fickleness of the sentiments behind the reaction.

Worse, as the years went on he came to take a good reception for granted and, admittedly often out of tiredness as well, behaved perfunctorily and unpunctually. This was noticed. As Prime Minister, David Lloyd George had taken the Prince's side against his father over the India journey in the early 1920s, but by 1934 had to take him firmly in hand to prevent him offending the people of Caernarfon with his cavalier behaviour.[3]

Edward's private life also dismayed his father. It was in distinct contrast to George V's marriage to the formidable Mary of Teck, which was irreproachably faithful and also the product of what seemed like the dynastic calculations of a bygone age. She had been his elder brother's fiancée, but George had unhesitatingly married her when his brother died. She adopted the same credo of unflinching respect for royal duty as her husband. Edward remained obstinately a bachelor and this seemed to his parents a great missed opportunity. There was a simple pragmatic aspect to the question: the lack of a wife was seen widely as a distinct handicap for someone who would bear the burdens of kingship. Being the most yearned-for bachelor in the world might have fuelled the celebrity hysteria around Edward, but marriage might have brought more solid benefits. Successful marriages had dramatically improved the lives of two of George V's younger sons, as well as giving a powerful boost to the public image of the royal family. The Duke of York had married a strong and loyal woman from the upper reaches of Britain's aristocracy, who did much to rescue him from the handicaps of a crippling stammer, a violent temper and a deep sense of his own inferiority. The marriage had also ensured the royal succession with a pair of healthy and attractive daughters. The Duke of Kent's marriage to the glamorous Princess Marina marked a clear turn away from the sexual promiscuity and drug-taking of his youth.

By contrast, Edward's personal life was the source of potential scandal or even worse that lay beneath the glamorous bachelor image. One affair in particular offered a dire warning of the dangers. As an officer in the Grenadier Guards on the Western Front during the First World War he had conducted a lengthy liaison with Marguerite Alibert, a superior Parisian prostitute, to whom he wrote ardent love letters, which she held onto with the habitual foresight of her profession. She went on to marry an Egyptian prince but, in 1923, she shot him dead in London. She was acquitted of murder and there is some evidence that she was able to buy the verdict by handing over these letters.[4] Had any hint of the relationship between Edward and Marguerite reached the wider public at the time of her trial, the scandal would have been immense, and infinitely worse had any part of the story emerged of how his letters had been retrieved. After the war, his behaviour calmed down somewhat, but he was stuck on the sexual merry-go-round of the shiftless upper classes, vividly depicted in the plays of Noël Coward and novels of Evelyn Waugh. Through the 1920s, he maintained a long-term and discreet affair with Mrs Freda Dudley Ward, the wife of an MP. It provided him with a degree of stability but did not deter him from a string of casual seductions, often undertaken with a flagrant lack of discretion. In 1930, Edward had replaced Mrs Ward with the American-born Lady Furness in another illicit but entirely conventional relationship. His father was so upset at this latest sign that his heir had no plans to conform to conventional notions of family life that he tried a long man-to-man conversation with his son in 1932. George V warned him that the revelation of his adulterous affairs would hurt his popularity and tried to convince him of the advantages of marriage. George V overreached himself and took Edward to task for his social circle as well. Afterwards, Edward claimed to accept that his father's strictures on his private life were fair, but resented deeply his remarks on his personal friends. He continued as before on both the sexual and friendship fronts. Thereafter, his father had lapsed into gloomy predictions of the damage that his son would wreak when he succeeded to the throne.

Edward's private life did not improve. In 1934, he had acquired another long-term girlfriend, who was several steps down from her predecessors in almost every respect. Mrs Wallis Simpson was again of American origin, of modest social and financial status. Her husband through whom she had acquired British nationality had had to apply for British nationality himself and abandon American citizenship in order to serve in the British Army. Worst of all, she was already a divorcee. In 1930s Britain, divorce carried an immense social stigma; divorcees were largely excluded from the higher levels of Society and public service. The legal process of divorce was complex and expensive, in part because of the innate conservatism of Britain's legal system and in part because it served as a deterrent. Mrs Simpson's drawbacks were clear to anyone aware of the relationship. Those close to him could see that he was utterly devoted to her and coming ever further under her thumb. Gradually she was monopolising him and cutting him off from his brothers and their families. He had turned from irresponsible womanising to ardent monogamy. He was determined to marry Mrs Simpson.

He kept his intention firmly secret, but with hindsight there were clues that Edward saw a more permanent attachment. The most striking was a present he gave Mrs Simpson for Christmas in 1934. Struck by her interest in his own Cairn Terriers, Cora and Jaggs, he gave her one of her own. They called him Slipper and he became an important part of their lives. He also showered her with hugely expensive jewellery, but Slipper was almost a family member, destined to be seen as the 'principal guest at the Wedding'.[5] At around the same time he took Mrs Simpson to a palace reception to celebrate the engagement of his younger brother, even though his father had struck her name off a list of guests that he had proposed.[6] He even succeeded in introducing her to his mother. It was the only time that they were to meet.

Concern about Edward went further than distaste for his habits and attitudes; Edward's personality was so erratic that a number of responsible people thought that he was downright insane. This was exaggerated, but it was noticeable to most people close to him that his personality was somehow not fully formed. Moreover, once the crisis that led to his abdication got under way, placing him under continuous stress, there were widespread fears that he would suffer some kind of breakdown or harm himself. Oceans of ink have been drained in attempts to analyse Edward's character, but for the purposes of this story a few aspects that forcibly struck many of his contemporaries will suffice. To many he appeared never to have matured fully; his development seemed to have stopped in his early teens. His future wife, Wallis Simpson, arguably better placed than anyone to know, called him

'Peter Pan'. Edward's guiding principle seemed to be the child's instinct to push the boundaries to find out what he could 'get away with'.[7] This phrase recurs too frequently in what Edward said and wrote for it to be written off as a mere truism; it hints strongly at an inability to develop rounded adult relationships of mutual comprehension, of give and take. He was by any standards a monster of egocentricity and breathtakingly stubborn. Once he had decided on something he would not accept argument or criticism. Those around him were expected to comply blindly. Anything else was disloyalty. Like Mr Toad in *The Wind in the Willows*, he moved from one dominating enthusiasm to another, pursuing them with blind and total devotion whilst they lasted. These included, variously, horse riding, golf, gardening, drink, casual sex and, finally, something that would change his life for ever: an unreasoning obsession with one woman.

Had Edward been a wealthy aristocratic playboy and nothing more, none of this would have mattered to anyone but friends and family, but he was the heir to the throne, and in the first half of the twentieth century, the monarch played a far more important part in politics than today, even though it was very restricted and hidden to the general public. This gave a further edge to worries about Edward's flaws: the fear that he might not be up to the job. On this score his father had set him a very high benchmark as a successful constitutional monarch. To many, George V seemed a relic of the past with his country-squire style, old-fashioned dress ideas and a quaint enthusiasm for stamp collecting, but in the eyes of Britain's political and administrative elite, Edward had much to do before he matched his father. As Prince of Wales, Edward's modernistic appeal struck a chord with the young and the populace at large, but the less conspicuous merits of George V ranked higher in Westminster and Whitehall, where he was revered for his impeccable handling of the succession of grave challenges he had faced from the moment he succeeded to the throne in 1911: the constitutional crisis triggered by Lloyd George's 'People's Budget'; near-civil war in Ireland triggered by plans for Home Rule; the slaughter of the First World War; the collapse of his cousin's Russian Empire into murderous communist revolution; the, to many, terrifying innovation of Britain's first

Labour government in 1924; the collapse of the second Labour government in 1931 and the formation of a coalition government to tackle the immense economic problems that had brought it down. Any one of these might have proved fatal to the monarchy or severely damaging to the country. George V's deep-seated instinct for compromise and reconciliation was exactly what was required, and behind the scenes he strove in almost every case to apply it. Coupled with his personal rectitude, faith in the constitution and a usually sound judgement of character, this instinct had produced a pitch-perfect performance as King; his skills would one day be missed.[8]

The real power of monarchy continued to dwindle, but in 1931, its symbolic importance had been boosted. In the wake of the First World War, the old structure of the British Empire firmly run from London was no longer tenable and the Statute of Westminster had given the Dominions – Australia, Canada, New Zealand, South Africa and Southern Ireland – full legislative autonomy. They operated their own armed forces. A common allegiance to the monarch was the only formal tie that bound them. The Imperial Conference of 1932 in Ottawa had singularly failed to translate nebulous ideas of community into economic cooperation to tackle the Great Slump. The status of India was a running sore. After a bitter fight in Parliament it was to receive some autonomy, but this was only just in the process of being implemented and there was no certainty that it would satisfy the people of India, where the campaign for independence had not slackened. By the close of George V's reign the British Empire was in a fragile state and the monarch faced unprecedented challenges.

The scope for an inept successor to do damage was great. In the early 1930s, Britain faced a range of acute risks. Britain's economic recovery from the Great Slump was precarious, and elsewhere in the world extreme politics were challenging stability and democracy. Less than ten years before, the General Strike had seemed to many to portend full-scale revolution. Home-grown fascism and communism lurked on the fringes. Stable democracies were in a shrinking minority in Europe. The international situation was growing steadily more desperate with all-out war on the horizon. It was up to the professional politicians to devise ways to tackle these problems, but the sovereign would have to support them. Above all, he had to avoid compromising their efforts in any way. As well as being a decorous figurehead, Edward would probably be faced with complex and demanding political choices. He showed little promise of being as effective as his father. Whilst George V was stable (to the point of being boring) Edward was erratic; he was far too willing to speak out publicly on topics that concerned him. Perversely Edward's huge success as crowd-pleaser increased the risks. The powers that be always prefer an inconspicuous and unadventurous figurehead to one with stronger pulling power but less restraint.

On occasion Edward appeared positively to relish striking an unconventional if not downright shocking attitude on political questions, as well as expressing his views openly and indiscreetly. In 1934, he attended a grand dinner for 200 or so guests given by a City of London livery company, the Worshipful Company of Stationers and Newspaper Makers, of which he had been the Master since the previous year. It was attended by a number of diplomats and, quite conventionally, the Prince exchanged a few words with each of them when they withdrew to the smoking room after the meal. Politeness dictated that these include Ivan Maisky, the Soviet ambassador, although in the eyes of many he represented a blood-soaked tyranny that had murdered the Prince's relatives. Edward went far beyond the requirements of diplomatic etiquette and 'engaged [Maisky] in a long and inappropriately serious conversation'.[9] He insisted to the ambassador that England was devoted to peace, but went well beyond the limits usually permitted to royalty in expressing their views on the diplomatic situation by saying the same of France and, remarkably, Germany. For a quarter of an hour or so the assembled diplomats and members of the British Establishment, headed by the Archbishop of Canterbury, exchanged glances and whispers in a state of shock.

Edward was certainly no one's idea of a safe pair of hands – a few stray incidents gave a vivid foretaste of the kind of trouble he could cause if left to his own devices. As early as the late 1920s, concern had been expressed at his open sympathy for the wretched conditions of coal-miners, but these had come from mine-owners. There was far worse in 1935, when he made two speeches within three days that showed a frightening inclination to put his own stamp on foreign policy. Speaking to the British Legion, he advocated sending a delegation of members to Germany as 'there would be no more suitable body or organisation of men to stretch forth the hand of friendship to the Germans than we ex-Servicemen who fought them in the Great War and have now forgotten all about that'.[10] He was almost immediately criticised by his father for mixing in politics, especially foreign affairs, above all when his views conflicted with those of the Foreign Office.[11] Edward was quite unabashed at the furore and made it clear to the German ambassador that he had wanted to influence policy by bypassing the government and overriding 'the timidity and hesitation which ... were characteristic of politicians, [and] were much slower in achieving results than a frank word spoken at the right moment, even though it might exceed the bounds of reserve normally maintained'.[12]

As the speech coincided with a ticklish phase in the Anglo-German naval negotiations in which France was justifiably concerned that Britain might be looking after her own interest at the expense of France, it caused embarrassment on all sides. Two days later, the Prince compounded the damage with a speech at Berkhamsted School, in which he sounded downright militaristic to the extent of anticipating another war. He had been enraged by a report that the London County Council, then led by the prominent Labour politician Herbert Morrison, had forbidden the use of even wooden dummy rifles by the pupils' military cadet groups (Officer Training Corps or OTC) within its jurisdiction:

> I was met by, and inspected, a very smart guard of honour. I understand that over 70 per cent. of the school are members of the Corps. and that you have done very well in shooting. We live in very interesting times now, and it takes people with different ideas to make up a community, but it is always a mystery to me that a certain number of misguided people – I will even go as far as to call them cranks – should feel that the only way in which they can express the feeling we all have of abhorrence of war, and of the appalling distress to the whole world which another war

> would bring, is by discouraging, and if they are in authority prohibiting, any form of healthy discipline and training.[13]

The Berkhamsted speech enraged pacifist sentiment led by the veteran Labour MP George Lansbury and the British Legion speech was embarrassing enough to be discussed in Cabinet.[14] To head the Prince off from assisting the government with further exercises in personal diplomacy, the Cabinet agreed that his father should show him the minutes of the meeting so he would know the complications that he had caused.[15] George V had been very annoyed at the constitutional impropriety of the Prince's speech but he would not have objected to the underlying sentiment.[16] Far more discreetly he was lobbying the Foreign Office in favour of agreement with Germany.[17] It is not even certain whether George V passed on the government's concern, but from then on Edward abstained from further attempts at personal diplomacy.

Edward's flaws were clear to insiders from a very early stage and there was very serious concern as to whether he would be a disastrous liability when he became King. The most important of these insiders, Stanley Baldwin, was the Prime Minister during Edward's brief reign and for much of his time as Prince of Wales. Long before Mrs Simpson came on the scene Baldwin admitted these fears as vividly as a senior politician can be imagined as doing. In 1927, he accompanied Edward on a royal visit to Canada and this gave the Prince's chief courtier an opportunity discreetly to share his own doubts about him. Alan 'Tommy' Lascelles had started his long service to the royal family as private secretary to the Prince of Wales in 1920.[18] To begin with, the Prince's legendary charm had counted for far more than the huge differences in their characters and Lascelles had liked and respected his employer. Lascelles was intellectual, discreet, upright and moral; in short the epitome of a successful modern courtier; he was practically the only one of the Prince's staff who went on to very senior office in the royal household. In a few years, Lascelles had come to resent Edward's drinking, womanising and pursuit of selfish pleasure to the extent that he began to doubt seriously whether Edward was up to his duty at all.

His concerns were so severe that he nerved himself to break with rules and protocol and share them with the Prime Minister. The group were staying at Government House in Ottawa, a rambling and gloomy palace. Baldwin had a small sitting room at the end of a passage on the first floor where he agreed to meet Lascelles for a 'secret colloquy'.[19] Lascelles began by telling the Prime Minister directly that 'unless he [the Prince] mended his ways, would soon become no fit wearer of the British Crown' and finished his comments with the melodramatic confession that he thought 'the best thing that could happen to him, and to the country, would be for him to break his neck'. The Prince was a very aggressive horse rider who had already suffered a number of bad accidents, so this was not a remote possibility. Nonetheless it is a fair indication of the strain under which Lascelles had been placed that he gave way to such an outburst, for which he expected 'to get [his] head bitten off' by the Prime Minister. He was taken aback when Baldwin replied, 'God forgive me, I have often thought the same' and promised that he would 'talk straightly to the Prince at an early opportunity'. However, there is no evidence that he ever delivered on the promise.

Baldwin was not a malicious man, so it is unlikely that he actively wished harm to come to the Prince. He was just pessimistic as to whether Edward's personality would allow him to be a successful monarch, and hoped that the country would somehow be spared the consequences. There was also an element of self-interest in Baldwin's thinking. He knew that there was a fair chance that he would be Prime Minister when Edward succeeded to the throne, putting the question of his fitness or otherwise for the job to the acid test. Baldwin could see that whoever was Prime Minister would face an unprecedentedly difficult task. He might even have decided already that it was an impossible task, that there simply was no way that Edward could be brought to behave. If so, this might explain why Baldwin did not deliver on his promise to give the Prince a serious talking to. Nothing in the subsequent record suggests that Baldwin would have been wrong to have despaired. Lascelles stuck it out for another couple of years, but resigned in disgust in 1929 and allowed himself to deliver to Edward a frank account of his shortcomings. The Prince thanked him with every appearance of amiability and gave not the slightest sign that the diatribe had made any impression on him. Lascelles would not be the last to try to reform Edward and fail.

The incident that provoked Lascelles's resignation also showed how Edward had come to a less than flattering opinion of Baldwin. To begin with, he had gushed apparently sincere praise for his Prime Minister, but this had ebbed.[20] George V fell seriously ill whilst Edward was in the bush on a tour of East Africa in 1928. Baldwin was then Prime Minister and sent Edward increasingly urgent cables begging him to return to Britain, but Edward did not believe them: 'I don't believe a word of it. It's just some election-dodge of old Baldwin's. It doesn't mean a thing.'[21] The Prince was entirely wrong, but his outburst shows that he had somehow spotted Baldwin's usually well-concealed capacity for self-dramatisation and linked it to the Prime Minister's trade as a politician.

The problem of Edward was still on the table in 1935, when Baldwin re-entered Downing Street for his third and final premiership. Indeed, it was at the very first Cabinet meeting that he chaired after becoming Prime Minister again that the Prince's British Legion speech was discussed. He knew that he was at the end of his political career and could look at things in terms of the next generation. To Sir Horace Wilson, his closest civil service adviser and already a long-standing collaborator, Baldwin mapped out three tasks for his term in office: to postpone or prevent war through an understanding with Germany, to create 'the most favourable conditions for his successor' as leader of the Conservative Party and to 'enable the Prince of Wales (should he succeed to the throne) to make a favourable start as King'.[22] It would be a thankless and difficult task and not one that Baldwin relished. He freely admitted that 'he had always hoped that the King [George V] wouldn't die in his time as P.M.'[23] It is also extremely striking that he had already considered the possibility that Edward might not become King. The exact words that Baldwin used to set out his tasks and how the conversation came about have been lost for ever; all that survives is Wilson's paraphrase into cautious, non-committal civil service prose. Wilson's notes were written with the benefit of hindsight after the event, but Baldwin had long had his doubts as to whether Edward 'would stay the course'.[24] It was a short step to recognising that Edward had no appetite for the throne, and Baldwin may have hinted this to Wilson. When the crisis broke, political calculation, if nothing else, dictated that Baldwin treat Edward as worthy of the throne, but there was no sign that he was optimistic that Edward would prove his doubts to be wrong.

A few weeks after the abdication Sir Horace Wilson set down to write a long account of the crisis, setting out the government's side to the affair. He opened his draft with the episode of Baldwin's three tasks. It was a crucial point, but it was also a very sensitive thing to disclose, and it begged the massive question of what Baldwin might actually have done to smooth the way for Edward.[25] There is almost no evidence that he tried to make Edward improve his behaviour. When Wilson reviewed his draft, it was clear that the admission would lay Baldwin open to the charge that he should have intervened actively with Edward. The whole episode was thus left out of the final version. Many in Baldwin's political and civil service entourage would not have hesitated to level this kind of charge. Baldwin was the supreme example of the reactive Prime Minister. He had the patience and strong nerves required to postpone hard action until he judged the time was ripe to move. This drove many around him to the utmost frustration. They accused him of not making decisions because he was too idle. They failed to understand that Baldwin took his responsibilities as Prime Minister with immense seriousness, that he recognised the huge risks latent in any course of action and wanted to be as certain as possible that he was doing the right thing. He was all too successful in concealing this inner torment behind a façade of bluff insouciance and, to this day, a reputation for laziness lingers around him. Baldwin's cautious political style provoked a dangerous overreaction. The people who accused him of idleness came to believe that pre-emptive action, the more vigorous the better, was almost invariably the correct option.

The new government was not completely inactive, but all that it did about Edward in 1935 was to initiate a far more limited precautionary strategy. The Special Branch of the Metropolitan Police was put on the job of finding out about Mrs Simpson and her husband, Ernest. It was far from the first time that it had handled this kind of task. Since the late nineteenth century it had been protecting members of the royal family from the consequences of their more wayward instincts. Most recently its detectives had helped cover up the many indiscretions in the private life of the Duke of Kent. The fear that Edward's liaison with Mrs Simpson might cause severe embarrassment or leave him vulnerable to blackmail was a more or less routine reflex for the powers that be. The Marguerite Alibert episode was proof enough of Edward's capacity for dangerous indiscretion.

Detectives were sent to sniff around the Simpsons' household and their previous addresses and they produced a suitably squalid picture.[26] Their reports reflect amply the social, moral and racial attitudes of the time. Mr Ernest Simpson was a member of the 'bounder' class and openly boasted of the advantages that turning a blind eye to the affair would bring – ludicrously, he imagined he would be given a peerage. He could not even hold his drink. His wife was living far above the couple's means and was only jealous of other women round the Prince because she feared she would lose out financially. An Austro-Hungarian woman was a particular target. The poor opinion of the couple was reinforced by the fact that they were regarded by some people as Jews. In fact this was true of Ernest, although he himself might have been unaware of it. Most useful of all, the police reported some damning information on Mrs Simpson. Before marrying Ernest, she was accused of having been 'fond of the company of men' and of having had many 'affairs'. We can almost see the twitch of the lace curtain and hear the disapproving hushed whispers of strait-laced neighbours. Even more excitingly, the detectives had heard that she was being unfaithful not only to her husband but to Edward as well. She had a lover called Guy Trundle on the side. Just to complete the unsavoury picture, she was even giving him money. In the parlance of the day, he was her kept man. The stories were detailed and intimate; they suggest that the detectives had informants inside or very close to the Simpson household. The Simpsons did not seem to inspire much loyalty.

It will probably never be known just how true the police reports were apart from Edward's cash gifts to Mrs Simpson, for which there is evidence elsewhere. What matters in trying to understand how the crisis evolved is that no one in authority doubted the accusations, and they coloured the already hostile view of Mrs Simpson held within government. She appeared to have the lowest morals imaginable. It hardly needed to be spelled out that, by the standards of the time, Mrs Simpson was little better than a prostitute and her husband little better than her pimp. Sex was a cash commodity and she was recycling her income from Edward to indulge in Trundle. When the previously unthinkable idea of a marriage between Edward and Mrs Simpson did arise, this helps explain why a good number of people did not expect that it would last. It was another very potent reason to oppose the marriage, which one hardline minister believed 'could only end in disillusionment and disgust'.[27] The Trundle story also gave the government their own tool for discreet blackmail or at least a means of blackening Mrs Simpson's already dubious image.

The Special Branch detectives seem to have stretched the truth so as to present as unfavourable a picture as possible. They made much of the Simpsons' friendship with the Society hostess Emerald Cunard, mentioning in particular her connections to two scandalous women.[28] She was described as a great friend of Alice 'Kiki' Preston, a sexually promiscuous cocaine addict known as the 'girl with the silver syringe', who had an affair with the Prince's brother George and supposedly introduced him to drugs. Just how close she was to Lady Cunard is hard to establish but, in reality, Edward, in one of the very rare entirely altruistic acts of his life, had devoted considerable effort to rescuing George from such influences. Even more questionably, the detectives mentioned Emerald's daughter Nancy, who committed the unforgivable sin, by the standards of the time, of openly having black lovers, as well as publicly advocating racial equality. As mother and daughter had become bitterly estranged some years before over Nancy's support for the avant-garde film-maker Luis Buñuel and public appearances with her black lover Henry Crowder, this looks little better than a smear.[29]

Baldwin had good excuse not to have done anything about Edward when he returned to Downing Street; there were far more urgent calls on his attention. Fascist Italy's invasion of Abyssinia was the first of a series of international crises that culminated in the Second World War. A general election was due in Britain that autumn. Moreover, nothing noticeable changed in Edward's relationship with Mrs Simpson, so things were at least not getting worse. It is, however, tempting to speculate that the police reports might have lulled the government into something of a false sense of security. They presented the Simpsons as such low grade and vulnerable people that they ought not to be seen as a serious threat. If Downing Street had fallen into any such complacency, it was matched by a sense of hopelessness at Buckingham Palace. Neither parents nor politicians actually did anything and the question of Edward was allowed to drift for the rest of George V's reign. The Establishment rather lapsed into a sense of collective denial. The King was relatively young – he only turned seventy in 1935 – and there was no immediate reason to fear for his life. A number of courtiers expected him to live to a ripe age, which would defer the question of Edward by a good number of years. But this had more to do with wishful thinking than any considered examination of George V's medical history. He had nearly died of septicaemia in 1928 and was a heavy smoker.

Paradoxically, George V's illness was hijacked by optimists with a strong literary bent. Edward was recalled from Africa to what many thought was his father's deathbed, but as soon as he entered the room George V regained conscious and curtly asked his son, 'What the devil are you doing here?'[30] It was like the scene in Shakespeare's *Henry IV* when the old King, also on his deathbed, catches his dissolute son trying on a crown and triggers an argument that marks the start of Prince Hal's road to redemption and his proper recognition of the duties of kingship, which he goes on to fulfil magnificently as Henry V. The parallels between Prince Hal and Edward seemed all too neat to a surprisingly large number of people, who were sucked into the deluded hope that when Edward came to the throne, he too would experience a similar conversion to full cognisance of the obligations that it brought and banish the worthless companions of his misspent youth.

CHAPTER 2

THE PRIME MINISTER AND THE SUPER-CIVIL SERVANT

S.B. felt the job too heavy, and ... suggested Wilson should come and help him.
There was nothing more to it than that – no new title, no definition of function
... Other ministers and Departments of State would watch the new departure
with jealous eyes. Ministers in particular would be hot against any attempt
to subordinate them to any sort of Super-Civil Servant...
RAYMOND STREAT, DIARY, 26 JULY 1935

I T IS ALMOST a truism of British politics, notably in the Conservative Party, that leaders are chosen because of what they are not much
more than because of what they are. They are often the least unattractive
alternative to an individual or group of individuals who are actively loathed
and rejected. Stanley Baldwin rose to the top of politics on a groundswell
of backbench hatred for the man who put them in office in 1916 and kept
them there for six years. Gratitude is rarely a feature in such choices. David
Lloyd George had broken with Henry Asquith, who led the Liberal Party
to which they both belonged, and replaced him as Prime Minister with the
support of the Conservatives in 1916. Lloyd George offered the war-winning
dynamism so noticeably lacking in Asquith and he amply delivered on

the promise, but once he was in power he did not play by the established rules. He did not pick his preferred supporters from the ranks of traditional Conservatives. Indeed, some of his key ministers were deeply suspect and were seen as unprincipled political adventurers: Winston Churchill, who had defected to the Liberals in 1904; F. E. Smith, brilliant lawyer and violent opponent of any weakening of Ireland's ties to Britain; and a gaggle of press lords. Traditional Conservatives distrusted these men for their opportunism, but distaste for their varying permutations of dubious finances, irregular sexual activity and heavy drinking added a moralistic layer to this disapproval. Lloyd George's style of leadership seemed to be contrary to every tradition of the Conservative Party. It was highly personalised and was funded by a series of dubious measures including the sale of honours. Baldwin memorably described Lloyd George's government as a 'thieves' kitchen'.[1]

By 1922, Lloyd George had exhausted whatever fund of goodwill he had once enjoyed. The press barons, never the most trustworthy of allies, had already deserted him. He had conspicuously failed to build a 'land fit for heroes' and was threatening to drag Britain into futile diplomatic and military adventures in the relics of the Ottoman Empire. In October the backbenchers of the Conservative Party met at Carlton House and decided to put an end to the coalition. The memory of the coup is still hallowed in the Conservative Party through the 1922 Committee, which continues to serve as a powerful conduit to remind the party's leaders that they ignore rank-and-file sentiment at their extreme peril. Lloyd George was replaced as Prime Minister by Andrew Bonar Law, the most senior of the rebels, with Baldwin as Chancellor of the Exchequer. After a few months as Prime Minister, Bonar Law was diagnosed with terminal throat cancer and Baldwin was the obvious choice to succeed him at 10 Downing Street even though he had scant experience of being a minister of any kind. F. E. Smith sneered that the new government consisted of 'second-class brains'. Baldwin is credited with responding that this was better than a government of 'second-class characters' although this is sometimes attributed to Lord Robert Cecil. Whether he actually said this or not, the sentiment provides the leitmotif for Baldwin's leadership. He marked a return to stability and balance after a decade of turbulence. Baldwin was (and still is) widely criticised and mocked for his lack of inspiration and charisma, but that was precisely what appealed to both professional politicians and voters of the era.

Baldwin became the defining politician of Britain between the wars. He was either Prime Minister or a true deputy Prime Minister for ten years and led the Conservative Party into four general elections in the fourteen years of his leadership, but he is one of the very few modern Prime Ministers of whom it can plausibly be claimed that he had no ambition for the job. He had been fully prepared to leave politics entirely if the Carlton House coup had gone wrong. He certainly had no particular grand schemes or dreams that he wanted to realise when he got into 10 Downing Street. He believed that his political duty was to identify and implement the wishes of the British public. Insofar as he felt that he had any particular talent for the job, he believed that he had the ability to read the collective mind of Britain. His bitterest feud was with the press barons, whom he accused of usurping this role by claiming to speak for their readers.

In the months after the Carlton House coup, the coalition ministers returned to the fold, more or less chastened. Only Lloyd George remained in the wilderness for the remainder of his life, a dwindling force on the political scene. The political world that he had built disappeared almost overnight as his heavyweight supporters switched their allegiance to the new regime, but in one corner of the machinery of government his legacy proved remarkably enduring and created an immovable internal opposition to Baldwin. In 1919, Lloyd George gave a single individual, Sir Warren Fisher, clear responsibility for running the entire civil service, replacing the chaotic and ambiguous arrangements that had gone before. This was badly needed. The First World War had given a huge fillip to the massive expansion of the civil service through the nineteenth century. It had become by far the largest single employer in the country and it reached into corners of people's lives undreamed of a few decades before. The civil service was becoming a political liability and badly needed to be taken in hand. Things that had been acceptable in the crisis of total war were out of place as the country returned to what people hoped would be the normality of peace. The press barons had withdrawn from government in the final year of the war, but their ambitions to influence politics remained strong. Even whilst Lloyd George was still Prime Minister, Viscount Harmsworth, proprietor of the *Daily Mail*, had launched a venomous and highly effective campaign against what he saw as government overspending under the slogans 'squandermania' and the 'Road to Ruin'. Lloyd George hoped that Fisher would ward off Harmsworth's growing assault on the government for the size and cost of the civil service by instituting a more manageable regime.[2]

Fisher's appointment was typical of Lloyd George's methods. He gave a man in whom he had confidence a loosely defined task and left him to get on with it under minimal supervision. Fisher had already proved his value to Lloyd George twice when he built from scratch bureaucratic operations to translate Lloyd George's political vision into hard practical reality. Lloyd George had practically staked his career on the National Insurance Act of 1911, Britain's most extensive piece of social legislation ever, covering most of the working population. Early attempts to build an organisation to administer it had fallen into confusion and had Fisher not rescued them with spectacular efficiency, it would have been politically disastrous for Lloyd George. Fisher revered Lloyd George personally and he was, like Lloyd George, an outsider, having begun his career far down the civil service pecking order in the Inland Revenue and twice failed to secure a transfer to the Treasury, the premier department of the civil service and its intellectual powerhouse. Anyway, he had no taste for abstract consideration of high policy; he was much closer to Lloyd George's ideal of 'men of push and go', business entrepreneurs whom he brought into government and administration. Fisher described his own talents as those of a department store 'floor-walker'. Although he was only thirty-nine, he appeared a perfect man for the job and was appointed as the top civil servant in the Treasury to '*act as* permanent Head of the Civil Service' [author's italics].[3]

Fisher did not display the traditional calm, detached, conservative and Olympian characteristics of a top-level civil servant. Instead, he was highly strung and volatile. He took violent likes and dislikes to individuals, which he elevated into a management philosophy under which a competent individual – one of whom he approved – was capable of any task irrespective of technical knowledge or experience. He wrote and spoke in the gushing Edwardian-era style larded with 'dears' and 'loves', notably addressing Neville Chamberlain, his political boss, as 'My Dear Neville'.[4] He had progressive views for his day; he was an early advocate of promoting women to senior positions and tolerant of divorce in an era when it could and did wreck careers. In 1922, he complained to the Lord Chancellor when the invitation of Sir Basil Blackett, one of the most senior civil servants in the Treasury, to a palace garden party was cancelled merely because Blackett had been in the divorce courts.[5] This attitude perhaps reflected Fisher's own unhappy home life. He separated from his wife acrimoniously and lived the rest of his life as a quasi-bachelor in a circle of like-minded cronies.

Fisher proved a severe disappointment as a cost-cutter and had probably never believed that it was his job to be one. He was driven by a quite different and far greater set of ambitions for himself, his post and the civil service as a whole. Had they been completely fulfilled he would have been second only to the Prime Minister in power and authority, with the added advantage of job security until retirement at the age of sixty. He saw himself as the undisputed boss of the entire public service, subject only to the Prime Minister's authority. He was scathing about Cabinet government as a method of producing policy driven by the aims of ministers, whom he castigated as 'unrelated individuals with no recognition of a corporate trust and concerned each one only to force his own schemes (or megalomania)'.[6] This left civil servants (Fisher manifestly to the fore) 'restricted to impotent albeit disgusted, observation of this example of how not to run the business of this country'. He fought to strip ministers of any say in which civil servants were in charge of their departments. He also tried to force ministers to clear their spending plans with the Treasury – in effect Fisher himself – before they were presented to Cabinet. He wanted to become established as the Prime Minister's principal adviser on every topic under the sun and dreamed up a daft constitutional argument that awarded himself this job by right. He fought to bring the Foreign Office under his direct control, but in its established, patrician style it simply ignored him. Fisher's ambitions went further than Whitehall; he classed the civil service as 'the Fourth Crown Service' on a par with the armed forces and awarded himself equivalent status to their chiefs.

Fisher was driven by a burning desire to do what was best for the country and had no doubt that he was the man to judge what was best. Even in the words of the businessman and later government minister, Lord Woolton, who claimed a close friendship with him and later defended him in an acrimonious parliamentary debate:

> He was a man of profound convictions and little tolerance. To him the greatness of Britain took precedence over all other issues, public or personal. He was ruthless in his dealings with either civil servants or Ministers – including the Prime Minister – if he thought that their actions were not contributing to his conception of Britain's proper position in the world...[7]

Fisher operated entirely by his own rules, completely ignoring codes and conventions as to how civil servants should behave with politicians. He briefed whichever senior ministers he got on well with. If he happened to have a good relationship with the Chancellor of the Exchequer, he would fulfil his duties as his civil service adviser; if he did not – as happened with Winston Churchill whom he considered a 'blight' – he bypassed him.[8] Fisher also meddled directly in politics; he worked resolutely to promote the cause of Neville Chamberlain, whom he considered a far better minister than Baldwin.

As a regular civil servant Fisher was unaffected by the defenestration of Lloyd George, his political patron, in 1922, which actually opened the way for his next gambits to consolidate his power in Whitehall. He tried to bring under his control the one crucial piece of the machinery, the Cabinet Secretariat, which operated autonomously as the personal fiefdom of the first Cabinet Secretary Sir Maurice Hankey, who had also acted as Lloyd George's personal adviser, much as Fisher dreamed of being adviser to all Prime

Ministers. Hankey had a very high personal reputation for competence and integrity so Fisher's move failed but he used the next change of government to begin using the title 'Head of the Civil Service' as his official designation and not merely as an informal adjunct to his job at the Treasury. Under this new banner, he renewed his assault on Hankey's standing by boosting his own position on the Committee of Imperial Defence, Britain's top military planning body, which Hankey cherished as his original springboard to power in Whitehall.

Predictably, Fisher's high-handedness made him enemies and, in 1926, he became the target of a parliamentary campaign triggered by his assault on Hankey. It was vigorously supported by George V, who held Hankey in high regard and was outraged at Fisher's pretensions, notably at Fisher calling himself 'Head of the Civil Service'. Not only had royal approval never been sought for the new title, but it referred to the 'Civil Service' rather than 'His Majesty's Civil Service' as though it were Fisher's own personal enterprise. The weaknesses in the government case were mercilessly skewered in some remarkably sarcastic letters from the palace to which Downing Street struggled to respond adequately.[9] Baldwin had an easier job of defending Fisher in the ensuing House of Commons debate against an astonishingly inept attack by some very third-rate debaters, but this marked the end of Fisher's drive to expand his own powers. Thereafter he behaved more circumspectly and devoted himself to lesser goals, notably to reforming the Prime Minister's personal staff arrangements. In part this was a piece of badly needed modernisation but also, predictably, a land-grab on behalf of the regular civil service and by extension Fisher himself.

Before the Second World War the Prime Minister was supported by a staff little bigger than that available to a provincial bishop. It was ludicrously inadequate to handle the volume of work of a twentieth-century head of government. By custom the Prime Minister had three private secretaries, only one of whom was a professional civil servant, and a fairly junior one at that. No qualifications or experience were required of the others; the Prime Minister simply chose them on whatever grounds happened to appeal, usually family or personal acquaintance. Fisher set out to transform the

Prime Minister's personal staff from a pool of amateur patronage into the exclusive preserve of professional civil servants, answerable of course to himself. Fisher's first step was to eliminate the most objectionable survivor of the old regime, Colonel Sir Ronald Waterhouse. Waterhouse was devious, duplicitous and an obvious relic of how things were done in the Lloyd George era. Fisher tried to buy him off with the offer of a directorship of the Suez Canal Company, one of the juiciest near sinecures available. This failed, but eventually an unsuitable marriage saw him off; Baldwin's wife Lucy was extremely strait-laced on such matters. Fisher's next step was to upgrade the Prime Minister's staff simply by installing more senior and more dynamic civil servants as private secretaries, but here he was less successful. Fisher's first pick was Robert Vansittart of the Foreign Office, but he had no opportunity to establish himself in the post properly. His appointment lasted only two years, serving two different Prime Ministers – it was brought to a premature end when Fisher had the opportunity to parachute him into the top position at the Foreign Office. Moreover, Vansittart was a prime example of Fisher's often suspect judgement of individuals; he rivalled Fisher for high-handedness, but was devoid of his low cunning. Fisher's second pick as a heavyweight private secretary to the Prime Minister, James Barlow, was a far better administrator, who went on to reach the top of the Treasury, but his appointment began in near farce.[10] The then Prime Minister, Ramsay MacDonald, was morbidly suspicious of the civil service as a whole, and frantic efforts had to be made to conceal from him the fact that Barlow was Fisher's own nominee. MacDonald and Barlow did not get on well personally and Barlow was happy to move back to the Treasury after barely a year.

It was not until in 1935, when MacDonald stepped down as Prime Minister and Baldwin returned to 10 Downing Street, that Fisher was able to take a radical step towards creating a perfect civil service cocoon around the Prime Minister. The signs were propitious. At the age of sixty-seven, Baldwin was tired and knew it. As deputy Prime Minister in MacDonald's coalition government and leader of the dominant Conservative Party he had borne much of the political burden since 1931. Stepping up to the official top job meant an enormous increase in his workload. The Prime Minister bore a massive administrative burden and Baldwin had neither the skills nor the taste to bear it alone. Baldwin's heart lay in the House of Commons and not in the meeting rooms of Whitehall. Fisher came up with a remarkably simple solution. A top-level civil servant whom Baldwin already knew and trusted would be attached to the staff at 10 Downing Street: '[e]xperience had shown … the need of an experienced official at No. 10 on the P.M.'s Staff who knew the machine of government. The burden on the P.M. was such that he needed this help more and more.'[11] He would have no official job title, defined remit or set term of office. He would just help the Prime Minister however he could and however the Prime Minister thought he could. The man who was chosen – according to one account, specifically asked for by Baldwin – was Sir Horace Wilson.

Senior civil servants hold mixed opinions of the ministers they serve, but are usually exceptionally discreet in how these are expressed. Fisher, however, was openly contemptuous of politicians individually and in general. Baldwin was a particular target of his criticism for what he saw as idleness and moral cowardice: 'S.B.'s tendency whenever he saw a job of work or some responsibility was to bolt … I must admit he does it with remarkable skill.'[12] Like many, Fisher failed to recognise that delaying action or decision was central to Baldwin's political methods. Doubtless Fisher hoped that Wilson would hold Baldwin's nose to the grindstone.

Wilson was an example of how the civil service was a pioneer in terms of social mobility. He had been born in the unfashionable seaside resort of Bournemouth to parents at the higher end of the working class: a cabinet maker and a boarding-house keeper. He had entered the civil service at its most junior grade, boy clerk, after only basic schooling. He had enough ambition, brain and commitment to earn a university degree at night school whilst he was already working. Unlike Fisher, he had the calm, detached style of the traditional senior civil servant, but this had been honed in a far rougher environment. He had developed great skill as an industrial negotiator and conciliator in the poisonous and often violent world of labour relations before the First World War. He had proven his worth to

Baldwin during the General Strike, when he had been one of the inner circle around the Prime Minister as the chief civil servant of the Ministry of Labour. Wilson had generally supported a hard line, and it was he who had imposed the final humiliation on the strike leaders by insisting that they conceded defeat to him personally before they were even allowed to surrender formally to the Prime Minister.[13] It is improbable that this was his own initiative and, perhaps, a lesson to him, that civil servants sometimes have to do the politicians' dirty work for them. His career had taken a wrong turning in 1929, when he became the civil service front man of a futile political initiative to tackle the growing catastrophe of unemployment. It soon collapsed but Wilson was far too able a civil servant to lose. The grand-sounding but entirely unspecific job of 'Chief Industrial Adviser' was devised to keep him on the civil service payroll, but this accidentally created huge confusion amongst historians as to what he actually did. It was the only official title he held for the next nine years, and it more or less accurately described his work for the first five of them when he was the civil service's chief odd-job man for economic affairs, but it was quite unrelated to the work he did at Downing Street.

Wilson was a far more restful individual than Fisher. He had a gentle if faintly acerbic sense of humour and an understated charm that won him long-lasting friends amongst the men he dealt with at all levels of government and business. He had an entirely stable and contented home life and was an enthusiastic evangelical Christian. He had none of the abrasiveness that made so many enemies for Fisher, but he had one great flaw: he had unshakable confidence in the correctness of his judgement, and barely ever admitted error.[14] His memoranda are calm, measured and models of clarity, but they almost invariably either assume unarguable premises or arrive at unqualified conclusions.

Wilson was immediately aware of both the strengths and weaknesses of his new position at Downing Street and discussed them frankly with an old friend, Raymond Streat, on a peaceful summer stroll through the Sussex lanes near his weekend cottage. In contrast to Fisher's self-interested constitutional theorising, he concentrated on the nitty-gritty of how jobs work and how small motives can be as important as large ones. He knew there was no guarantee that his job would continue when Baldwin's premiership ended, which most observers expected would only be in a very few years. He feared that he might be resented by both ministers and his civil service colleagues, suspicious that something approaching the French *chef de cabinet* (chief of staff) system would diminish their power. He also foresaw that part of his job would be to act as a buffer between the Prime Minister and other members of the government, and that a time would come when it would come down to a question of raw power: 'What will happen … when I have to say "No" to some minister who wants a "Yes" from S.B., I do not know.'[15] He believed he could spare the Prime Minister much work because of how well he thought he knew Baldwin's mind. Worryingly, he thought that this mind-reading skill alone was sufficient; he did not ask himself at what point he would need to refer questions to the Prime Minister. This was the seed of a more dangerous arrogance than Fisher's.

It was up to Wilson to make what he could of the job. He stood higher in the civil service hierarchy than anyone else who had been based at 10 Downing Street, but his standing was ambiguous. He had ceased being a head of department – and a junior one at that – years before, and since then had been almost in limbo. The informal status of his new job might have been due to the fact that Fisher recognised a risk that the new man in Downing Street would hold potentially phenomenal power and that this would be reinforced if he was given a clear official title and rank. If this was so, Fisher was being prescient; within a couple of years Wilson would eclipse him entirely, but for the time his job bore all the signs of a temporary posting. According to the civil service list, he was merely 'attached for service at 10 Downing Street'. He was clearly junior to Fisher and was not going to achieve anything without his support, but together they had the potential to be a formidable partnership: proximity to the Prime Minister allied to domination of the entire civil service machine. For the first two or three years the partnership did work very well.

Whilst Wilson had neither job title nor detailed remit, he was given one priceless advantage in the mechanics of bureaucratic power: a small office immediately next to the Cabinet Room overlooking Horse Guards Parade. As one later Downing Street insider has written:

> It was seen as the key room because of its access … The point was its location with access to all ministers coming to wait in the lobby outside the cabinet room and knowing when cabinet meetings were ending and Prime Minister free. Access equals power.[16]

Later occupants included such virtuosi of translating access to the Prime Minister into power and influence far beyond that of their official jobs such as Brendan Bracken and Marcia Williams. A muted but sustained struggle amongst the members of the entourage of incoming Prime Ministers to be the one to occupy the room has been a regular feature of changes of government. Baldwin preferred to work in the intimacy of his library upstairs at No. 10, which somewhat diluted the tactical value of Wilson's office, but it was a formidable location nonetheless. The contrast between their offices was emblematic of the differences in the way he and Fisher held the levers of power. Wilson operated quietly in the background, ever alert to the realities of power. Even when he had become far better known, he was classed first and foremost as an *éminence grise*. Fisher operated from the splendour of the Permanent Secretary's office in Treasury Chambers and cheerfully talked down to even the highest in the land.

Wilson's first half year at Downing Street was quiet. The Prime Minister's attention was dominated by diplomacy and party politics, matters in which the home civil service was little involved. Immediately after Baldwin arrived in Downing Street he had to prepare for the general election later in the year that the national government won comfortably. More menacingly, the invasion of Abyssinia opened the series of diplomatic crises that culminated in the Second World War. This did not stop Wilson making his presence felt in Downing Street. Compared to his political counterpart as the Prime Minister's odd-job man, he seemed to embody a shift in power from politicians to the civil service. Eustace Percy had been appointed as Minister without Portfolio by Baldwin, who had a largely inexplicable soft spot for him. He had a seat in Cabinet but no very clear remit and, crucially, no access to civil service support. Non-departmental ministers are often entrusted with important one-off tasks, but this depends on the tasks and competition from elsewhere in the machine of government to undertake them. After a few frustrating and miserable months in office he resigned in April 1936. According to a seasoned Whitehall insider, 'Probably the existence of Horace Wilson on the P.M.'s staff made Percy all the more superfluous.'[17] Wilson's arrival in Downing Street also marked the beginning of the final eclipse from power of Hankey, who found himself cut out of the new order.

Things stepped up several gears when George V died in early 1936 and the new machinery of government had the opportunity to show how it could operate in a full-blown crisis, as the uncertainty over Edward's fitness for the throne that had long hovered under the horizon became an acute question for Baldwin. It was not, though, the kind of problem that Fisher's machine had been designed to deal with. Baldwin was confronted with elemental dilemmas, essentially the same as had confronted the chief advisers to monarchs down the ages. The sovereign was set on a foolish and dangerous course from which he had to be deflected. It came down to the dialogue between two individuals. The huge machinery of a modern state was redundant. The civil service could bring no relevant experience or technical expertise to the table. But power and influence are never lightly forsaken and Fisher and Wilson were no exception to this rule. There is no evidence that either ever met Edward on other than purely formal occasions, but what mattered to them was their position vis-à-vis the Prime Minister. It was not one that either was going to sacrifice willingly.

CHAPTER 3

ALMOST IMPOSSIBLE
TO APPEAL TO REASON

*Lord Wigram made it clear that, in his view, we were dealing with a case
where it was almost impossible to appeal to reason or judgement and
he gave no hope that anything that might be said would be effective*
SIR HORACE WILSON, ABDICATION NOTES[1]

THE DREAM THAT the country would be spared for some time
the question of coping with Edward as King vanished almost without warning when George V fell ill quite suddenly in January 1936,
and it became clear that he had only days to live. This left the two individuals most deeply concerned – Queen Mary and Baldwin – with little time
to make any serious preparations for the new reign.

Whatever private grief she was feeling, the Queen was strong enough to
decide that Shakespearean optimism was not enough and that the politicians
had to face up to their responsibilities. As ever, duty came first. She knew the
man for the job. Family, courtiers, Cabinet ministers and the Archbishop of
Canterbury had gathered around the King's deathbed at Sandringham on
the last day of his life, 20 January 1936, but it was Sir Maurice Hankey whom
she took into her confidence and with whom she shared her fears.[2] As well

as being Cabinet Secretary, Hankey was Clerk to the Privy Council so he had a major part to play in the formal arrangements, but he also was a long-standing friend and confidant of the royal couple. The Queen summoned him to her private quarters and made it plain that action was required. First she wanted to know whether the Prime Minister had done anything to take her son in hand. In Hankey's delicately phrased diary entry, she 'indicated a doubt as to whether the Prince had fully realised his responsibilities, and how far he would have to alter his manner of living and so forth'. She had clearly noted that Baldwin had so far done nothing to correct the situation, and Hankey understood that she expected the Prime Minister to guide Edward firmly in the right direction. In particular, she was anxious that he raise the question of his staff. The raffish band of chancers and lightweights around the Prince had long been a source of worry to his father. She hinted to Hankey that the Prime Minister should try to ensure that her husband's senior courtiers were kept on, in particular his private secretary Lord Wigram and Wigram's assistant Major Alec Hardinge. Both had faithfully served King George for many years and earned the confidence of the royal couple.

Queen Mary had been unfair to behave as though Baldwin were doing nothing to steer her son in the right direction. On the same day that she was sharing her disquiet with Hankey, Baldwin raised – admittedly very tentatively – the question of Edward's private life with one man who might just have established a worthwhile dialogue with him. Duff Cooper, the Secretary of State for War, was the only senior politician amongst Edward's personal friends.[3] He was about Edward's age, which made him one of the youngest – and most glamorous – members of a Cabinet that was distinctly long in the tooth. He was a womaniser on an epic scale, so unlikely to be troubled by questions of pure morality. Baldwin summoned him to the Cabinet Room at Downing Street and expressed his unease at Edward's relationship with Mrs Simpson. He was scared of the public reaction if it were to become widely known. Baldwin had a low personal opinion of Mrs Simpson but his fears were bluntly pragmatic. He told Cooper he would not have minded, 'if she were what I call a respectable whore' who was kept in secret and did not monopolise his time.

Baldwin and Cooper were caught in a Mexican stand-off. The Prime Minister did not openly ask Cooper to intervene with the King, and Cooper did not volunteer to. As far as Cooper could make out the only practical point of the conversation was to nudge him towards advising Mrs Simpson to leave the country, temporarily at least. Sending an unsuitable partner abroad was the Establishment's instinctive and routine first move to deal with an undesirable entanglement. If nothing else, it would dampen the scandal and might even bring an end to the relationship, but it was neither an imaginative nor realistic solution to the problem. Cooper knew enough of Edward and his relationship with Mrs Simpson to foresee immediately that any such attempt on his part would not merely fail but would never be forgiven by Edward. Cooper was almost certainly right to doubt the scheme would work, and cannot be faulted for holding back, but with hindsight he might have explained himself more forcefully. As it was, the simplistic idea of getting Mrs Simpson out of the country remained on the government agenda with unfortunate consequences.

Baldwin gave no sign of great surprise or disappointment that Duff Cooper was not going to help, but he was under severe strain and needed a stiff whisky as he climbed the stairs of Downing Street to the library and the next item on his agenda: preparing the radio broadcast that he would make after King George's death.[4] Baldwin was in a deeply pessimistic mood as he discussed the arrangements with his speechwriter and long-standing confidant Thomas Jones. He did not relish the task of mentoring Edward at all: 'You know what a scrimshanker* I am. I had rather hoped to escape the responsibility of having to take charge of the Prince as King … I am less confident about him than Lucy [his wife] is.' He saw no prospect of assistance from anyone around the Prince, 'nor is there any man who can handle him'. With a note of desperation, he expressed a hope that the Queen would continue to live at Buckingham Palace. When Jones tried to persuade him that responsibility would reform Edward, Baldwin was not convinced.

One aspect of Baldwin's political style that fed the frustration of his more

---

* shirker

activist colleagues was his failure to share his analysis of the position as it evolved. He succeeded so well that he rather gave the impression that he was either shirking an obvious solution or, possibly worse, was confused as to what the problem was.[5] His gloomy remarks to Jones give possibly the best idea of the problem as he saw it. There was little hope of a happy outcome, so his job was to manage the consequences of an unhappy one. Only Edward could save himself.

However little confidence he might have felt in the outcome, Baldwin supported Queen Mary's desire to protect her son from himself. Two days later, after George V had died, Baldwin was still repeating the hope that the Queen 'would act as hostess and keep an eye on him [Edward]' with the additional hope that Wigram would be kept on.[6] It is a safe bet that Hankey had passed on the Queen's thoughts on the point to Baldwin. It is unknown whether Baldwin did actually ask the new King to keep his late father's secretaries, but in the event he did. It must have come as a relief to the Queen, but it was anything but a solution, and rapidly proved to be a blind alley. The Queen appears to have thoroughly exaggerated their potential for influencing her son to the good or mitigating the ill effects of his instincts. Edward was prepared to keep Wigram and Hardinge, but this had nothing to do with falling in with his mother's programme for reforming his behaviour. They provided window-dressing and not much else. The secretaries' main job is the highly delicate one of acting as a conduit between the sovereign and the government, and it was a dialogue that Edward saw as going in one direction only. He had no desire to form the same kind of partnership of trust with his secretaries that his father and grandfather had done; they were part of the irksome world of royal duties. He did not plan to be directed by the government, so was doubtless happy that men of Wigram's and Hardinge's standing would be there to represent him in government circles. It is a register of his egocentricity that he imagined they would automatically transfer their full devotion to him irrespective of personalities – that they would unquestioningly use their standing and influence in Downing Street on his behalf.

On the very first day of his reign, Edward showed his contempt for tradition and flagged to insiders how important a part Mrs Simpson was going to play in the new reign. Traditionally, the new sovereign does not attend his or her own formal proclamation as monarch. Like so much in royal ritual, the original purpose has been lost in the mists of time, and all that is at stake is a willingness to be bound by the past. What made Edward's decision to watch his proclamation from a window at St James's Palace truly shocking was that he had invited the Simpsons to accompany him. This made a bad impression on his friend Duff Cooper, who recognised that this kind of behaviour was already attracting criticism.[7] Not only had Mrs Simpson been spotted by members of Society, but she had also been caught on film, although the press maintained a discreet silence on this, as it was doing over the entire affair.

Criticism of the new King quickly sparked a heavily coded debate in the upper reaches of the Court and the Establishment. Edward VIII's relationship with the Church of England had got off to a bad start when the Archbishop of Canterbury had called on him soon after his accession. Cosmo Gordon Lang was everything Edward disliked about the Establishment: conservative, unctuous yet ambitious. He had won a place in the esteem of George V, who had a strong and simple Christian faith, but his son had none. Lang made the fatal error of telling the new King that he had often discussed his 'conduct' with his late father and claimed that he had taken Edward's side.[8] It was a singularly inept attempt to present himself as a supporter of the King, whilst reminding him that his father disapproved of his behaviour. The debate was taken up publicly by Albert Baillie, the long-serving Dean of St George's Chapel Windsor in his first sermon of the new reign.[9] Baillie had served the royal family since Queen Victoria but his loyalties were deeply influenced by a feud with the monstrous Canon Dalton, George V's boyhood tutor, who had remained a powerful influence at Court.[10] Baillie insisted that Edward should not be criticised for not being an 'imitation' of his father. He recognised that George V's settled Christian faith was the product of an earlier, more stable age and implicitly excused Edward's more lax approach to religious observance.

Baldwin sensed that all was not well with the King at the time of his accession, and felt that he had a 'hunted' look in his face.[11] At the time, Baldwin could not find a reason, but after the abdication he concluded that the King had realised 'that he had missed an opportunity to get out and would now find it more difficult to do so'. The idea is supported by the courtier Alan 'Tommy' Lascelles, who had served almost ten years as Edward's private secretary when he was Prince of Wales and re-joined the royal household at the end of George V's reign. Lascelles believed that Edward had wanted to avoid becoming King and to withdraw into private life but had changed his mind when he learned the terms of his father's will, which left him lit-tle money.[12] In Lascelles's jaundiced view, Edward now wanted to milk his kingship for what he could. These accounts are quoted to support the belief that Edward never wanted to be King. This may have been true up to the start of his reign, but thereafter there is no real evidence. It conflicts with Edward's enthusiasm for the idea of Mrs Simpson becoming his Queen. Moreover, Baldwin's admission that he had not suspected any unwillingness to accede to the throne is testimony to how hard Edward fought to remain on the throne when the crisis developed.

Baldwin was deeply worried about the new King, but this was only one amongst a host of far more urgent problems that was to occupy him over the following months, above all in foreign affairs. Just before King George died, the government had been rocked by the scandal of the Hoare–Laval pact, which seemed to condone Mussolini's invasion of Abyssinia in a cyni-cal great power carve-up. In March, Germany reoccupied the Rhineland, confronting western statesmen with the hideous reality of Hitler's policy of aggression. In July came the Spanish Civil War. Baldwin had to defend his performance against the attacks of Conservative elder statesman, Sir Austen Chamberlain. Domestic politics were quieter, but the Budget in April ushered in a financial scandal that led a month later to the disgrace and painful resignation of Jimmy Thomas, a highly popular if excessively colourful Cabinet minister. These difficulties may have acted as active deter-rent from trying to do anything about the King. Baldwin's extreme worry about the King showed he appreciated the risks of the situation but he was pessimistic that active measures would succeed and he also recognised that he could not force the pace even if he knew the affair would almost certainly end unhappily. His true goal never went further than that of minimising the pain when the end came, 'getting through without a row'.[13] It was a realistic but pessimistic and uninspiring goal, and one that he could hardly explain in detail to the steady trickle of insiders who nagged him to take action in the first months of Edward's reign.

One of the first calls for action took things back to the sordid world set out in the reports from the Special Branch. Ernest Simpson's ambitions appeared to have become more realistic than his fantasies of ennoblement, but just as alarming. Whilst he was still Prince of Wales, Edward had arranged for Simpson to be admitted to his own highly prestigious Freemasons' lodge. This was doubly questionable; outright blackmail might explain why the seducer should do the cuckold such a great favour and there was the normal suspicion that Simpson was merely interested in furthering his business activities by joining the lodge. Such suspicions prompted other members to complain to its president, Sir Maurice Jenks, a former Lord Mayor of the City of London, who obtained a pledge from Edward under Masonic oath that there was nothing between him and Mrs Simpson. Soon after Edward's accession, Ernest Simpson came to Jenks with an extraordinary tale. Not merely did Edward wish to marry Mrs Simpson but he (Simpson) was willing to leave the country to facilitate the necessary divorce. As if this were not enough, Simpson wanted to discuss the matter personally with the Prime Minister. Jenks reported this all to J. C. C. Davidson, a relatively junior minister but a close confidant of Baldwin.[14] Even though he found Simpson's claim that Edward wanted to marry his wife 'unbelievable', Davidson saw enough to convince him that an unpleasant conspiracy was afoot; his response was unequivocal: 'Convinced Blackmail sticks out at every stage ... I advocate most drastic steps (deportation) ... S and Mrs S, who is obviously a gold digger, have got him on toast.' Ernest Simpson was in fact a British citizen, so it would not have been possible to deport them anyway and Davidson failed to convince Baldwin to act. The Simpsons were behaving suspiciously, but there was no evidence that they were criminals. Even though the King had an extremely unsuitable mistress, there was nothing that Downing Street could do about it. Moreover, Baldwin appeared to share Davidson's disbelief in the idea of Edward marrying Mrs Simpson.

Mrs Simpson's image of seediness went beyond the tawdriness of commercial sex. From an early stage it had acquired a national security dimension thanks largely to the efforts of Joachim von Ribbentrop. Probably the stupidest and least competent member of Nazi Germany's political leaders, he was nonetheless the Nazi Party's supposed expert on foreign affairs. He was rather more cosmopolitan and polished than the other leaders, but that is to say very little as they were overwhelmingly provincial, petit bourgeois and monoglot. He was and still is sneeringly referred to as a 'champagne salesman', but even this is an exaggeration. His horrible and domineering wife was a member of the Henkell family who owned Germany's best-established sparkling wine maker, but his in-laws recognised his worthlessness and refused him a partnership. He was, though, allowed to bail out their Berlin sales agent financially, so, in reality, he only dealt in champagne's humbler German cousin, *Sekt*. He had two solid albeit negative qualifications for his job: he was entirely subservient to Hitler, who made all material decisions on foreign policy, and he was not a member of Germany's foreign service establishment, which was genuinely aristocratic (von Ribbentrop's noble status was of recent and suspect origin) and conservative, thus repugnant to the Nazis. He combined unbounded faith in his own judgement with near-total ignorance of the countries on which he was so happy to pronounce. In particular, he simply did not know how British politics operated despite having made lengthy visits in 1934 and 1935. On the second of these visits he had successfully conducted the negotiations of the Anglo-German Naval Treaty, which gave him a quite unfounded reputation as a master diplomat. Otherwise he had merely concentrated on cultivating those (relatively few) politicians who were very friendly towards Germany, and members of high Society. Amongst the latter was one of the era's great hostesses, Emerald Cunard, who had been instrumental in advancing Mrs Simpson in Society. She found him attractive as a man and responded to his advances. The witless MP and diarist Chips Channon contrived to see the Prince's British Legion speech as their work in a weirdly eighteenth-century fantasy of diplomacy:

Much gossip about the Prince of Wales' [*sic*] alleged Nazi leanings; he is alleged to have been influenced by Emerald (who is rather éprise with Herr Ribbentrop) through Mrs Simpson … He has just made an extraordinary speech to the British Legion advocating friendship with Germany; it is only a gesture, but a gesture that may be taken seriously in Germany and elsewhere. If only the Chancelleries of Europe knew that his speech was the result of Emerald Cunard's intrigues, themselves inspired by Herr Ribbentrop's dimple![15]

According to one account, it was Mrs Simpson who arranged for the Prince to meet von Ribbentrop at Lady Cunard's some time in 1935, to the great annoyance of the Foreign Office.[16] Hitler and von Ribbentrop conceived a great faith in the prospects for using Edward to swing British policy onto a pro-German axis, misreading his personal affinity for Germany and his potential for influence under the British constitution.

One of the legacies of Edward's British Legion speech had been a deep anxiety on the part of the notably anti-German head of the Foreign Office, Sir Robert Vansittart, who saw the hand of Lady Cunard as well as more traditional diplomats at the German Embassy and a campaign of active German propaganda.[17] Unusually for a senior diplomat Vansittart was an enthusiast for secret intelligence sources and was well informed because he was personally handling his own spy in the German diplomatic community: Klop Ustinov, the Embassy's press adviser and father of the actor Peter Ustinov.[18] Ustinov defected to the British but he continued to handle an even more valuable MI5 asset: one of the Embassy's accredited diplomats, Wolfgang zu Putlitz. Vansittart was intrigued by Mrs Simpson's part in Edward's life and, in December 1935, had made a point of inviting them to his grand house at Denham Place in Buckinghamshire.[19] Mrs Simpson quickly recognised that this invitation from an only slight acquaintance was meant to give him the opportunity to inspect her closely. His verdict was unfavourable, and early in the new reign Vansittart made a determined attempt to alert the palace to the dangers he saw. Wigram was summoned to a meeting at the Prime Minister's room in the House of Commons with

Vansittart and the country's highest-ranking civil servants: Fisher, Hankey.[20] The venue lent the discussion an air of Prime Ministerial authority, but it was the civil servants who supplied the urgency. According to Vansittart's information the King '"discusses everything" with Mrs. Simpson ... [who] is said to be in the pocket of the German ambassador'. Baldwin had declined to act, although his confidant J. C. C. Davidson credited the story of Mrs Simpson's relations with the German ambassador, von Hoesch.[21]

Wigram took little persuading that the country faced a major problem. He was an early, determined and indiscreet adversary of Mrs Simpson, complaining to Sir John Reith, 'If only we could bump off that woman, but I can't do that myself.'[22] He also held distinctly alarmist views on Edward's stability. Lascelles overheard him muttering out loud to himself, 'He's mad – he's mad. We shall have to lock him up.'[23] Wigram went to see Baldwin shortly after the meeting with the civil servants and pleaded with him to intervene.[24] Baldwin brushed him off with the claim that doing nothing was the best course, as such problems tended to resolve themselves. Baldwin cannot have believed this idiocy, but Wigram might have thought that he did. He certainly understood that Baldwin was not going to do anything active, and went to see Fisher, who was convinced that action was urgently needed. Fisher saw the lack of intervention as evidence that the Prime Minister was being 'too lazy' on a question that involved the 'fate of the Empire'.[25] Fisher's frustration shows that he had already succumbed to the unreflecting belief that any action was preferable to none. It marked a growing rift at the top level of government between those who thought it was vital to take a hard line with the King immediately and a Prime Minister who showed no inclination to intervene.

Within a few weeks of the conference in the Prime Minister's room, Hitler's unilateral remilitarisation of the Rhineland in defiance of the Versailles and Locarno Treaties provoked a European diplomatic crisis but, curiously, there is no sign that there was any concern in official circles at the King's attitude towards foreign affairs. On the one hand, the arrival of a full-scale international panic over a concrete issue pushed an abstract and potential problem into the background, and on the other, the

British government appears to have remained ignorant of the attention that the German Embassy was devoting to the King. In both official and unofficial German eyes, he might have passed for a significant player. Von Hoesch, the ambassador, reported formally that the Court saw scope for a lasting settlement in the flimsy negotiating proposals with which Germany followed up its fait accompli, and that it had indicated to the government that no serious complications were to be allowed to develop.[26] On the same day, according to his memoirs, the German Embassy's press adviser, Fritz Hesse, was invited to listen in to a phone conversation between the King and the ambassador in which the King boasted of having threatened to abdicate if there was war and to have put Baldwin in his place.[27] It is far from clear what foundation, if any, there was to either of these. Hesse's story is especially suspect as the events were supposedly triggered by rumours of a British military mobilisation, of which there was at no point the slightest possibility, and occurred only four days after the remilitarisation when the British attitude was tentative and mainly concerned to head France off from any resolute action. There is no record of the King giving an audience to Baldwin in the relevant time frame. However, Hesse insisted ever after, when confronted with sceptical comment, that the telephone conversation had taken place, and cited numerous witnesses from the Embassy to support him.[28]

The clue to the true purpose of the ambassador's despatch and the telephone call could lie in an analysis of the relationship between Hesse and the accredited diplomats. Hesse had been sent from Berlin at von Ribbentrop's behest and was suspected, probably accurately, of having been sent to keep an eye on the conservative apolitical professional diplomats.[29] The most plausible explanation for his being asked to listen in to the phone call was to ensure that word of it got back informally to von Ribbentrop in Berlin. Von Hoesch may have wanted to cover his back against potential accusations by von Ribbentrop that he was failing to exploit the good relationship that he (von Ribbentrop) had nurtured with the King at a moment of great need. The garish phone call incident would have lent colour to the guarded and, quite possibly dishonest, despatch. Hesse did not know the King and failed at first to recognise the voice, so it is just possible that the whole thing was a charade. Certainly more junior diplomats were not above such manoeuvres.[30] Whatever the truth is, von Ribbentrop retained his deluded faith in the potential for using Edward as a tool of Anglo-German rapprochement. He later claimed that this was strong enough to make him overcome his doubts and accept the job of ambassador to London when von Hoesch died suddenly a few weeks later.[31]

The civil servants had been worried that the German Embassy might have sight of government papers via Mrs Simpson, but this was a facet of broader concern at the new King's casual attitude to his constitutional duties.[32] George V had read assiduously and promptly the government papers that were sent to him for comment and responded accordingly. Edward rapidly demonstrated how different he was from his father; he returned papers long after they were sent to him and, worse, displayed minimal respect for their security and confidentiality. Some showed marks where cocktail glasses had stood on them.

When he came to prepare his account of the crisis very soon after it ended, Wilson was concerned that the government might be accused of having failed to act soon enough.

> It seemed to me that one possible criticism which the historian of the
> future might be tempted to make, would be that we did not appear to
> have begun soon enough to bring influence to bear upon the King to
> induce him to change his mind and that by the time we did take action
> a position had arisen which gave less hope of success.[33]

Bureaucrats rarely set out even hypothetical criticism of the work of the governments they serve, so it is hard to escape the conclusion that Wilson believed that the government was decidedly vulnerable on this score and, quite possibly, had felt so from the beginning. Wilson was being far more discreet than Fisher, but he was writing for the official record, not talk-ing privately. At a number of points in his notes, he reports conversations with the Prime Minister as a subtle method of underlining the fact that a decision taken reflected Baldwin's own judgement rather than a broader consensus. Baldwin's response to the accusation of delay was to tell Wil-son that Wigram had warned him early in the year that the King intended to marry Mrs Simpson, destroying his (Baldwin's) hopes that acceding to the throne would change the King's mind.

Wilson's fear that the government might be accused of failing to tackle the problem promptly made him drop the account of the list of priorities that Baldwin had shared with him in the summer of 1935 from the final ver-sion of his notes; he could not afford to admit that Edward gave grounds for concern well before his accession. The final version opens in the summer of 1936 but, in one of its many pieces of jumbled chronology, moves back to the early part of Edward's reign to mark the start of the acute phase of concern with the moment when Wigram told Baldwin of his fears.

The first major step toward outright crisis was noticeable to only a hand-ful of the closest insiders. By custom, senior courtiers remained in place for the first six or so months of a new reign to allow the new monarch to set-tle it. It thus did not arouse much outside attention when Wigram decided to resign his post in May, which was announced in July. Only the hand-ful of individuals aware of Queen Mary's determination that her son keep Wigram would have spotted anything untoward. Soon after he decided to go, Wigram visited Downing Street and treated Baldwin and Wilson to a litany of his complaints. He was propelled by a catalogue of misdeeds, but above all by Edward's 'subservience to Mrs. Simpson's wishes'.[34] Wigram blamed a large programme of insensitive and highly unpopular cost cuts that the King had instituted in the royal palaces on his desire to have more money for her. Lurking behind Wigram's decision to turn his back on his royal master was outright despair at the King's imperviousness to anything but his own desires, which came through even in the restrained prose of Wilson's notes: 'It was almost impossible to appeal to reason or judge-ment and [Wigram] gave no hope that anything that might be said would be effective.' Usually, Wilson maintained a decorous silence over Edward's character and this is practically the only direct criticism of his personality either made or quoted in his notes, and it is all the more striking for that. The logical implication of Wigram's verdict served as the unspoken slogan for the hardliners as the crisis unfolded: if the King was impervious to reason, force would provide the only solution.

Edward was put out by Wigram's departure, not because he was sympathetic to him, but because, like many egocentrics, he failed to comprehend that true loyalty has to be earned and saw anything other than blind obedience as betrayal. Wigram had been a conveniently reputable figurehead, and his resignation confronted Edward with the difficulty of finding a private secretary with sufficient credibility in Downing Street who could also cope with Mrs Simpson. One of Edward's long-standing courtiers, Admiral Halsey, had already been dismissed because he criticised her.[35] Edward's first choice as Wigram's replacement was Sir Godfrey Thomas, his assistant private secretary, who had worked for him for the best part of twenty years. Thomas, however, knew full well that the senior post would be anything but comfortable, and declined. Rather as had happened with 'Tommy' Lascelles, who had despaired of working for Edward in 1929, long and close acquaintanceship with his royal master inspired severe caution. This left Edward with Alec Hardinge, who had been assistant to Wigram and his predecessor, Stamfordham, since 1920. Even though he was only a few years older than Edward, Hardinge belonged firmly to the upright certainties of George V's Court. His family had a long and distinguished record of public and royal service. He himself had fought bravely in the First World War, in which he had been seriously injured. He liked Edward personally – perhaps another victim of his dangerous charm – but he deplored Mrs Simpson's all-pervading and dominant influence on the King.[36] Chips Channon MP, a fair representative of the social circle in which Edward and Mrs Simpson moved, took it for granted that Hardinge and other such 'dreary narrow-minded fogies' would be sacked when Edward became King.[37]

It was Hardinge's personal tragedy that he followed his perceived duty towards the royal family and accepted the job. He had little direct experience of working with Edward, unlike Lascelles, who had re-joined the Court as assistant secretary to George V in 1935, and Godfrey. Hardinge had practical rather than people skills; according to Lascelles, his 'great administrative and executive talents as a King's secretary, compensated, on balance for his complete inability to establish friendly, or even civil relations with the great majority of his fellow-men...'[38] Hardinge's chances of success were further eroded by his outspoken and indiscreet criticism of Edward and his circle, some of which found its way back to the target.[39] Edward was morbidly sensitive to adverse comment, either about himself or Mrs Simpson. It is improbable that there was anyone who could have created a genuine dialogue between Edward and Downing Street, but it fell to Hardinge to make the attempt.

Wigram's departure was the clearest evidence of doubts about the King to the highest levels of government, but he was also dissipating the fund of goodwill with which he had begun his reign in other ways as well. The most striking example was his savage economy drive in the royal household.[40] It had long been run chaotically and inefficiently, but the King's measures appeared to be no more than penny-pinching rather than a reasoned reform. Worse, the contrast between his meanness towards his servants contrasted vividly with the huge sums of money he lavished on Mrs Simpson. The brunt was borne by the palaces of Sandringham and Balmoral, which were his personal charge and cost. It did not help that he had no affinity for either place. The King also strove to punish courtiers who expressed any reservations about Mrs Simpson. His long-standing equerry Admiral Halsey was dismissed, and he conducted a vendetta against Louis Greig, a friend of his brother the Duke of York, whose unfavourable comments on her appeared to have reached his ears.[41]

Edward VIII had no patience with the encrusted and arbitrary practices that had grown up around the sovereign. He manifested his contempt for ceremony and tradition by insisting that a clutch of privileged bodies with the ancient right of presenting a Loyal Address should be given a single royal reply in a group and not one each. It was established practice to alternate the profile of the sovereign's head used on coins and postage

stamps; left profile for one sovereign then right profile for his or her successor. In Edward's case this would have meant using his right profile but
he felt it was less flattering and insisted his left profile be used. Edward
VIII stamps carried the left profile but no coins were ever circulated.
It was a case of witless vanity versus pointless tradition. He offended the
senior infantry regiment of the British Army, the Grenadier Guards in which
he had also served. The Grenadiers had expected to be honoured by the
first royal review of the reign, but he reviewed the Welsh Guards – a mere
fifth in seniority – two days before them.[42] Much of this was fatuous and
barely damaging, but it all demonstrated an overbearing self-centredness
and thoughtlessness towards the feelings of others.

The King's relationship with the Archbishop of Canterbury got no better when the question of a national memorial for George V came under
discussion. Lang promoted vigorously a grandiose scheme to create a
large esplanade between Westminster Abbey and the Houses of Parliament, supposedly as a fitting place for a statue of the late King.[43] It would
have involved the wholesale demolition of about a hectare of old buildings.
In reality, Lang's scheme was a naked attempt to promote the Church's
position in political life:

> If there is one place in London which can be described as very specially
> a centre of our national and Imperial life it is surely the great area which
> contains Westminster Abbey, the sacred shrine of its history and the glo-
> ries of Parliament, the scene of its Government.[44]

The King and his brothers supported a rival scheme for public playing fields
across the country, which was eventually preferred. Quite how much Lang
might have resented this is unclear, but the King certainly came to believe
– wrongly – that Lang worked against him in the crisis that was to come.

Edward certainly did not see Wigram's departure as a reason to moderate his behaviour; in fact it coincided with the next step in his plan to
make Mrs Simpson his Queen. Whilst Edward was still Prince of Wales,
Mrs Simpson had been almost entirely confined to the bachelor world that

he created with its centre at his private house, Fort Belvedere. It was his refuge from the royal side of his life and the world of his official duties. But now he set out to introduce Mrs Simpson into the semi-public and ordered world of Court. His first step was to invite the Simpsons to the very first formal dinner of his reign at York House for Derby Day in May 1936. Their names thus appeared in the Court Circular, invariably reproduced in *The Times* and read intently by anyone who was anyone in British Society and wanted to know what was going on in the very top bracket. To an extent unimaginable today, inviting the Simpsons signalled that they belonged to this elite. The invitation was not merely intended as the first push of a pawn up the social chessboard. Edward wanted Baldwin to meet his 'future wife'.[45] According to her memoirs, this was the first time that he told her that he intended to marry her. If true, it was an unconventional proposal of marriage, in which the bride-to-be was still married to someone else and was also offered no choice in the matter. Perhaps he simply assumed that Mrs Simpson would want to marry him as much as he wanted to marry her. He was determined to marry her, whatever opposition there might be. She claimed to have seen the inevitable difficulties and told Edward, 'The idea is impossible. They'll never let you.' Edward seemed to relish the challenge, although he had no clear idea of how he was going to do this: 'I'm well aware of all that but rest assured, I will manage it somehow.' Like the naughty child trying it on with its parents, he was just looking towards the next turn of the screw.

The idea of marriage remained a secret between Edward and Mrs Simpson. Quite apart from the broader question of overcoming the likely resistance of government and family to such a marriage, the oddities of Britain's divorce law at the time meant there was a very strong practical reason for Edward to keep his relationship with Mrs Simpson as quiet as possible. According to the law, the 'innocent' spouse had to take action against the 'guilty' spouse. Evidence or even suspicion that the 'innocent' spouse was involved with anyone else threatened their 'innocent' status, which could and frequently did wreck divorces. One of the government law officers, the King's Proctor, was tasked with sniffing out any suspect divorces and had a healthy success rate in blocking those he discovered. There was a distinct danger that Edward's plan to marry Mrs Simpson would fall at the first fence: securing her divorce from Ernest. It was around the time of the York House dinner that Edward had prompted Mrs Simpson to begin divorce proceedings. It was imperative to keep their relationship quiet. It was possible for the 'innocent' party to ask the judge in the case for 'a discretion' in respect of adultery of their own. But this would almost certainly have brought the King's relationship with her into the light.

It is an open question as to whether the York House dinner increased the number of people in Britain aware of Edward's relationship with Mrs Simpson, but it certainly stoked the outrage that the affair provoked. Horror was amplified by inviting the flamboyant Society hostess Emerald Cunard as well. Lady Cunard was also originally American and had been an early supporter of Mrs Simpson's in London Society. She used her husband's money from shipping to support the musical career of her lover Sir Thomas Beecham. Her salon was faintly bohemian and a touch disreputable. Sir John Reith, the dourly sanctimonious Director General of the BBC and a close ally of Fisher's, was appalled to see both on the guest list; the sight of the names in *The Times* caused him near-physical agony: 'Lady Cunard, an evil woman who was never at the late King's parties. Mr and Mrs E Simpson. It is too horrible and it is serious and sad beyond calculation.'[46] There was a powerful element of outright snobbism in resentment at the invitations to Mrs Simpson and Lady Cunard. Nancy Astor, the American-born MP and a divorcee herself, 'deplore[d] the fact that any but the best Virginian families should be received at Court'.[47] At the level of crude social tactics, the King had succeeding in ambushing the Baldwins, who had no forewarning of the Simpsons' (or Lady Cunard's) presence, although the manoeuvre was sufficiently shocking for it to be believed that Baldwin had almost fled the dinner when he saw Mrs Simpson.[48] It is unlikely that he would have done anything so offensive, but the matter was serious enough to be discussed in Downing Street. The only clue as to what was said is Wilson's frustratingly impersonal remark: 'There was some uneasiness at the thought that her name should be included in the Court Circular, but her husband's name was also included…'[49] The most plausible reading of this is that Wilson expressed his anxiety, but the Prime Minister was mollified because the social decencies were being respected. Mrs Simpson might still hold on to the status of 'respectable whore'.

In July, Mrs Simpson was again scandalously invited to a Court dinner, this time – even more scandalously – without her husband. Reith muttered once more, musing that an unfit monarch supported the argument for a republic. There was also an indication that alarm was spreading at the higher levels of the political world. Baldwin's predecessor as Prime Minister, Ramsay MacDonald, was well past the peak of his political power and failing mentally, but the need to maintain the charade of a national government embracing the Labour movement had dictated that he remain in the Cabinet, albeit in a token quasi-sinecure of Lord President of the Council, which brought him into extensive contact with Court circles. He complained of the King's 'appalling obstinacy' and how the affair was 'making a bad effect on the country'.[50] MacDonald's worries were nebulous and it is hard to gauge how strongly or broadly they were shared by other senior politicians. Neville Chamberlain, who emerged as the chief advocate of taking a hard line with the King when the crisis proper began, did not mention the King at all in either his diary or his letters to his sisters between April and the autumn. In Downing Street, though, worry continued to grow. Once again, the imprecision of Wilson's notes is frustrating. By the 'latter part of the summer', Baldwin was 'increasingly anxious as to the way in which the matter might develop'.[51] Quite what might have been feared is not clear, but the thing that set the alarm bells ringing was the news that the King was going on holiday and taking Mrs Simpson with him. By August, Wilson had told his wife he was very worried, but by then Baldwin was on a prolonged convalescence from acute strain.[52]

Downing Street was not wrong to be perturbed. The next move in the King's relationship with Mrs Simpson transformed it from a secret amongst a relatively small number of people in Britain into an international cause célèbre. It destroyed whatever chance that there might have been of the matter being dealt with in decorous, British silence. He took Mrs Simpson

on holiday with him in a way that could not fail to attract enormous attention. This took things out of the control not only of Downing Street but
also Edward himself, quite possibly to his surprise. In a number of respects
he was behaving responsibly and cooperatively, at least by his own standards. He and Mrs Simpson had gone on holiday together the two previous
summers; all that was different was that he was now King. These holidays
were private to the extent that they did not feature in the Court Circular and
so were less openly provocative than the York House dinners, which appear
as conscious attempts to advance Mrs Simpson on the social chessboard.
Edward was also sufficiently alert to any appearance of impropriety for Ernest
Simpson to be invited to accompany his wife. Edward deferred not once but
twice to Foreign Office advice. Originally, he had planned to rent a villa in
the south of France, but the Foreign Office convinced itself that the outbreak
of civil war in Spain made that area excessively sensitive. It might also have
been deterred by the election of the left-wing Front Populaire government,
which drew support from the Communist Party. The villa holiday was cancelled and the King chartered a luxurious yacht, the *Nahlin*, from its owner
Lady Yule for a cruise in the eastern Mediterranean. The Foreign Office then
successfully objected to a plan for the *Nahlin* to collect its guests from Fascist Italy, which the Italian ministry for foreign affairs recognised would have
been a symbolic softening of official British policy.[53] Instead, they boarded at
a small port in Yugoslavia. Moreover, the King undertook to perform a slight,
but not negligible, diplomatic mission in combining the voyage with private
visits to a series of the local rulers, in particular Kemal Atatürk of Turkey.
Having fought Turkey in the First World War and come near to war in 1922,
this was a powerful token of a more friendly approach from Britain. The
whole exercise sent a strong signal of British desire to maintain alliances in
the region to Italian diplomats who followed the voyage closely.[54] The presence of a Cabinet minister, Duff Cooper, on the *Nahlin* added another layer
of superficial respectability.

As an informal foreign policy exercise, the *Nahlin*'s cruise was a solid
success, with Edward exercising his usual charm on his hosts. Some of
them were surprised that the King of England should travel openly with

his mistress, but as he was travelling privately and incognito as 'Duke of Lancaster', it all fell into a very grey area of protocol. Otherwise, the cruise was a catastrophe. The diplomatic achievements were swamped by the massive international press coverage of the King's romance. British journalists believed that a tacit deal between the King and leading newspaper proprietors meant that the voluntary press silence on the King's affair would apply to the holiday. The British blackout was maintained, but no such consideration applied to the US and European newspapers. Until then they had had very little to get their teeth into, but the *Nahlin* cruise changed this utterly. Photographs of Edward, bare-chested, strolling in the sunlight and walking hand-in-hand with Mrs Simpson were the sensation of the summer. British prestige abroad was severely hurt by this catastrophic loss of royal dignity. Mussolini himself followed the cruise, sniffing that the King's behaviour was '*troppo democratico*'.[55] Letters began to flow into Downing Street and other Establishment addresses. The ludicrous move of cutting the offending articles out of foreign newspapers imported into Britain merely made things worse. Worst of all, in Wilson's eyes, *Cavalcade*, a lightweight British magazine, revealed Mrs Simpson's presence on the *Nahlin*.[56] Even though *Cavalcade* did not discuss her relationship with the King, this was the first crack in the wall of British press silence.

One part of the cruise that attracted favourable and open publicity at the time was later to hurt the King badly. Perversely enough, it was one that reflected his better side, his sense of solidarity with former combatants. As the *Nahlin* reached Gallipoli, the King visited the graves of the British and Empire servicemen who had died trying to storm the peninsula twenty years before in one of the most savage and futile battles of the First World War. Many had fought in the legendary ANZAC corps from Australia and New Zealand, whose name had become a byword for the sacrifice of Dominion citizens on behalf of the mother country. Given the King's reverence for his comrades in arms it was practically inevitable that he should want to pay his respects to the fallen. His visits to the memorials were fully covered in the British press. The Turkish government was entirely supportive of a dignified act of remembrance. It was only when the crisis got under way that Mrs Simpson's presence appeared as an act of gross disrespect, entirely cancelling out the goodwill generated at the time.

The mass of publicity shook Mrs Simpson. Waiting for her as she travelled back to Britain through Paris at the end of the holiday was a wad of clippings from the US papers. This prompted her to write to Edward, making a half-hearted attempt to split from him and to return to the unchallenging world of her husband and a 'calm, congenial life'.[57] He responded with a threat of suicide. Faced with Edward's obsession, Mrs Simpson's letter led to nothing, but he had learned that she was disturbed by the thought of attracting press attention. He could not, of course, repair the damage done by the *Nahlin* cruise, but within a few weeks, his desire to protect Mrs Simpson's privacy led him down a very dangerous path indeed.

The disaster of the *Nahlin* cruise did not make Edward moderate his behaviour when he was back in the apparently safer environment of his home country. He continued to escalate his challenge to established decencies. Having scandalised or delighted the non-British world with his idea of a good holiday, he proceeded to vandalise the British idea of an appropriate holiday for its sovereign. Since Queen Victoria's day, tradition had dictated that in September the sovereign went to Balmoral, which had acquired an almost sacred aura in the iconography of the House of Windsor as the cornerstone of its largely imaginary Scottishness. Edward did not go so far as to outrage his Court by not going in 1936, but what he did might have been even worse. Balmoral was part of the monarch's official programme and the names of guests featured in the Court Circular, so the affront would be as severe as the York House dinners and probably worse given Balmoral's particular status. The sovereign customarily invited well-established worthies, most notably the Prime Minister, to Balmoral. Edward chose lightweight cronies from Fort Belvedere instead.

Edward's guest list for Balmoral could, just, be dismissed as another turn of the screw on Society, but he capped it with a piece of grotesque insensitivity and bad manners, which seemed almost perfectly designed to cause the maximum offence to the ordinary public. He had been invited to perform the entirely natural and undemanding task of opening the new

Aberdeen Infirmary on 26 September. He had laid the foundation stone on the building in 1928 as Prince of Wales. He declined to perform the opening on the flimsy pretext that he was still in mourning for his father and left the task to his oldest brother, the Duke of York. As if to rub in his apparent contempt for his Scottish subjects, on the day of the ceremony he personally drove to Aberdeen railway station to collect Mrs Simpson when she arrived from London. The *Aberdeen Evening Express* reported the two events side-by-side in an unstated but merciless denunciation of the relative priorities of the royal brothers.[58] The article did not mention Mrs Simpson by name, but made a point of describing the King's doings as 'unexpected' and drew an unspoken but damning contrast between the crowd of thousands at the Infirmary and the handful of railway employees who saw the King at the station, implying, probably accurately, that he had hoped not to be spotted. He added insult to injury by driving a Ford car rather than one from a British-owned company, but this registered only on Lord Nuffield.[59] Even the feather-brain socialite Chips Channon, a normally uncritical friend to both of the couple, rated Edward's behaviour as 'almost brazen … Aberdeen will never forgive him.'[60] It also created a deeply unfavourable and alarmist impression in Downing Street.

The King used the visit to Balmoral to prepare for the burgeoning political crisis. One of his guests and possibly the only one who would have featured on anything other than the social pages of the newspapers was Esmond Harmsworth, one of the few of his friends who counted for something in the wider world. His father and uncle were the Harmsworth brothers, the prototypes of Britain's press barons, who had become fabulously wealthy as proprietors of mass-market newspapers, above all the *Daily Mail*. They had also parlayed their newspaper readership into transient political power under Lloyd George's coalition government, but had been left out in the cold following the Carlton House coup. Harmsworth's father, Viscount Rothermere, was clearly the junior in the partnership and after his brother's death in 1922 had been left in something of a limbo. He operated in loose alliance with his notional competitor Lord Beaverbrook, who had earned his undying gratitude for the sympathy he showed when Rothermere lost his two older sons during the War. Harmsworth had been brought into politics by his father as a mouthpiece for the venomous 'anti-waste' campaign against government spending that Rothermere launched after the War. He was elected to Parliament in 1919 as the baby of the House at the age of only nineteen, but he was hindered rather than helped by his father's increasingly eccentric views; ludicrously, Rothermere had tried to extort a Cabinet post for his son in 1922. Harmsworth remained as an MP until 1929, but his energies were increasingly devoted to managing the family newspaper business competently in the teeth of his father's erratic practices. He pursued the lucrative strategy of buying up provincial newspapers and since 1934 had been chairman of the proprietors' trade body, the Newspaper Proprietors' Association. Harmsworth was also a figure at the top level of Café Society, where his education, good looks and sporting prowess practically guaranteed success. At Balmoral, he and the King discussed politics, probably assessing senior politicians in terms of their likely behaviour in a confrontation with the King. The King told Harmsworth how much he disliked Sir John Simon, the Home Secretary.[61] Simon did indeed emerge as one of the leading hardliners in the following weeks.

Mrs Simpson's visit to Balmoral brought her into uncomfortable proximity with the wife of the King's oldest brother, the Duchess of York. Relations between the two were poor; before she arrived on the scene, the Yorks had seen much of Edward and had even entertained him and Lady Furness as a couple. Mrs Simpson treated the Duchess as a figure of fun and, according to one author, had earned her undying enmity by delivering a cruel impersonation of her in front of a group of people.[62] If any of this came to Downing Street's attention, it has left no trace in the record.

It is hardly likely that the Aberdeen episode was intended as a provocation; it brought Edward nothing whatsoever. It was an example of the complete thoughtlessness that led him to neglect the possibility that the British press would abandon its self-disciplined silence when it reported Mrs Simpson's divorce action barely a fortnight after his return from Balmoral. The court case would present the press with a temptingly hard domestic news item, and even the vaguest public mention of the King in connection with it would be too horrible to contemplate. One of the most formidable predators of the British political and media jungles sensed vulnerable prey and began to stalk. On Monday 12 October, Theodore Goddard, Mrs Simpson's solicitor, received a telephone call from the press magnate Lord Beaverbrook, warning him that one of his newspapers, the *Evening Standard*, had the story of the divorce case and intended to publish it.[63] Goddard tried to persuade Beaverbrook to give his client privacy, but he received a studiedly non-committal reply.

Beaverbrook was one of the great trouble-makers of his time. He took an impish delight in manipulating men and events from behind the scenes. He now began a discreet auction for his assistance in keeping the press quiet. There had long been an uneasy stand-off between him and Edward, who, like any celebrity, understood something of the dangers of getting too close to the media. In 1928, Edward played golf with Robert Bruce Lockhart, the former spy and now one of the star journalists in the Beaverbrook empire, who noted in his diary that 'the Prince does not like Beaverbrook, says he wants to get everyone under his thumb and, if he cannot get them, he tries to down them'.[64] In 1929, Beaverbrook had opened one potential channel of communication to Edward by hiring Mike Wardell, a close friend of the Prince, despite his only very humble business qualifications. Whilst this helped establish Beaverbrook firmly in the same social set as Edward, direct contact was modest. In his memoir of the abdication, Beaverbrook is ambiguous as to how actively he had sought Edward's friendship. He did invite him to dinner, but claimed that the other guests 'were made up of my own group of friends and had not been gathered for the purpose of entertaining the Prince of Wales. Dean Inge and his wife were among them.'[65] The 'gloomy Dean's' blend of intellectual Christianity and social conservatism might have been calculated to repel Edward. However, when Edward became King, Beaverbrook saw the prospect of a 'new outlook in public life' and broke his habit of not attending formal functions and attended Edward's Accession Council, making great play of what he presented as the great sacrifice of donning his, admittedly uncomfortable, Privy Councillor's uniform.

Beaverbrook was calculating that the benefits of putting the King under an obligation would have been far greater than the benefits of a good news story, and he took full advantage when Edward showed how desperate he was to shield Mrs Simpson from publicity. He personally telephoned Beaverbrook to ask for a meeting the day after his telephone conversation with Goddard. Beaverbrook made full use of the King's invitation to 'name your own time' and set the appointment for three days later, Friday 16 October.[66] In his memoir he explained away the delay with a claim that he needed urgent dental treatment, but the historian A. J. P. Taylor, who edited the memoir and openly revered Beaverbrook, was for once sceptical and pointed out that Beaverbrook's appointments diary for the days between mentions no dentist but does mention Ernest Simpson late in the afternoon of Thursday 15th.[67] It seems that Beaverbrook wanted to make the King sweat a little and to check on the relationship between him and Mrs Simpson before committing himself to suppressing what might have been a very major story indeed.

There is a small hint that the King might have been somewhat reluctant to see Beaverbrook, perhaps because of his previous distrust, perhaps because he dimly foresaw the political cost. On the Thursday, Mrs Simpson nagged him by post to perform 'Friday's job' and secure appropriately low-key press coverage.[68] Against this, there was ample reason to seek Beaverbrook's help. The King's plea to Beaverbrook was heartfelt and focused on his desire to protect Mrs Simpson, 'ill, unhappy, and distressed at the thought of notoriety'.[69] Beaverbrook accepted and in his usual style swung into action, bringing in Esmond Harmsworth, his fellow press proprietor. The Harmsworths' *Daily Mail* and Beaverbrook's *Daily Express* stood together as the great popular newspapers of their day, reviled by conservative politicians; their owners tried to translate their huge circulations into political influence. Beaverbrook and Harmsworth approached other national and local newspapers and won them over to a policy of restraint. Beaverbrook overcame the doubts of Sir Walter Layton of the left-leaning *News Chronicle*, which held the line of silence. Edward was ever afterwards immensely grateful for Beaverbrook's assistance but, in reality, Beaverbrook had got much for very little. His habitual exercise in dramatically exaggerated activity masked a far more modest performance. The silence of the *News Chronicle* was Beaverbrook's only solid achievement. There is no indication that he even contacted either *The Times* or the *Daily Telegraph*, the two dominant Establishment papers. They were conservative papers who supported the government and were far more likely to follow an official lead than that of competitors whom they despised anyway. Geoffrey Dawson, editor of *The Times*, knew that his paper '"will have to do something about the King and Mrs. Simpson". But that the Prime Minister must tell him what he wishes done.'[70] It is unlikely that either would have broken the silence spontaneously. The Labour *Daily Herald* also kept silent without intervention; the Labour Party leader had decided not to fish in the troubled waters of the King's affairs.

Intentionally or otherwise, the King had made a significant political choice in calling Beaverbrook to his assistance. There was a gulf between those papers who supported the government and those who didn't. Beaverbrook was the most extreme example. He was a bitter enemy of Baldwin, who had signally failed to give him the same privileged position that he held during the brief premiership of his fellow Canadian and business partner, Andrew Bonar Law. Bonar Law had benefited financially from the relationship, and Beaverbrook in terms of backstairs political influence. Beaverbrook had also been a leading light in Lloyd George's coalition government, the 'thieves' kitchen', loathed by the traditional Conservatives championed by Baldwin. Beaverbrook's genuine enthusiasm for the Empire had led him to campaign vigorously against Baldwin on the issue of Empire Free Trade. When Baldwin famously denounced the press for exercising 'power without responsibility, the prerogative of the harlot throughout the ages', he was aiming squarely at Beaverbrook. At the start of Edward's reign Beaverbrook was suspected of plotting with Winston Churchill, then struggling to return from the political wilderness, to remove Baldwin.[71] At this stage, the King was concerned only to protect Mrs Simpson, but he had unthinkingly stepped into the camp of the government's opponents. He had strayed into a singularly venomous political feud. It was to have serious consequences.[72]

CHAPTER 4

A JOB IS ASSIGNED
TO THE PRIME MINISTER

As to the particular job in connection with a 'serting' lady assigned to
the P.M. he has done it but I can't make out that he clinched anything...
NEVILLE CHAMBERLAIN TO HIS SISTER IDA, 24 OCTOBER 1936

T HERE WAS A gulf between Stanley Baldwin's public persona and
the reality. He cultivated the image of a bluff and stolid Midlands
businessman and country lover, the epitome of a rank-and-file
Conservative MP. Beneath this façade, he was acute and highly strung.
People unfamiliar with his true personality might have thought that outside events were barely registering on him. In reality, he would agonise over
the best way to tackle a given problem until he was confident of the right
move. Baldwin paid for this habit in two quite different ways. Even close
colleagues mistook his inactivity for nonchalant idleness. Some, notably
Neville Chamberlain then Chancellor of the Exchequer and his de facto
deputy, were driven to near fury and nursed a growing contempt for Baldwin based on a complete misunderstanding of the man and his methods.
Baldwin's resolute concealment of his doubts also put him under huge
mental stress. Contrary to Chamberlain's contemptuous opinion, Baldwin

took his responsibilities as Prime Minister immensely seriously. As he aged, Baldwin found the burden a heavy one and by the summer of 1936 he was close to a nervous breakdown. Of the various accidents that shaped the abdication crisis, this was one of the most significant. Just as the *Nahlin* cruise was propelling the King's relationship with Mrs Simpson into global consciousness and transforming a significant scandal into a major problem for the government, the Prime Minister was not available to tackle it.

The strains of dealing with the international situation had taken Baldwin to the verge of collapse. Since he had become Prime Minister in 1935, the pressure had been almost unremitting. Diplomatic crises had come one on top of another beginning with the invasion of Abyssinia. Confronted by its first major test, the League of Nations failed abjectly to deliver on its promise of harmonious and peaceful resolution to this kind of challenge. Not only was Britain politically unprepared to rebuild the old order in Europe, but the crisis threw into stark relief the extent of her military weakness after years of minimal spending on the armed forces. In March 1936, Nazi Germany reoccupied the Rhineland in a flagrant breach of the Versailles Treaty. Even if Britain had seriously wanted to intervene, it lacked both the diplomatic and the military power to do so. The outbreak of the Spanish Civil War added another layer of complexity and danger. Baldwin found himself struggling with the dilemma that baffled British statesmen until Hitler's invasion of France in May 1940 gave Britain no option other than fighting an all-out war against the fascist dictatorships on its own.

In late July, Lord Dawson, the most eminent doctor in the country, strongly advised Baldwin to take three months of complete rest.[1] Baldwin did not get his full three months, but he dropped out of all political activity to an extent inconceivable for a modern head of government. For more than two months he was away from Downing Street, unaccompanied by either politicians or civil servants. He was almost completely out of contact; the telephones of the time were unreliable and insecure, and letters or personal visits were the only method of contact. He spent August at Gregynog Hall, an isolated mansion in Wales owned by the Davies sisters, devout Methodists deeply involved in the revival of Welsh culture but entirely uninvolved in the greater affairs of the country. They were friends of Tom Jones, former assistant secretary to the Cabinet and Baldwin's confidant and speech-writer. In honour of the Prime Minister and to the delight of their butler, they suspended their usual absolute ban on alcohol.[2] Baldwin toured the Welsh Marches, exploring his ancestral homelands.[3] It is far from certain that he was more than dimly aware of the full scale of the *Nahlin* debacle. Baldwin's only recorded serious contact with his official life was a visit by Tommy Dugdale, his parliamentary private secretary.[4] Dugdale's drive from his home in North Yorkshire was sufficiently epic by the standards of 1930s motoring to remain a strong shared memory, but what prompted him to make the journey remains a frustrating mystery although it was planned some days in advance, suggesting the business was not urgent.

Baldwin's next destination brought him back nearer to London, both literally and figuratively. Blickling Hall in Norfolk was the home of Lord Lothian, an intimate member of Lloyd George's circle and a former minis-ter. Official life began to press Baldwin again. Tom Jones, Horace Wilson and Maurice Hankey came down separately from London to see him. But there is no positive evidence that suggests that the King's affairs were even mentioned. Jones briefed the Prime Minister on his recent visit to Hitler and floated a scheme for a summit meeting.[5] All that Hankey remembered of his visit to Blickling in old age was that Baldwin had promised him a peerage there, but that the promise was forgotten amidst the abdication crisis that ensued, which implies that Hankey believed that the crisis began later.[6] Of the three visitors, Wilson was the most preoccupied about the King, but there is no hint whatever in current or later accounts as to what he talked about with Baldwin. Wilson visited Blickling on 16 September, even before the minor scandal of the King's choice of guests at Balmoral had broken and weeks after the *Nahlin* cruise had vanished from the news.[7] If he did bring up the subject of the King, the conversation was inconclu-sive. The only indication that the crisis was under way lies in the memories of the servants' hall at Blickling, but this is not decisive.[8] It may reflect what the servants gossiped about amongst themselves or a gloss of memory. Mrs Baldwin made a great impression with her tip of £25 to the staff, immense by the standards of the day, perhaps unintentionally creating a sense that great matters were afoot.

Baldwin's absence from London left a void at the centre of government for the critical period that the King's behaviour began to appear as a flagrant challenge to convention. But could he have done anything? Before Baldwin left on his convalescence, Hardinge recognised that 'the Prime Minister's natural reluctance to interfere in the private life of the Sovereign … was reinforced by the fact that no constitutional issue could arise as long as Mrs Simpson remained married to Mr Simpson'.[9] British Prime Ministers had never advised sovereigns on their private lives, only on marriage. Only if the King proposed to marry Mrs Simpson (or anyone else) would practice have demanded that he consult the Prime Minister. Notwithstanding, Baldwin's absence from Downing Street isolated him from two forces that would have pushed him towards action: the growing stream of letters from concerned members of the public and Horace Wilson. It was at least hypothetically possible that the King might have been warned against inviting Mrs Simpson on the *Nahlin* cruise or to Balmoral, the two episodes that most shocked opinion. Wilson knew about Mrs Simpson's presence on the *Nahlin* before the cruise began. Had Baldwin been in Downing Street, it is a near certainty that Wilson would have tried his hardest to make the Prime Minister act given the extent of his fears. When Baldwin briefly passed through London on his way from Gregynog to Blickling, Wilson was itching to broach the King's affairs but deferred to Lord Dawson's view that Baldwin should be kept from public business.[10]

If there ever had been any opportunity to persuade the King to behave decorously before he triggered a full-scale crisis, it had gone by the time Baldwin returned to Downing Street on Tuesday 13 October. He was much restored by his weeks of rest, most fortunately given the trial that awaited him. The scandal of the King's private life had escalated into a crisis. What had been a painful and degrading spectacle now appeared to pose acute risks, and the Prime Minister was the only man in a position to do anything. Baldwin was very soon made aware of this. The mountain of letters had been building up over the summer and offered brutal, physical testimony to the level of public revulsion at the King's behaviour. This was soon reinforced by urgent warnings from senior figures from the Establishment. When he attended what proved to be an entirely routine audience with the King on Wednesday 14th, Hardinge expressed his concerns to the Prime Minister both before and after the audience itself.[11]

Concerns were even graver in Downing Street, where Wilson was particularly incensed at the King's behaviour over the opening of the Aberdeen Infirmary, which he saw as a dangerous provocation of public opinion. Wilson did not specifically mention the press coverage of the incident in his notes, but seems to have recognised that the King's affair could no longer be kept secret. Worse, he began to believe 'that before very long public opinion would be provoked to an outburst'.[12] Wilson's fears that Mrs Simpson would provoke public disorder were extreme and exaggerated and it is difficult to find anyone who shared them to anything like the same extent. There is no sign that Baldwin shared them at all and Wilson gives no hard supporting evidence, say reports from Police Chief Constables. He was not shy of disclosing intelligence material when it backed up his case elsewhere. It is easy to guess why Wilson was so sensitive on this topic. He had made his name as an industrial negotiator before the First World War, when strikes had become so violent that the army had to be called in to keep the peace. Potential mob violence was real enough to him and stood in stark contrast to the vague anxieties expressed elsewhere, which blended moral and social outrage with a sense of British prestige somehow being damaged. Wilson's fear that there would be a violent public reaction against Mrs Simpson continued throughout the crisis. It was so extreme that he imagined that any breach in the press silence would trigger violence. When Wilson briefed Baldwin on the same day as his conversation with Hardinge, his warnings were even starker: 'Opinion was developing throughout the country in a way that might have unfavourable reactions upon the position of the King.' The time-bomb of Mrs Simpson's divorce case was also set to explode.

There are a handful of pointers to the possibility that Whitehall might somehow have got advance warning of the divorce case. Wilson's notes avoid giving a precise date by jumping from discussions of the King's 'association' with Mrs Simpson straight to the news of the divorce case reaching the newspapers. Baldwin's arrangements for resuming his duties on his return from Blickling were changed at the last moment. Chamberlain complained to his sister on 11 October that he had learned only from the newspapers that Baldwin was returning to Downing Street the following day, a considerable acceleration of his original plan to base himself at Chequers and only come to London for Cabinet meetings.[13] When Chamberlain probed Hankey on the reason for this change, he was evasive. The civil servants certainly withheld firm news of the divorce case from Baldwin when he arrived in Downing Street, so the same might well have applied to advance warning of the case, even more so if this had been acquired by unavowable means. One potential source of a leak was Mrs Simpson's solicitor, Theodore Goddard, who went on to display distinctly ambiguous loyalties towards his client and the government.

Baldwin did not immediately commit himself to intervene with the King when he spoke to Wilson, but he did agree that Wilson should be put in direct contact with the royal household.[14] This strengthened Wilson's personal role and deeply affected how the government handled the affair. The individual allocation of tasks as a crisis unfolds is not just a mundane matter of chance and careerism. It is part of a process that bakes sets of prejudices and instincts into the way the crisis is handled. After two months of enforced inactivity in the face of the King's dangerous and reckless behaviour, Wilson was now in a position to begin to treat the matter with the urgency that it deserved. Baldwin was still held back from tackling the King directly by the constitutional niceties of the position, but it was now acknowledged that there was a severe threat to national stability, which called for exceptional measures.

The day after the audience, Wilson had lunch with Hardinge, which seems to have been the first substantial conversation between the two men. They were both deeply perturbed about the King and desperately anxious that something should be done; to begin with at least, they worked to achieve this. This was a significant recasting of the pattern of contact between the royal household and Downing Street. In the past, the Prime Minister himself had generally spoken directly to the sovereign's private secretary on matters of importance, but Wilson's position in Downing Street was a novelty and the whole situation was unusual in the extreme. Given the gravity of the issue and the likely complexity of the questions that would have to be dealt with, it would have been unwise to rely on a single high-level channel of communication, so there was a strong practical argument for creating another one. The move was perfectly legitimate and justifiable, although it is striking that Baldwin should have given the task to a civil servant and not a senior minister. It helps explain why it was only some weeks later that politicians other than the Prime Minister became involved. It gives rise to suspicion that Wilson himself suggested the move and that his notes misstated the facts by claiming that the lunch was '[a]t the Prime Minister's suggestion'.[15] An extra channel of communication to the King was not a bad idea, but the weak relationship between the King and Hardinge compromised it. When Wilson came to produce an account of the crisis after the abdication, it is barely surprising that he eliminated the lunch and his subsequent dialogue with Hardinge from the definitive version.

Bringing Wilson into contact with Hardinge was a quite ordinary piece of crisis management, but Wilson and Baldwin agreed another move that was far more radical. MI5, Britain's domestic security service, was tasked with putting the King under surveillance. The unchallenged and legitimate head of state was to be treated as a potential threat to national security. Wilson's bland description of the move in his notes both understates colossally the significance of the move and provides a clue as to how the conversation between the Prime Minister and Wilson actually went: 'The Prime Minister decided to make certain enquiries with a view to determining how best to approach the King on the subject.'[16] It is one of the points where Wilson's notes contradict themselves clumsily, and unintentionally point towards something that they were trying to conceal. As written, the notes imply that the MI5 operation was conceived to brief the Prime Minister for a single conversation with the King, but the remainder of the notes contain many references to a steady flow of intelligence on the King's camp. The notion of a limited MI5 involvement with a single, precise goal has the flavour of the thin end of a dishonest wedge that Wilson might have used to prise open the Prime Minister's scruples over spying on his King. There is no evidence that Baldwin was briefed on the MI5 or any other intelligence operation as the crisis unfolded, so it is perfectly possible that these were essentially intended for the civil servants. The best guess is that Sir Vernon Kell, the head of MI5, reported orally to Fisher or Wilson and they drew their own conclusions and passed these or the raw intelligence on as they saw fit. The MI5 operation was almost certainly Wilson's initiative; nothing that Baldwin wrote or said afterwards suggests that he was even aware of the information that it was supplying, and there is clear evidence that he had little sympathy for the intelligence-led approach himself. Dugdale's wife wrote: 'S.B. showed signs of his half Highland ancestry by being very suspicious of him [Dugdale] and Horace Wilson, for they did much delving into the gangster side of this affair; the seamy side not politic for the P.M. to know about.'[17]

Established just before the First World War to defend Britain against foreign, mainly German, espionage, MI5's role had expanded into fighting, mainly Soviet, subversion; its existence was not publicly acknowledged and it operated under minimal supervision with no formal terms of reference, even secret ones. It had been founded in 1909 under Kell's leadership, and both the organisation and the man had become trusted features of the Whitehall landscape. MI5's internal history went rather further than Wilson's notes in acknowledging the part that it played in the abdication with a blend of pride that it had been entrusted with so sensitive a task and an implicit recognition of the paradox that it involved.

> There have been, however, on rare occasions more important matters, the investigation of which has been entrusted to the Security Service as a special measure. For example, certain delicate enquiries were made under the Prime Minister's directions in connection with the abdication of King Edward VIII. These were matters touching on the constitution and ultimate issues of sovereignty and were very far removed from any question of guarding the King's realm from penetration by external enemies or

of rebellion by a section of the King's subjects. They involved its inner-
most integrity and the enquiries were entrusted to the Security Service
because no other suitable machinery existed for the purpose while its
head, Sir Vernon Kell, had during a long period of service earned the
respect and confidence of the highest authorities.[18]

If MI5 was not targeting foreign powers or treasonous Britons, that left
only the King himself as the target. The head of state was a short step away
from being classed as an enemy of the state. Quite who MI5 ranked as 'the
highest authorities' is unstated, but the term points to a broad respect
for Kell that ran the length of Whitehall to the men who had the task of
dealing with the King, notably Wilson. The head of the civil service, Sir
Warren Fisher, was also one of the group handling the flow of intelligence
from MI5. Whitehall was on the side of the angels fighting the dark forces
of Buckingham Palace.

Ten years before, Baldwin and Wilson had worked in close partnership
to address a major crisis with a large constitutional dimension. In 1926,
they had faced the General Strike, when outright political revolution was
in the air. In both cases there was a clear threat to national stability, but
there were vast differences between the two as exercises in political calculation and management: what happened in the General Strike depended
on choices by many individuals and organisations; what happened in the
abdication crisis depended overwhelmingly on a single individual. There
was also a clear threat of external subversion in the General Strike from the
Soviet Union, which openly supported militants, so secret intelligence was
a vital tool for the government.[19] It was necessary and inevitable that the
government should use the intelligence services to cope with the General
Strike; the same cannot be said of the abdication. The stakes were high, but
the use of covert intelligence against the King cast the crisis – at least from
Wilson's standpoint – in a confrontational pattern almost from the start.
It was a classic example of how the intelligence dimension of an episode
can play a far more active part in how it develops than merely through the
information it provides. Treating the King as the threat to stability meant

that anyone who seemed to support him would be tarred with the same brush. If an intelligence service is tasked with combating a particular threat, it is inevitable that its responses will focus on that threat and in doing so will magnify the threat.

Whatever its origins and motives, the MI5 operation had barely begun when the crisis passed the point of no return. On the evening of the day after Baldwin's first audience with the King, the news of the divorce case reached Fleet Street, presumably as someone at Ipswich Assizes tipped off a journalistic contact that the case had been entered for a hearing. This placed the affair in the public domain even though the British press maintained its self-imposed embargo on the King and Mrs Simpson. Wilson's comment that 'it would no longer be possible to avoid press comment and public discussion' underestimated the self-restraint of Fleet Street, but reveals the mindset of the civil servants who were dominating the government response to the affair. Provided it could be addressed secretly by the small group already well in the know, there was little risk; the risk began once the ignorant and irresponsible got in on the act. It was a short step from public awareness to mob violence. The all-out crisis had begun.

HIDDEN
CRISIS

CHAPTER 5

PROVOKING AN OUTBURST

In particular, the action of the King in inviting Mrs. Simpson
(without Mr. Simpson) to go to Balmoral Castle, and even more his action
in meeting her train at Aberdeen Station on the very day when he said he
would not have time to open the Aberdeen Infirmary, had led to the most
unfavourable comment throughout Scotland. It seemed clear that before
very long public opinion would be provoked to an outburst.
SIR HORACE WILSON, ABDICATION NOTES[1]

THE DEFINITE NEWS of the divorce case, which broke publicly on the evening of Thursday 15 October, transformed the affair from a scandal into a crisis. It opened the hideous possibility that the King might marry Mrs Simpson and not just keep her as a scandalous mistress. At this stage, the possibility was abstract and remote, but it was still enough to cause near panic. Throughout the crisis it was taken as axiomatic that she was simply unthinkable as a royal wife. At no point did anyone in authority try to analyse her pros and cons, or, as it would doubtless have appeared, try to establish whether she had any redeeming features. She had an array of disadvantages. First and foremost, she was divorced. Divorce was only just becoming acceptable at all and divorcees were excluded from much of respectable Society. They were not received at Court. Double divorcees were exceedingly rare.

The status of divorcees was larded with double standards and hypocrisy. Divorce was not an absolute bar to acceptability in high Society, as is sometimes supposed, although the most rigorous standards would have been applied to the King's wife. Nancy Astor, Britain's first sitting woman MP, was a divorcee, but this did not hurt her social position. Divorce was even tolerable in Downing Street, as Tommy Dugdale, Baldwin's parliamentary private secretary, was kept in position even though he married a divorcee just before the crisis broke. Sir Warren Fisher was one of Mrs Simpson's most committed opponents, but he did not object to the principle of divorce and had shown unusual courage in sheltering divorced colleagues from ostracism. Under the social norms of the day, divorcees had to work their passage back into acceptability through a healthy period of decorous inconspicuousness. The King's ever-less discreet behaviour with Mrs Simpson was the opposite of anything that might have won her rehabilitation in conservative eyes.

There were other considerations working against Mrs Simpson. She had established herself in British high Society, but at its frivolous and hedonistic end, rather than the conservative and aristocratic world that neighboured the Court. Her patroness, Emerald Cunard, was despised by the likes of Sir John Reith, and she was tarred with the same brush. She seemed to be a woman who had come from nowhere. Very few British observers were in a position to judge the lineage of old Baltimore families like Mrs Simpson's. Perversely, American women who entered British Society were expected to have large and recently earned family fortunes and were tolerated in direct proportion to their wealth. Here Mrs Simpson had nothing to offer. In an age when sexual morality and social consciousness were deeply intertwined, her advance through Society appeared as immorality rewarded, even to the vast majority who had not seen the lurid police reports. Mrs Simpson was routinely described as a second (or even third) rate woman. This was a moral judgement. The wife of Labour politician Jimmy Thomas refused to be introduced to a 'whore'.[2]

National origin also told against her. She was routinely referred to contemptuously as an American, although it is harder to detect what else lay behind this. It was an era where national and racial stereotypes were accepted unquestioningly, but it is hard to find instances in which Mrs Simpson was accused of a specific national flaw apart from one moment in the crisis when her exaggeration of the number of threatening letters she received was ascribed to 'American megalomania'. When the crisis broke publicly, even the usually liberal newspaper the *Manchester Guardian* editorialised venomously that the King was 'anxious to become the third husband of a lady of American birth who became a British subject by her second marriage'.[3]

On the positive side of the ledger, Mrs Simpson had made Edward cut down his drinking, which was appreciated by his mother, who had feared drink would become a serious problem and render him ridiculous. His secretary 'Tommy' Lascelles had been put off by his drinking too, but there is no evidence that concern had been widespread. Otherwise, Mrs Simpson had almost no redeeming features. She undertook no charitable or cultural activities that might have diluted the image of a woman purely focused on Society.

The news of the divorce case was so alarming that the civil servants decided, in Warren Fisher's words, that 'this was so serious that H. Wilson was to go to Chequers to see the P.M. & arrange with him to see the King on Sunday & tell him that the proceedings must be stopped'.[4] Even by Fisher's demanding standards this was high-handed. The civil servants had sat on the news for at least a day and a half before even telling the Prime Minister, and on their own authority briefed a senior minister about it the day before they planned to tell the Prime Minister.[5] The word 'arrange' appears to be barely a euphemism for 'instruct'; it was soon being said at the top level of government that the job had been 'assigned' to the Prime Minister.[6] Two senior civil servants had decided between them how the matter should be handled and intended to tell the Prime Minister where his duty lay. In turn, the Prime Minister was to tell the sovereign to intervene in a legal action between two of his subjects with whom he had no other formal connection. Fisher's ability to make up the constitutional rules as he went along had clearly not weakened over the years. He had given no thought to what would happen if the King refused meekly to obey a peremptory instruction from Baldwin. Neither Fisher nor Wilson had more than a passing acquaintance with the King, but the idea that Baldwin, who knew him well, might be better able to judge how to handle a matter of extreme delicacy does not seem to have occurred to them. This is marked by the same simplistic mindset evident in the decision to bring in MI5. The King was little better than a delinquent and unreliable subordinate of the Prime Minister who could and should be treated roughly when he stepped out of line. Of course, the King's own cavalier and irresponsible behaviour invited such a response, but the imperious tone that Fisher and Wilson thought appropriate was hardly the way to start a constructive dialogue. It baked another layer of antagonism into the conception of the problem held by the civil servants.

The weekend after the news of the divorce, Baldwin was subjected to sustained attempts to convince him to persuade the King to make Mrs Simpson abandon her case. Wilson went to Chequers and finally told the Prime Minister what the civil servants had known for at least two days: that Mrs Simpson had formally begun divorce proceedings.[7] The pressure was stepped up when Baldwin went on to a very grand house party at Cumberland Lodge in Windsor Great Park, the home of Lord Fitzalan, staunch Catholic and Tory grandee. Fitzalan's nephew, the Duke of Norfolk, and the Marquess of Salisbury added further aristocratic and political weight, which was rounded off by the respectable press baron, Lord Kemsley. All shared deep disquiet about the King. The party was completed by Hardinge, who had been asked to Cumberland Lodge after writing to the Prime Minister on the Friday expressing his anxiety. He put his case to Baldwin in a private conversation after lunch on the Saturday.[8] Baldwin crumbled under this massed assault and tried to arrange an audience with the King on the Sunday morning. In the event this proved impossible, because the King was engaged in a dangerous, illicit and inevitably secret visit to Mrs Simpson in Felixstowe, where she was staying temporarily to qualify for jurisdiction under the Ipswich Assizes. Eventually an audience was fixed for the Tuesday morning.

During the interlude, Fisher stepped up his efforts to put his own stamp on how the crisis was handled in another way: by cultivating an ally for his

hardline approach at the top level of politics. Fisher's formal job was Permanent Secretary to the Treasury, so Neville Chamberlain was notionally his
direct political master and the ideal candidate for the job. He was a persistent critic of Baldwin's seemingly passive approach to problems, which he
castigated as mere idleness, and shared the civil servants' inclination towards
a hard and proactive line with the King. He was an ideal ally in the Cabinet.
Like Baldwin, he had come to the top level of politics relatively late in life
when the Carlton House coup upset the existing Conservative hierarchy. He
had been born into a great albeit short-lived political dynasty, but had seemed
doomed to play a minor role, vainly trying to rebuild the family's finances in a
miserable sisal farming experiment in the Bahamas, then superintending the
municipal affairs of the family stronghold in Birmingham. He had become
Chancellor of the Exchequer in the national government in 1931, bearing
much of the administrative workload, whilst the Prime Minister Ramsay
MacDonald took diplomacy and Baldwin took domestic politics. He was
an assiduous and successful administrator, but took minimal interest in the
human side of politics. It is easy to understand why Fisher held him in high
regard. Once he had decided what the correct policy was, he worked tire-
lessly and unrelentingly to implement it. Anyone who disagreed was treated
as an idiotic obstacle or worse. He was the most likely successor to Baldwin.

On his own authority, Fisher began to brief Chamberlain almost at the
outset of the crisis. Fisher told Chamberlain about Mrs Simpson's divorce
case very soon after he learned about it himself and even before he told the
Prime Minister.[9] Fisher was also happy to encourage Chamberlain in the
belief that he (Chamberlain) would do a better job of defending national
stability from an erring sovereign. For some months, Chamberlain had
nourished the rather questionable idea that he was better qualified than
Baldwin to handle the King. A few weeks after the accession, he had been
told both that the King 'had "formed a high opinion of his Chancellor's
good sense and ability and I hope that it is so, as it may be useful"' but,
according to an 'unimpeachable' source, could not '"bear to sit in the same
room as Baldwin"'.[10] The King certainly found his Prime Minister's manner irksome sometimes, but his supposedly high opinion of Chamberlain

is corroborated nowhere. On the one recorded occasion in which the King mentioned Chamberlain, it was simply as a reliable ally of the Prime Minister. Chamberlain was both childishly vain and jealous of Baldwin, so whoever brought him these stories had clearly found a receptive audience. He was also amenable to the idea fed to him by Fisher that Baldwin was neglecting his duty by not taking a more resolute and proactive stance with the King.

Baldwin finally saw the King at Fort Belvedere on the morning of Tuesday 20 October. It was by any standards a momentous encounter: the Prime Minister faced the challenge of persuading a self-willed and stubborn sovereign to recognise that his personal conduct was putting his throne at risk. It is hardly surprising that Baldwin felt the need of a drink strongly enough to ask the King for whisky and soda. The conversation itself proved to be an anti-climax and its results fell well short of the dramatic reversal in his behaviour that Fisher imagined could be achieved. The King politely heard out his Prime Minister as he showed him samples of the foreign newspaper articles that were causing so much alarm, but he refused to intervene in what he described as a private matter between Mrs Simpson and her husband. The closest that they came to confrontation was when Baldwin told the King, 'I don't believe you can go on like this and get away with it.'[11] Baldwin had deliberately picked the phrase 'get away with it', knowing that it was one of the King's favourite expressions, and he touched enough of a nerve for the King to ask Baldwin what he meant by it. Here Baldwin pulled a punch and told the King that he was referring to how Mrs Simpson had been promoted socially; he did not mention the risk of marriage, and the exchange left no impression on the King. It is unclear whether the King fully appreciated the depth of public and political unease in Britain and the Empire that Baldwin set out; he certainly did not acknowledge it in his conversation. Either the King was so wrapped up with Mrs Simpson that he was simply impervious to any negative aspect to the relationship or he was pursuing a strategy, conscious or otherwise, of delaying any serious discussion until he was in a position to present the government with marriage as a fait accompli. Both would explain the King's nonchalance, and it is far from certain that Baldwin would have penetrated the carapace by adopting a harsher tone. As it was, the King appears to have misread Baldwin's quite genuine expression of sympathy with the human dimension of his predicament as a sign of readiness to accept the King's solution. It could have seemed to the King that he was going to 'get away with it' once again.

Baldwin may have stopped short of speaking to the King brutally because he overestimated the King's opinion of him. One of the drawbacks of the King's devastating charm was that it tempted people on whom it was being used to believe that they enjoyed his friendship and esteem. This included very senior politicians, notably Baldwin and Winston Churchill. Even Adolf Hitler was not immune and imagined political sympathy on the part of the then Duke of Windsor.[12] More junior men who had long been in his service and had been presented with ample proof of the selfishness underneath the charm also found it hard to resist. In reality, the King was driven to distraction by Baldwin's tic of flicking out his fingers and cracking the joints, which he claimed to have first noticed on the Canadian trip nine years before. The only human who counted for anything to him at a personal level was Wallis Simpson.

Wilson was uniquely well informed about the audience. Soon after coming back from the Fort, Baldwin gave Wilson his side of the story. Wilson seems to have been the very first person to hear it. He also heard how the King thought that the talk had gone. MI5 proved to be remarkably efficient and reported the King's version of the conversation to Wilson soon after he had heard Baldwin's account of it.[13] As the King's phones were not tapped until the final days of the crisis, this suggests that MI5 was either monumentally lucky or already possessed a line to a potential agent or agents with good access to what the King was saying when it was given the job of investigating him. MI5's success was not just a flash in the pan, as the flow of reports continued throughout the crisis.

Wilson was immediately struck by a gulf between the two versions of the conversation, and this left him 'very much perturbed'.[14] MI5 told Wilson that the King felt 'the interview had been very friendly indeed and, that far from endeavouring to oppose the King's wishes, the Prime Minister had shown every sympathy with the King's personal difficulties'. This was certainly not the message that Baldwin had told Wilson that he had delivered to the King: 'that he was embarking on a course of action which would affront the people of the country and would arouse their opposition'. Astoundingly, Wilson's first instinct was to put the discrepancy between the two accounts down to Baldwin's version being incomplete or inaccurate. Wilson appears here to be an early adherent to the cult of secret intelligence, which assumes that information obtained surreptitiously is automatically more accurate than information given voluntarily. In effect, MI5 was spying on the Prime Minister as well as the King, and Wilson was more inclined to trust its report of a conversation, covertly and indirectly obtained from one notoriously erratic participant, than one freely given to him by the other participant, the Prime Minister. Wilson's notes suggest he held so low an opinion of the Prime Minister that he assumed that Baldwin had pulled his punches with the King:

> At the time it looked as if the Prime Minister might perhaps have been so anxious not to break the contact between the King and himself as to have given the impression that he, the Prime Minister, did not take a grave view of the consequences of the continuance of the King's association with Mrs. Simpson.

Wilson's confidence in the Prime Minister's willingness to do the necessary dirty work was shaken.

Wilson's idea of what dirty work was needed also went well beyond Baldwin's: it was harsher and more absolute. Baldwin merely wanted the divorce stopped and to warn the King against 'a continuance of the present state of affairs', flaunting Mrs Simpson semi-publicly,[15] but Wilson went far further: 'It was sufficient therefore for the Prime Minister to convey to the King the impression ... that in his opinion the people just would not tolerate Mrs. Simpson.'[16] From the outset, Wilson believed that the only solution was for the King to dismiss her entirely; the possibility that the problem might be defused by the King behaving with far greater discretion in his relationship did not seem to merit consideration. Wilson might have judged that the King was simply incapable of such discretion, but it looks much more as though he was projecting his own preconceptions of what was acceptable or not and thus narrowing the options that he thought were available to the Prime Minister.

After the crisis, Wilson admitted that the discrepancy between Baldwin's account and the King's own (via MI5) arose because 'the King's infatuation for Mrs. Simpson was such as to make him quite oblivious of the realities of the situation and to make him incapable of seeing any other considerations in their proper perspective'.[17] At the time, though, he and Fisher concluded that the dialogue between the King and the Prime Minister alone was not able to head off the crisis. They set out to put pressure on Mrs Simpson herself to abandon her divorce case. An emphatic message should be sent to her warning her 'of the dangerous situation which might arise once a decree nisi had been granted'.[18] Down the years, senior civil servants have found themselves discreetly undertaking a variety of sensitive missions on behalf of the government, but few can have been as sensitive as this. There is a great question mark over Baldwin's involvement in it. He gave a number of ostensibly indiscreet but, in reality, carefully selective, oral accounts of the crisis, but none of them mentioned the approach to Mrs Simpson. This does not mean that the Prime Minister had no intimation. Wilson's notes on the crisis carefully mention when the Prime Minister approved a potentially contentious step, but they do not discuss the genesis of the approach via Theodore Goddard, Mrs Simpson's solicitor, at all. The best guess is that Baldwin gave some very tacit endorsement to a move that the civil servants themselves strongly believed was necessary. When the scheme ultimately failed, Wilson did inform Baldwin. As the exercise involved a highly questionable attempt to use a citizen's lawyer to influence her behaviour, there was every reason for Baldwin to have wanted to avoid being linked to it and Wilson would also have wanted to play down the government's role.

The civil servants' first step was to see if the channel of communication with the royal household established by Wilson's lunch with Hardinge could be used, and they sounded him out on sending a warning to Mrs Simpson.[19] Hardinge had no relationship to speak of with her and nothing came of this. The civil servants then cast around for another way to get their message to

Mrs Simpson. Fisher even considered seriously speaking to Mrs Simpson himself.[20] Sadly, this idea came to nothing and we can only imagine the epicene Edwardian-era British civil servant trying to explain to a hard-edged and mercenary American-born socialite that it was her civic duty to abandon the juiciest piece of prey that was ever likely to come her way. Short of building a line of contact through Mrs Simpson's social circle, which was quite alien to the civil servants, this left Fisher with almost no alternative. On Saturday 24 October, Fisher summoned Goddard to see him.[21]

Goddard played a decidedly ambiguous part in the abdication. It is perhaps an indication of the sensitivity of the topic that nothing resembling the 'personal and confidential note' about Goddard to which Wilson referred in his notes has been released publicly.[22] He was introduced to Mrs Simpson by Walter Monckton, a highly successful lawyer and friend of the King from their days together at Oxford, and one of his legal advisers.[23] Monckton also operated in rarefied spheres of governmental work as an adviser on Imperial constitutional issues to one of India's princely rulers. Goddard was, though, only Monckton's second choice for the job, and his first choice gives a rather better clue as to what Monckton thought was appropriate. At the time, Theobald Mathew was the son of an eminent lawyer and a well-established City solicitor who went on to serve for twenty years as Director of Public Prosecutions, during which he enthusiastically promoted thorough enforcement of the law against homosexuality and pornography. Mathew was a devout Catholic, which might explain why he declined the job. Goddard was a self-made man and far less of an Establishment figure than Mathew, but he proved to be entirely reliable from the government point of view. He was no stranger to the sensitive world where politics and the law met, having acted for the Dominions Secretary Jimmy Thomas in the judicial inquiry into the leak of Budget secrets during the spring of 1936 that led to Thomas's disgrace. He advised Mrs Simpson on the technical aspects of her divorce, but did not develop any broader or more personal relationship with her. By contrast, he did become a friend of Fisher, who tried to obtain a knighthood for him ten years after the abdication on the grounds of his services to the government during the crisis.[24]

Of course it is not often that a solicitor finds himself acting for the sovereign's lover in a divorce case, but it is still striking that Goddard should have accepted the invitation to talk to Fisher without, apparently, asking his client beforehand. Almost from the start of his conversation with Fisher, Goddard was at pains to emphasise that patriotism coloured his view of the affair. In his account of this episode, Goddard carefully avoids specifying what Fisher asked him to do when he called him in; Goddard clearly understood the dubious ethics of even countenancing a request from a third party, however mighty, to persuade his client to drop a case, and claims to have resisted doing what Fisher asked.[25] Fisher called in Wilson, Vansittart and other colleagues, presumably including Hankey, to back him up. Goddard later claimed that he managed to convince all of them except Wilson that it was none of his business to advise Mrs Simpson on any hypothetical plans for marriage she might entertain after divorce. This is at best an incomplete description of what happened. Working back from reports of the conversation and Goddard's own incomplete account, it appears that what Fisher asked Goddard to do was not only to persuade Mrs Simpson to withdraw her divorce petition, but also to drop any idea of marrying the King and to leave the country.[26] Goddard had placed himself in a false position. His sole concern should have been to advise his client what was in her best interests, yet the criterion for his advice seemed to be the national interest or at least what he and Fisher thought was the national interest. There is no indication that he disclosed to Mrs Simpson that he was also speaking for the top level of the civil service. She did not mention the incident at all, even indirectly in her memoirs, maintaining the fiction that almost everything had come as a complete surprise to her.

The conversation with Mrs Simpson was not a comforting experience for Goddard.[27] She told him bluntly that she was totally committed to the divorce, for which she put the entire blame on her husband. Goddard was even more firmly rebuffed on the question of her marrying the King. When he was unwise enough to 'express his own vision of the damage to the throne if a marriage shd. take place (and Goddard told W that as an Englishman he felt this v. strongly & expressed it as strongly as he felt)' he was treated

to Mrs Simpson at her worst. She 'blazed out at him What do you take me
for [?]. I would never think of it. I am trying to help him. Can you deny that
I have helped him[?]' She stopped short of denying that the King wanted
to marry her, but wanted to head discussion away from the topic by con-
centrating on how she was helping him, boasting that she had made him
give up drinking spirits in favour of light beer only. At this stage she might
genuinely have thought that marriage was not a serious possibility despite
what the King had told her back in May when planning the dinner at York
House. Her next comment does suggest that she saw herself as no more
than a temporary feature in his life: '[s]ome day I shall just fade out & be
prepared to go'. Goddard was convinced she was sincere. The King's track
record certainly would not have suggested that he was inclined towards
long-term commitment. This provided a measure of hope to compensate
for the disappointments of the interview, which he had to report to the civil
servants. It proved to be an entirely false hope and, worse, the disappointment that followed further poisoned the hardliners' view of Mrs Simpson.

Although she refused to stop the divorce, Fisher and Goddard believed
that Mrs Simpson had agreed to leave the country. This was a major comfort
to Fisher, but quite how they came to this conclusion is one of the smaller,
but still significant, mysteries of the abdication. Fisher further seems to have
taken this as some kind of formal and binding commitment given to the
top level of British government and, again, it is far from clear why he did
so. The best account of the conversation is indirect and far from conclu-
sive. According to Chamberlain's diary, Fisher reported to him Goddard's
version of his conversation with Mrs Simpson: that 'after the [divorce] proceedings were over he was going to get Mrs Simpson away to France for
six weeks and thereafter he would try and persuade her to spend as much
time abroad as possible'. Nothing is mentioned about how Mrs Simpson
took this suggestion and there is no sign that she had made any plans to
leave the country at this point. When, weeks later, she did leave for France,
circumstances had changed radically. The crisis had broken publicly and
she was shattered by the publicity and fearful for her own safety. Accommodation had to be found at short notice.

It would have been quite routine for Goddard to advise Mrs Simpson to go abroad. This was the only part of what he tried to persuade her to do that was not manifestly driven by his conversation with Fisher. Leaving the country was a quite normal method of escaping the baleful attentions of the King's Proctor after the decree nisi. Divorce was a luxury product in those days and it could almost be assumed that a petitioner would have the money for a prolonged stay abroad. This also meshed nicely with the social mores of the time, which attached the greater scandal to proceedings in open court. Unless Goddard had disclosed to Mrs Simpson on whose behalf he was talking – for which there is no evidence at all – whatever she said about the idea of going to France would merely have been a response to her lawyer's advice. She may simply have been answering evasively until she could discuss the question with the King. Many years later, her long-standing private secretary commented that she 'occasionally gives the impression she has said yes, when in fact she has said no'.[28] Perhaps it was as simple as this. She was not to know that what she told her lawyer would be fed back to the highest levels of the bureaucracy and the government, and treated as a binding commitment.

The balance of probability is that Goddard simply overestimated his influence on his client and expected her to follow his advice. After his failure to persuade Mrs Simpson to drop the divorce entirely, Goddard might also have felt under some pressure to offer some consolation to Fisher and thus exaggerated the definiteness of what Mrs Simpson told him. In turn, Fisher took this all at face value and drew some very rosy conclusions. Wilson might have been more cautious, and he described what Mrs Simpson said to Goddard as 'the assurances *which I had understood* had been given through Theodore Goddard to the effect that Mrs. Simpson had grasped the realities of the position and *was likely* to go away' [author's italics].[29] But this was written weeks after these hopes had been shattered, and he might simply have wanted to protect his own reputation.

Whatever reservations Wilson might have had, they were not shared with Fisher, who spent the following week in a happy glow of achievement at having defused the crisis, certainly in the short term and perhaps permanently if Mrs Simpson did indeed 'fade out'. Fisher did not keep this to himself and extended the rickety edifice that he had built on these unsolid foundations when he passed on his new-found confidence to Neville Chamberlain, who was equally uncritical. Fisher further boosted Chamberlain's spirits with a titbit from the flow of MI5 intelligence, telling him 'very secretly that the K[ing] knew of this interview'.[30] From this, Chamberlain drew the conclusion that the King accepted the idea of Mrs Simpson leaving the country. On the basis of very scant evidence indeed, Fisher and Chamberlain had come to believe that after the scandals of the summer, the King and Mrs Simpson would behave with all the discretion that their position demanded.

The civil servants could also take some comfort from something else that Mrs Simpson told Goddard, which proved to be entirely misleading, although here the blame falls squarely on her. She claimed to him that she would never contemplate marrying the King, which might, just, have been the literal truth about her own thinking, but suppressed the far more important fact that the King was determined to marry her.[31]

Fisher was able to ease Chamberlain's mind on a quite different question. He had been fretting at the possibility that the King might marry Mrs Simpson morganatically, that is without her becoming Queen and keeping any hypothetical children out of the line of succession.[32] It was an established practice amongst the royalty of Continental Europe, although it was usually adopted when a member of a royal family married someone not of royal blood. Many if not most people of the period would have been familiar with the morganatic marriage between Archduke Franz Ferdinand, heir to the throne of Austria–Hungary, and Countess Sophie Chotek, a perfectly respectable lady but just not royal, who went on to be famously murdered together in Sarajevo. Chamberlain had seen a 'dangerous possibility' that the formula might be applied to Mrs Simpson, but Fisher had researched the question and could tell Chamberlain that 'any woman who the King marries is ipso facto Queen Consort'.[33] Chamberlain displayed a touching faith in the immutability of current practice if it suited his tastes and concluded that this made a morganatic marriage 'out of the question'.

CHAPTER 6

A REAL JOLT

Things had gone back. Mrs. S. had spent the week-end at
Fort Belvedere. [Baldwin] thought it was necessary to give
the King a real jolt to bring him to realise the situation.
NEVILLE CHAMBERLAIN, DIARY, 2 NOVEMBER 1936

WHEN MRS SIMPSON'S divorce case was heard in Ipswich on Tuesday 27 October, the world's press was out in force, but there were no unpleasant surprises for the government or the King. Nothing was mentioned in court to link her to the King. The case was reported briefly and factually in the British newspapers as though it were a quite unexceptional divorce. There was no mention of the King. Beaverbrook was credited with having 'engineered the gentlemen's agreement with the Press Lords'.[1] Inevitably, the foreign press gave the story extensive coverage with no restraints on mentioning the connection between the King and Mrs Simpson, parodied in the legendary headline 'King's Moll Renoed in Wolsley's Home Town', which was enthusiastically circulated in British Society showing how scandalously vulgar the elite found it all.[2] To the powers that be it was also an unpleasant foretaste of what could happen if the story reached the British press.

The court hearing itself went smoothly on the pattern of most similar undefended divorce cases, although there were enough unusual features to excite some suspicions. It was never explained satisfactorily why the case was not heard in London, where Mrs Simpson lived. Instead it was heard as a 'country' case, a supposedly cheaper and more convenient way of conducting a divorce case that had recently been introduced. This logic was undermined because the case could not be heard at Maidenhead, the court closest to Bray where Ernest Simpson's adultery had occurred at the Hotel de Paris, and thus most accessible for the witnesses. The best alternative was in Ipswich, which in some eyes had been chosen because it was supposedly remote from London. Any notion that the case was being heard in Ipswich to minimise publicity and cost was torpedoed by Goddard's choice of barrister to present the case, Sir Norman Birkett KC, one of the country's most prominent (and expensive) courtroom advocates. The feature of the case that the judge, Mr Justice Hawke, was most irked about, however, was the uncertainty over the identity of the woman found in bed with Ernest Simpson. She was in fact Mrs Simpson's former friend Mary Raffray, who went on to marry Ernest Simpson. His reluctance to disclose her identity was a gentlemanly instinct but apt to be misconstrued, especially in such a high-profile case. It was usual for a couple to agree – illegally – to divorce and arrange for one to be 'caught' in bed with someone else hired for the purpose. Typically, they were young women willing to earn a modest amount of money in a faintly insalubrious fashion. Keeping quiet as to the co-respondent's true identities was part of the deal. As the British press had yet to break its silence at that point, there was practically no comment, although the details were well enough known to lead a good many members of the public to write to the legal authorities to complain two months later when the King's involvement became public. Perhaps curiously, the hardliners did not complain about any of this, although one senior Cabinet member, Ramsay MacDonald, did complain that the case was a 'stretch of law & justice' and believed that it would be a scandal if the King's Proctor did not intervene.[3] This appears to be nothing more than outrage at routine illegality.

The British press behaved itself; the King did not. Within days of the divorce case it was clear that the cosy fantasy that Fisher and Chamberlain had erected on the flimsy foundations of Goddard's conversation with Mrs Simpson and their misreading of the MI5 report had collapsed. Not merely did Mrs Simpson remain on the British side of the Channel, but the couple did not behave even with the reticence and decorum customary for people anxious to transform the half divorce of a decree nisi into a full divorce. Mrs Simpson spent the weekend after the divorce case at Fort Belvedere and dined twice with the King in London. Hardinge was plunged into a mood of deep pessimism and now feared that the King would have to abdicate.[4] He brought the bad news of the King's behaviour to Baldwin at Downing Street on Monday 2 November.[5] There was even worse to come, as Fisher discovered when he dined with Goddard on the Tuesday. Mrs Simpson had made it clear to him that she had no intention of leaving the country; her 'assurances … had had to be withdrawn' by inference after she had put the idea to the King. Moreover, the King had forbidden her 'to see anyone on the subject again'.[6] The idea of getting Mrs Simpson out of the country that Goddard and Fisher had cooked up together had proved to be a tactical blunder. As was to become even more painfully clear, the King reacted furiously against the proposal, which he found extremely offensive and demeaning.

The first attempt to resolve the crisis by talking to Mrs Simpson had ended in a fiasco. It had been handled at best incompetently and with minimal consideration or forethought. The dialogue was conducted through an intermediary who had only a brief and limited relationship with Mrs Simpson. The blame lies squarely with Fisher, although Wilson shares some of it. There is, of course, no certainty that if the government's contact with Mrs Simpson had been handled any differently, the outcome would have been any happier, but an astute intermediary or one who knew her well could have spotted that she had motives of her own, which could have been played on to defuse the crisis. She was far less committed to the idea of marriage than the King, and it might even have been unwelcome to her. There is no reason to suppose that an elegant and well-funded withdrawal from the relationship would have distressed her. She also shared the government's horror of public scandal. She was deeply disturbed by the massive publicity over the *Nahlin* cruise and had a powerful motive to behave in ways that did not attract press attention. Even if it had not been possible to persuade her to give up the King at this stage, she could easily have been persuaded to make the King behave discreetly.

Mrs Simpson's decision to remain in Britain made Fisher appear a fool several times over. He had drawn a falsely optimistic conclusion from what Goddard had told him and then passed this on to Chamberlain. Fisher had read too much into the MI5 report that the King knew of the conversation between Mrs Simpson and Goddard, and he thought that it meant the King approved the plan. Fisher and Goddard had been exposed as prisoners of their own excessive optimism, but naturally they blamed Mrs Simpson. Goddard saw her behaviour as a rank breach of trust – 'he has lost all faith in her' – and Fisher and Chamberlain shared this view.[7]

There is no sign that Baldwin had been swallowed into Fisher's bubble of delusional hope, or that he suffered the same degree of shock when it burst, but he was sufficiently concerned by the turn of events to muse on more robust action than had been taken so far. On 2 November he told Chamberlain that 'He thought it was necessary to give the King a real jolt to bring him to realise the situation' and thought that it might even be delivered through a discreet press campaign by 'the more responsible newspapers'.[8] In the event nothing occurred, which suggests that Baldwin may have been more interested in persuading Chamberlain that he was prepared to take some resolute action. In reality, he still saw the six-month gap between granting the decree nisi and the decree absolute as a breathing space.[9]

> As the next step in the divorce proceedings would not, in the ordinary course, be reached for six months, and as he was most anxious that the King should have every possible opportunity for reflection, the Prime Minister decided that it was better to give time for the views he had expressed to the King on 20 October to have their effect on the King's mind.[10]

Baldwin did, though, take one practical step that, arguably, he should have taken months before. He sought professional advice on his legal options in an unprecedented constitutional position. The government's senior law officer, Attorney General Sir Donald Somervell, dealt rapidly and easily with two of the points that had arisen: the government had to approve the King's choice of a bride, and an abdication could simply be effected through an Act of Parliament.[11] Somervell accepted that the only written law covering the King's marriage barred him from marrying a Catholic, but firmly stated that 'the marriage of a King was of such concern to the State that it would be an unconstitutional act for a King to marry contrary to the advice of his ministers'. Baldwin also wanted his opinion on a much less obvious issue, which was bubbling beneath the surface: the possibility that the King's Proctor might intervene in Mrs Simpson's divorce. Someone in government thought this provided a potential tool to end the government's difficulties at a stroke by torpedoing her divorce and eliminating the risk that she and the King might marry.[12] Somervell saw two immense flaws in this idea, one subtly constitutional and the other common sense. There is a well-established but little-known doctrine that the British monarch cannot be subjected to action in his or her own courts. When Somervell made the automatic assumption that the King was the only person with whom Mrs Simpson could be accused of 'misconduct', he did not believe that it was an accusation that could be brought to court. Perhaps more tellingly, Somervell knew that if the constitutional point were wrong and a court case did ensue, it would be squalid:

> I had no doubt a feeling that whatever was to be the solution to the prob-
> lem the King's Proctor appearing with a bevy of valets and chambermaids
> before Merriman [the President of the Divorce Court] to prove that the
> reigning Monarch had been seen going down the passage etc. was not
> the right one.[13]

For the time being, Somervell's advice removed the thought of bringing in the King's Proctor as a way of cutting the Gordian knot, but this was far from the last anyone was to hear of the scheme.

Few would have questioned Somervell's advice that the King's marriage fell squarely in the area of topics on which the Prime Minister had a right to advise the King, but it was a far more contentious question whether he could or should advise the King on his private life, in practice on his relationship with Mrs Simpson. This aspect of the problem was passed on to Sir Maurice Gwyer, the senior Parliamentary Counsel, who was junior to Somervell in the hierarchy of law officers, but an expert on constitutional law. He had edited the standard legal text book on the subject.

The opinion that Gwyer delivered on 5 November was everything that the hardliners could have hoped for.[14] It sets out a doctrine that the sovereign is ultimately powerless against the politicians. Not merely did it deprive Baldwin of the argument against taking action that he had been repeating since the summer, but it told him that it was his duty to take action:

> It would be the constitutional right and duty of Ministers to advise the King to abandon a course of conduct which, though it fell exclusively within the sphere of his private life … lowered the Monarch in the estimation of his people …
>
> Ministers have to act as interpreters of public opinion; and if they are satisfied that public opinion generally is strongly behind the advice which they think that they ought to give, I cannot doubt that constitutional principle not only empowers, but requires, them to tender it.[15]

After concluding that it was for ministers to decide whether any particular issue were grave enough for ministers to apply the 'ultimate sanction' of resignation, Gwyer went well beyond a straightforward legal analysis of what he believed the government could do. He also examined the political options involved and argued that ministers would not tender advice under these circumstances unless they had 'secured the concurrence of the leaders of the Opposition'. This would compel the King 'either to accept the advice tendered to him or to abdicate'. Put simply, the politicians could sack the monarch if he or she disagreed with them. Gwyer rounded off his opinion by covering the final base and addressed the ugly possibility that the King might simply flee the country as James II had done in 1688. In that case, Parliament could declare the throne vacant and hand it to the next in line of succession.

Even before Gwyer had delivered his opinion, Fisher and Wilson had set in motion what Baldwin's biographers described as 'a most striking exercise of back-stage power' aimed at forcing his hand.[16] The civil servants were in the grip of an overwhelming belief that the crisis was so urgent that normal rules could be set aside. Under the shock of what they saw as Mrs Simpson's broken promise, Fisher and Wilson despaired of persuading the Prime Minister to act ruthlessly, and set out to engineer a Cabinet revolt against the Prime Minister's policy of inaction. They called on Chamberlain on the afternoon of 4 November and began by breaking the bad news about the King's behaviour that they had gathered from Goddard, some of which Chamberlain already knew from talking to Baldwin.[17] It was not hard to persuade Chamberlain that the hour for action had come or that he was the man for the hour. They began by working on Chamberlain with snippets from the MI5 reports claiming that the 'K had spoken with amusement of his interview with S.B. & it wd. be of no use for him to see him again'. They followed this up with the rather more surprising claim that Goddard thought that he (Chamberlain) was the only man who might be able to prevent the King from taking 'some rash action', presumably marrying Mrs Simpson.[18] Chamberlain was so happy to be told that the King mocked Baldwin but respected him that he did not question the highly dubious proposition that the King was discussing individual Cabinet ministers with Mrs Simpson and that she, in turn, was gossiping to her solicitor about this.

Amongst Chamberlain's various flaws was ludicrous vanity, which made him a soft target for this kind of operation. His letters to his sisters take a childish delight in anything that he thought showed him in a better light than other men. Fisher and Wilson hit their target squarely. A week later, Chamberlain was reporting to his sister Goddard's supposed assessment of his unique influence over the King that he had learned from Fisher, with some additional embellishment, suitably flattering to his sense of self-worth: that 'some very near [to the King] say it is of no use to repeat the warning unless it is given by the C[hancellor] of E[xchequer] for whom, they say H.M. has a wholesome respect'.[19] Fisher seems to have given an exaggerated account of Goddard's relationship with the King. Fisher and Wilson had been building on foundations laid some months before by the unnamed individual with his 'unimpeachable' source, who had talked up Chamberlain's belief that he was the man to tackle the King, and talked down the relationship between Baldwin and the King.[20] The general similarity of the two sets of comments leaves the suspicion that Fisher was the origin of both, and that he had been sufficiently far-sighted to bolster Chamberlain's confidence in his superior qualifications as King-tamer well in advance of deciding that he was required to mount a revolt against Baldwin's approach.

Gwyer's opinion added fuel to the fire by providing a constitutional blank cheque for precisely the kind of action that the hardliners were pushing for.[21] When Fisher sent Chamberlain a copy, he, hardly surprisingly, felt it was 'a masterly letter'.[22] Not only did it tell the Prime Minister that he had the power to advise the King on his personal life, but told him it was his duty to do so. It was precisely such a duty that the hardliners accused Baldwin of shirking. Frustration with the King's behaviour and Baldwin's temporising had reached such a pitch that the hardliners began to push for a step of unprecedented constitutional ambition. Not merely did the civil servants encourage the Chancellor to mount a revolt against the Prime Minister, but they had already decided what the revolt should achieve: the Prime Minister was to order the King to end his relationship with Mrs Simpson; 'that the K. be formally advised to reorder his private life in writing & then seen by S.B. myself [Chamberlain], the speaker & Halifax'.[23] Wilson was driven by his vision of the 'growing resentment of the public at the thought of the King's association with Mrs. Simpson'.[24] Wilson was not deterred by the absence of obvious signs of this, but fell back on detecting the mysterious force of 'quiet and non-vocal opinion … against the King's proposal'.[25] Quite what the King was supposed to be proposing at this stage is far from clear. Wilson may simply have muddled his chronology and been referring to the proposal for a morganatic marriage, which did not arise for another fortnight. Chamberlain seems to have had no qualms about being given a programme of political action by civil servants and immediately fell in with the plan precisely as set out by Fisher and Wilson. The civil servants were despatched to draft the advice to the King, and Chamberlain went to see Baldwin to tell him how the crisis should be handled. Baldwin again temporised with the remarkably lame view that any move should be postponed until after the opening debate of the upcoming Parliamentary session.[26] However, he raised no objection to a meeting with the group of ministers proposed by Fisher as a delegation to the King together with Sir John Simon and Ramsay MacDonald. It is not clear who suggested adding these two, but they were not natural allies of Baldwin's policy of delay.

The civil servants' next move forced the pace yet again and greatly lessened whatever hope there might have been of finding an amicable solution between the King and the government. In parallel to intriguing with Chamberlain to force the Prime Minister to give the King an ultimatum, they moved on to apply indirect pressure on the King through his private secretary, Alec Hardinge, who for a week or so became one of the key figures in the crisis. It is uncertain whether this began entirely on the civil servants' initiative or whether the Prime Minister had some intimation that Hardinge was being primed. As might have happened with the approach to Mrs Simpson through Goddard, Baldwin may have been working to avoid taking any demonstrable responsibility for a potentially contentious step. The initial contacts were so sensitive that Hardinge's wife masked the identities of Fisher and Wilson from any accidental reader of her diary under the imaginary title of 'the High Co. liaison officers'.[27] Hardinge was given – firmly off-the-record – a picture of how things were developing. The civil servants' account was so distorted as to be almost fiction: the whole government – Baldwin included by implication – had reached the point of exasperation, so a constitutional crisis was imminent; the 'Government are not prepared to carry on'.[28] The civil servants did not disclose that Baldwin had not fallen in with the hardliners' desire to send the King an ultimatum, and on Saturday 7 November they showed Hardinge the draft advice they had prepared on Chamberlain's instructions, but claimed that they had prepared it 'for the Prime Minister', which stretches truth to the

breaking point.[29] Moreover, the draft demanded that the King terminate
his relationship with Mrs Simpson forthwith, which had never been one
of Baldwin's goals. Whilst the Prime Minister would have been content
for the King to conduct a discreet liaison with a 'respectable whore', the
hardliners wanted the relationship to end entirely. Ostensibly, they wanted
Hardinge's comments, but more likely they hoped that he would pass the
word to the King that the time was close for him to make the crucial choice.

The civil servants added an extra layer of spurious urgency by claiming
that formal intervention by the King's Proctor in Mrs Simpson's divorce
was in imminent prospect. Here intervention was being spun as a threat
and not an opportunity: it would bring the King's name into open court and
destroy the public silence on the affair. Again, they were far ahead of reality.
Only two people had written to the King's Proctor at that date, only one of
whom made anything approaching a specific allegation, and neither stated
any intention of filing a formal affidavit.[30] Nonetheless, Hardinge was told
that two affidavits had already been filed. Either the civil servants' imagination had run away with them or they were lying outright. Hardinge took
the assertion at face value, and the threat of intervention preyed on him as
much as the threat of a constitutional crisis.

Hardinge was horrified. He spotted immediately that threat of formal
advice to the King would have been the prelude to abdication and was
something that Baldwin had carefully avoided thus far. He also saw the weakness of the government's case for advising the King on 'a mere association
with a woman'.[31] It is unlikely that he had seen Gwyer's hawkish analysis
of the government's rights and duties, so he took the common-sense view
that the government should not use its constitutional power to force the
King to drop a mistress completely just because the affair caused a scandal.
At first the civil servants declined Hardinge's urging to 'tone down the
draft and make the approach a more informal one', but they did accept
the idea that Chamberlain should mediate on the dispute.[32] If, as is suggested in his wife's memoir, it was Hardinge who proposed Chamberlain,
Fisher and Wilson must have rubbed their hands in secret glee. Hardinge
seems to have been entirely unaware that Chamberlain was not only already

deeply engaged but was already convinced that an ultimatum was indeed required and was highly unlikely to dissent from the civil servants' views.

In the event Fisher did take up Hardinge's idea of an informal approach, albeit in an entirely token form. He sent his draft of an informal letter to Chamberlain with a covering letter that passed it off as a mere refinement of the plan rather than an attempt to fend off a constitutional crisis. He also sent the draft of a letter of formal advice, together with a copy of Gwyer's uncompromising advice that it was the government's duty to take stern measures:

> Alec Hardinge came to see me this morning, very privately, with a suggestion which is, I think, well worth consideration.
>
> The interview of 20 Oct. [between the King and Baldwin] was a pleasant chatty affair which failed (naturally enough) to leave any impression; indeed might well have lent itself to the inference that the visitor [Baldwin] was not really taking a very serious view.
>
> Therefore, before the ultimatum we have been considering is launched, shd. there not be an intermediate stage, half way in form between the first causerie & the full formality. With this idea in mind A.H. sketched out the enclosed which strikes me as rather good. Of course if it proved fruitless, the final document, & audience, wd. follow.
>
> [in margin at end of letter] Of course I assured Hardinge that he has <u>not</u> been in the picture
>
> Yours ever
>
> WARREN

The 'intermediate' letter was only informal in the sense that it threatened the King with formal advice.[33] Otherwise, it was an insultingly phrased denunciation of the King's conduct and a peremptory instruction to send Mrs Simpson out of the country. Fisher's statement that Hardinge had 'sketched' it out is dubious and was more likely intended to serve as grounds for claiming that steps were taken only after consultation with the King's private secretary. It would have allowed the government to claim that its first written communication with the King on the topic of Mrs Simpson had not been formal advice. Fisher's comment that 'I assured Hardinge that he has <u>not</u> been in the picture' is further proof of the sensitivity of the dialogue, with a distinct hint that Fisher was trying to dilute responsibility for what was going on. It opens the possibility that Fisher himself might not have been authorised to talk to Hardinge and was keen to keep this under wraps. There is little evidence that Baldwin used speciously off-the-record briefings himself.

Chamberlain and the civil servants had been so consumed by their belief that only tough action would work that they had lost touch with political reality. After a single informal and inconclusive conversation between the King and the Prime Minister on the topic of Mrs Simpson, they wanted the government to take the most extreme action available to it. Chamberlain did revise the 'informal' draft extensively, toning down some of its more blatantly confrontational language, but the substance was unchanged. It is tempting to speculate that the drafts were written with the deliberate intention of provoking the King into refusing the advice. At all events their author had no hesitation at the thought of forcing the King's abdication. When Baldwin eventually saw a copy of the draft, he showed it to his crony J. C. C. Davidson, who was appalled: 'If his memorandum had ever seen the light of day it would have destroyed public confidence in the Government ... I was terrified that, if we had another constitutional crisis after S. B. went, Chamberlain would have handled it in the same blundering, insensitive manner.'[34]

As well as indirectly inviting the Prime Minister to put a pistol at the King's head, Wilson and Fisher fed Chamberlain the same alarmist story that they had given to Hardinge: that intervention by the King's Proctor was imminent. They were not quite so lucky with Chamberlain. Unlike Hardinge, he appears to have probed Fisher on the factual basis for the statement in the draft, 'that already two affidavits have been put in by outside parties requiring the intervention of the King's Proctor'.[35] Fisher must have backed down and Chamberlain amended the draft to read 'two affidavits by outside parties are being prepared for submission'.[36] Even this formulation was incorrect; neither of the first two letter-writers filed an affidavit and the only formal intervention was not made until over three weeks later and never got as far as an affidavit. Had the Prime Minister signed even the amended draft of the 'informal' letter, he would have laid himself open to an accusation of lying to the King.

In the days following his conversation with Fisher and Wilson, Chamberlain set out to brief his cabal of hardline ministers for the meeting with Baldwin. He began with Halifax, Leader of the House of Lords, Lord Privy Seal and the archetype of the respectable Tory grandee, and moved onto Sir John Simon, the Home Secretary.[37] He was sure enough that they would support him that he showed them the drafts in advance. Halifax and Simon were men of whom Chamberlain thoroughly approved and they were to become leading lights in the government he formed the following year when he took over as Prime Minister. Just to make doubly sure of the outcome of the meeting, the idea of including the Speaker was dropped and a reliably hardline minister was added to the list: Walter Runciman, President of the Board of Trade, another spent political force, but whom Baldwin respected for his position amongst the nonconformist churches, a bastion of far stricter morality than the Church of England. This still left Baldwin in a minority of one with his conciliatory and patient line towards the King. The little group met for the first time on Wednesday 11 November, but this seems to have been no more than a preliminary discussion, and the substantial meeting was set for the morning of Friday 13 November. If all went to Chamberlain's plan, Baldwin would be steam-rollered into sending the ultimatum.

Baldwin was also coming under pressure from other directions. On Thursday 12 November he had received a letter from Howell Gwynne, the editor of Britain's staidest newspaper the *Morning Chronicle* and the longest-serving national newspaper editor.[38] As the doyen of Fleet Street he was by default the obvious conduit for mainstream newspapers to pass on their opinions to Downing Street. According to the letter, Gwynne's colleagues had warned him that it was increasingly difficult for them to maintain the 'Great Silence' on the King and Mrs Simpson. Nothing in particular had happened to challenge the press' self-censorship and Gwynne provided no

evidence regarding which of his colleagues were concerned, so it is suspicious that his letter should have coincided almost exactly with the cabal's
big push. In a rather different way he was sending the same message as the
hardliners: time was running out for the Prime Minister to keep deferring
resolute action. For the time being, Gwynne was content to advise other
editors to maintain silence, but ultimately the government had to give a
lead. How large a part Gwynne's letter played in spurring Baldwin into
action can only be guessed, but it was treated seriously enough for Baldwin to agree to see Gwynne at Downing Street the following afternoon.
There was still a faint hope of settling everything in discreet silence, so it
was worth a small effort to preserve.

Consultations with representatives of the Dominions were also pointing toward tough action. Under the Statute of Westminster of 1931, the
Dominions had acquired significant autonomy. In particular, any change in
the relationship with the Crown required their approval. In practice they
would follow the lead of the mother country, but this could not be taken for
granted. Mackenzie King, the Prime Minister of Canada, happened to be
visiting Britain and agreed that a marriage with Mrs Simpson could break
up the Empire.[39] Mackenzie King claimed that he had spoken forthrightly
to the King about the state of feeling in his country. This claim proved to
be fictional, as Wilson ruthlessly exposed, but the conservative sentiment in
Canada was real enough. The Australian High Commissioner and former
Prime Minister Stanley Bruce visited Baldwin at Chequers whilst efforts
to chivvy Baldwin into action were at their most intense. Bruce recognised
that the audience of 20 October had been a failure and wanted Baldwin
to put the question directly to the King as to whether he wanted to marry
Mrs Simpson, and to threaten to resign if he said yes.[40]

The pressure that the hardliners had been building up finally found a
release valve and escaped in a way that unarguably delivered a 'real jolt'
to the King. This fell to Hardinge. Since the previous week, he had been
agonising over how to deal with the risk that Fisher's ultimatum would be
issued in its full high-handed and tactless glory, almost inevitably triggering a full-blown constitutional crisis. Hardinge's thoughts seem to have

crystallised when Baldwin called him to Downing Street after dinner on the evening of Thursday 12 November, supposedly to ask him whether there had been any change in the King's relationship with Mrs Simpson.[41] Perhaps Baldwin had won himself two days' reprieve when he first met the cabal the previous day by raising the possibility that the King's behaviour might just have improved over the previous week. Such a vanishingly faint hope cannot have been Baldwin's only reason for speaking to Hardinge again – he wanted him to warn the King just how serious the situation was. Hardinge was left with the impression that the story of an imminent constitutional crisis was entirely accurate. Baldwin confirmed to him that the group of ministers was meeting the following day and Hardinge seems to have assumed wrongly that they were meeting to ratify a decision to send formal advice that had already been taken in practice. There had always been a risk, albeit distant and hypothetical, that the government might resign, but summoning Hardinge to Downing Street for a late-night conference signalled that there was something more urgent happening. Baldwin was exploiting Chamberlain's initiative in organising the ministers' meeting to provide a narrative of impending conflict.

After an anxious night, Hardinge sat down to compose a letter to the King to try to persuade him to defuse the crisis. He talked over the question with two of his juniors in the royal household, 'Tommy' Lascelles and Sir Godfrey Thomas, who had a much longer and closer acquaintance-ship with the King.[42] They endorsed the need to warn the King and how it should be done. In comparison with the work of Fisher and Chamber-lain, Hardinge's letter is a masterpiece of tact and conciliation.[43] It gave as much weight to the risk that the press would break its silence as anything else, but it carried a warning of impending constitutional crisis by going straight from mentioning the minister's meeting that day to 'the resignation of the Government – an eventuality which can by no means be excluded…'

The only possible solution was for the King to send Mrs Simpson abroad forthwith. Hardinge's letter fell short of demanding that the King termi-nate the relationship entirely, as the civil servants wanted, but otherwise gave the King the same message as Fisher's drafts. Hardinge concluded with a postscript about his shooting plans for the weekend and where he could be contacted.

The risk that the press would break its silence was a powerful factor in Hardinge's decision to write. He feared intervention by the King's Proctor because of the publicity it would bring. On the morning he wrote the letter he spoke to Geoffrey Dawson, editor of *The Times*, who told him he would break the story once there was no doubt that the King wanted to marry Mrs Simpson.[44] Even though this was well ahead of the game at this point, Hardinge attempted to restrain him and showed him his letter as proof that resolute measures were in hand and that it would be better to give them time to bear fruit.

Ever afterwards, Hardinge took full responsibility for the letter and its contents and insisted that it was entirely his own initiative, protecting Lascelles and Thomas as well as the civil servants. His wife played down the government's involvement to the point of disappearance in her memoir. This stretches the truth. Baldwin was aware that Hardinge planned to warn the King and he certainly gave explicit approval for him to tell the King that ministers were meeting to discuss his case. Helen Hardinge's memoir states that her husband had gone to Downing Street on the Friday '[t]o find out if the Prime Minister had any objection to his passing on to the King the information which he had given my husband in the strictest confidence the night before'.[45]

She does not explicitly confirm that Downing Street cleared the despatch of the letter, although this is implied. She also omitted from her memoir the fact that Hardinge had been told – presumably by Wilson – that his letter was also discussed at the meeting of ministers, implying further depth in government approval.[46] Neither of the ministers who left accounts of the meeting mention the letter or anything like it, which creates a suspicion that Hardinge was misled. Intriguingly, Wilson makes a point in his notes of stating that no record was made of the meeting as it was 'secret in character', which begs the question as to why it should have been more confidential than any other discussion within government.[47]

What is far from clear is whether Baldwin actually saw the letter before it was sent rather than simply approving the principle of telling the King about the meeting of ministers. There is no evidence that he ever saw the actual text of the letter then or afterwards, and it is uncertain that this was quite the message that he hoped would be delivered. The direct ultimatum implied in Hardinge's letter was far away from Baldwin's approach throughout the crisis. When Baldwin finally saw Fisher's drafts, he recognised that they were no more than a 'curt ultimatum', which he summarily suppressed.[48] Moreover Baldwin's sole recorded reference to Hardinge's letter mentioned only the fact of a meeting of ministers: 'The King has been told there has practically been a Cabinet meeting to consider his case…'[49] Baldwin may have thought that the fact of the ministers' meeting in itself should have given the King sufficient proof of how serious things were.

The two available accounts appear to contradict each other as to whether Baldwin saw Hardinge's letter. According to Hardinge, 'I did not see him [Baldwin] personally but I showed a copy of the letter to one of his staff', manifestly Wilson.[50] Wilson's notes say:

> This letter was written by Major Hardinge on Friday, 13 November. He brought it to the Prime Minister, enquiring whether Mr. Baldwin saw any objection to his reference to possible action by Ministers. I was present when Major Hardinge saw the Prime Minister. It was pointed out that Major Hardinge was accepting considerable responsibility in communicating with the King on the lines proposed.[51]

But like everything that Wilson wrote, it is well to read the passage very carefully. He does not state outright that Baldwin saw the letter and the phrase 'possible action by Ministers' is studiedly ambiguous: it could refer to anything from their holding a meeting simply to discuss the situation, to actual resignation. Wilson had no scruples about muddling the sequence of events elsewhere in his notes, and may well have merged fragments of two different conversations taken out of order: one between just himself and Hardinge on the Friday when he gave his warning, and the other on the Thursday evening with Baldwin there as well, when the idea of a letter was discussed in principle. This is borne out by the draft version of Wilson's notes, which differs from the final version in stating that it was he and not Baldwin who advised Hardinge: 'I was present when Major Hardinge saw the Prime Minister and pointed out that Major Hardinge was accepting a considerable responsibility in communicating with the King on the lines proposed.'[52] It is far more likely that a civil servant would have given the King's private secretary such blunt advice only in a private two-way conversation. It strains credulity that the Prime Minister would simply have taken a back seat whilst Wilson talked like this. The final version avoids this trap and gives the warning even more authority by implicitly putting it into the Prime Minister's mouth.

The danger of an immediate constitutional crisis of which Fisher and Wilson had warned Hardinge was exaggerated to the point of invention. Baldwin squashed with consummate ease the hardliners' scheme to provoke one. The ministers' meeting on the morning of Friday 13 November proved a complete damp squib, at least from the point of view of its promoters. Fisher's draft letters were simply presented to the group; Baldwin, MacDonald and Runciman had not seen them before.[53] As an attempt to present Baldwin with a fait accompli, this failed entirely. Chamberlain did not try to insist to Baldwin that the letters be sent. Afterwards, Chamberlain tried to mask – to himself as much as anyone else – this loss of nerve by claiming that all but Baldwin agreed 'that the situation brooked no delay'.[54] Baldwin merely said that he would take the letters to Chequers for further consideration and the drafts were consigned to oblivion. If Hardinge's letter was in fact discussed at the meeting, the cabal may have held back from insisting that the ultimatum be sent because they saw it as a concrete way in which the King was being sent a clear signal that ministers were deeply concerned. However, neither of the ministers who left accounts of the meeting mention the letter at all. According to Ramsay MacDonald, the meeting decided that Sir John Simon should also see the King's Proctor about intervention.[55] MacDonald had been suspicious of the divorce so this was probably his idea, although it does not appear to have led to any action.

The meeting did serve another purpose. It allowed Baldwin to assure

Gwynne when he saw him that afternoon 'that he and certain of his colleagues had the matter under ~~careful~~ [struck out by hand] consideration'.[56] For a couple of days, the Prime Minister had headed off both a ministerial revolt and the conservative press's urgent demand for a lead. However, it soon proved that this time had been very dearly bought.

The events of the fortnight following the divorce case in Ipswich were probably the most sensitive in the whole abdication crisis. Or, at least, they are the ones that Wilson worked hardest to obfuscate. The government's response to the crisis was at its most dysfunctional. The civil servants manipulated a senior minister into mounting a revolt against the Prime Minister on the grounds that his approach to the problem was wrong. They also fed a distorted version of the government's response to the crisis to the King's private secretary with the ultimately successful hope that this would reach the King. It did reach him in a form that was to all intents and purposes an ultimatum. Baldwin played an ambiguous part in approving Hardinge's letter; he might have seen the idea as a way of giving the King a 'real jolt', but kept himself well away from executing the plan. Wilson had very good reason to ensure that none of this ever became known.

Wilson's most obvious goal was to pin as much blame as possible on Hardinge. Hardinge is set up as the fall guy, a loose cannon whose headstrong letter sabotages a carefully calculated scheme by Downing Street. The role of the civil servants and Chamberlain vanishes completely. Hardinge is the one individual who is openly and remorselessly criticised throughout Wilson's notes; they say nothing good of him at all.

> It seems doubtful whether the decision to appoint Major Hardinge to succeed Lord Wigram was a wise one. Even if, had there been more time, Major Hardinge could have gained the confidence of the King (about which there must be considerable doubt) he certainly had not done so by the time the storm broke. His feelings seem to have led him to make

remarks that were to say the least of it tactless and some of them were said to have been retailed to the King. And his letter of the 13th November – however well intentioned – may very well have made the worst possible impression.[57]

The portrayal of Hardinge as a lone wolf begins at the start of the crisis. The lunch on 12 October intended to set up a line of communication between Wilson and Hardinge is mentioned in the draft but disappears from the final version as does Hardinge's visit to Downing Street on 2 November when he told Baldwin of the King's continued misbehaviour. His letter is presented as coming out of the blue and spoiling a prepared plan to approach the King once his long-planned visit to south Wales had filled his head with 'Kingly' thoughts: '…action by Major Hardinge, however, led to an acceleration of these plans' as though waiting until the King's return from Wales were part of a carefully thought out roadmap and not yet another prevarication by the Prime Minister.

Wilson's comments about Hardinge's letter are outstandingly hypocritical considering that he and Fisher had already tried to have Mrs Simpson sent abroad and they were working to persuade the Prime Minister to send the King an even blunter ultimatum. He also accidentally lets slip the mask, in his anxiety to heap the maximum blame on Hardinge. Wilson made a point of spelling out that Hardinge's call for the King to send Mrs Simpson abroad was his own initiative: that he '…added a plea *on his own behalf* [author's italics] that the King should ease the situation by arranging for Mrs. Simpson to leave the country'. First, this practically acknowledges that the letter carried a message from the government. If one part of the letter was on Hardinge's behalf, on whose behalf was the rest of it? Second, Wilson had good reason to disassociate the government from the idea of pressurising the King to send Mrs Simpson abroad. As he and Fisher had discovered through MI5 so painfully a few days before, the King was violently hostile. By contrast, there is no reason why Hardinge should have been aware of this hostility, as he had barely discussed Mrs Simpson with the King and there is no indication that the civil servants had warned him of the sensitivity of the issue. When Wilson saw the copy of Hardinge's letter, he did not alert him. As the civil servants were aiming for a more radical outcome in the form of a complete termination of the King's relationship with Mrs Simpson, Wilson may not have thought that it mattered. The hardliners by this stage had no qualms about provoking the King.

Ever afterwards, Hardinge detested Wilson and some years later told Sir John Reith, 'H. J. Wilson he can't abide, distrusts him profoundly and says his influence is all wrong'.[58] In the language of the time, Fisher and Wilson had carted him, egging him into writing an inflammatory letter to the King on the basis of their wildly and dishonestly exaggerated version of the crisis and, when the letter failed to make the King change his ways, Wilson made him the scapegoat.

Another part of Wilson's project was to hide what he and Fisher had done and, by extension, the machinations of Chamberlain's cabal of ministers, which was practically their own creation. In particular he wanted to blur the picture of what happened in the second week of November when the crisis that they had manufactured culminated in Hardinge's letter. Practically everything in his account distorts events by misstatement, contrived ambiguity, muddied chronology and outright suppression of embarrassing episodes. Predictably enough, all of the civil servants' private conversations with Hardinge and Chamberlain simply do not feature in his notes at all. The notes come perilously close to an outright lie when Wilson mentions the meetings of the cabal for the first time by implying falsely that the initiative came from Baldwin: 'the Prime Minister mentioned the matter to some of his senior colleagues' on 11 and 13 November. The ultimatum is presented as though it were only one of a number of courses of action discussed at the meeting. Baldwin's disagreement with the cabal rates barely a phrase, and a very anodyne one at that: '[t]he Prime Minister's own view was that the better course...' Just to head anyone off from inferring a connection between Baldwin's discussions with the cabal and Hardinge's letter, Wilson throws a largely irrelevant paragraph about the King's diary of official engagements into the narrative to split up the paragraphs about the two events.

Wilson also minimises the influence of the pressure from newspaper editors. In the draft, Gwynne expressly told the Prime Minister that the press's continued silence depended on the government taking resolute action and that the Prime Minister was able to give him comfort on this point. All that survives of this in the final text of Wilson's notes is that 'the Prime Minister was considering what it might be possible for him to do'. Even more flagrantly, the whole episode of Gwynne's letter and subsequent meeting with Baldwin is shifted to the very beginning of the final version of the notes ostensibly as part of a broader discussion of the press's attitude throughout the crisis and thus widely separated from the account of Hardinge's letter. It was unlucky for Wilson that the key date was a Friday the 13th and thus noticeable to even a moderately superstitious reader when it appeared at widely separated points in the notes.

Hardinge's letter and the events that led to it were a closely kept secret, which remained hidden until the then Duke of Windsor published his memoirs in 1951. The cover-up began whilst the crisis was still at its height. When Baldwin finally discussed the question of the King in Cabinet two weeks later, nothing was mentioned of them at all. A seriously distorted picture of the episode was fed to the King's lawyer, Walter Monckton, who was playing a vital role in the final phases of the crisis as the link between the King and Downing Street. He was trusted by both sides, but not far enough for Downing Street to disclose the full story. The King had shown Monckton Hardinge's letter, but Monckton did not make a copy, and took away the false memory that the letter told the King that it was the Cabinet itself that was to discuss the question. He must have queried this point at Downing Street and someone, most likely Wilson, his chief contact there, had told him accurately but misleadingly that the Cabinet had not discussed the question, withholding the crucial fact of the meeting of ministers on Friday 13 November.[59] Monckton thus thought that Hardinge's letter to the King was factually incorrect.

Chamberlain was also misinformed about the contents of Hardinge's letter. He was told that the letter reflected what had become Wilson's hobby-horse, 'calling the K.'s attention to the growing resentment & apprehension in the country', whilst the letter actually referred to the likelihood of the press breaking silence.[60] Chamberlain was not told that the letter warned of the government's supposedly imminent resignation, but merely 'that ministers were in consultation about it [public disquiet]'. This is far closer to Baldwin's take on what the King had been told, which opens the possibility that Wilson was anxious to conceal this crucial aspect of what Hardinge wrote.

There remains a large question mark over what Baldwin actually knew. He probably did not see Hardinge's letter, but he knew much of the background. It was Hardinge's job to keep the King in touch with government thinking, and Baldwin may not have wished to appear to be dictating how this was done. It could be a normal instance of a politician knowing what had to be done, but wishing to avoid compromising himself too deeply. Baldwin could see through Wilson, and later on in the crisis, he played on this without scruple. It is practically impossible that he was utterly ignorant of what Wilson was up to. He awarded Wilson a GCB in his resignation honours, the highest grade of knighthood generally available to a civil servant, as a reward for his services during the crisis, which argues firmly against him having had qualms or resentment over what had been done.

CHAPTER 7

QUEEN OR NOTHING

Mind you if I can stay and marry Wallis is going to be Queen or nothing.
KING EDWARD VIII QUOTED IN DUFF COOPER'S DIARY

W HEN THE KING received Hardinge's letter after a tiring two
days visiting the Royal Navy, his first reaction was fury. If Baldwin, Wilson or Hardinge had imagined that Hardinge's letter
would upset him less than Fisher's crass ultimata, they had been proved
entirely wrong. The King immediately grasped the key fact that he was
being warned of the possible resignation of the government; he sensed
that a gun was being pointed at his head to make him drop Mrs Simpson.[1] He knew full well that Hardinge would not have told him about this
without the government's endorsement. His first reaction was to assume
that the letter had simply been written at Baldwin's behest, that 'Hardinge
was a tool, a catspaw'.[2] The King was wrong, but Downing Street must
take responsibility for the letter. Everyone there, Baldwin included, shared
responsibility for the fact of the letter and the warning that ministers were
meeting and the implicit claim that the government was close to resignation, which gave the letter the feel of an ultimatum.

Not only was the King offended at what he saw as an ultimatum, but he

took particular umbrage at the very point that Wilson could have warned
Hardinge about. The King was incensed at the suggestion that Mrs Simpson should be sent out of the country. On one level this inspired him to a
gush of cod-chivalric anger at 'the startling suggestion that I send from my
land, my realm, the woman I intended to marry'.[3] On a more mundane level
the proposal bracketed Mrs Simpson with his youngest brother's 'doxies',
the female companions of the Duke of Kent's disastrous wild years from
which the King had played a large part in rescuing him.

> The family got rid of my younger brother's girls. Scotland Yard could be
> quick, silent and invisible in those little jobs. No strong arm measures,
> mind you – only a firm suggestion. Then a bank address in a foreign land
> or a packet of five-pound notes. A state-room reservation and a departure
> in the dead of night, with an unobtrusive stranger a step or two behind
> to make sure that the tearful 'misunderstood' lady was on her way. I was
> having none of that.[4]

The King's first instinct was to sack Hardinge, but he was deterred by
Walter Monckton, to whom he showed the letter two days after he received
it.[5] Monckton warned him that dismissing Hardinge would instantly signal
to the outside world that the two had disagreed over Mrs Simpson. The
King's real motive was fury at what he perceived as an insult to Mrs Simpson, which overrode his objective recognition that Hardinge was merely
doing his duty in warning him of the government's concern. The Duke of
Windsor later complained of the 'cold formality' of the letter, although he
clearly did not have a warm relationship with Hardinge. Hardinge remained
in place, but in practice he was entirely side-lined and played no further
part in the crisis. Monckton took over as the intermediary between the
King and Downing Street.

It is doubtful whether the impasse over the King's relationship with
Mrs Simpson could ever have been resolved amicably. The King was committed to a strategy of acting as though there were nothing exceptionable
going on at all, and Baldwin was determined to postpone action as long

as possible. When the stalemate was broken it was more than likely that this would happen messily. After Hardinge's letter, any possibility of a harmonious conclusion disappeared. Provoking the King also triggered the impatience which was another feature of his immaturity. According to one of the drafts of his memoirs, '…if Alec Hardinge had truly reflected Mr Baldwin's attitude, then time could not wait. I must send for him at once and declare myself; tell him frankly that I intended to marry W.'[6] The King's instinctive unreflecting haste combined with acrimony and distrust to set the pattern for the next stages in the crisis.

The King later described Hardinge's letter as a challenge. In fact, he seems to have gone further and treated it almost as a declaration of war. He summoned Baldwin to an audience, but even before he had seen him, took a step that escalated the confrontation. He sought the advice and, implicitly, the support of the press baron Beaverbrook, Baldwin's irreconcilable enemy. It was a typical impetuous and unreflecting act by the King. Beaverbrook had appeared to be an ally over the question of press coverage of Mrs Simpson's divorce, and in the King's solipsistic world could be counted on to support him in the burgeoning conflict with the government. He had few alternatives. The King had very few friends amongst the great and the good of the land. Such worthies were part of the royal world that he held at arm's length from the unchallenging world of the people with whom he could relax at Fort Belvedere. It is quite possible that he was simply unaware of the full extent of the hostility between Baldwin and Beaverbrook, although he did recognise a darker aspect to Beaverbrook's personality.

Beaverbrook was willing to help the King, but by chance he could not be brought into play immediately. He had left England on an ocean liner bound for America on Saturday 14th for an indeterminate stay, purportedly to cure his chronic asthma in a drier climate. This had been announced publicly, but not directly to the King. Nothing shows better the extent of the King's egotism than his complaint to Beaverbrook in the telegram that he sent to him on board the *Bremen* that he had not informed him of his plans.[7] When the *Bremen* arrived in New York, the King followed up with further telegrams and telephone calls both directly and through Beaverbrook's staff, notably Mike Wardell, his friend at that court. The message was plain: the King wanted Beaverbrook back in Britain. Beaverbrook had shown he was the King's man by helping keep the press silent, so it was his duty to help with the next phase. Beaverbrook's memoir implies that he returned to Britain under pressure, but this is hardly credible.[8] He was a supreme opportunist and believed his skill lay in guiding crises to his advantage, so it would have been entirely against character for him not to have taken up the challenge. Exactly how the King expected Beaverbrook to help beyond giving his advice is unclear. He hinted to Duff Cooper that Beaverbrook's task would be to ensure that the story of the King's plan to marry would be broken in a favourable light in the press but, according to Beaverbrook, he might be 'consulted on wider issues'.[9] Beaverbrook was suspicious that telephone calls would be intercepted, so there was as good as no practical discussion whilst he was in New York, and there would be a hiatus of a few days whilst the *Bremen* returned to Europe with him on board. By the time he arrived, what would anyhow have been a tricky question of developing a worthwhile strategy had become even more complex.

Beaverbrook was not the only potential ally that the King had in mind. When the King summoned Baldwin to see him on the evening of the following day, Monday, he proposed that two Cabinet ministers who he had reason to think might be sympathetic to his cause should come as well, as though he were a duellist nominating his seconds.[10] He suggested that Baldwin bring his own, and mentioned Chamberlain and Halifax. In the event Baldwin declined and saw the King alone. This was in keeping with what Baldwin did throughout the crisis: keeping it as a dialogue between the two of them. It does not appear that he spotted the implication of the King's idea: to force some political debate on the matter. At that stage, Baldwin had no means of knowing how badly Hardinge's letter had miscarried and that the King was very close to open hostilities with the government.

Almost a month after their first inconclusive conversation about Mrs Simpson at Fort Belvedere, the Prime Minister came to Buckingham Palace at 6.30 p.m., Monday 16 November. This time there was no pretence that they were there to discuss anything other than the threat of a constitutional

crisis over Mrs Simpson, but there was an immediate breakdown in communication. Both wanted to tell the other something that was non-negotiable;
neither was there to discuss alternatives. The King had summoned Baldwin to tell him that he was going to marry Mrs Simpson, come what may.
The Prime Minister had come to tell the King that he could not marry Mrs
Simpson and remain on the throne, as public opinion would not countenance this. Baldwin began with a blunt statement of his position. The
King was irked to be, in his view, lectured on the duties of kingship, and
irritated by Baldwin's tic of cracking his fingers for emphasis. The King
cut him short by saying that if he was right about public opinion, he would
abdicate, as he was determined to marry Mrs Simpson.[11] He made willingly an admission that some, notably Stanley Bruce the Australian High
Commissioner, had thought would have to be forced out of him. He had
begun his serious dialogue with the government by painting himself into
a corner. When the King's allies tried to persuade him to stonewall against
the government later in the crisis, they were trying to make him reverse
the effect of this statement. In the King's eyes it was not an admission at
all; rather, it announced his intention to marry a woman of transcendent
merits. He never quite grasped how anyone could take a dim view of her.
He might also have miscalculated how much the government would fear
abdication. The King was fully aware of his own popularity with the public.

Baldwin took what the King said as a firm commitment to leave the
throne.[12] It did not seem to have occurred to him that anyone could challenge his reading of public opinion. It was practically an article of faith that
Mrs Simpson was unacceptable, and thus that to marry her, the King would
have to go. The King thought otherwise: that the country might accept her
as Queen. One draft of his memoirs went so far as to state, 'But of course
I was not going to accept without a challenge his bold statement that the
Cabinet and the country would not stand for the marriage'.[13] The exact
words the King used to answer Baldwin's claim and the tone in which they
were uttered have vanished beyond recall. A handful of words spoken over a
few seconds are inevitably subject to different hearings and memories. The
failure in communication rested on an omission by each participant. With

hindsight, the Prime Minister can be faulted for not trying to put some flesh on the bones of the King's willingness to abdicate. This would have revealed instantly the gulf in their different understandings of the conversation. But Baldwin had not lost all hope of keeping the King, and, according to Wilson's notes, closed the conversation by asking the King 'again to think the matter over'.[14] On his side the King deserves a greater share of the blame, because he did not make it plain to Baldwin that he disagreed with him as to whether public opinion would accept marriage to Mrs Simpson. When Baldwin regretted the 'grievous' decision he had taken, the King treated it as referring to his hypothetical willingness to abdicate rather than a firm commitment to do so. It is possible that the King foresaw a head-on confrontation and wanted to hide the outright disagreement until he had time to prepare.

Baldwin irritated the King by telling him that the country would not object strongly to him having a mistress. This seemed to the King to be the 'height of hypocrisy'.[15] It also implied that Mrs Simpson had loose enough morals to countenance such an arrangement, but, as the King insisted to Baldwin, 'Mrs. Simpson is a lady.'[16] Baldwin was taken aback; his view of Mrs Simpson was marked by the Special Branch reports of her sex life and it stood in stark contrast to the radiant image of female perfection that the King held of his intended bride. He was infatuated beyond reason. Baldwin rounded off his unintentional exercise in provoking the King by alluding to concerns over the validity of Mrs Simpson's divorce.[17]

Baldwin seems to have missed a couple of clues in what he heard that should have warned him that the King believed that things were far from settled. The King asked that Baldwin should not immediately mention 'his decision except to 2 or 3 trusted privy councillors'. He also asked for permission to speak to his two 'personal friends' in the Cabinet, whom he had nominated as his chosen seconds in the abortive proposal to make it a larger meeting: Sam Hoare and Duff Cooper.[18] He had been forbidden to have them as supporters in his audience with the Prime Minister, but there was still a long way to go, and he saw them as potential allies. When he told his wife about the conversation, Baldwin mentioned only the King's request to keep the news of his decision to a minimum of individuals without drawing any conclusion from this. He was similarly nonchalant about the King's wish to speak to Hoare and Duff Cooper, which he thought went no further than telling them of his decision. Neither Baldwin nor Chamberlain, to whom he mentioned the King's request, recognised that the King was trying to build a group of supporters.

Baldwin might have been misled by the King's superficial friendliness into failing to spot that they were teetering on the edge of open conflict, but he did recognise that the conversation had been far from perfect. In Lucy Baldwin's account:

> All the time the King was most charming, but S[tanley]. said he felt a streak of almost madness. The King simply could not understand & S. couldn't make him. The King was obsessed by a woman & that was the long & short of it – he said he couldn't do his work without her & that she was the best friend he had ever had & he couldn't live without her. S. was so impressed by the want of sanity & clear vision in it all that he feared that really he might completely go 'off it' if at the moment he was more directly opposed & Mrs. Simpson disappeared.[19]

The King took immediate advantage of the permission Baldwin had granted him to speak to Hoare and Duff Cooper, whom he summoned to the palace for the following day. Of the two, Hoare was by far the heavier hitter. He was ten years older than Duff Cooper and had been elected to Parliament before the First World War, in which he went on to serve as a senior intelligence operative. He had bribed Mussolini to support Italy's entry to the war on the Allied side. He was a leading figure amongst the Carlton House plotters against Lloyd George, which practically ensured him a place at the political top table. His chief drawback in the eyes of the other Conservative leaders was that he was known to be close to Beaverbrook. He also had a wider reputation for untrustworthiness fuelled by the unfortunate coincidence that a popular card game of the time, Slippery Sam, supplied an easy and telling nickname. He was one of the ministers who had a degree of social contact with the King. During his short period out of office after carrying the can for the debacle over the Hoare–Laval pact, Hoare had tried to cultivate the King and Mrs Simpson, and the King had invited him to shoot at Sandringham in October.[20] Hoare was then First Lord of the Admiralty and the King was deeply interested in the affairs of the Royal Navy, which had brought him into closer contact with Hoare than with other senior ministers. Hoare was anyway too astute a politician to see any advantage in backing the King, and made this entirely clear when they met that morning. Like Baldwin, Hoare left the conversation with the impression that abdication was inevitable. The King was far more direct in stating his determination to marry Mrs Simpson than in stating his difference in opinion with Baldwin on public opinion.

The King had a marginally more encouraging conversation with Duff Cooper that afternoon. Duff Cooper was almost the only person who thought that it might be possible for the King to marry Mrs Simpson, but it would depend on a cautious and patient programme, 'that, given time, while it would be very difficult, it might not prove impossible'.[21] The King should spend the next few months establishing himself on the throne and let Mrs Simpson slip out of the public eye for a year or more, by which time public opinion might have shifted to tolerance of a marriage. This was not enough for the King, who revealed the full extravagance and unreality of his own thinking. He had developed an *idée fixe* that it would be dishonest to take the coronation vows to uphold the principles of the Church of England whilst intending to breach them himself, and would countenance nothing but marrying before his coronation. Quite how this would have been less honest than taking the vows having breached them already is not a question he appears to have asked himself. It is possible that this guff masked an image that Edward had been nursing in his mind for a long time: that of a joint coronation ceremony as a surrogate state wedding. When he told Ernest Simpson and Rickatson-Hatt that he intended to marry Mrs Simpson in February, he appeared to be driven by such a vision: 'Do you really think that I would be crowned without Wallis by my side?'[22] He made it clear to Duff Cooper that the idea of any morganatic halfway house was unacceptable: 'Wallis is going to be Queen or nothing'. Duff Cooper got the impression that the King wanted to marry before his coronation and told him directly that the idea was 'plainly impossible'. The most superficial examination of what would have been involved shows that Duff Cooper was almost certainly correct. Only a few Anglican churches would marry divorcees, and they had a tawdry reputation. There would also have been only a couple of weeks at most between Mrs Simpson's divorce becoming final and the coronation. Quite apart from any consideration of Mrs Simpson's suitability, the marriage would have appeared indecently hasty. Yet there is an ambiguous passage in one draft of the Duke of Windsor's memoirs that suggests he thought it was possible: 'W therefore could not expect to obtain her freedom until April 27, 1937 ... With my coronation set for May 12, this seemed to allow ample time for me to work things out. But I was mistaken.'[23]

Over the next few days the King talked to his mother and his three surviving brothers and seems to have said the same as he had to Baldwin and the two ministers: that he absolutely intended to marry Mrs Simpson. Whatever the ministers might have said to him, the King still believed he could do so and remain on the throne. According to one account, he believed that the fortnight between Mrs Simpson's decree absolute and his coronation gave sufficient time to get married. He is reported as telling his mother: 'I'm going to marry Mrs. Simpson on April 27 and be crowned on May 12.'[24] Like Duff Cooper, she assumed that this was impossible and told him: 'But my dear David you cannot do any such thing.' The King acknowledged that he would abdicate to marry Mrs Simpson if necessary, but clung to his optimistic view. When he told the Duke of Kent that he was going to marry, his brother was unwise enough to doubt that she was fit to sit on the throne. The King made it clear that he did not contemplate a morganatic halfway house or anything like it.

> Duke: What will she call herself?
>
> King: Call herself? What do you think? 'Queen of England', of course!
>
> Duke: She's going to be Queen?
>
> King: Yes and Empress of India – the whole bag of tricks.[25]

To his brother, the King was 'cock-a-hoop, gay, happy and confident'.[26] However unrealistic as it might seem now, the King thought that there was at least a chance of pulling off the plan in its full extravagant scope. In April, he had succeeded in including provision for a Queen in the Civil List allowance paid to the royal family from public funds even though there was no talk of him marrying at that stage.[27] With hindsight, this was a manoeuvre designed to pre-empt any attempt by the politicians to use money to head him off from marrying Mrs Simpson. From the other side of the table, the picture looked very different.

The audience of 16 November had a mixed effect on Baldwin. On the one hand, he had been appalled at the depth of the King's infatuation with Mrs Simpson. As he told the Chief Whip that night, 'I have heard such things from my King tonight as I never thought to hear. I am going to bed.'[28] On the other hand, he could see a distant prospect of an outcome that provided a solution to his long-held fears about Edward's suitability for the throne. By chance, one of the first people Baldwin met after the audience was Duff Cooper, whom he told about what he still saw as the King's intention to abdicate, and went on to muse that the Duke of York might indeed be better fitted to kingship than his brother, 'just like his father'.[29] Baldwin was in a similar tentatively optimistic mood when he briefed Chamberlain the following morning as to what had gone on.[30] Baldwin could see the appeal of a smooth changeover, although he did not entirely exclude the possibility that the King might change his mind. He also recognised the vital point that if the King abdicated, it would have to be clearly of his own volition. This set the pattern for his dialogue with the King through the remaining weeks, when less patient men were desperate to pile pressure on the King. It was Chamberlain who was more concerned about the risks.

> S.B. observed it might be the easiest way out provided it was clearly understood that it was a voluntary act on the part of H.M. I said might we [...] not try to induce him to reconsider his decision in view of the dangers involved in a change. S.B. said we must consider all that but I thought he was relieved at the prospect of getting through without a row.[31]

Baldwin's appointments over the couple of days following his conversation with the King suggest that he was preparing to deal with the practical details that abdication would involve. He saw Queen Mary, the Duke of York and the Archbishop of Canterbury. Nothing was recorded of these conversations, but the fact that Wilson mentioned them in his notes shows that they concerned the King's affairs. By contrast there is no sign that Baldwin made any political preparations for an abdication. He does not seem to have told Chamberlain or any of his other Cabinet colleagues about these conversations. Chamberlain complained: 'The position described above remained the same all last week. S.B. informed me that the K. had told his brothers & the Queen but he did not apparently think it necessary to call any meeting of ministers or to see the K. again.'[32] There is no immediately obvious explanation for this. The most probable explanation is that his visceral sense of timing told him that the time was not quite ripe or that he thought that the King might still change his mind. He had told Wilson that he thought that the King's visit to south Wales at the end of the week would genuinely inspire 'kingly' thoughts and a consequent change in his view of his responsibilities.[33] To some extent this was a pretext for delay, but Baldwin was correct in expecting the visit to be a momentous event.

Once again Chamberlain was left fuming at Baldwin's inaction. Once again he started to gather matters into his own hands. This time he crossed something of a Rubicon in terms of the proprieties of how ministers should work with civil servants. When he had plotted with Fisher, Chamberlain at least had the excuse that he was nominally Fisher's political boss as Chancellor of the Exchequer, and fully entitled to seek his advice. Fisher's old pretensions to work for the Prime Minister alone could be set aside. There was no such justification when 'Feeling uneasy about this rather dilatory procedure I had a long talk with Horace Wilson on the time table and the work of presentation'.[34] It is unclear who took the initiative – Wilson's notes unsurprisingly make no reference to this conversation – but it is a safe bet that Wilson shared Chamberlain's desire for action. Chamberlain had entirely forgotten the caution at the thought of change that he had expressed to Baldwin when he had been told that the King was prepared to abdicate. He also seemed to have forgotten that the King had expressly asked that only a restricted number of ministers be told. He and Wilson had come to the view that it would be best if the King left with minimum comment or prior explanation. The 'presentation' that he discussed with Wilson was the presentation of an accomplished fact. As he put it later, '…I had hoped at one time that it would be possible to effect the whole transition by a sort of coup d'etat with no public discussion of the pros & cons…'[35] Or, as Wilson wrote in his notes, '…it was hoped that some way would be found out of the difficulty without publicity'. Unlike Baldwin, who understood that the key consideration was that the King should only abdicate by his own will, the hardliners wanted abdication to be forced through quickly and in absolute secrecy.

Chamberlain and Wilson wanted to set the seal on the hardliners' apparent triumph; the King had been treated firmly and had bowed to the voice of reason. It merely remained to translate the acknowledgement into a formal concession before the King had second thoughts. Even if they had been right, they were too late. By the time that Chamberlain and Wilson planned the King's disappearance into obscurity, things had moved on. If it had ever existed, the chance of quietly removing the King had vanished.

CHAPTER 8

THE UNDERWORLD GANGSTER ELEMENT

All the while the plot thickened and the underworld gangster element
(touched with an Arabian Nights' nightmare entertainment)
gathered strength.

NANCY DUGDALE, DIARY

B ALDWIN HAD WANTED to defer the crucial conversation with
the King until after a long-planned royal visit to the mining areas of
south Wales, which were still recovering from the brutal ravages of
the depression. He hoped that this trip would inspire 'kingly thoughts' in
Edward and make the King more amenable to reminders of his royal duty.
It was the last outing for the 'reform of Prince Hal' school of optimism.
The visit certainly proved to be a glorious farewell to Edward's kingship.
It showed him at his best, evidently moved by the plight of his subjects and
fully engaged with them. He was received rapturously. His simple statement 'Something must be done' instantly struck a chord as an instinct of
basic humanity moved by gruesome economic reality. It is a sad coda to his
reign that his call produced no more than a highly successful newspaper
subscription fund to buy toys for the children of the unemployed, which

were doubtless welcome but hardly a solution to the deep-rooted industrial problems of the region.

On his return to London, the King was engulfed by the more pressing problem caused by his desire to marry Mrs Simpson. Here his flaws dominated, making it painfully obvious that widespread doubts as to his fitness for a responsible job were accurate. He was impatient, headstrong and unreflecting. He flitted from one expedient to the next. He expected his friends to offer unconditional loyalty, but was deaf to their advice. He got the support he deserved. The only figures prepared to come out in support of him were at the fringes, driven by sometimes questionable motives. Extraordinarily, the hardliners at Downing Street were so deeply in thrall to paranoia and defective intelligence that they persuaded themselves that the resulting mess added up to a serious threat to constitutional stability.

The first outside attempt to get the King out of his difficulties by a manoeuvre, began behind his back whilst he was away in Wales. His friend Esmond Harmsworth thought that he had identified a way to allow the King to marry Mrs Simpson and to remain on the throne, but it was one that the King had already explicitly rejected: a morganatic marriage, one in which Mrs Simpson married the King but did not become Queen.[1] There was nothing particularly new in the idea of a morganatic marriage; it had been swirling around on both the government and the King's side as an abstract possibility for some time.[2] It offered the prospect of overcoming Mrs Simpson's unsuitability by tolerating her as the King's wife but not as the Queen. There was no established tradition of the practice in Britain, but it was far from unheard of.

Harmsworth was a friend to both of the couple, and recognised that the best prospect of trying for a morganatic marriage lay in winning Mrs Simpson over to the idea and letting her do the work of persuading the King to change his mind. On the second day of the King's visit to Wales, he invited her to lunch at Claridge's and put the idea of a morganatic marriage to her. In her memoirs, Mrs Simpson claimed that it came to her as something unexpected and unfamiliar, although she admitted a dim memory of a Hapsburg connection. Harmsworth had armed himself with a considerable amount of historical research on the topic of morganatic marriages and was ready for the challenge. Whatever her true basis of prior knowledge might have been, Mrs Simpson was sufficiently impressed by Harmsworth's pitch for the idea that she set to work on the King over dinner the following day when he had returned from Wales and over the weekend.[3] According to Beaverbrook's hostile account, she actively preferred a morganatic marriage to becoming Queen under any circumstances.[4] Her persuasion worked and the King agreed to put the idea forward to the government via Harmsworth, even though Walter Monckton warned him that the prospects of success were slim. Monckton had seen immediately an aspect to the plan that Harmsworth had either overlooked entirely or underestimated massively. A morganatic marriage would almost certainly require special legislation, and it would take the full support of the government to pass it.

Harmsworth had chosen his moment well to attack the King's scruples. Baldwin's blunt statement that marrying Mrs Simpson was not acceptable and the King's failure to win any real support from Duff Cooper and none at all from Hoare had brought home to him that his original game plan had been an abject failure. The powers that be were not simply going to stand aside and wait for him to present them with marriage to Mrs Simpson as a fait accompli; for once, he was not going to be allowed to 'get away with it'. As he put it in his memoirs: '…at this stage I was ready to welcome any reasonable suggestion that offered hope of allowing me to marry on the Throne without precipitating a political struggle.'[5] According to Mrs Simpson, he was rather more direct: 'I'll try anything in the spot I'm in now.'[6] Either way, it was hardly a ringing endorsement of the proposal.

In the eyes of the government, the whole morganatic scheme had a murky aspect from the start. Newspapers in the US, notably ones belonging to William Randolph Hearst's resolutely Anglophobe publishing empire, had been running stories that seemed to imply insider knowledge of the morganatic proposal even before Harmsworth had mentioned the idea to Baldwin, and some mentioned that Mrs Simpson was to become a Duchess rather than Queen. The US press articles could be traced back to the Simpsons themselves. One part of the intelligence operation against her and the King about which the least has come into the public domain, was the interception of international telegrams. It appears that Post Office clerks given cables to send simply passed these on to the Home Office, if they appeared sensitive.[7] The supposedly private company responsible for Britain's international cable traffic, Cable & Wireless Ltd., was secretly controlled by the government, and operated its network as an arm of the state. It had numerous connections to the state's security apparatus. The government knew for a fact that Mrs Simpson was exchanging cables with the Hearst group.[8] Baldwin told Bruce that 'Mr. Simpson has an alliance with Hearst to write the thing up on the basis of a marriage of the King with an American subject would cement Anglo-American relations'.[9] MI5 further reported that Hearst was paying for the information it was being fed. It was not an appealing picture of crude mercenary motives combined with an attempt to pressure the government through a hostile foreign press organisation.

It was unlikely that the government would endorse the morganatic scheme anyway, but Harmsworth chose to combine it with an attempt to use the Rothermere newspapers to try to bully Baldwin as his father and Beaverbrook had tried to unsuccessfully over the Empire Free Trade issue five years previously. On the Monday after the King's return from Wales, Harmsworth's *Daily Mail* published an editorial comment, which drew an unfavourable contrast between the King's obviously heartfelt engagement with the unemployed and the allegedly callous indifference of ministers and civil servants in the committee rooms of Whitehall. Later legend, in part cultivated by the then Duke of Windsor, has it that there was a genuine disagreement between King and government on social and economic policy, but in reality, his declaration that 'Something must be done' never went further than sentiment. The only senior minister who complained about what the King had said was Labour's Ramsay MacDonald, who objected to its constitutional impropriety rather than its sentiments of social justice. MacDonald feared that the King's statement might be seen as binding on the government and also suspected that this might be a way of 'cloaking his [the King's] other troubles'.[10]

It shows how little the King understood of political realities and how precipitately he was behaving, that he allowed Harmsworth's initiative to go ahead in the way that its author thought best. Once the King had accepted the idea of the morganatic scheme, he gave no thought as to how it might be presented effectively to the government. Mrs Simpson might have found Harmsworth impressive, but it would have been hard to find anyone in Britain less suited to the job of persuading the Prime Minister to consider the morganatic scheme seriously. Harmsworth, of course, represented the kind of press proprietor whom Baldwin despised in general and as a would-be force in politics in particular, so he started the conversation at a considerable disadvantage. Like MacDonald, Baldwin also saw through the attempt to restage the Empire Free Trade campaign, as he told Tom Jones: 'The *Daily Mail* is flying kites over the south Wales visit but really with the marriage business in mind.'[11] If the Harmsworths imagined that the *Daily Mail* leader would frighten the government with a foretaste of what the popular press could do if it did not cooperate, they grossly overestimated their influence. Baldwin had seen off the press barons in a much harder fight over Empire Free Trade.

By coincidence, just as Harmsworth was tasked with pitching the morganatic scheme to the government, Downing Street was trying to speak to him in his capacity as chairman of the Newspaper Proprietors' Association in order to sound him out about the industry's willingness to remain silent about the King and Mrs Simpson. For a couple of days, Harmsworth dodged messages from the government, presumably to give time for the *Daily Mail* leader to appear, and it was not until that Monday that he came to Downing Street. Wilson's notes are not written for comic effect, but it is difficult to believe that he was not aware of the farcical side to the interview between the Prime Minister and Harmsworth, which might have come out of a P. G. Wodehouse novel in which an idiotic youth pesters an elderly peer with the supposed merits of some half-witted scheme. Once Harmsworth began to talk, it was obvious that he had no interest in press silence, but was desperate to broach the idea of a morganatic marriage. He seems to have paraded the same recently acquired erudition on the topic that he had deployed with Mrs Simpson to vastly less effect. The abdication is full of incidents of which the various participants gave different accounts afterwards, but none even remotely compare with the gulf between Baldwin's accounts of the meeting and those given by Harmsworth. Even in Hankey's restrained prose, it is obvious that Baldwin made no secret of his distaste for Harmsworth's importunity when he told the Cabinet about the conversation a few days later. According to the minutes, he also told Harmsworth firmly that it was for Parliament and not newspapers to decide whether a morganatic marriage was acceptable, and offered little hope that it would be agreeable. When Baldwin told the story to his niece, Monica, some months later, he gave full vent to his personal dislike of Harmsworth and the press lords.

> A disgustingly conceited fellow and yet curiously timid ... I told him that he and his filthy paper did not really <u>know</u> the mind of the English people: whereas I <u>did</u> ... 'I tell you that the English people will never accept the thing that you suggest' ... Harmsworth was frightfully funny though he didn't realise it.[12]

Even if Baldwin had been less blunt to Harmsworth than he told Monica, it is hard to understand how Harmsworth came to tell Mrs Simpson that Baldwin was 'interested but wary about committing himself', and the King that he was 'surprised, interested and noncommital'.[13] Harmsworth went to Downing Street to talk rather than to listen, but he seems not to have listened at all. That, or he was so embarrassed at his abject failure to bully the Prime Minister that he lied outright to his friends.

Yet again, the dialogue between the King and government was compromised by simple but serious misunderstandings. Baldwin seems to have thought that what he told Harmsworth was enough to put an end to the idea of a morganatic marriage and did nothing further. It is not even clear whether Harmsworth had told him that the proposal had been endorsed by the King; he seems to have thought that it was simply a scheme that he had dreamed up which he did not discuss with the King until after he had spoken to the Prime Minister. Baldwin was still labouring under the misapprehension that the King had given him a firm commitment to abdicate at their last conversation. On his side the King thought he had left the question open and appears to have accepted Harmsworth's version of his conversation with Baldwin. He was burning with impatience and took offence at the lack of an immediate response from Downing Street even though a moment's reflection would have told him that the government had been presented with a scheme with deep constitutional implications.[14] He summoned Baldwin to an audience on Wednesday 25 November; the first time that he had taken the initiative.

The King confirmed that he had spoken to Harmsworth and asked the Prime Minister to consider the idea of a morganatic marriage.[15] It was bad enough that the King appeared to be operating on the advice of a contemptible press baron, but to Baldwin it seemed that he was going back on a promise given at the audience on 16 November. Baldwin's reply to the King was not as emphatically negative as his reply to Harmsworth, but it was anything but encouraging. He blamed Harmsworth for the King's apparent change of mind and delivered a tirade on the unimportance of the *Daily Mail*'s assessment of public opinion. Baldwin did offer to sound out the political parties in Britain and the Dominions informally, but gave the King a pessimistic estimate of the prospects that the legislation necessary for a morganatic marriage would be approved. He also asked the King for a brief written summary setting out his vision of a morganatic marriage, which he agreed to but never delivered. Once again, he passed on to the King something that was weighing heavily on Wilson's mind, but which, if anything, might have deterred the King from abdication. Baldwin warned him that there might be 'a wave of fury' against Mrs Simpson if the King abdicated. It is not clear how much this registered on the King at the time, but over the course of subsequent audiences he began to feel that Baldwin was using threats against Mrs Simpson as a way of putting pressure on him. Arguably the most productive outcome to the meeting was that Baldwin's uncompromising attack on the *Daily Mail* scheme registered on the King and he distanced himself from Harmsworth's attempt to manufacture a constitutional crisis on a political issue; he 'expressed regret that certain articles had appeared in the press suggesting there was a divergence [of view with ministers]'.[16] That was the last anyone was to hear of Edward VIII as the champion of the unemployed against an uncaring government until well after the crisis had ended. The legend lingered on and has become embedded in various narratives of the era.[17]

The King was so deeply in the grip of his own impatience that he had not been prepared to wait the few days necessary for Beaverbrook, his only other worthwhile potential ally, to return to Europe before telling Baldwin that he intended to marry Mrs Simpson and then launching the morganatic marriage scheme. It is doubtful whether it would have changed much if he had waited, given Mrs Simpson's enthusiasm for the scheme, but as it was, the accident of timetabling meant that the King's campaign to stay on the throne was dislocated from the start and Beaverbrook found himself trying to cope with the consequences of two barely considered moves. When the *Bremen* arrived in Southampton on Thursday 27 November, Beaverbrook was driven directly to Fort Belvedere. Beaverbrook immediately proceeded to attack Harmsworth's idea of a morganatic marriage. He had instantly spotted the same weakness as Monckton: the proposal passed the initiative into the hands of the government, who would have to try to get Parliament to approve it, and they were under no compulsion to try very hard. Beaverbrook told the King that by raising the possibility of a morganatic marriage, he had 'put your head on the execution block. All that Baldwin has to do now is to swing the ax'.[18] Beaverbrook spent much effort in the coming days in unavailing attempts to retrieve the initiative that the King had handed to the government by acting so hastily. He was determined that the King should refer as little as possible to the politicians. He took the view that only the written law counted and that the King was free to marry whomever he wanted.[19] Even before they got round to substantial questions of tactics in the campaign, it was clear that jealousy and mutual suspicion would further hamper things. The King began by asking Beaverbrook to conceal from Harmsworth the fact he had returned to Britain at the King's request. He also appears to have withheld from Beaverbrook the fact that he had already sounded out his two supposed friends in Cabinet.

When Beaverbrook advised the King to find an ally to support him in Cabinet and seems to have offered to try to use his influence with Hoare on his behalf, there is no sign that the King warned him that he himself had tried already. Beaverbrook even went to see Hoare the same evening, but Hoare told him outright that he was opposed to a marriage of any kind.[20]

The King did not agree to Beaverbrook's advice to withdraw the morganatic scheme, but his arguments were persuasive enough for the King to find out whether Mrs Simpson would change her mind. It had anyway never been what he wanted. She, however, remained convinced and made it plain that she preferred morganatic marriage to becoming Queen. She relished the financial benefits and the prestige from her relationship with the King, but she shared his distaste for duties of royalty and was daunted by 'all that formality and responsibility'.[21] The King telephoned Beaverbrook at Stornoway House, his Mayfair mansion, with the bad news at 2 a.m. but, characteristically, was more interested in finding out whether Beaverbrook had succeeded with Hoare where he himself had failed. In turn, Beaverbrook's chief concern – apart from natural annoyance at being woken – was that the King was talking unrestrainedly over an open telephone line that Beaverbrook feared was being tapped by the government. In its way this phone call encapsulates many of the key features of the crisis: the King's inconsiderateness, duplicity and impatience; Mrs Simpson's dominant part in the relationship; the all-pervading presence of the secret services.

Somewhere in his discussion of the morganatic scheme with the King, Beaverbrook slipped in what might have seemed to be a trivial untruth, which was to have serious consequences. He told the King that the true author of the proposal was Winston Churchill. It was not an especially outrageous lie, certainly by Beaverbrook's standards. He and Churchill had already discussed what they called the 'Cornwall plan' (after the idea of making Mrs Simpson Duchess of Cornwall) and Beaverbrook freely admitted to him what he had told the King, although he went on to tell him that the King was enthusiastic, which was certainly not the full truth.[22] Moreover, Churchill and Beaverbrook were long-standing cronies. Beaverbrook's motives for the lie are obscure. Possibly Churchill was fleetingly taken with the idea of a morganatic marriage and Beaverbrook wanted to reinforce it. Possibly Beaverbrook felt he was already in competition with Churchill for the King's ear and wanted to foist onto him the responsibility for what he already recognised was a damaging proposal. This would also explain why he had misled Churchill on the King's support for the proposal. At the time the King believed Beaverbrook, and with his habitual lack of discretion told people around him that the morganatic scheme was Churchill's idea.

Beaverbrook's fear that phone lines were being tapped was – at that point – wide of the mark, but MI5 was collecting information via its informant network. Downing Street was quickly aware of what was happening in the King's camp or, at least, what the King thought was happening, and Wilson was soon treating the morganatic scheme as a ploy of what was soon being called the King's Party. At the outset he was cautious – 'There is some reason to believe that this idea [the morganatic proposal] originated with Mr. Winston Churchill' – but he was soon referring to it 'as the Churchill–Harmsworth proposal'.[23]As had happened before when MI5 was reporting on the plan to get to get Mrs Simpson out of the country, it repeated what the King was saying without considering whether the King was himself correctly informed. Fisher's intelligence-led over-optimism about Mrs Simpson's post-divorce plans had left few marks beyond the dents to Fisher's pride and a further deterioration in Mrs Simpson's deplorable reputation in Downing Street, but associating Churchill with the morganatic scheme had far more radical consequences. It fuelled paranoia in Downing Street, triggering fears of a close-knit conspiracy to manufacture a constitutional crisis for the benefit of a small group of political adventurers. In reality, the Harmsworths (father and son), Churchill and Beaverbrook were pursuing quite different goals: Esmond Harmsworth wanted to find a way for the King to marry Mrs Simpson and stay on the throne; Churchill wanted to keep the King on the throne; Beaverbrook was determined to force Baldwin's removal. The most famous version of Beaverbrook's motivation is Randolph Churchill's story that he said he wanted to 'bugger Baldwin'.[24] Years later Churchill and Beaverbrook were still bickering about what the abdication had been about. Early in the Second World War, Churchill, by then Prime Minister, accepted he might have been wrong in wanting to keep Edward VIII on the throne and that his brother was the right man, but Beaverbrook, then in the Cabinet, was still insisting that he had wanted to 'get rid of Baldwin'.[25] Esmond's father, Lord Rothermere, was caught between his son's loyalty to the King, his own loyalty to Beaverbrook and the dictates of good sense. Apart from Esmond, none had any affection for Mrs Simpson, and Beaverbrook positively disliked her. Moreover, there is scant evidence that there was any coordination between the Harmsworths on one side and Churchill and Beaverbrook on the other. Apart from a qualified claim from MI5 that Churchill was in touch with Esmond Harmsworth, there is no record of any contact and some indication that they were operating separately. Both parties talked of making Mrs Simpson a Duchess, but Esmond Harmsworth thought of making her Duchess of Lancaster, whilst Churchill and Beaverbrook had Cornwall in mind. However shaky they were, MI5's reports that Churchill was behind Harmsworth's morganatic scheme in close alliance with Beaverbrook provided the central narrative of the supposed conspiracy. From then on, the hardliners thought they were fighting for the control of the country and not merely dealing with a sovereign's wayward matrimonial instincts.

Churchill had unintentionally cast himself almost perfectly as the villainous leader of this conspiracy. At this stage in his career his reputation was at its lowest ebb. Almost from the beginning of his political life he had appeared erratic and untrustworthy. He had defected from the Conservatives to the Liberals in 1906 and defected back again after the war. After his disastrous handling of the Gallipoli campaign as First Lord of the Admiralty in 1915, he had briefly abandoned politics to command a battalion on the Western Front. In the early 1930s he had waged a bitter campaign against government plans to give India Dominion status. He championed rearmament and firmness to Nazi Germany; entirely correctly in hindsight, but in the teeth of almost unanimous pacifism. Many saw his opposition to Hitler as merely another opportunistic scheme. His tiny band of faithful followers included two MPs with extremely lurid reputations: Bob Boothby and

Brendan Bracken. He was in the curious position of holding great political stature – he had been a senior Cabinet minister on-and-off for twenty years – but was firmly outside the pale of respectable politics. The middle 1930s were Churchill's wilderness years, but his ambition to return to political power was undimmed. To a respectable Conservative such as Tommy Dugdale's wife, he was a 'potential snake in the grass, whose very freedom from loyalties makes him a "dark horse in a loose box"'.[26] When Churchill finally became Prime Minister, Rab Butler, a long-standing opponent, disdainfully claimed that '…the good clean tradition of English politics … had been sold to the greatest adventurer of modern political history'.[27]

The King's cause had a dangerous attraction to Churchill. In 1911, Churchill had been Home Secretary and had organised Edward's investiture as Prince of Wales. Ever since, he had viewed him with a friendly eye. To some extent, he was fatally taken in by Edward's charm, which worked on him long after the abdication. In the words of Lascelles who knew both men well: 'Winston's sentimental loyalty to the D. of W. was based on a tragic false premise – viz. that he (W.) really *knew* the Duke – which he never did.'[28] Throughout the crisis, Churchill's actions were marked by a quixotic personal loyalty to the young King. In the summer of 1936, Churchill was still close enough to the King to write a speech for him to deliver at a ceremony for Canadian veterans at Vimy Ridge, but like many relationships, his had suffered from the advent of Mrs Simpson. In July, this became an outright breach when Monckton sought Churchill's advice about whether Mrs Simpson should divorce and whether she should be invited to Balmoral. Doubtless, Monckton hoped that Churchill would use his influence to try to deter the King. Churchill did not intervene directly, but firmly advised Monckton against both ideas. Churchill was unaware that the King and Mrs Simpson had decided by early May that she would visit Balmoral.[29] Churchill's opposition was enough for Mrs Simpson to class him as 'against her', and contact ceased until the crisis broke.[30]

In the aftermath of the crisis, Churchill played up his doubts about Mrs Simpson, at one point claiming 'never for one instant did I contemplate such a dreadful possibility [Mrs Simpson as Queen]'.[31] In fact, Churchill's attitude to the King's affair with Mrs Simpson was considerably more ambivalent. Hardinge's wife described his attitude at a dinner party early in the reign:

> Winston Churchill was one of the few people around the dinner table that night who found Mrs Simpson acceptable. Curiously enough, he considered that she just did not matter and had no great significance; he believed that, in the ultimate analysis of the Monarchy, she simply did not count one way or the other. Moral and social considerations apart, he considered her presence to be irrelevant to King Edward's performance as Sovereign.[32]

He said at least once that he saw no difficulty in the King marrying 'his cutie'.[33] It entirely escaped him that the choice of a royal consort went far beyond a personal choice. In the eyes of a moderately sympathetic MP, he took the line 'let the King choose his girl'.[34] From early in the crisis, Churchill had attracted suspicion by holding back from the consensus that the King's behaviour had to change. He had declined to join a delegation of senior Privy Councillors organised by the arch-conservative grandee Lord Salisbury that saw Baldwin on 17 November to express their disquiet at the King's behaviour and, implicitly, at the failure of the government to do anything about it. His next step away from the common line was even more drastic. Around the time that the morganatic marriage was proposed, Baldwin had begun to take precautionary steps against the risk that the King might decline formal advice and force the resignation of the government. As though following the script written by Gwyer in his analysis of the constitutional position, he had set out to obtain 'the concurrence of the leaders of the Opposition' to issuing formal advice; in practice, commitments not to form an alternative government. Clement Attlee, the recently chosen leader of the Labour Party, and Archibald Sinclair of the opposition Liberals fell in practically unhesitatingly. Churchill appears to have stopped well short of giving such a promise; 'his outlook was rather different', although he would support the government.[35] He was more cooperative when Baldwin, according to Beaverbrook, 'specifically and positively banned' him from seeing the King, from which he does not appear to have demurred.[36]

Churchill's willingness to support the King against the government was a catastrophic error of judgement, and it showed him in his best and in his worst light: passionately espousing what he saw as a just cause, but with minimal political calculation and a degree of naked opportunism. His old political sparring partner Leo Amery faced the difficulty of reaching a final verdict on these contradictions in his diary:

> Winston is never so excited as when he [is] doing a ramp for his own private ends ... Winston has thought this a wonderful opportunity of scuppering B[aldwin]. by the help of Harmsworth and Beaverbrook. What a fool he is when it comes to any question of political judgement![37]

Amery softened his opinion four days later after Churchill was shouted down in the House of Commons: 'I may have been a little unjust to Winston in thinking his action entirely due to the desire to work up an anti-Baldwin campaign. He is personally very fond of the King and the thought of the King's difficulties may also have helped to upset his judgement.'[38]

Churchill was also an obvious bogey-man for more junior ministers fearful of their positions should the government change. As the recognition that a major crisis was afoot spread to the lower end of the Cabinet table, he featured largely in the nebulous forebodings of ministers. Even before Esmond Harmsworth launched the morganatic scheme, Leslie Hore-Belisha, the Secretary for War, was babbling drunkenly that 'the Conservatives will resign, and that the premiership will be hawked about to anyone who will take it and that Winston Churchill will summon a party meeting, create a new party and rule the country!'[39] The Minister for Agriculture, Walter Elliot, more soberly in both senses, was 'full of fears as to what Winston Churchill would do in conjunction with Lord Beaverbrook as to forming a King's party'.[40]

Churchill, Beaverbrook and the Harmsworths were soon lumped together under the damning epithet of the 'King's Party', with its echoes of irresponsible, anti-democratic factionalism from the time of the English Civil War. It is not clear who first coined the phrase, but it probably first appeared in the *Daily Telegraph*, the newspaper closest to the government through the crisis.[41] It was inevitable that Civil War era notions would come back into fashion when hints of dissent between King and Parliament arose. Wilson was certainly an early adopter and used it almost invariably in his notes to refer to the King's supporters. The word 'Party' conveniently emphasised the idea of coherence and common purpose, which was conspicuously lacking in reality. To the hardliners in Downing Street, they were 'gangsters' plotting evil deeds. By failing to rally round to the Prime Minister's line unambiguously, Churchill had branded himself as a threat to national security in Wilson's eyes.

The combination of Churchill with the press lords was an appalling prospect. Again, Tommy Dugdale's wife combined the insider view from Downing Street and the authentic voice of traditional Tory squirearchy:

> The King, having kept bad company, had bad advisers. Lord Beaverbrook of the Daily Express and the Evening Standard; Mr. Esmond Harmsworth (son of Lord Rothermere) of the Daily Mail and the Evening News; and Mr. Winston Churchill of nothing in particular, but whose name carries a certain publicity. None of these men is English in the sense that Mr. Baldwin is English … They are three men in public life unashamedly out for themselves, all wanting to make personal capital out of a public tragedy.[42]

Chamberlain had no reason to doubt it when Baldwin had told him that he was definitely going to abdicate after the audience provoked by Hardinge's letter. The King's apparent change of mind came as a 'bombshell' to Chamberlain when Fisher told him about it on the morning of 25 November.[43] Once again, a civil servant proved to be far in advance of the government's second-ranked minister. The news ended the second phase of Chamberlain's intrigue, which had got as far as persuading Baldwin to accept another meeting with the cabal for the following day, presumably to implement the plans for effecting an abdication rapidly and secretly that Chamberlain and Wilson had been drawing. Instead, all the cabal got was a briefing by the Prime Minister on Downing Street's vision of the background to the morganatic scheme and the King's Party. Chamberlain was instantly suspicious of the morganatic scheme, which he saw as merely 'prelude to the further steps of making Mrs. S. Queen with full rights'.[44] He was less obviously perturbed at the threat supposedly posed by the King's Party, but did take the precaution of warning his half-brother off. Sir Austen Chamberlain was still one of the Conservative Party's elder statesmen and had openly criticised Baldwin's feeble foreign policy earlier in the year, but he entirely supported the government's line toward the King. Neville then returned to the charge of making the idea of abdication into a hard fact by pushing through the practical arrangements:

> I asked [Baldwin] if we should not now set the procedure legislation timetable &c as I was apprehensive that the K. would not stay even if we got him back to abdication & we ought to be ready to act swiftly. S.B. agreed vaguely but at once changed the subject.[45]

Baldwin's stonewalling against Chamberlain's chivvying shows how far he was prepared to go to put the full responsibility for abdication on the King's shoulders alone. Moreover, he still did not see abdication as entirely inevitable. He was far less alarmist than Wilson and saw far more clearly the real risks than Chamberlain. Dugdale's wife drew a contrast between Baldwin's 'statesmanlike assurance' and 'courage to carry inaction where others would run', and the hardliners.[46] He had no fear of the King's Party. Baldwin was aware that Churchill and Beaverbrook were working together and did see a degree of conspiracy in the activities of the King's supporters, but his attention was predictably focused on the press lords: 'There is a "set" which is backing the marriage. I don't know but I suspect that the Beaverbrook–Rothermere press will take that line.'[47] He was unremitting in his contempt for Harmsworth, but read quite correctly Churchill's weakness and ineptitude as an intriguer:

> I know my Winston. When he came to see me he looked like a cat that has been caught coming out of the dairy & thinks you haven't seen her but you had. And again when L.G. [Lloyd George] is out for mischief you can see the wash of his periscope but when W. is trying to torpedo you half his hull is out of water.[48]

Baldwin's political flank rested on very solid ground. He could depend on the support of the main opposition party. The day after the King asked Baldwin to consider the morganatic scheme formally, Baldwin had asked Attlee outright whether he would be prepared to form an alternative government. Even though Attlee had been in office only a few months and had been a far from obvious choice as leader, he unhesitatingly gave a commitment not to, without even asking anyone else in the Labour Party, still less consulting the National Executive Committee, its formal controlling body. Afterwards, he explained himself to the National Executive Committee in a long memorandum, but there is practically no sign that he had judged the party's opinion incorrectly. Sir Walter Citrine, the pragmatic General Secretary of the Trades Union Congress, had already told Baldwin that he was reading Labour opinion correctly when he visited Chequers soon after Baldwin's first conversation with the King, and endorsed his strategy.[49] Some of the party's more intellectual wing including Hugh Dalton, who had stood against Attlee in the leadership contest, were tempted to exploit the King's image as a champion of the industrial poor, but the Labour movement as a whole was still very conservative on social questions at the time. Its nonconformist roots showed through.[50] Attlee's decision to fall into line behind the government was one of the crucial decisions in the crisis. Even judged by the harsh standards of political expediency, it was the right one; the balance of risk and reward was overwhelmingly against taking any risk. The King was left with no prospect of support from the political mainstream. Churchill later expressed his outrage that

Baldwin had gone directly to Attlee without any public airing of the matter, but it is hard to find any constitutional flaw in what he did. The only difficulty he encountered within the Labour Party was to be accused by the left-winger Aneurin Bevan that he had been overly deferential to the monarchy.[51]

CHAPTER 9

THE BATTLE FOR THE THRONE

*The Battle for the Throne has begun. On Wednesday evening (I know all that
follows to be true, though not six people in the Kingdom are so informed),
Mr. Baldwin spent one hour and forty minutes ... with the King and
gave him the ultimatum that the Government would resign, and that
the press could no longer be restrained from attacking the King,
if he did not abandon the idea of marrying Mrs. Simpson.*
CHIPS CHANNON, DIARY, 28 NOVEMBER 1936

O N THURSDAY 26 November, Baldwin changed his mind on a
very important point. He decided that the time had come to bring
the full Cabinet into the debate on how to handle the crisis. The
number of insiders expanded dramatically. Up to then, barely ten individuals in government had known anything approaching the full picture.
Everyone else, Cabinet ministers included, had been no better informed
than any member of the public in touch with Society gossip. Like the hardliners, Baldwin had hoped to settle the problem in private, albeit without
pushing for a solution, but he now saw the chances dwindling. Just the day
before, he had turned down the idea of informing the Cabinet because he
judged that it was too prone to leaks, and with the large number of people

involved, the story would get out. The easy explanation for Baldwin's change of mind is that he had concluded that the story was going to get out anyway, that he had abandoned any hope of settling the affair informally with an absolute minimum of discussion. It meant that he had become more pessimistic. Almost any outcome that involved public knowledge would not be a happy one; in practice this meant either a full-blown constitutional crisis or abdication. Baldwin wanted neither, but there was only a limited amount that he could do to prevent either. In both cases, Baldwin knew that he would need his whole government fully in his confidence, so like a good chess-player, he reluctantly made a move that was inevitable, before circumstances forced him to.

No single event triggered Baldwin's decision. The King's request for the morganatic proposal to be considered formally was probably the most important individual factor, but it was not the most important one. The only practical decision taken at the Cabinet meeting, when it occurred, was to refer the question of a morganatic marriage to the Dominion governments, although the substance of the proposal itself was not discussed at the meeting.[1] The Statute of Westminster had created a constitution for the Empire in 1931, which gave the Dominions an explicit right of approval for 'any alteration in the law touching the Succession to the Throne or the Royal Style and Titles', so this was a necessary formality. More important, the crisis had grown to an extent that made Baldwin decide that it could no longer be handled by the tiny number of individuals directly involved up to then. MI5 intelligence and outright rumour were stoking fears of a constitutional crisis engineered by Winston Churchill and the King's Party for their own ends. According to one report, a group of the younger Cabinet members had met to discuss what line to take on the question, frustrated that the Prime Minister was not providing a lead. The foreign press had also interested itself in the question again, this time in potentially a far more sinister fashion than retailing prurient gossip.

The discussion at the Cabinet meeting itself on Friday 27 November showed that Baldwin's timing had again been near perfect. He was well ahead of the curve and was able to control the discussion practically as he wished. When he sat down to write his own account of the crisis a few weeks later, Duff Cooper was struck by the similarity between Baldwin's performance at that first Cabinet meeting on the question and his masterly performance at the House of Commons a fortnight afterwards.[2] Baldwin delivered the same uninflected narrative of the events up until then, with no apparent overlay of analysis or obvious attempt at persuasion. Encased in the neutral narrative was a progression to a more or less inevitable conclusion. In the same way that he explained to Parliament why the abdication could not have been avoided, Baldwin was setting out to the Cabinet why the crisis was likely to end in abdication without spelling out or labouring so deeply pessimistic a message. One of the younger Cabinet members who had been part of the rumoured conclave was easily won back to the fold, and left the meeting full of praise for the Prime Minister's performance.[3]

Baldwin did not torpedo the morganatic proposal so much as letting it sink on its own. He had hobbled the idea before the Cabinet got to the topic by pointing out the stark fact that morganatic marriage was entirely contrary to established practice. He quoted himself telling the King that 'Public opinion, neither in the United Kingdom nor in in the Dominions would stand for it [marriage], for the reason that the Wife of the King automatically became Queen'.[4] The 'compromise' proposal of a morganatic marriage was damned instantly because it came from Esmond Harmsworth. Baldwin described Harmsworth's *Daily Mail* as 'the worst judge in England of what people were thinking'. As even Esmond Harmsworth acknowledged that the morganatic scheme would involve legislation, Baldwin exposed its most glaring weakness. It is unlikely that anyone around the table would have questioned Baldwin's judgement that Parliament would not vote for it. The only minister to say anything in favour of the scheme was Duff Cooper, who, perhaps unhelpfully for his cause, cited the example of Archduke Franz Ferdinand as a precedent. He was the only minister to speak out for the King at all, but he admitted that 'There seemed to be general agreement that the morganatic proposal was unthinkable'.[5] The Cabinet did not, however, come to any formal conclusion on the scheme, but agreed to seek the views of the Dominion governments.[6]

Along the way, Baldwin had adroitly slipped in some highly telling points in the guise of simple anecdote. He repeated something that he had been told by Bruce, the Australian High Commissioner, which had made a deep impression on him. Bruce had spoken to an ANZAC veteran who was appalled at the King 'taking that woman to Gallipoli'.[7] In the subtlest possible way, Baldwin was hinting at the concealed depths of wickedness that the Special Branch had discovered in Mrs Simpson. If her character was so bad that her mere presence defiled the graves at Gallipoli for a former soldier from the rough-and-ready Dominions, she must be pretty bad. Baldwin squeezed an extra point from the story with a much larger significance. The veteran was a New Zealander, so that was another Dominion that the Prime Minister was lining up against Mrs Simpson, even before they pronounced formally on the question of a morganatic marriage. Baldwin delivered one of the most crucial parts of his presentation by pretending that it was an after-thought that he had almost forgotten about. He told the ministers that Attlee was firmly behind his position, so any political support for the King was only going to come from the fringes of politics.

The meeting was subject to the deepest secrecy. The story had been spread that the Cabinet meeting had been called to discuss an urgent question relating to the supply of arms in the Spanish Civil War. Baldwin made a point of telling ministers how important secrecy was. The concern for confidentiality even extended to Maurice Hankey's record of the meeting, which did not mention some things that were discussed, most notably the menace of the King's Party, which was very much on the minds of the men at the meeting and found its way into one private account of the discussion:

> But his [the King's] present intention seemed to be to refuse to withdraw from his position. It was pointed out ... that this might involve the resignation of the Government and that in this case it would give rise to a Constitutional issue of the first magnitude, viz the King *v.* the Government. It seems that the King has been encouraged to believe that Winston Churchill would, in these circumstances, be prepared to form

> an alternative government. If this were true, there would be a grave risk
> of the country being divided into two camps...[8]

Quite who raised the spectre of a government resignation was unclear, but it has the ring of coming from the inner circle. The comment squares with what was actually happening. Beaverbrook was touting Churchill to the King as a potential supporter, not necessarily with Churchill's approval or even knowledge.

There was a further and very telling layer of secrecy to Hankey's record of the meeting. It was not even classed as a formal minute, rather it was a 'Note' for the Prime Minister and only a single copy was to be kept 'under the personal care of the Secretary'.[9] It was not circulated to ministers or to the King, who routinely received the minutes of Cabinet meetings. Twenty years before, Hankey's minutes had taken over from the time-honoured system of the Prime Minister simply writing a letter to the monarch to tell him what the Cabinet had discussed, but now he was being completely excluded. When the King opened the red box sent by the Cabinet Secretariat in which he used to receive the Cabinet minutes the following day it came as a double shock to him. Not merely did the minutes not contain an answer to his question about a morganatic marriage, but all they did was to state in a few words that the entire Cabinet had assembled to agree that the Foreign Secretary would assist the Trade Secretary in a debate on a bill to regulate the shipping of arms to Spain. It was an obvious sham, reporting at most a few minutes' discussion and devoid of serious content. The true significance of what the Prime Minister had sent him was clear to the King and he was infuriated. Of course, he had no right to expect a rapid answer on so complex a point, especially as he had not sent the Prime Minister the written proposal that he had promised, but it was a potent symbol of the gulf that had opened between the King and what was still nominally his government.

Baldwin's decision to call the Cabinet meant that he had acknowledged that it would no longer be possible to hold the secret until something had been settled, but despite Baldwin's scepticism, the story did not explode.

Apart from one well-informed courtier, no one at the select house party in Wales to which Duff Cooper went straight after the Cabinet meeting was in the know. Garbled rumours, though, continued to swirl about of the conflict between the King and the government. A friend of one MP had been told by her uncle that the Privy Council would resign en masse unless the King abdicated.[10] Chips Channon was fed a deliciously distorted account of the King's audience with Baldwin that was incorrect on almost every point:

> The Battle for the Throne has begun. On Wednesday evening (I know all that follows to be true, though not six people in the Kingdom are so informed), Mr. Baldwin spent one hour and forty minutes ... with the King and gave him his ultimatum that the Government would resign, and that the press could no longer be restrained from attacking the King, if he did not abandon all idea of marrying Mrs. Simpson ... [The King] refused point blank and asked for time to consult his friends. 'Who are they?' Mr. Baldwin demanded ... 'Lord Beaverbrook,' the King retorted. The Prime Minister gasped and departed.[11]

The most likely source for this farrago was Beaverbrook's mistress, Mrs Jean Norton, adding a layer of confusion to her lover's inventions. Channon did not even appear to have picked up that there was a Cabinet meeting. The one solid nugget of fact was that Beaverbrook was the King's only declared or active ally.

The week after Beaverbrook's return from New York was the high point of his involvement in the crisis and, on the surface, there were aspects to it that he could relish. He was the friend and confidant of the King, called on to use his power, influence and contacts to keep him on the throne. He could indulge in an orgy of high-pressure phone calls and sweeping promises. If all went well, he would be established as one of the powers in the land and the favoured counsellor of the monarch. Even better, he had the opportunity to defenestrate and humiliate Stanley Baldwin. The reality was very different. He was the prisoner of the King who was already committed to a programme with which Beaverbrook disagreed, and deaf to any suggestions that he might make, as well as having no interest whatever in Beaverbrook's plots to remove Baldwin. According to Mrs Norton: 'Beaverbrook, while enjoying his role of Mr. Fixit and the power he now holds in his horny hands, is nearly distraught…'[12] The problem was the King himself: '…he has no sense of reality and whenever Beaverbrook, whom he looks on as a supporter, gives him adverse advice, the King not only refuses to believe it, or take it, but actually only says to his advisers and solicitors: "Lord Beaverbrook was in a bad temper last night."' He tried to make the King undo the damage that he had already done to his chances by asking Baldwin to consider the morganatic proposal. As Beaverbrook had spotted immediately this was the move that placed the King's fate irrevocably in the government's hands, but having let the genie out of the bottle it was impossible to put it back in. Even more fatal in Beaverbrook's eyes was when he learned from Hoare that the King had condoned the question being referred to the Dominions. With his Canadian background, Beaverbrook was well aware that social attitudes in the Empire outside Britain were more conservative. The King was persuaded to ask the Prime Minister via Walter Monckton to withdraw the request, but Baldwin skewered this move when he asked Monckton whether this meant that the King had abandoned his plans for marriage completely; Monckton could not answer the question. Nothing had changed; all that Monckton was asking the Prime Minister was the impossible, to turn the clock back. In the end Beaverbrook ended up with more or less the same fatuous dream as the King: marrying in secrecy just before the coronation and then springing the challenge on the government.

Beaverbrook consoled himself with fantasies of assembling an alternative government once the constitutional crisis swept Baldwin away. In his memoir of the crisis, he made much of the idea of bringing in Archibald Sinclair, leader of the opposition Liberals, as alternative Prime Minister, but this was no more than a daydream; there is no sign that he even spoke to Sinclair at the time.[13] As he reluctantly concluded, Churchill was the only even vaguely possible candidate. How far Churchill went along with Beaverbrook's plans is far from clear, but there does not appear to have been any very active conspiracy. Churchill was certainly in constant touch with Beaverbrook, but there is no indication that he had broken his undertaking to Baldwin not to communicate with the King. The only time he did anything that looked like canvassing support for the King was delivering an impassioned but ineffectual tirade to Duff Cooper a few days after the Cabinet meeting.[14]

In between attempts to lure the King out of his dreamland and musing on how to organise his own government, Beaverbrook was in constant contact with Hoare. It was the closest he came to serious political action. Beaverbrook bombarded Hoare with a great deal of self-serving twaddle and the occasional revealing snippet of truth, all of which found its way back to Chamberlain and much of it to Baldwin. Beaverbrook imagined that Hoare's support for the government could be compromised, but his skills as a political intriguer were negligible. As Clement Attlee had recognised immediately, the King was a lost cause politically, and no professional politician with anything at all to lose was going to take it up. All Beaverbrook achieved was to heighten the mistrust of Churchill and reveal that the King had already lost interest in the morganatic scheme. He also admitted to Hoare that he disliked Mrs Simpson. The only worthwhile piece of information from the government side that Beaverbrook picked up from Hoare was that a Cabinet meeting had been fixed for Wednesday 2 December and that it would decide on the morganatic proposal. As well as a hopelessly uncooperative King, Beaverbrook now faced a deadline.

Beaverbrook entirely failed to change the King's mind or to garner significant political support for him, but he did rather better with a far more deeply hidden part of his operation, which for very different motives aimed to achieve the same thing as the government hardliners had been trying to do for some weeks: to get Mrs Simpson out of the way. Helping the King and doing what the King wanted were quite different things, and this was what doomed the efforts of his friends. The King would have been furious at Beaverbrook's dislike of Mrs Simpson and beside himself if he had discovered that Beaverbrook was scheming to send her abroad. Beaverbrook understood that separating her from the King was the only thing that gave him a chance of staying on the throne. Mrs Simpson became the target of a campaign of anonymous hostile letters and a brick was thrown through the window of her house on Cumberland Terrace near Regent's Park. Many years later, Beaverbrook proudly implied that he had had a hand in the last incident, and it features as one of the key turning points in the crisis in a book about the then Duchess of Windsor by a writer closely linked to Beaverbrook.[15] Having failed in all of the serious goals of his conspiracies, it was as though Beaverbrook took consolation from the thought that he had succeeded in this nasty little scheme. Even here, he would have been deluding himself: the window was broken after she had left the house for ever; neither she nor the Duke of Windsor mentioned it in their memoirs.[16] The poison-pen letters and the strangers gathering on the foggy pavement outside the house, though, were real enough, and Baldwin's warning to the King of 'a wave of fury' against her ate deeply into whatever physical courage Mrs Simpson possessed. The final straw came when the King learned of a nebulous and completely insubstantial story of a bomb plot that the Metropolitan Police investigated, which even he dismissed as ridiculous.[17] On the evening of Friday 27 November, he drove up from Surrey to collect her, her dog Slipper and her Aunt Bessie, to take them away from London and its menaces to the security and isolation of Fort Belvedere. It brought a sudden end to Mrs Simpson's career as a London socialite; the dinner party she had planned for the King and the Channons that evening was only cancelled at 4.30 p.m.[18]

The couple were finally installed together in the Fort under the token chaperonage of Aunt Bessie, where they could spend what proved to be one final weekend together in England. Mrs Simpson recognised immediately that the atmosphere had changed for the worse: '…this was no longer the enchanted Fort; it was the Fort beleaguered.'[19] It was ever more claustrophobic. It had been his refuge from the burdens of kingship, but it was now almost a bunker. The only member of his court to remain with him at Fort Belvedere was a fairly recent arrival, Ulick Alexander, Keeper of the Privy Purse, in effect the household steward. The King's only notable visitor from the older, happier days was the rather ambiguous figure of

Bernard Rickatson-Hatt, a good friend of Ernest Simpson. In his capacity of a senior editor at Reuters News Agency, he played a small part in enforcing the news blackout and provided the King with Fleet Street gossip.[20]

The King was constantly on the phone to his allies but, in reality, they were all waiting powerlessly. Beaverbrook delivered the hardly surprising news from Hoare that the government expected the press silence to break soon. On the Sunday afternoon, the King finally told Mrs Simpson directly of his predicament: that in practice he was faced with the choice of giving her up or abdicating. She comforted him with the glimmer of an idea. She saw a chance of using American political methods to escape the trap: using radio to address the public directly, bypassing the politicians.[21] It was still a relatively young medium, but President Roosevelt had recognised its potential whilst still governor of New York. He had used the medium to appeal directly to the public in his battle to overcome strong Republican opposition to his policies, but calling his broadcasts 'fireside chats' he had adroitly softened their function as a tool in party politics. She was much taken by what seemed to her to be a way of breaking the impasse on the King's terms. In later years she complained that the King could have kept his throne if only he had used a 'first class public-relations man from New York'.[22]

For the time being, the couple kept this idea to themselves, but by the Monday night it was clear to his allies that the campaign to keep the King on the throne was in desperate trouble and that a radical change in approach was needed. Beaverbrook hosted a dinner party for Esmond Harmsworth, Monckton and Lord Brownlow, known as 'Perry', one of Edward's courtiers and, more importantly, one of Beaverbrook's network of semi-dependents. The main conclusion of the dinner, and probably the reason for holding it in the first place, was to persuade Brownlow to take a message from the King's supporters directly to Mrs Simpson.[23] They had recognised that the only 'avenue of approach to the demented love-sick sovereign was Wallis Simpson herself'.[24] Brownlow was bullied into taking approximately the same message to Mrs Simpson that the hardliners had tried to send: to 'warn her confidentially that the country will not accept the marriage, and that she must go away for a few weeks, and allow the talk to simmer down, and to put all thoughts of marriage out of the King's mind'.[25] Brownlow 'reluctantly but very patriotically' agreed, but discovered that the King had put her beyond his – or anyone else's – reach. Her departure from Cumberland Terrace for Fort Belvedere, for which Beaverbrook was unwittingly responsible, was almost the only move in the crisis that the King succeeded in keeping secret for any length of time.

As the King's supposed allies were plotting to break up the relationship on which he had staked everything, the sky over London and the home counties was lit by a gigantic glow in the south. The Crystal Palace, a relic of the optimism of Queen Victoria's reign, which had been mouldering sadly in the dreary suburb to which it had been moved after the glories of the Great Exhibition in Hyde Park, had caught fire and was utterly destroyed. Seldom has a pure accident held such an ominous quality. The symbolism runs doubly deep if there is any truth in the unverified, but widely repeated, story that Winston Churchill broke his journey to his country home, Chartwell, to join the estimated 100,000 spectators who flocked to Sydenham Hill to savour the spectacle, and remarked: 'This is the end of an age.'[26] Under the naval designation of 'HMS Crystal Palace', it had served as a depot for the Royal Navy Division, which had featured in the attempt that Churchill had made as First Lord of the Admiralty to muscle into the land fighting in the early weeks of the First World War.[27] In one of his more futile and damaging errors of judgement, he visited the Belgian port of Antwerp, which the division was helping to defend against a German siege, and proposed to Prime Minister Henry Asquith that he swap his Cabinet post for the command of the Allied land forces there. The offer was refused. His involvement in the abdication crisis was to be no happier.

OPEN
CRISIS

CHAPTER 10

A FIRESIDE CHAT

David had mentioned that if there was only some way by which he could make his position known to the people of Britain and the Dominions, their decent and loyal sentiments would be felt in Downing Street, and the present picture would be quickly reversed. The thought struck me that possibly the only way, and certainly the most effective way ... was for him to make a radio broadcast to the nation and to the Empire telling his story and letting them hear his voice. In suggesting this idea, I was not unmindful of the extraordinary impact on public opinion of President Roosevelt's 'fireside chats'...
THE DUCHESS OF WINDSOR, *THE HEART HAS ITS REASONS*

WHILST BALDWIN WAITED for the Dominions to answer the government's telegrams asking for their view of the morganatic proposal, he was looking ahead to the moment when the crisis broke publicly. He knew that the dam could not hold for ever, and was taking the necessary steps to ensure that press coverage would help the government's cause. He was even considering making his first move through the press, although he wanted to wait for the Dominions to give their answers 'before taking any action, which might begin with a press campaign provided the Berry Press & the provincial papers were prepared to take part in it.

We should then see what the real feeling of the country was.'[1] Baldwin opened contact with some of the major proprietors beginning with Lord Kemsley, the head of the Berry family. When the crisis burst publicly, it was to be Berry's papers that worked most closely with the government. Baldwin even asked Beaverbrook to act in line with the other papers – in practice to support the government – via Hoare, but he can have had little hope of success. Beaverbrook grandiosely declared that he had taken the King's shilling and was a King's man.[2]

The King, too, was looking ahead to the moment that the press broke its silence, but in a considerably less calm state. With Mrs Simpson ensconced at Fort Belvedere, he could now see constantly and at first hand the stress that she was under. He raged that the 'damned politicians were making Wallis ill', oblivious to his own responsibility.[3] But he never wavered in his intention; Beaverbrook described him repeating again and again: 'No marriage, no coronation.'[4] He was determined to shield her from further press coverage when the fatal moment arrived in the evening of Tuesday 1 December. Beaverbrook telephoned with the bad news. That morning, Alfred Blunt, the Bishop of Bradford, had spoken about the coronation in his address to a diocesan conference. He later vehemently denied that it had been his intention, but his words could be read as implying that the King was not obviously the most active or committed supporter of the Christian religion. This caught the attention of a local newspaper reporter who was there, and the story went out on the Press Association's national newswire. Beaverbrook discovered that the *Yorkshire Post*, one of Britain's most important regional newspapers, was going to run the story together with an editorial comment that pointed out the Bishop's hidden or unconscious message to the King. Arthur Mann, the editor of the *Yorkshire Post*, was a member of the press establishment and he had been fully briefed on what the government thought of the King's Party by Geoffrey Dawson, the editor of *The Times*, the week before.[5] It was a near certainty that the other newspapers would follow suit, and Beaverbrook wanted the King's authority to launch a campaign that supported his position vigorously against the government's. He refused.

Beaverbrook knew that the end of press silence had changed the game completely; he tried to convince the King that he would now have to fight to keep his throne, and offered his help in the fight. It was the moment for which he had been waiting. He told the King that the initial public reaction would be hostile to him, but that his friends in the press were his only means of turning the tide, that 'the criticism could not be halted unless the King allowed his friends amongst the publishers to counter strongly and promptly'.[6] Beaverbrook relished the idea of an all-out struggle between the King and the government, which he fantasised would end in abject defeat for the Prime Minister. The notion that such a conflict would be bitterly divisive for the country did not occur to him. All that mattered was that the 'King's affair' offered a chance to damage Baldwin.

Mercifully, the King turned Beaverbrook down. He later gave two substantial reasons for doing so. Firstly, 'to avoid the responsibility of splitting the nation and jeopardising the Monarchy on the issue of my personal happiness'.[7] This was the closest he came to recognising some form of adult responsibility for his actions during the crisis, although his curious phraseology insinuated that the government was actually doing the splitting. Secondly, he wanted to shield Mrs Simpson from 'the full blast of sensationalism about to overwhelm us'.[8] An open conflict would attract a hostile press for Mrs Simpson and that was the factor that counted most for him. He wanted to keep his throne and to marry Mrs Simpson, but the second objective counted for more. She was violently hostile to the thought of any press publicity, and that is precisely what Beaverbrook's dreamed-for newspaper campaign for the King against the government would have involved. In her eyes, the purpose of Beaverbrook had always been to stop press coverage and not to promote it.

Beaverbrook was not impressed with the King's reasoning, and the King sensed that he had failed to rise to his ally's 'natural belligerence' and had left him frustrated.[9] Beaverbrook's complaint that 'our cock won't fight' underscores this and gives a sense of the rough-and-tumble view of politics that drove Beaverbrook.[10] The King was a plaything in a game between real men. To Beaverbrook, the crisis was a great missed opportunity for a profitable fight. When the King's memoirs were being written, Beaver-brook fed the ghost writer with (dubious) newspaper circulation figures that purported to show that those supporting the King had 12,500,000 readers compared to 8,500,000 for those opposing him.[11] These were no more than a measure of the power available to each side in a journalistic civil war that was never fought, but which Beaverbrook hoped to trigger. He thought that it was a war that he would have won. The King quoted the figures in his memoir, but bent their meaning to suggest that he and not Baldwin might have better assessed what the majority of people would accept. He also allowed himself another parade of his 'consideration for my constitutional obligations', inviting readers to be amazed at his moderation in declining to use so powerful a weapon.[12]

The end of the press silence was far worse for the King than the government for a number of reasons. It made a clear solution urgently necessary, which destroyed his chances of spinning things out until he could spring an unheralded marriage on the government. Worse, the actual press coverage that appeared dispelled whatever dreams the King might have had that his personal popularity would dominate journalists' thinking and swamp any consideration of Mrs Simpson's suitability. He was particularly hurt by the *Birmingham Post*, which had followed the lead of the *Yorkshire Post*. He had been due to visit the Midlands and may have expected a repetition of his success in south Wales.

The process of formulating telegrams to the Dominion governments and letting them consider their answers inevitably took some days. Because of the difference in time zones, those to Australia and New Zealand arrived late on their Friday afternoon. According to one story, there was a further delay because the New Zealand government also had to learn who Mrs Simpson was and why she was responsible for all this fuss.[13]

As Beaverbrook had feared, the King's willingness to refer the morganatic proposal to the Dominions hurt his cause severely. The damage went well beyond simply delivering a negative answer on the narrow question of the form of marriage. In practice, the Dominion governments had been given a forum for their comment on the larger aspects of the affair, and their replies were far from encouraging. As their telegrams came in over the next few days, they showed minimal inclination to take a different line to the British government; if anything, they were more hostile to the King. None approved the idea of a morganatic marriage; none even suggested that it was urgently necessary to find an alternative to abdication.[14] The reply from Australia was the worst for the King. Its High Commissioner in London, Stanley Bruce, was already firmly in the camp of the hardliners and a powerful voice in Baldwin's ear, and Joseph Lyons, the Prime Minister of Australia, was a Roman Catholic and hostile to divorce anyway. His message implied that the King had already forfeited his right to the throne by his behaviour and that abdication was the only solution: '…his strong view [was] that situation now passed possibility of compromise, i.e. that even should H.M. now drop proposal of marriage nevertheless abdication should take place since in Mr. Lyons' view public confidence in Australia is so shaken that no other course is possible.'[15] Only Ireland's Prime Minister tried to wriggle out of the responsibility for taking a view, with the feeble and ingenious claim that as the matter involved divorce, which was not an institution recognised in his entirely Catholic country, he was not qualified to give an opinion.[16] The Cabinet Secretary, Maurice Hankey, brought him back to earth with the *reductio ad absurdum* of this analysis: that the rest of the Empire would accept abdication, leaving Edward VIII as the King of Ireland only.

The Dominion telegrams, especially the one from Australia, hardened Baldwin's belief that abdication was the most likely outcome, but he still stuck firmly to his strategy of not trying to force the issue; he was determined to keep open the possibility for the King to change his mind.[17] He did take care to keep Neville Chamberlain abreast of his growing pessimism, but all that he asked of the Cabinet when it met on Wednesday 2 December was authority to tell the King that there was no realistic prospect of a morganatic marriage. He did not seek to debate any other options.

Word of the decision was taken to the King immediately after the Cabinet meeting by Walter Monckton. The refusal to pursue the morganatic proposal was a disappointment for the King, but not because it had ever been his preferred solution. It had just offered the mirage of an easy way out for him. Now that it had vanished, he was faced by the brutal fact that none of his governments would accept Mrs Simpson as Queen. He was not yet ready to face reality squarely, but the disappearance of the morganatic option ended any hope the King had had that he would be allowed to have his cake and eat it. When Baldwin brought him the news formally at Fort Belvedere, he talked the King through his options: the King ruled out giving up Mrs Simpson; the Prime Minister ruled out either a morganatic marriage or for her to become Queen; neither ruled out abdication, but they did not discuss it either. This was not the end of the King's difficulties. He now had to face up to the consequences of two major tactical errors that had fatally undermined his position: his headstrong determination to marry before his coronation and having admitted to Baldwin that he definitely wanted to marry Mrs Simpson. These missteps stopped him from using the one strategy that might have saved him the throne: stonewalling and leaving the government to decide whether it could take the risk of breaching convention and intervening in his private life. Worse, he was now forced to make choices before Mrs Simpson was actually free to marry him at all. Her divorce could not be finalised for about five months, and until then it could still be blocked by intervention by the King's Proctor. The King had entirely failed to take this risk into account before then and it was now far too late to rebuild his plans to allow for it. It was a point that Walter Monckton had known that the King should have considered, to avoid the risk of falling between two stools: abdicating in order to marry Mrs Simpson, but finding that she was trapped in her marriage to Ernest and unable to marry him.[18] Monckton's warnings had finally registered and, once again, he had left himself few options. All he could do was to ask Baldwin for a guarantee that her decree nisi would be made absolute, implicitly before he abdicated, but the Prime Minister told him outright that this was impossible.[19] It would require political interference in the judicial process, which, then as now, was sacrosanct.

On every significant point, the initiative was now firmly in the government's hands. The King's position was almost hopeless, but he believed that he had now found another high card in his hand and he wanted to play it. When Baldwin came to tell him formally of the Cabinet's decision early that evening, he talked little about the morganatic proposal itself, but he did return to the unspoken – and on Baldwin's side, unrecognised – disagreement over the Prime Minister's right to speak for public opinion. It was the question that had been left hanging after the audience three weeks before, after Hardinge's letter. In the King's eyes, Baldwin was merely expressing an opinion on a question that had not been put to the electorate.[20] It was a fair question, but one which would have been far more effective had it been opened far earlier in the crisis. By this stage, Baldwin was able to brush it away easily with an elementary lesson in the mechanisms of parliamentary democracy. He explained that Attlee had told him firmly that Labour MPs would not vote for the idea and the Chief Whip's soundings on the government benches had shown a similar lack of support. The King stopped short of disagreeing outright with the Prime Minister, but he was not convinced. As Baldwin put it to the Cabinet: 'The King had not appeared much impressed by all this.'[21]

The King was determined to back his own judgement of public opinion against that of his Prime Minister. He had already come up with a rival method of applying democracy to the question of his marriage to Mrs Simpson, and now sprang on Baldwin the idea of a radio broadcast in which he could set out his case. The King had done little about a broadcast since Mrs Simpson had made the suggestion on the previous Sunday, but its appeal had been growing. It had the added attraction to the King that it would give him the chance to pre-empt any criticism of Mrs Simpson in a hostile press. At this stage, Baldwin seems to have been caught off-guard by the proposal and did not challenge the King's right to broadcast, but only pointed out that as not everyone in the country had heard of her, a broadcast would draw attention to her with possibly disastrous consequences. 'He would have to mention her name. Everyone would want to know who she was and all about her, and the newspapers would be full of gossip.'[22]

As well as dealing with the collapse of the morganatic scheme, the King had to cope with the end of the press silence. He had begun the audience by accusing Baldwin of having orchestrated the move, as Beaverbrook had told him. He accepted Baldwin's emphatic denial, but as the audience neared its end he came back to the newspaper coverage, which was clearly preying on him. He kept picking up his copy of the *Birmingham Post* and complaining to Baldwin: 'They don't want me.' The delusion fostered by the rapturous public reception that he was accustomed to receiving was being shattered. He was no longer above criticism, 'admiration and allegiance are not blind hero-worship' and a direct statement that the 'Stuart maxim that "The King can do no wrong" was no longer accepted'.[23] The coverage in the provincial papers was only the start, and the King guessed that coverage would become even more hostile the following morning when the national papers took up the story. Above all, he feared the line that *The Times* would take. He had been told – presumably by Beaverbrook – that it would publish an editorial that was violently hostile to Mrs Simpson. He was reduced to the humiliation of asking the Prime Minister through Monckton to intercede and prevent its publication. Monckton thought that Mrs Simpson imagined that it was in the King's power to censor the press and that the King was prepared to go along with this. The Prime Minister had no more authority to issue orders to a newspaper than to the divorce courts, but did telephone Dawson to pass on the King's concerns. In fact, the editorial that *The Times* had prepared went no further than referring to 'a marriage incompatible with the Throne' and making it clear that it would support the government.[24] Baldwin got the King to accept that he would be satisfied if he (Baldwin) read the article before it appeared. Dawson consented and sent the proof by messenger to Downing Street, but in one of those farcical moments in which the abdication abounds, everyone had gone to bed by the time it arrived, no one read it and it was entirely forgotten. By this stage, stress and cumulative exhaustion were already blurring judgements.

The King remained in a highly emotional and depressed state after Baldwin had left. He called Beaverbrook, and in a long and one-sided conversation he spoke as if he had definitely decided to abdicate and to retire into private life. This was probably as close to despair as he came. Over the coming days his spirits revived and fluctuated, and with them his thoughts for the future. He was utterly certain that he wanted to marry Mrs Simpson, but unsure and indecisive about anything else. In the remorseless eyes of the government hardliners, he appeared feckless and unreliable.

CHAPTER 11

OBSESSED TO GET AWAY

From the moment he took his seat beside W. in the motor, Lord Brownlow
subtley [sic] and persistently worked on W.s mind. He even tried to talk her out
of leaving Great Britain at all. But she was obsessed with the desire of putting
the English Channel between herself and me: 'A lot of incidents in British
history have terminated in the Channel. Maybe this one will!'

Duke of Windsor, draft memoirs[1]

WHEN THE NATIONAL newspapers took up the story on the morning of Thursday 3 December, it was not *The Times* that had the most impact at Fort Belvedere. It was an unnamed, illustrated paper that splashed a photo of Mrs Simpson across its front page. She was appalled; not only was she sensitive to publicity in itself, but she feared violence and this seemed to be an incitement. She had already been warned by the police that they saw risk of 'some lunatic throwing vitriol at her'.[2] This was a testimony to the imaginative powers of the Metropolitan Police rather than anything else – the only physical threat that is recorded was the supposed bomb plot – but it helped confirm Mrs Simpson in the decision she had made the previous evening to leave the country.[3] Terror of an attack combined with the same horror at seeing her name splashed across the papers that had oppressed her at the end of the *Nahlin* cruise. All she wanted was to get as far away from it all as quickly as possible. To the King she 'was obsessed with the desire of putting the English Channel between herself and me'.[4] Obedient as ever to her wishes, the King made no protest, but he might also have been aware that she would try to prevent him from abdicating in order to marry her. He certainly claimed that the decision on whether to abdicate was his and his alone.[5]

Mrs Simpson's decision to leave the country for France was what the government hardliners and the King's allies had been scheming to bring about. The hardliners had been trying to make this happen almost since the beginning of the crisis, and the King's allies for the previous week. It came far too late for the effect that the hardliners had desired: the discreet disappearance of Mrs Simpson from the scene and the end of the scandal. Through a series of miscalculations, bad luck and, possibly, her own indiscretion, her flight to France fuelled the story rather than dampening it. Everything was fixed at almost the last minute, so this is hardly surprising; once again the King made bad decisions because of tiredness and minimal discussion. It was the King who took complete control of the arrangements, which he made with his usual precipitation. The man he had chosen to escort Mrs Simpson was given no more than forty minutes at Fort Belvedere before starting the journey.[6] Her old friends Katherine and Herman Rogers had a villa in the south of France outside Cannes, and this seemed to offer an easily arranged and comfortable place for her to stay, but she had to get there first. She disliked flying and he did not consider her going by train, presumably because it was thought to be insecure. This left a car journey of well over 1,000 kilometres across France. It was to take two days and a night to complete, which gave the press pack ample time to mount a full scale pursuit in force. According to one account, Mrs Simpson herself compromised the secrecy of the journey by telling two American journalists (out of 'Southern politeness') that she was leaving for France, to explain why she could not give them the interview she had promised.[7] The choice of vehicle also proved to be a weakness. It was the Buick that the King had given to Mrs Simpson; modern, comfortable and powerful, but a type extremely rare in France and easily recognised. Worse, the export document gave the owner's name as Mrs Ernest Simpson, which instantly destroyed the plan to travel under the alias of Mrs Harris, the name she had used for the ferry crossing from Newhaven. Her arrival in Dieppe was immediately and conspicuously signalled to the French customs personnel, who seem to have passed the information on to the press. To cap it all, the Buick's registration number was CUL 547, which by bad luck made the car doubly unmissable. *Cul* translates as 'arse' in French, and is used as a slang shorthand for sexual affairs. No attempt was made to inform the French government of her journey, so there was no possibility of help from the authorities; indeed there was a strong suspicion that the French police kept the press informed of where to find Mrs Simpson.[8] As a small concession to practicality, it was decided to leave Slipper behind, and he was able to keep the King company for the final traumatic days of the crisis and his own journey into exile by the more comfortable and dignified means of a Royal Navy destroyer and a private Pullman carriage.

As an extra security precaution, the King agreed with Mrs Simpson an elementary set of code names for the main players to conceal their identities in phone calls. They were closer to family nicknames in flavour and probably provide a better clue as to how the couple felt about the individuals than they offered as a means of concealment. Their names for Beaverbrook and Baldwin contrasted aptly: Beaverbrook was 'Tornado' and Baldwin was 'Crutch'.[9] Churchill was known simply by his initials, 'W. S. C.', somehow emblematic of his ambiguous role. The couple's names for the King's family members display a degree of acid. His undistinguished military brother the Duke of Gloucester was 'The Unknown Warrior' and his oldest brother's wife was 'Glamis Monster', in an early foretaste of acrimony between her and the Duchess of Windsor.[10] Glamis was her birthplace and home to her great-grandparents, who had had a baby boy who died on the day he was born. According to much later stories, he was born severely deformed and this, in turn, sparked a host of quaint and gruesome legends.

The plan to send Mrs Simpson to Cannes by road guaranteed her a long, stressful and exhausting journey, which provided ample copy for

the gleefully pursuing journalists, but the King's next part of the organisation also quite unintentionally introduced a further series of complications
that contributed to the chaotic developments of the final days of the crisis. It nearly led her to try seriously to give him up so as to let him keep
the throne. To escort her on her journey to Cannes, the King chose none
other than Lord Brownlow – 'Perry' – who, two days before, had agreed to
persuade her to leave the King on behalf of Beaverbrook and Harmsworth.
The King knew that Brownlow and Beaverbrook were on good terms –
Brownlow had arranged Beaverbrook's first meeting with Mrs Simpson on
5 November[11] – but the King was unaware that Beaverbrook was working
to break up his relationship with her, so he saw Brownlow's closeness to
Beaverbrook as a positive advantage for the job.[12] He just seemed a loyal
and discreet courtier. Brownlow had the added attraction of being one of
the court who had a good relationship with Mrs Simpson. The King was
so obsessed by the need for secrecy that he forbade Brownlow from telling
even his wife why he was leaving the country. Brownlow loyally obeyed the
King on this point and was nonplussed when Channon telephoned him at
Cannes a few days later, unaware that his destination had become an open
secret in London.[13] The party was completed by his personal chauffeur,
George Ladbrook, and one of the royal bodyguards, Inspector Evans, for
Mrs Simpson's protection.

Mrs Simpson's departure for France left the King even more isolated.
On her way through France, they regularly talked by telephone, but had
to battle with the poor quality of the network and, before she arrived at
Cannes, the pursuing journalists. At one point, two of her escorts had to
stage a loud conversation outside the booth, which held the hotel's only
telephone, to defeat eavesdroppers. Her power to influence the King was
drastically reduced, and he was thrown back onto his own very shaky judgement. Brownlow spotted the risk that 'her absence from him – at very long
range – would only increase the confusion and uncertainty of his personal
conduct of the crisis', and soon after they had left Fort Belvedere, tried to
persuade her to go into hiding at his country home at Belton in Lincolnshire
instead of going to Cannes.[14] Unlike Beaverbrook and, weeks before him,

Sir Warren Fisher, Brownlow understood that Mrs Simpson was the only person with any power to influence the King. His obedience to the King's orders was resolute but selective, and he was willing to disobey when he thought they would hurt his master. According to Mrs Simpson's account, he was afraid that the King would decide to abdicate, and was prepared to risk a permanent breach with him to prevent this.[15] Mrs Simpson refused to disobey the King, claiming that it was not in her power to stop him. Whether Brownlow was moved by a genuine desire to do the best by the King or because his real loyalty lay with Beaverbrook hardly matters; for the next few days, her closest companion was in practice working to break up the relationship.

The King had already practically retreated to Fort Belvedere; he never spent a night anywhere else in Britain as King. He was almost entirely isolated there. He had never had any friends, in the true sense, on whom he could lean, but a large Court and an undemanding social circle had offered a palliative. The King was now thrown back on Ulick Alexander and his lawyers: Walter Monckton, who had agreed to stay with him on the evening of Mrs Simpson's departure for France, and George Allen. A handful of servants completed his retinue. Monckton had taken over from Hardinge as the intermediary between the King and the government and he was also the link-between for the King and Beaverbrook. Monckton was a man whom almost everyone liked and trusted; the King was no exception. He was certainly a steadying influence on some of the King's wilder impulses, but it was far too late for anyone to fulfil the fantasies that his mother had entertained at the start of his reign, of sensible and conservative advisers who would improve the King's behaviour for good. Like any lawyer, Monckton was anxious to protect his client's interests (although, in keeping with tradition, he did not charge the King) and, once the morganatic idea evaporated, tacitly began to prepare to negotiate terms for the King's abdication. Monckton's first move was to try to throttle back the incipient confrontation between the King and the government. On the day of Mrs Simpson's departure, he told Beaverbrook via Brownlow that he would stop seeing him:

He [Monckton] cannot talk with me [Beaverbrook] any more. He wants
to negotiate the terms of the King's abdication and he does not intend
to prejudice those negotiations by the suggestions that he is allied with
me. Although he wants to avert the abdication, he considers on balance
that he should sever himself sufficiently from those opposing the government's views to escape the danger of any impedimenta in the financial
arrangements.[16]

The crisis was moving so fast that Mrs Simpson's flight, which would have
been of the highest importance a few days before, left barely a ripple in the
government. On the Wednesday evening, Monckton had tipped Downing
Street off to the prospect that Mrs Simpson was heading for Cannes, but
her actual departure late on the Thursday was not detected, according to
Dugdale's later account, because her car used the back drive of Fort Belvedere.[17] Downing Street anyway knew within hours that she had left for
Cannes.[18] This failure sparked neither recrimination nor regret. Moreover,
her flight does not appear to have sparked any of the exultation that it would
have done in government circles a few weeks or even days before. Things
had gone well past the point when the departure of the King's scandalous
mistress into Continental obscurity was going to help.

The end of the press silence had radically changed the crisis. Public
knowledge and interest created pressure for a quick and clear decision that
had been absent before whilst the King's affair was restricted to a tiny handful of insiders. Inevitably, the matter would be raised in Parliament. The
Labour Party and its leader Clement Attlee had no intention of challenging
Baldwin, but Attlee still had to go through the motions of holding the government to account. He put arguably the gentlest possible question to the
Prime Minister by asking him whether any constitutional difficulties had
arisen and whether he would make a statement. Baldwin was able to deny to a
hushed and attentive House that any difficulty existed, but did make clear that
the situation was delicate.[19] Far more important than the token activities of

the official opposition was that public awareness of the crisis allowed Churchill to break cover completely. Churchill believed that Parliament should have
the final say in the matter and demanded openly that Parliament discuss it.
He had already been calling insistently, but privately, to the Prime Minister
through Sir Horace Wilson, demanding that nothing 'irrevocable' should
be done without some statement having been made to Parliament.[20] He was
trying to block any possibility that the news of abdication might simply be
sprung on the House with no debate or even advance warning, much as
Chamberlain and Wilson had hoped to do. According to one MP, Churchill
was nearly in tears when he spoke, but his sentiment was in tune with the
mood of the House and his fellow MPs cheered him.[21] Baldwin's reply was
again entirely non-committal. These brief exchanges did nothing to dispel
the mood of tension in Parliament, and when the Commons were summoned
to the Lords by Black Rod there was a surge of expectation that abdication
was going to be announced.[22] In the stress of the moment, MPs had forgotten that this was merely a routine step, in this case to give the Royal Assent
to an Act regulating the shipment of munitions to Spain. By chance it was
the second time that the tangled path of the government's response to the
Spanish Civil War had crossed its handling of the royal crisis, in a healthy
reminder of how attention to serious international events was being sacri-
ficed to a trivial question of the King's love life.

Letting Mrs Simpson leave the country was a major surrender by the
King; it was something he had been trying to prevent almost from the start
and, as his repugnance for the idea makes plain, could easily be construed
as an admission that she was unworthy. He had not, however, abandoned
the fight, and he threw himself into one more frantic attempt to keep the
throne and marry Mrs Simpson. Even before she had left Fort Belvedere
he had set to writing the text of the broadcast that he proposed to make to
Britain. The hostile tone of much of the press coverage that morning had
given him an added impetus to pursue the idea. 'The broadcast that the
night before had been a vague and abstract notion became for me a burning
necessity.'[23] As ever when presented with an idea that seized his interest and
imagination, he took it up wholeheartedly. A surge of enthusiasm swamped

the despondency of the night before. What he wrote was a heartfelt plea that he should be allowed '…something that the fundamental law of the realm allowed my subjects, but that the Prime Minister proposed to deny me'.[24] Quite how the British public were to express their opinion on the matter was left entirely open. Perhaps the King imagined that the radiantly powerful justice of his case would unleash spontaneous demonstrations of support, which would compel Baldwin to yield. Probably his thinking was entirely vague and unstructured. In what was to prove a severe tactical error, he accepted the possibility of a morganatic marriage – 'Neither Mrs. Simpson nor I have ever sought to insist that she should be Queen'. Doubtless the King thought it should be open to the public to decide if they wanted Queen Wallis by whatever osmotic process they used to decide on the marriage. He did not seem to appreciate that he was reviving a proposal that had been specifically rejected by his governments around the Empire. He also introduced a refinement to the plan entirely of his own, which gives us a clue to the effect of the cumulative stresses of the previous weeks: he would leave the country – the Alps were his first thought of a destination – whilst his people considered their verdict. 'I feel it is best to go away for a while, so that you may reflect calmly and quietly, but without undue delay, on what I have said.'[25] As well as offering the country constitutional chaos, he was awarding himself a badly needed holiday. He was also slipping in another layer of emotional blackmail, insinuating a 'no' vote would condemn him to exile. The last words of the broadcast were as blatant an appeal for a 'yes' vote as anything from a professional politician: 'Nothing is nearer to my heart than that I should return…'

The King was now behaving in a profoundly irrational fashion. He was trying to appeal to the public over the head of the government in a radio broadcast whilst holding his press baron allies back from launching the same appeal in their newspapers. The explanation is simple and damning: one was a step that Mrs Simpson wanted, the other was one that she was opposed to. His subservience to her meant he could not approach his position logically and assess the options available on either moral or pragmatic grounds. It is just possible that the Duke of Windsor's later claim that he refused Beaverbrook permission to launch an all-out campaign in part because he did not want to divide the country is not necessarily entirely hypocritical. He was sufficiently unintelligent and under Mrs Simpson's thumb to take any plan she came up with as infallibly good and thus not in need of any further assessment. She, in turn, seems to have assumed that a broadcast would protect her own image in a way that newspaper coverage did not. She would, of course, have been able to dictate the contents of a broadcast to the King whilst she would not be able to do the same with newspaper articles. By accident and quite untouched by patriotism, she had made the right choice for the country. Her preference for a broadcast over a newspaper campaign saved the country from open conflict. The King had ended up with the worst of both worlds: committed to a plan the government could block easily and deprived of the use of a weapon that they could not. This was all hidden from the government, which saw in the plan for the broadcast evidence that the King wanted to fight and feared that it would produce a press campaign as well.

In many ways, the broadcast scheme was a rerun of the King's enthusiasm for the morganatic idea after Mrs Simpson had adopted it, with the difference that this time it was her own suggestion and he himself was passionately excited about it. His desire to make the broadcast was so extreme that one of his household thought he was 'quite "insane" on this issue'.[26] He immediately set about trying to organise the practical details. The first step was to tell the Prime Minister what he intended to do, and Baldwin was summoned to an audience at 6 p.m. on Thursday 3 December at Buckingham Palace. Despite the constitutional issues involved, the King seems to have thought that Baldwin's assent would be a formality. As had happened with the morganatic scheme, the King had made up his mind and did not want or seek any advice as to the wisdom of his plan. He behaved with the same unthinking impetuosity and launched the plan with no significant outside advice. His lawyers Walter Monckton and George Allen were allowed to help him polish the draft, but there is no sign that he wanted an opinion on whether the idea was a good one or not, still less on how to implement it.

The King also sent his assistant private secretary, Sir Godfrey Thomas, to Sir John Reith, Director General of the BBC, to put in hand the practical preparations for the broadcast. When Thomas arrived at Reith's office late on the Thursday afternoon he was in such a bad state that Reith had a whisky and soda sent up for him. Thomas told Reith that the King was going to ask the Prime Minister for permission for the broadcast, so they seem to have deferred any discussion of practicalities until it was given. Unknown to the King or Thomas, Reith was already one step ahead of them. Sir Horace Wilson had been informed of the King's thoughts of making a broadcast soon after the King first told Baldwin on the Wednesday night, and had wanted to warn Reith immediately but could not find his home telephone number. Somehow Reith had independently picked up the possibility that the King might want to broadcast and had sought direction from his patron in the civil service, Sir Warren Fisher, the following morning, Thursday. Reith was summoned to see Fisher and Wilson, who told him to say that '...we must consult the P.M. before agreeing' should the King ask to make a broadcast.[27]

The King's preparations for the audience with the Prime Minister to ask for permission to broadcast were so inconsiderate as to verge on insulting, and it began in an atmosphere of grim farce. The time was put back to 9 p.m., to give the King time to say goodbye to Mrs Simpson at Fort Belvedere before her long journey and to travel to Buckingham Palace. This message was given to Downing Street by Bateman, the former Royal Navy telegraphist whom the King had taken on to man a private switchboard at Buckingham Palace as part of the drive for security inspired by Beaverbrook's obsessive fear of phone taps.[28] He was already the object of suspicion in Baldwin's entourage and it was seen as offensive for someone so junior to be used as the conduit between monarch and Prime Minister.[29] The King's household at Fort Belvedere was so small and the circumstances so exceptional that this was a pardonable breach of etiquette, but the reaction shows how little personal sympathy there was for the King at Downing Street. Baldwin and Dugdale were left with most of the evening to kill and first went for a drive in Hyde Park, which was enlivened by a collision with another car, and then to dinner at Buck's Club, where the waiters tried to stop the Prime Minister from smoking his pipe in the dining room.[30] When Baldwin was allowed to come to Buckingham Palace he was sent to the back entrance and, in a final humiliation, made to climb in through a window. As seemed to happen so often with the King's attempts to preserve secrecy, all these arrangements failed and a press photographer caught a photo-flash picture of Baldwin huddled in the back of his small car. It is a tribute to Baldwin's equanimity that he took all this in his stride and conducted the audience with calm and courtesy, although he did treat the following morning's Cabinet meeting to an account of some of the unconventional preliminaries.[31]

The King began the audience by thrusting a copy of the draft of his broadcast into the Prime Minister's hands, but if he had entertained any hope that he would simply be allowed to make the broadcast, Baldwin dashed them firmly. The question was one for the Cabinet to decide, but after reminding the King that he had already told him that the members of the Cabinet, the leaders of the opposition and the Dominion Prime Ministers were opposed to marriage, he told him bluntly that the broadcast would be '...to go over the heads of his ministers and talk direct to the people ... a thoroughly unconstitutional procedure'.[32] The King was abashed enough to acknowledge the constitutional point, but Baldwin was not finished with his objections. The broadcast could even hurt the King's cause: '...the King would be telling millions of people throughout the world, including a vast number of women that he wanted to marry a married woman.' It should have been clear to the King that the whole idea of a broadcast was hopelessly flawed, but as Baldwin described the King's reaction: 'This was another instance of a certain lack of comprehension which he had observed in the King.' There was no serious possibility that the broadcast would happen, but the King was so insistent that Baldwin agreed to discuss the idea in Cabinet the following morning, where it would inevitably be buried with full constitutional honours.

The King certainly failed to understand that there was practically no possibility that he would be allowed to make the broadcast and he ploughed on undeterred, apparently assuming that the Cabinet would approve. After the audience just before midnight, he told Godfrey Thomas to telephone Sir John Reith to tell him to arrange broadcasting facilities at Windsor Castle because '...the King would probably broadcast tomorrow [Friday] night – the PM agreeing'.[33] Thomas had only the King's account of the conversation with Baldwin to go on, so may have been misled as to whether the broadcast had been approved, but after his conversation with the civil servants that morning, Reith was not going to do anything without clear evidence that the Prime Minister approved. All he did was to inform Fisher and Wilson of Thomas's midnight call the following morning, Friday.

At this point the King's matrimonial concerns collided head-on with a far more important question for Britain's future. By coincidence, on the evening of Thursday 3 December a huge public meeting was taking place at the Albert Hall. It was the culmination of a plan launched by Churchill in October to create a platform for advocates of rearmament from across the political spectrum to present their arguments.[34] Churchill had very quickly recognised that Hitler posed immense danger, and since 1934 had been advocating that Britain rearm in order to face the threat. He was far in advance of the government's own very cautious measures of rearmament, and of public opinion, which was still overwhelmingly pacifist. Churchill's goal for the meeting was to establish a consensus in favour of rearmament and demonstrate that it drew support from all areas of political thought. It was organised under the auspices of the League of Nations Union, who sent a high-level representative. The League was still immensely respected in Britain and viewed as offering a mechanism to resolve disputes between nations peacefully. The slogan for the meeting, 'Arms and the Covenant', explicitly referred to the League of Nations Covenant, and emphasised the need to back its measures with armed force if necessary as had conspicuously not been the case in the League's futile and humiliating attempts to protect Abyssinia from Italian aggression earlier in 1936. So as to further broaden the appeal, Churchill insisted that it was chaired by Sir Walter Citrine, General Secretary of the Trades Union Congress, who was, to say the least, not one of Churchill's natural allies. Ten years before, Churchill had been one of the then government's most hardline opponents of the

General Strike. Churchill was aiming at a curious fracture in politics on the Left. Sentiment in favour of rearmament was stronger amongst the unions than the Labour Party itself; doubtless the self-interest of workers in military-related industries played a part. Churchill had also succeeded in attracting a range of figures across the political spectrum: Sir Archibald Sinclair of the opposition Liberals and dissident Conservatives from both the right wing, Lord Lloyd, and the left wing, Harold Macmillan.[35]

The timing was almost perfect. Three weeks before, Baldwin had contrived simultaneously to confess that his defence policy had been tainted with electioneering dishonesty and to admit that rearmament was an urgent necessity. Before the 1935 election, he had promised the country there would be no 'great armaments', but on 12 November in a speech to Parliament that he admitted was one of 'appalling frankness', he confessed that this promise had deliberately misled an electorate which he judged would have been hostile to military spending. In reality, Baldwin acknowledged that it was a necessary response to the scale of Nazi German rearmament. But for the abdication crisis, the phrase 'appalling frankness', which aroused widespread contempt and suspicion, could easily have become the epitaph of a singularly mediocre political career.

Under other circumstances the meeting might have had a major impact on public opinion and even accelerated rearmament, but from the outset its prospects were poisoned by the crisis over Mrs Simpson. Citrine had already made clear to Churchill that he backed Baldwin's line over her, but Churchill had reserved his position.[36] Churchill arrived late at the Albert Hall full of thoughts of making a statement in favour of the King.[37] He knew about the King's plan to broadcast, that the King was determined to argue his case. Churchill told Citrine that he would be expected to make a statement. In effect, he was proposing to hijack his own meeting to support an entirely different cause. Citrine told him directly that if he did say anything in favour of the King, he would speak against him. This did deter Churchill from giving open support to the King against Baldwin, but he did make a point of mentioning the King in a neutral context. Churchill's efforts in organising the meeting and Citrine's efforts to keep Churchill went for nothing. Newspaper coverage of the meeting the following day was swamped by the crisis. There was no follow-through, and brief unity amongst political opponents lasted for that evening only.

The government's outright opposition to a broadcast by the King was entirely predictable, but even his friends were no more than tepid about the idea. They were anyway given very little opportunity to form or express an opinion. The King seems to have told Beaverbrook about his intention to make a broadcast in their many telephone conversations on the Wednesday and Thursday, but the conversation on the point was one-sided.[38] It was only after his conversation with Baldwin at Buckingham Palace that the King took Beaverbrook further into his confidence. Perhaps he had recognised that he might need help to put over the message that he wanted to broadcast. Immediately after the audience, Monckton was sent to see Beaverbrook at Stornoway House with a draft of the broadcast and instructions that Beaverbrook was to discuss the draft with Churchill.[39] It was not made clear to Beaverbrook that the King had already raised the idea with the Prime Minister. Beaverbrook had been irritated that the King had launched the morganatic scheme without reference to him, and the King had every reason to expect that Beaverbrook would have been similarly upset to discover that the broadcast proposal had been made to the Prime Minister without referring to him.

It was near midnight on Thursday 3rd when Beaverbrook and Churchill finally met to discuss the King's draft. They both agreed that the King should not give the text to Baldwin, but should simply read it to him, presumably on tactical grounds that the government would be able to pick the written text to pieces at its leisure even if they had no intention of letting it be broadcast. They knew that his chance of actually making the broadcast was vanishingly small, so delivering the text to Baldwin would merely have gifted the government advance warning of the case that he might find another way to present. They did not know that the King had already handed his draft to the Prime Minister. As it was, they recognised immediately that what the King proposed to say was 'contrary to constitutional custom in Britain' and, in almost exactly the same words that Baldwin himself used at the Cabinet meeting the following morning, 'was in effect an appeal over the heads of the Cabinet'.[40] The one and only change that they recommended was stylistic: to replace the word 'Britishers' with the phrase 'British men and women'. Despite all this, Beaverbrook and Churchill were prepared to advise the King if the broadcast did indeed take place, although Beaverbrook later implied that this was only because the King had lied to him outright in saying that he had not shown the draft to Baldwin.[41]

CHAPTER 12

A PISTOL AT HIS HEAD

The Prime Minister thought there was a certain degree of danger in keeping
the House of Commons in session without having anything to say to them.
He did not want to put a pistol at the head of the King in this matter
Minutes of Cabinet meeting on 4 December 1936

WHILST IT LASTED, both the King and the government had been happy with the press silence, although the government had come around to seeing potential advantages from it breaking. When the silence ended, the advantage shifted firmly against the King. His unstated and barely thought-out project of biding his time in silence until the spring of the following year, when Mrs Simpson would be free to marry him and he would be able to confront the government with her as his wife immediately before his coronation, had vanished into oblivion. Apart from his confirmed allies, the press did not approve. The succession of panicky initiatives that the King launched daily was a cruel proof that he had no fall-back strategy. Like an animal caught in a trap, he was fighting blindly against having to make a choice between the throne and marriage to Mrs Simpson.

There is no sign that the government as a whole was aware that the King was near the end of his tether. If Baldwin did, he kept this to himself. The hardliners failed to understand that the King's indecision and panicky initiatives were the symptoms of despair; he had never been popular amongst them and he had already burned through whatever fund of sympathy he might have had. They interpreted the shifts in the King's position as evidence of untrustworthiness rather than the alternation of pessimism and petulant defiance. Chamberlain saw the King's anxiety on the Wednesday night to make a broadcast to the Empire 'to tell them that he intended to marry Mrs. S. but without announcing his abdication' as a deeply suspicious sign, and when he put the request directly to the Prime Minister the following evening it was yet another instance of his reneging on a promise to abdicate: 'As I had feared H.M. had turned right round again.'[1] The King had achieved nothing except to feed the impatience for him finally to go.

It was not just the King himself whom the hardliners criticised. They blamed the King's Party for his changes in mind. He appeared to have lived up to the fears that Monckton had expressed on the Wednesday night that he would 'listen again to his bad advisers Esmond & Max. The tragedy was that he had no friends & that was why he turned in his desperation to men who comforted him by suggesting that he could count on the country rallying to him.'[2] In the eyes of the hardliners, the crisis was beginning to morph from the problems arising from the complications of the King's private life into an all-out battle with unscrupulous men bent on manipulating the constitution to achieve power. The immediate focus of this concern was the press. The end of the press silence had transformed the crisis into a public one and the only practical way in which the public could be reached in those days was through the newspapers. The King's allies were newspapermen and their titles addressed the politically fickle mass market, whilst the government's newspaper allies addressed the reliable upper end of the market. There was a significant undeclared middle ground in between. Downing Street and the hardliners were unsettled by the possibility of an all-out campaign for the King against the government that Beaverbrook wanted to mount but, unknown to the government, was blocked by the King from mounting. In the same way that they were imagining evidence of treachery on the King's part, they were imagining signs of a newspaper assault against the government. Downing Street was immensely sensitive to the stance taken by the newspapers, and its reading of the Harmsworth and Beaverbrook papers of Friday 4 December was that they had come out on the King's side.[3] Beaverbrook's incurred particular odium for repeating their master's mantra that the King did not require ministers' approval for marriage. Downing Street was being oversensitive. Whatever shift there might have been in the stances of the *Express* or the *Daily Mail* was imperceptible to a senior backbencher and firm supporter of the government's line on Mrs Simpson, Leo Amery, who saw them as 'sitting on the fence'.[4] Downing Street did not appear to take much comfort from the line taken by the Labour movement's *Daily Herald*, which followed its political leaders in broadly backing the government.

The hardliners were exaggerating the danger, but it did exist. Beaverbrook was keen to unleash an assault and set about organising his own potential allies. He had not been deterred from pursuing the King's cause by his downbeat conversation with him on the Wednesday night: 'On the Thursday morning I went to work on the newspaper proprietors likely to support our cause.'[5] What the government did not know was the extent to which Beaverbrook was handicapped by the King. Like many before him, he was now confronted by the King's unshakeable obstinacy:

> I was personally forbidden by the King to explain that no constitutional situation had arisen. He was the source of my information and I had to obey him.
>
> All through these days the King constantly interfered with the presentation of the case by the newspapers which he could influence. For days the papers which I control were completely ineffective on that account. And here let me dispel any misunderstanding. That influence was entirely directed (1) to dampening down controversy; (2) to avoiding conflict with the government and Mr. Baldwin, and (3) to limiting as far as possible the references to Mrs. Simpson. All three seemed to be major propositions with him, in moments when abdication should have been the principal consideration.[6]

Beaverbrook stopped short of saying that toppling Baldwin should also have been a consideration, but his sneer at the King's desire to avoid a fight with the government betrays his true agenda. Beaverbrook never seems to have grasped that he had been brought into the affair because Mrs Simpson thought he could keep the press silent about her, and everything else was secondary. This was also hidden to senior staff of the Beaverbrook organisation, who felt that their boss was behaving indecisively and should have come out wholeheartedly in favour of the King, albeit because they scented an opportunity for large extra sales and not because they supported the King.[7]

The disagreement between the King and Beaverbrook was not the only fault line within the King's Party. Beaverbrook envied the greater freedom enjoyed by Harmsworth, who was not restrained by direct contact with the King, but he did not appear to be aware that Harmsworth was not entirely his own master.[8] The *Sunday Dispatch* was a fading star in the journalistic firmament, but its editor, Collin Brooks, was a trusted personal adviser to Lord Rothermere. Brooks refused point-blank when Harmsworth asked him to write an article supporting the King.[9] Ultimately, the father remained in charge, however passionate his son might have been to help the King.

Perversely enough, it was the *News Chronicle*, the newspaper with only a very weak connection to the King's Party, that was causing the government the greatest concern. Unlike the *Daily Mail* and the *Daily Express*, whose proprietors were fully in touch with what was passing between King and government, Sir Walter Layton, owner of the *News Chronicle*, had only Beaverbrook's appeals for help to go on, and Beaverbrook cannot have given him a full or frank account of what had happened to the morganatic proposal when he saw him on the Thursday to solicit his help.[10] His paper was the only one that had come out immediately in favour of the morganatic proposal on the Thursday – in the government's eyes 'the one amazing exception' – presumably left unaware by Beaverbrook that the government had buried the idea the day before.[11] The attitude of the *News Chronicle* was disappointing, as at one level it should have been a natural ally to the government's moralistic stance. It had strong ties to nonconformism, which was supposedly solidly aligned against the marriage to

Mrs Simpson as well as holding left-of-centre political views. In the Friday edition, the *News Chronicle* had tempered its view by accepting that the King should follow ministerial advice, but in Downing Street's eyes at least, the Beaverbrook and Harmsworth newspapers had swung behind the morganatic proposal.

Sir Horace Wilson's reading of the situation was even more extreme and focused on the proposed broadcast. He 'knew from other sources that the King was being urged to press his request: it was one phase of the attempt to set up a "King's Party"'.[12] Having teetered on the edge of inaccuracy since the inception of the operation, MI5's reports had finally come up with a picture that was almost the opposite of reality. Wilson was painting the King's allies as the enthusiastic promoters of a constitutionally dubious project, rather than the hapless followers of another hare-brained scheme that had been half-explained to them too late for them to give any meaningful advice on it. This fitted comfortably with the near-paranoid image that Wilson had formed of an unscrupulous and resolute conspiracy to topple the government by whatever means it could find. MI5 had either fallen into the classic intelligence trap of allowing their informant to work out which way their thinking went and inventing material which would be well received because it confirmed this preconception, or it had accepted as true material that was simply wrong. Given the King's blind and overwhelming enthusiasm throughout the Thursday for the idea of a broadcast, it is quite possible that he had convinced himself that his allies would share this enthusiasm and had told this to MI5's informant. Perhaps it was a combination of both. Yet again, the government – or at least its hardliners – found itself making decisions on the basis of narrowly procured and untested covert intelligence rather than analysing the verifiable facts that were available to it.

When the Cabinet met at 10.30 in the morning of Friday 4 December at the Prime Minister's room in Parliament with the ostensible purpose of discussing the King's wish to broadcast, the crisis had taken on a quite different aspect since the meeting two days before. The previous meetings had been little more than confidential briefing sessions on how the Prime Minister was dealing with the King. The Cabinet now faced a public crisis and began to operate as a body to make decisions, albeit in an increasingly chaotic atmosphere. There were two items on the agenda. One was a piece of formal Cabinet business: to respond to the King's request to make a broadcast. The other was informal and unstated: Baldwin wanted to flag to the Cabinet that abdication was the most likely outcome to the crisis. He began, as he had done at the previous meetings of the Cabinet on the crisis, with a narrative of events. Significantly, he then went through, in detail, the four options that he had presented to the King on the Wednesday: renunciation of Mrs Simpson, marriage in defiance of the government, morganatic marriage or abdication, presented in a way that led to the almost inescapable conclusion that abdication was by far the most likely outcome. Baldwin and the King had discussed these options and one or the other had dismissed each of them as impossible except for abdication and marriage to Mrs Simpson. As to the formal business of the meeting, he had only brought the broadcast to the Cabinet for discussion because '[t]he King had used every argument to urge the broadcast and asked him [Baldwin] to consider it. He had promised to do so.'[13] The discussion was a formality; there was no doubt in anyone's mind that the proposal was unconstitutional. Even Duff Cooper, the nearest thing that the King had to a supporter in the Cabinet, knew this:

> There was no doubt ... in the mind of any member of the Cabinet that this broadcast could not be allowed. So long as the King is King, every utterance that he makes must be on the advice of Ministers who must take full responsibility for every word. If, therefore, we could not advise him to make this speech, we could not allow him to.[14]

The mood and dynamics of any discussion can be fragile things especially in as fraught a situation as the Cabinet faced that day, and they are as vulnerable to accident as to deliberate intervention. It would have been a simple matter to drive the final nail in the broadcast's coffin by reading out the King's draft, but Sir John Simon had forgotten to bring it with him. However, he had remembered to bring his own analysis of the legal position, with which he proceeded to divert his colleagues when Lord Swinton was unwise enough to ask him what it was. If there had ever been any risk of the ministers not grasping that the King's request was impossible, it was firmly laid to rest. Simon's failure to bring the King's draft was the first step on an ever-steeper downward slope that was to take the meeting a long way from another orderly sitting that followed the Prime Minister's script. The hiatus whilst the draft of the broadcast was sent for broke the smooth flow of the meeting and, by chance, coincided with the intrusion of parliamentary vulgarity on the orderliness of Cabinet. A message was brought in that Attlee wanted to follow up his gentle enquiry of the previous day and ask another question in the House, and the Prime Minister was duty bound to leave the Cabinet meeting, and deliver an answer even if it was as empty as his previous one. When Baldwin arrived in the Chamber and replied to Attlee, Churchill then pressed again his demand of the previous day, with equal lack of success. The whole proceeding took no more than quarter of an hour.

The discussion resumed and Simon read the King's draft using it as a launch pad for a two-pronged assault on the King. He tutted at the King's ignorance of constitutional law, so lamentable in someone who had been taught law at Oxford University by no less a luminary than Sir William Anson, the author of that standard work on the topic, *The Law and Custom of the Constitution*. An ignorance, Simon insinuated, which was shared by the King's lawyer and Oxford contemporary, Walter Monckton. Simon then moved on from Inns of Court cattiness to the more telling point that the King appeared to have backtracked on his willingness to abdicate. The King's claim, 'I could not go on bearing the heavy burdens that constantly rest on me as King unless I could be strengthened in the task by a happy married life; and so I am firmly resolved to marry the woman I love when she is free to marry me', showed that he still aimed to marry Mrs Simpson and remain on the throne. Despite the verdict of the Dominion governments and what Baldwin had told him about its prospects in Britain, he was also still pursuing a morganatic marriage: 'Neither Mrs. Simpson nor I have ever sought to insist that she should be Queen.' Not only did this sound like an attempt to appeal over the government's head to be allowed to make a morganatic marriage, but the scheme was now inextricably linked to the King's Party, and as such anathema to the hardliners.[15]

The combination of the constitutional position and what the King actually intended to say should have been sufficient to dispose of the proposal in short order, but a mix of punctiliousness and political ambition added another twist to the discussion. The Imperial complication made itself felt, once again more by accident than by design. Perhaps inevitably the question was raised by the Dominions Secretary, Malcolm MacDonald, son of Ramsay MacDonald and one of the youngest members of the Cabinet. His father had insisted that he be a member, otherwise his political claim to the position was minimal. He was naturally alert to the Empire dimension to the issue and keen to make his mark as a politician in his own right and not merely as a dynastic appendage. He pitched in by expressing his doubt that the British Cabinet could advise on such a constitutional question without 'consultation with the Dominions', and this triggered an unfocused and rambling debate as to how the obstacle could be overcome that drew in about half the ministers present. His point was quite true, but it did not help find a solution to the urgent problem, so somewhere between a fifth and a quarter of the Cabinet's discussion that morning was taken up by the Dominion dimension. Little by little the talk broadened out to ticklish and more detailed questions of how the advice against the broadcast was to be delivered and even how the abdication itself was to be effected. Whenever it looked as though a conclusion had been reached, MacDonald steered the conversation back round to the Dominions.

Whilst this was going on, events at the other end of Whitehall were about to change the tenor of the meeting one more time. The hardline civil servants, possibly in collusion with Chamberlain, found a pretext to heighten the tension. Earlier that morning Sir John Reith had telephoned Wilson and Fisher to tell them of Godfrey Thomas's midnight phone call asking him to make the practical preparations for a broadcast by the King. Reith was unable to reach Wilson immediately, but left a message at Downing Street requesting some official statement to broadcast. Reith did not ask for instructions as to what he should do about the broadcast: after his earlier conversations with Fisher and Wilson, it was perfectly clear that he would only initiate the broadcast with the government's authority.[16] When Fisher and Wilson did call Reith back, they confirmed that no such authorisation had been given, so there was no risk of an uncontrolled broadcast. That should have been the end of the matter, but the civil servants still decided that the incident was important enough to interrupt a Cabinet meeting.[17] How they could have concluded that there was an urgent threat is mysterious. At first glance it did seem to be an attempt by the King to defy, or at least pre-empt, the Cabinet's decision, but on closer examination the concern appears to be badly overdone. The connection between the King's Party and the broadcast was tenuous to say the least. The clue to the true purpose of the civil servants' intervention is that the message they sent to the House of Commons was delivered to Neville Chamberlain, their ally in Cabinet, rather than to the Prime Minister.

Chamberlain was called out of the room around noon to take the message and re-entered in a *coup de théâtre* with an announcement that played to the unfocused and latent fears of many of the ministers that the King's affair would be exploited to trigger a full-scale constitutional crisis aimed at forcing a change of government. Curiously, Chamberlain did not even mention the King's proposed broadcast. Instead, he warned the Cabinet in general terms of a conspiracy by the King's Party. In Maurice Hankey's cautious prose, Chamberlain 'had learnt from the Chief Whip that Mr. Winston Churchill and Lord Beaverbrook were in close consultation and were working together on the lines adopted by the *Daily Mail*, the *Daily Express* and the *News Chronicle*'.[18] In Duff Cooper's memory, the conspiracy that was reported to the Cabinet embraced the King himself: '...the King was busily engaged in taking counsel with Max and Winston.'[19]

None of the accounts of the meeting attempted to give a verbatim account of what Chamberlain said, but his intervention transformed the meeting from a rambling discussion of ways and means into an outright crisis session. There is a distinct flavour of stage-management to the way in which the hardliners had exploited Thomas's midnight call as a tool to inject a panic factor. Somewhere along the line things had become exaggerated and what Chamberlain said to the Cabinet was very different to the events that had triggered the message being sent to him, but it is impossible to trace at what point this change occurred. No copy appears to have survived of the message that Wilson sent to the House of Commons, so it is not even clear whether it described Thomas's midnight call or merely said a conspiracy was afoot. It is tempting to speculate that the message did indeed mention the broadcast, but Chamberlain decided not to mention it because its value as a panic factor had been severely eroded. Earlier in the meeting Lord Halifax had asked Baldwin whether there was any risk of the King in his overwrought state defying the Cabinet and going direct to Sir John Reith. Baldwin told him firmly that the King would only be allowed to broadcast with the government's authorisation.

Chamberlain's intervention put the hardliners firmly in charge of the meeting with he himself leading the charge to force the King's hand and make his choice almost immediately, in practice to abdicate. 'The Prime Minister should bring His Majesty sharply up to the point that he must make his decision that very day.'[20] He raised the dangerous spectre of the King's Party: 'some irresponsible people [who advised the King] that he could get away with it.' The implicit threat that they posed was linked to the vital urgency of severe measures: 'In the interests of the Country and of the Empire it was impossible to delay any longer.' Moreover he was not just acting on his own analysis of the situation: '...the Parliamentary Secretary to the Treasury [the Chief Whip] had received a private message from a well-informed person who said that the Cabinet should play all their cards now.' After months of biting his lip at what he saw as Baldwin's temporising, Chamberlain could give full rein to his instinctive desire to tell the King that enough was enough. Support amongst the other ministers was practically unanimous. Halifax proposed that the King be threatened directly with the government's resignation if he did not make his mind up and at least one other minister echoed the proposal. Leslie Hore-Belisha spoke for the self-interest of the junior members of the Cabinet with the terrifying prospect that the King's Party might rapidly deprive them of their jobs: '…if the Government were to resign before the weekend, the King might be able to obtain other Ministers who would advise him to go on with his course.'

Baldwin fought a doomed solo rear-guard action to hold the hardliners at bay. Even his admission that he had told the King informally that it would be better for him to go had been more or less ignored. He got no support at all when he told the Cabinet 'He did not want to put a pistol at the head of the King in this matter'. That, it seemed, was exactly what the overwhelming majority of his colleagues wanted to do. No one came to the Prime Minister's assistance. Duff Cooper made no contribution to the discussion. He had been squashed in his attempts to speak out for the King at the two previous meetings and he was swinging away from his previous support for the King anyway. At a dinner party given by the Channons that evening, everyone else was a 'Cavalier' but Duff Cooper was 'revolted by the King's selfish stupidity'.[21] Even the news that a line was open to the King's Party in the shape of an invitation from Winston Churchill to the Chief Whip for lunch failed to calm the fears of Baldwin's colleagues.

Almost every member of the Cabinet was certain that not only did something have to be done, but it had to be seen to be done. The government would have to say something. Gradually the urge to make some kind of statement took the upper hand over the urge to wring an immediate decision out of the King. The possibility that the government might soon resign if the King did not buckle had been raised a number of times, but no head of enthusiasm for an outright ultimatum had developed. In the mysterious way that ideas emerge unheralded from group conversations, the idea began to take shape that the Prime Minister should make some statement to the House before it adjourned for the weekend at 4 p.m. that day. The proposal would not block the possibility of insisting the King should be forced to decide and was certainly not in any way touted as a middle way. The most dovish argument that anyone came up with was Sam Hoare's that it would buy the Cabinet an extra day or so that it could give the King to choose. In reality, a statement by the Prime Minister offered a more effective way of putting pressure on the King than giving him an ultimatum in private. It would, of course, be a public announcement, and it was Simon, the courtroom lawyer, who spotted the opportunity to hold the King's feet to the fire. Reviving the morganatic proposal in the draft broadcast had opened a weak flank in the King's position, which could be attacked ruthlessly. The statement would make entirely plain that the morganatic proposal was impossible: 'It would also enable the Government to get the position clearly to the public and the Empire that Mrs. Simpson could only become the wife of either the King or of a private person who had been King.' It went without saying that Mrs Simpson was not acceptable as a Queen so this was virtually a statement that the King had to abdicate if he wanted to marry. The House of Commons and the world were to be given a summary of the alternatives available to the King with which Baldwin had begun the meeting, the stark choice of renouncing Mrs Simpson or abdicating. Baldwin's faint plea that he 'saw some risk in starting in three hours' time to make a statement without adequate opportunity to think the whole matter over' was brushed aside. The Cabinet wanted the King to choose, and it made a formal decision that the Prime Minister should make a statement. The hardliners had won, but their victory was not quite total; Baldwin was to urge the King to choose soon, but he was not to deliver an outright ultimatum with a deadline of midnight, instead:

> That the Prime Minister should the same day represent to the King the dangerous political situation which might arise throughout the Empire if the present uncertainty as to His Majesty's intentions in the matters arising out of his intention to marry continued, and should ask His Majesty to notify his decisions … at the earliest practicable moment, and, if possible, in time for announcements to be made in Parliament on Monday, December 7th…[22]

Baldwin's hand had been partially forced, but the Cabinet had not forced him to send an outright ultimatum. The Cabinet could disperse with a sense of having pushed the Prime Minister into a resolute move, but it would be some hours before it took effect, and the spectre of the King's Party was still stalking the land.

Its two leaders kept up the fighting talk over separate lunches with representatives of the government. Churchill subjected the Chief Whip, David Margesson, to a variation on the same overblown rant to which he had treated Duff Cooper to the effect that the King was being ill-treated and pushed into a corner.[23] Beaverbrook talked up the strength that the King had drawn from press support but kept quiet about the fact that Monckton had just cut off communication with him and that the King had given him to understand that he was going to abdicate. He did, though, give faint clues of the weakness of the King's Party's position, in two shifts in his own position. He introduced the idea 'that the crisis might yet be resolved by an act of renunciation on the part of Mrs. Simpson'.[24] In effect, he was trying to capitalise in advance on Lord Brownlow's effort to persuade Mrs Simpson to give up the King, which Beaverbrook had set in train when it became obvious that the King was not going to give his party the help it wanted. The unmistakable sign that the King's Party was on the ropes came when Beaverbrook tried to swing Hoare round to 'tak[ing] a greater interest in the cause of His Majesty' on the grounds that he was a 'likely selection' if the King had to send someone else as Prime Minister.[25] It is a tribute to Beaverbrook's delusional confidence in his status of kingmaker that he was now hawking the incumbency of 10 Downing Street to his third candidate in the space of a week and that he should imagine that Hoare would be taken in. It was not a temptation that Hoare found any difficulty in resisting, and the King's Party had to continue with its proven line-up.

More junior members of the government overrated the strength of the King's Party just as badly as the hardliners. When Chamberlain had made his dramatic re-entry to the Cabinet meeting that morning he had had easy material with which to work. Rumours of what the King's Party were up to had also reached the back benches, albeit in rather less alarmist fashion. Leo Amery offered his support to Baldwin against 'rumours that had reached me that Winston was trying to work a big intrigue through the press'.[26] However doomed and feeble the King's Party might have been in reality, there were still acute fears of the havoc it might wreak as became clear when a group of the younger members of the Cabinet known as the 'Servants' Hall', which included Hore-Belisha, gathered to discuss the situation. Churchill remained the prime bogey-man. Their fears rivalled the worst imaginings of the established hardliners. Duff Cooper was one of the group, but he had been far closer to the heart of the affair almost since the beginning and he was taken aback:

> ...that some of them took a much more alarmist view than they had expressed in the Cabinet. They thought a coup d'état was not impossible. They suggested that the King might accept the Prime Minister's resignation and send for Winston. It was not impossible for Winston to form a Government; he might come out with a popular programme for speeding up re-armament and more drastic measures for dealing with the distressed areas. If he were defeated in the House of Commons he could go to the country. The prospects of a General Election on the King's marriage were not agreeable to contemplate. An attempt might even be made to upset the Parliamentary system altogether. It had disappeared in other countries recently: why not in this? Beaverbrook and Rothermere would work with Winston: so would the Fascists; so might some elements of the left.[27]

Malcom MacDonald's self-important interjections into the Cabinet's discussion had been a grating distraction as the ministers struggled to find a solution, but there was a sound kernel of truth in his insistence that the Dominions be involved in the process, and one of the meeting's formal decisions was to inform the Dominions. The first task that fell to Baldwin after the Cabinet meeting was thus to tell his Dominions colleagues that the British government had decided to take action unilaterally. It was unlikely that any of them would disagree with what was planned, but attention had to be paid to the Statute of Westminster. Baldwin's telegram to

Joseph Lyons, the Australian Prime Minister, hinted strongly that Cabinet had forced his hand by juxtaposing the statement of the British Cabinet's decision with his personal apology: 'Cabinet therefore feel that it is necessary that I should make a statement in the House of Commons before it adjourns this afternoon until Monday ... I greatly regret not being able to consult you prior to the statement...'[28]

The King's reaction when Monckton brought him the news from the Cabinet meeting that the broadcast would be blocked shows that Simon had been entirely correct in questioning the King's ability to understand the constitutional position. The King had been fully braced for the government to reject the broadcast, but he was surprised at the elementary constitutional arguments lying behind the refusal. The fact that a broadcast would have been an appeal over the head of the government, which had been instantly obvious to both ministers and the King's allies, entirely escaped him; to the King, Baldwin had acted because he was scared of losing. 'To let me address my people would have involved risks that Mr. Baldwin and his colleagues were apparently unwilling to take. With its rejection disappeared my only possible means of rallying the whole nation.'[29] Quite how this ambition could have been squared with the King's professed desire to avoid strife is mysterious.

Baldwin's statement to Parliament had been drafted by Sir John Simon and bears the imprint of lawyerly finality, disposing for good of the morganatic proposal:

> Suggestions have appeared in certain organs of the Press yesterday and again to-day that if the King decided to marry, his wife need not become Queen. These ideas are without any Constitutional foundation. There is no such thing as what is called a morganatic marriage known to our law. ... The King himself requires no consent from any other authority to make his marriage legal, but, as I have said, the lady whom he marries ... necessarily becomes Queen. She herself, therefore, enjoys all the status, rights and privileges which, both by positive law and by custom, attach to that position ... and her children would be in the direct line of succession to the Throne.

The only possible way in which this result could be avoided would be by legislation dealing with a particular case. His Majesty's Government are not prepared to introduce such legislation. Moreover, the matters to be dealt with are of common concern to the Commonwealth as a whole, and such a change could not be effected without the assent of all the Dominions. I am satisfied, from inquiries I have made, that this assent would not be forthcoming. I have felt it right to make this statement before the House adjourns to-day in order to remove a widespread misunderstanding. At this moment I have no other statement to make.[30]

When Baldwin delivered the statement at 4 p.m., it was received with cheers in the House but it revolted Churchill, to whom it seemed like part of a monstrously unfair cabal against the King. Immediately afterwards Amery

went into the smoking room where I found Winston completely on the rampage, saying that he was for the King and was not going to have him strangled in the dark by Ministers and bumped off without a chance of saying a word to Parliament or to the country in his own defence etc. etc.[31]

A more measured criticism came from the King's friend Chips Channon, who criticised Baldwin's 'unsmiling and ungracious' delivery of a statement 'which slams the door to any possible compromise'.[32] Baldwin's statement was the first piece of hard official comment on what was going on, and the House of Commons had been awaiting it tensely from the moment that it was announced. The direct and unambiguous statement was what was needed. The House as a whole was just as keen as the hardliners to bring the affair to an early close.

The statement was the high point in the hardliners' campaign for tough, active measures towards the King. They were beginning to recognise the inherent risks in their more extreme positions. When Chamberlain was told what Churchill had said to Margesson, he thought ahead to how the conspirators might present their case: 'The plan was to represent S.B. as having forced the K. to take a vital decision without adequate time for consideration and to protest against this "bumping off" of a friendless and impassioned youth who was passionately & romantically in love'.[33] Chamberlain spotted the danger that Churchill might claim that the King had been forced into a corner, and he developed second thoughts as to the wisdom of the Prime Minister actually delivering the ultimatum for which he had been pushing at the Cabinet meeting that morning. He had finally understood the basic flaw in the hardliners' position, which had been obvious to Baldwin throughout and which had driven his strategy of letting the King make his own decision. Chamberlain claimed in his diary to have made Baldwin reassemble the Cabinet and soften the decision that it had taken on the point:

> Some prudence would be required in forcing the issue since with an unscrupulous & desperate K. and a man like W. determined to take any risks in forming a Govt & trying to soothe the country with some vague undertaking from Mrs. S. or the K. or both there was a real danger that we might find we had left the helm too soon. … I then got S.B. to assemble the Cabinet again & I proposed that we should modify our morning's decision to this extent, that no ultimatum shd. be delivered but that the K. should be told of the Cabinet's view that the situation admitted of no long delay, that we should like to have his decision by tomorrow (Saturday) night but that in any case it ought not to be withheld for more than a few days. This proposal appeared to be received with some relief & was unanimously agreed to.[34]

Hankey's minutes of the Cabinet meeting mention Chamberlain arguing for a deadline on Saturday night and also refer to some slight changes having been made after the meeting to the formal advice that the Cabinet was to give on the broadcast, but nothing about any recall meeting took place. That said it is hard to read any indication of consensus having been reached from the minutes and it is possible that the formal Cabinet conclusion as to what the Prime Minister should tell the King reflected some discussion afterwards.

Even though Monckton had warned him in advance, the King took Baldwin's statement as a body-blow. Coming as it did only a few hours after the Prime Minister had repeated his non-committal answer to Attlee's question as to whether there was a conflict between sovereign and government – hours in which there had been no material discussion between the King and the government – it was an escalation that came from the blue. As had happened with Hardinge's letter, the Commons announcement appeared to the King to ratchet up gratuitously the confrontation between him and the government. In his memoirs, the then Duke of Windsor insinuated that Baldwin had sprung a surprise: 'Thus Mr. Baldwin dealt the first crushing blow … A few hours later, in the House of Commons, he struck again.'[35] Even stripping away the loaded language and *suggestio falsi* it is clear that the King was shaken by the statement. Once again the hardliners had ended up injecting a confrontational element into the dialogue because they disagreed with the way Baldwin was handling the affair and were unconcerned as to how it would look when they forced their own strategy. Publicly discarding the morganatic proposal was in practice an ultimatum, and no attempt had been made to prepare the ground: '…there was to be no conciliation, no palliation, no marriage. The challenge was unequivocal. It was abdication for me or resignation for him.'[36] The discussions in the Cabinet meeting that morning were, of course, hidden to the King, and he blamed the statement entirely on the Prime Minister, almost exactly reversing the true course of events: 'Now he maneuvered [*sic*] with a swiftness and directness that astonished even his colleagues.' The misreading of what had happened would be comic but for its contribution to the fund of bitterness against the government that was already accumulating. Even when he was given a copy of Simon's unarguable analysis of the constitutional position, the King sought to blame the move on tactical considerations, letting slip his delusion that the public would have supported him. He wrote in his memoirs:

> But the learned expressions … struck me, on second thought, as being a less than adequate explanation of why my proposal had not been accepted.

Mr Baldwin may have prided himself on his knowledge and understanding of what the British people thought and felt. But it was now
abundantly clear that he wanted no test of their sentiments at this critical moment. He and his colleagues were therefore guarding themselves
at every vulnerable point.

Once again a firmly held misunderstanding on one side of what the other
was up to fuelled the conflict.

Unbeknownst to the government the King had been very close to accepting that abdication was inevitable. He had bowed to Monckton's advice
and begun to back away from the King's Party and acrimony with the government. He had allowed Monckton to break off contact with Beaverbrook
as a first step in negotiating terms for his departure.

Along with Hardinge's letter, Baldwin's House of Commons statement
on the Friday afternoon was probably one of the key turning points in the
crisis. Wilson was at pains to use his notes to mask the true sequence of
events and considerations that led to both, above all to mask the way in
which the hardliners had hijacked the government's handling of the affair
to put pressure on the King. The Friday statement presented a different
problem, because everything to do with the Hardinge letter episode was
still shrouded in the deepest secrecy, whereas nothing could be more public than what Baldwin and Churchill had said in the House of Commons.
Rather than merely hiding something entirely, Wilson had to fend off Churchill's implicit allegation that pressure had been put on the King. As the
hardliners – Wilson included – had been scheming and clamouring for
precisely this to be done and had largely succeeded at the Friday Cabinet
meeting, he faced something of a challenge developing an alternative narrative that reduced the events to an innocuous story of dignified discussion.

Wilson's key strategy was to paint a picture in which the Commons statement was simply aimed at silencing a newspaper campaign mounted by

the King's Party in favour of the morganatic marriage, rather than a lightly disguised ultimatum to the King himself:

> A section of the press supported the 'compromise' which we had come to regard as the Churchill–Harmsworth proposal i.e. that the King might marry Mrs. Simpson but that she should not become Queen. It was necessary to remove any misunderstanding on this point…[37]

The Beaverbrook and Harmsworth newspapers were an easy target. They could be dismissed as the mere '"froth of Fleet Street" which was running counter to solid English opinion.'[38] From this Wilson moved onto a denunciation of Churchill who 'sought to convey the impression that the Government were trying to bring pressure upon the King to accelerate his decision'. To some extent the Wilson version of the story was honestly intended. Downing Street could not see beyond Beaverbrook's fiction that the morganatic proposal was Churchill's own idea – which was reaching them through Hoare's conversations with its author and was topped up by MI5 reports – to the far more nuanced reality of the limitations under which the King's allies were operating in their attempt to keep the King on the throne and that they, like the government, would much have preferred to see the back of Mrs Simpson for good.

In order to sustain his account, Wilson made one major and glaring omission. Everything to do with how the morganatic proposal had been handled between the King asking Baldwin for it to be considered and the Friday afternoon, was excluded from his notes. Only someone with access to the minutes of the Cabinet meetings on the Wednesday and the Friday could have seen that part of the story. A reader who relied on the notes alone was left with the impression that the morganatic proposal was still live on the Friday afternoon and would have had no reason to see that the King had been told it was not practical and, at least on the Wednesday evening, had accepted this without protest. This is mildly charitable towards the King by masking his apparent bad faith in returning to the morganatic proposal in his draft broadcast, but it is far outweighed by the damning implication that the morganatic proposal was a concerted effort by the King, Churchill and his press allies. By presenting the morganatic marriage as little more than a press ramp, Wilson's notes also leave hanging the question of what might have been said directly to the King about the proposal. This is their most glaring flaw as a coherent narrative.

CHAPTER 13
MY FIRST BLUNDER

Realising, on reflection, and learning more of the apparent activities of
Mr. Churchill and of the leaders of the Harmsworth and Beaverbrook press,
that the King's interview with Mr. Churchill might be used harmfully, the
Prime Minister felt that perhaps he ought to have objected to the King's proposal.
'I have made my first blunder', he said next day. I ventured to differ if the
Prime Minister had in fact objected to the interview the King might
have felt that an attempt was being made to isolate him.*
SIR HORACE WILSON, DRAFT ABDICATION NOTES[1]

W HEN BALDWIN CAME to Fort Belvedere on the afternoon of
Friday 4 December to tell him formally that the Cabinet had
ruled out the broadcast, the King had calmed somewhat from
the high agitation of the previous audience, but he was still in a nervous
mood. He took the news that he would not be allowed to make a broadcast with the same superficial equanimity as he had taken the news that the
morganatic proposal was to be blocked. All he asked on the topic was that

---

* Amended by hand to '"I have made my first blunder", he said next day. But if the Prime
Minister…'

the Prime Minister himself make a statement to Parliament on the Monday explaining the situation. Over the weekend much thought and deliberation was to be expended on what the Prime Minister might say, but this proved to be one of the blind alleys of the crisis. Every possible variant of the statement concealed pitfalls when it was examined in detail and the idea was overtaken by events. Moreover, the King seems to have come up with the idea without great reflection. It is far from clear what he hoped a statement from the Prime Minister would do for him and cannot have attached great importance to the idea as there is no record that he mentioned it to his allies and he himself did not refer to it again. Astonishingly, he still seemed to be fantasising that he would be able to make Mrs Simpson his Queen as it would be 'fun for her'.[2]

Baldwin failed to notice that the King was nursing a deep grievance at the statement that he had made in Parliament that afternoon, which they do not seem to have discussed at all. He was more concerned to make plain to the King that he had to make a decision soon even though there was no set deadline. As a result neither he nor anyone else subsequently recognised that the surprise the King chose to spring on the Prime Minister that evening was his way of fighting back against what seemed to him to be the injustice of the Friday afternoon statement to Parliament. The government had won every round so far. First the morganatic proposal had been blocked and then his briefly cherished project of a broadcast. It was just not fair; the King was deep in a wallow of resentful self-pity. The Prime Minister had at his beck and call every manner of adviser and worthy to help him develop and sustain his arguments, but he, the King, had no one.[3] Even before Baldwin arrived, the King had decided to do something to remedy the situation, and this time he had acted without asking the Prime Minister. He was not risking a third snub on the grounds that the constitution left the monarch virtually powerless. He simply told Baldwin what he had done and left it to the Prime Minister to challenge the fait accompli if he dared.

What the King had done was to decide to ask Churchill to dinner that very evening. Immediately after the House of Commons statement, Monckton had checked whether Churchill was available.[4] In the charged atmosphere of the final stage of the crisis, it was an act of provocation and possibly outright defiance. The Prime Minister chose not to pick up the gauntlet and did not demur, silently granting the King permission to talk to Churchill.[5] The King had in fact been braced for a refusal, as a formal invitation was only issued to Churchill afterwards.[6] With hindsight we can see how small a risk Baldwin was taking. He did not fear Churchill's skills as a political intriguer. There is no sign that he ever shared the fears of the King's Party's conspiracy that were haunting the hardliners of Downing Street and the fringes of the Cabinet. But it was still a brave decision to make without preparation. At the very least he knew that it would be challenged from within his own ranks. The dinner had no material effect on the outcome of the crisis, but it was the one episode that can be said to have affected the broader course of history because of the damage it did to Churchill's standing just at the moment when Britain needed a strong voice warning of the dangers of Nazi Germany. The eclipse of the Albert Hall meeting was a tactical upset, but Churchill's private and public support for the King ensured that he would remain a marginal figure in politics for years to come. The episode shows the extremes of Churchill's character – at his best in his passionate loyalty to the King and his sense that the King was being treated unfairly, and at his worst in his bad judgement and opportunism. It also shows the King at his very worst: duplicitous, unreflecting, selfish and entirely irresponsible. The whole idea for his conversation with Churchill was little more than a piece of petulant self-assertion.

As was his habit, Churchill spent the first part of the dinner listening. The King concealed from him how close he was to making his choice between marrying Mrs Simpson and keeping the throne. Instead he gave the impression that he was determined not to abdicate. He began by treating Churchill to how he would have complained to Baldwin about the disparity in their power had he been free to do so:

> You can see anyone you like. You can send for anyone you like. You can
> consult with any number of people. You can arrange with the newspapers
> and with the Church; you can bring the Dominions High Commissioners

together; you can set the Whips to work upon the M.P.'s. But I cannot
see anyone except those you send me, like the Archbishop of Canterbury or Mr. Geoffrey Dawson of the 'Times'. I want to see someone who
is independent of all that. I want to see Mr. Churchill.[7]

Quite how the King persuaded himself that Baldwin had inflicted Lang or
Dawson on him is a mystery, as he had no contact with either of them during
the crisis. What he said next crossed the threshold into deliberate dishonesty:
'I have not abdicated. I never used the word abdication in my conversation
with the Prime Minister. I had Monckton in the room with his permission all
the time and he will bear me out.'[8] It is possible that this was literally true, but
as the King had often told the Prime Minister that he was willing to 'go' it is
no more than a quibble. The King was clearly asking for Churchill's help in
fighting the government against forcing an abdication. There is no sign that
the King asked for Churchill's advice as to how to cope with his predicament.
The only advice he might have wanted was how to fight. Above all he wanted
Churchill as an ally and, in his account at least, Churchill was prepared for
the sacrifice and risk this entailed: 'he proposed to join his fortunes with
mine under circumstances that were bound to damage his standing with his
own party'.[9] He told Churchill about the fate of the broadcast proposal and
rounded things off by telling him he wanted a fortnight to think things over,
ideally in Switzerland with a 'couple of equerries'.[10]

Churchill had decided before the conversation to emphasise what he
saw as the strong point in the King's position. He had time on his side. The
government could not force the pace. Churchill was unsparing towards
the government: 'The Cabinet, Winston argued, … had taken advantage
of my agitation and the confused state of public opinion to push me off the
Throne.'[11] According to one draft of his memoirs, Churchill advised the King
to dare the government to make the first move: 'Retire to Windsor Castle.
Close the gates. Pull up the drawbridge. Challenge Mr. Baldwin to throw
you out if he dares.'[12] If there had to be an open constitutional fight, it was
the King who should win it: 'A popular King with a first-hand knowledge
of the Empire and the world, he insisted, was immeasurably more important

than a politician of expediency and procrastination. If any stepping down was to be done, let Baldwin do it.'[13] The weakness of Churchill's advice lay in its insistence on a legalistic point that entirely ignored the political reality of the crisis that had developed. Churchill argued that until Mrs Simpson's divorce became final, there was no issue on which the government could advise him. All the King needed to do was to insist to Baldwin that he should be given time. It was a variant of the strategy that Duff Cooper had urged on the King two weeks before, and he showed no more indication to accept the advice from Churchill than he had from Duff Cooper.

The King was equally uninterested in another extempore component that Churchill added to the plan for keeping him on the throne, which he devised when he appreciated the strain under which the King was operating. The King had begun the evening sheltered behind a mask of insouciance: 'H.M. was most gay and debonair for the first quarter of an hour and no one would have thought this a serious crisis.'[14] But as the conversation continued it was ever more obvious to Churchill that the prolonged strain was taking its toll on the King: '…it was obvious that the personal strain he had been so long under and which was now at its climax had exhausted him to a most painful degree.' To Churchill the King was giving signs of impending complete breakdown: 'He twice in my presence completely lost the thread of what he was saying, and appeared to me to be driven to the last extremity of endurance.'[15] The King, Churchill thought, should plead mental exhaustion and get peace and quiet. After all, the Prime Minister had just taken a two month break on medical advice. The King should call in the country's two most eminent physicians, Lords Dawson and Horder, who could certify his state. If he were to take this break, however, it would have to be in Britain. Churchill was emphatic that the King's idea of going to Switzerland would be seen practically as an act of desertion and it would be assumed that he had left the country to see Mrs Simpson. The King denied that he planned to see Mrs Simpson, but insisted that he needed a break in the Alps.

Churchill failed to win the King round to his plan to stonewall against the government, but he did restore his spirits. The King took strength from Churchill's enthusiasm and confidence. He relished Churchill's rhetorical language and imagery. In particular, he was taken by Churchill's emphasis on the splendour of the institution of monarchy in a way that contrasted, to the King's ears at least, with Baldwin's defensive and formalistic conception. When Churchill had left, the King treated Monckton to an affectionate impersonation of him exhorting in an almost military metaphor, 'We must have time for the battalions to mass. We may win, we may not. Who can say?'[16] The King had sloughed off the panicked hopelessness that had afflicted him since Wednesday, and there was a flicker of an inclination to fight. He telephoned Beaverbrook personally to tell him that Churchill would go to see him at Stornoway House immediately when he got back to London.[17] The King's acquiescence in Monckton's decision to break off communication with Beaverbrook had not lasted long, and Beaverbrook took it briefly as a sign that the fight was back on.

Fortunately for the country, the King's surge of pugnacity was short-lived. After a sleepless night of reflection, he decided to face reality. On the Saturday morning, he told Monckton to warn Baldwin that he intended to tell him that he had decided to go at the audience scheduled for the Saturday afternoon. He did not, however, do anything to alert Churchill or Beaverbrook to this decision. This bears the stamp of the King's ineptitude as an amateur but still cynical politician. The King's decision to abdicate was subject to one crucial proviso and it is hard to escape the conclusion that the King was happy to keep Churchill and Beaverbrook in play until he was confident that it had been secured.

Churchill was still riding on the crest of optimism and bellicosity that had swelled during his dinner with the King, but when he arrived at Stornoway House at 2 a.m. it did not prove to be the moment that the King's allies launched an all-out campaign to save him. The conversation was inconclusive. Beaverbrook had become jealous that Churchill seemed to have displaced him in the King's favour even though he was by then blaming this all directly on Baldwin: 'So it was a Good Friday for Churchill who was being consulted directly for the first time, and a Bad Friday for me since I was being tossed out of the Council Chamber.'[18] All that Beaverbrook could see was that the King was cutting off contact with him at the same time as he was establishing contact with Churchill.

Beaverbrook's dreams of using the King to provoke an all-out battle with Baldwin were fading, but he clung on to the hopes for the Brownlow plan.[19] He was already losing faith in the King's combativeness after Monckton had told him that contact was to cease. Earlier that night he had told Channon, 'Our cock would be all right if only he would fight, but at the moment he will not even crow'.[20] Persuading Mrs Simpson to give up the King was looking like a far more certain way to keep the King on the throne, and Beaverbrook pressed it on Churchill as the correct line to take. Churchill, however, wanted to work directly on the King to stop him from abdicating, and told Beaverbrook that he was going to write to Baldwin. They parted with no agreement as to what to do.

The final blow to Beaverbrook's enthusiasm for an all-out fight came the following morning. The message that Monckton brought to Downing Street that the King had decided to abdicate gave the government the ammunition for a move to head off the King's Party. By chance it seems to have forced a wedge into the gap that had been opening between Churchill and Beaverbrook since their conversation of the early hours. Having been told by Monckton that negotiations between the King and the government were well advanced when he cut off contact, Beaverbrook was now to be told that they had practically concluded. Simon went to see Beaverbrook at Stornoway House to tell him that there was no point in trying to continue the struggle; the King had given up, and it was only a matter of a short time before the King was gone. Simon delivered a list ticking off how each serious obstacle had been overcome:

1. That an accommodation had been reached

2. That a Bill was in preparation solving the difficulties attending on the divorce

3. That the King would abdicate at once.[21]

Simon's call at Stornoway House was a matter of the greatest delicacy. There is no hint of it in any document, official or otherwise, from the government side. Beaverbrook is the only source for the incident, but if he can be believed, he was being fed a story that was significantly in advance of what had actually been achieved at that point. In reality, there was still much to be done, in particular the King had given at most a conditional agreement to abdicating. Beaverbrook was aware of the sensitivity and was unsure as to how much to say of it; he referred coyly to a 'member of the Cabinet'. It is anyway striking that he was not told by Hoare, his usual intermediary with the Cabinet, but the one member of the Cabinet who was entrusted with the most ticklish parts of the government's work over the next few days. These included lying outright to a journalist to block a story that the government did not want to appear. The government was still afraid of a large-scale press campaign supporting the King's views against its own, and could well have judged that the risk of anticipating a happy outcome to its negotiations with the King was worthwhile to head off the most likely architect of such a campaign; failure of the negotiations would have taken the country into entirely uncharted territory. If it was a gamble, it paid off; Beaverbrook appears to have taken Simon's account at face value.

Monckton's message from the King opened a chink of light at the end of the tunnel for Baldwin, but there was no guarantee that it would be reached or even how far away it might be. Baldwin could not know of the dissention within the King's Party and how its strategy was hamstrung by the King's unwillingness to commit himself to an all-out fight, but he knew the hard-liners on the government side would question his judgement in acceding to the King speaking to Churchill and that he would need to head off criticism before it developed. To do this he picked almost the oldest gambit in the book: defusing criticism by making it himself and inviting his interlocutor to tell him that he was wrong. Wilson created the first opening for this little piece of theatre the following morning with the blood-curdling warnings of '…the apparent activities of Mr. Churchill, and of the leaders of the Harmsworth and Beaverbrook press, [and] that the King's interview with Mr. Churchill might be used harmfully...'[22] Baldwin figuratively held his head in his hands and confessed, 'I have made my first blunder.' Wilson changed tack smartly and loyally disagreed with him on the grounds that 'the King might have felt that any attempt was being made to isolate him' if the Prime Minister had objected.

Heartened by the success of this little ruse Baldwin repeated it on the whole Cabinet when it met at 10 a.m. that Saturday morning. It had been fine-tuned for the audience: 'I made a bloomer last night. I am very sorry for it. I realised it afterwards. I suppose I was tired at the time.'[23] He recited sympathetically the King's complaint that 'he had no friends to discuss the matter with' using almost the King's own phraseology to describe his plight, '...faced with the serried ranks of the Cabinet and Parliament...'[24] Duff Cooper observed the performance in fascination: 'He adopted with the vocabulary of the schoolroom, the appearance of a penitent schoolboy "owning up" to a delinquency.'[25] Baldwin did not even have to trot out Wilson's admission that the King might have complained of an attempt to isolate him. Ramsay MacDonald rose to the bait with a magisterial, flat and unambiguous endorsement of the Prime Minister's decision: 'May I be allowed, as your predecessor, to say that I very much doubt you were wrong in giving your consent.'[26] MacDonald's only reservation was that the King should not see Churchill again.

Baldwin had covered his flanks against immediate internal criticism from both his Cabinet colleagues and the civil servants, but it remained to be seen whether he had assessed the risks correctly. He had to give away a little more later on in the meeting when a number of ministers challenged him on how he would deal with exactly the strategy that Churchill was urging on the King: stonewalling on the grounds that Mrs Simpson was not free and that a marriage was impossible. Somehow the Labour Party newspaper the *Daily Herald* had picked up or guessed that the King's unofficial advisers were pointing him in that direction. It was certainly a risk which they should have been worried about. Even as convinced a hardliner as Sir John Simon acknowledged that it existed; it never took much to make Simon revert to his lawyer's habits and he admitted there would be a 'basis' for such a move – in other words it would be very hard to challenge in law, as Churchill was fully aware. Fortunately for the government it never had to decide how to respond; Baldwin had a good sense that it was not a strategy that appealed to the King. He could also hint to his colleagues that negotiations on terms of the abdication had begun and that he hoped to be able to get a clearer sense of how they were going when he saw the King again that afternoon.

Baldwin had been wise to anticipate an adverse reaction to Churchill becoming directly involved in the affair and this was amply proved when the Cabinet meeting was interrupted to bring in a copy of the personal letter that Churchill had told the King he was going to write to the Prime Minister. Baldwin read it out to the ministers. In typical Churchill style, it was overwrought and high-flown, giving Churchill's account of the King's overstretched mental state; his loss of the thread of the conversation had become elevated to 'two marked and prolonged "black outs" in which he completely lost the thread of the conversation'.[27] It concluded with the same plea for time that Churchill had been urging directly on the King: 'It would be a most cruel and wrong thing to extort a decision from him in his present state.' Churchill gave no indication of how much time he felt the King needed to make a decision and ministers recognised instantly that he wanted the King to stonewall. The point was answered by Simon, still wearing a lawyer's hat, but this time he was a street-fighting hard-man choosing from an armoury of legal low-blows and not a judicious quasi-academic expert on the constitution. If the King tried that on, he should be told that Mrs Simpson's divorce would be blocked. Halifax was even more radical; if the King attempted to stonewall, the Cabinet should take the ultimate step and give him formal advice. The King had done well not to follow Churchill's advice. The result would have been messy in the extreme if he had.

The hostile mood in the Cabinet was further fuelled by yet another piece of news that arrived from the outside world. It seemed that the second part of Churchill's programme for the King had been put into operation. By a roundabout route, Wilson had picked up a story that Lords Dawson and Horder had already been to see the King. It did not take him long to see a connection with the King's Party. The story as it reached Wilson was inaccurate, and Downing Street had very quickly established this, but it must have had some basis in fact. Drafts of the Duke of Windsor's memoirs refer vaguely to a doctor 'of the highest eminence and probity' having been prepared to certify his state and the fact that the rumour mentioned the same two doctors whom Churchill had suggested points to more than coincidence.[28] Once again the cry went up for the King to be made to make a decision, with Chamberlain well to the fore. Simon dropped any pretence of legal courtesies and proposed that any public statement should firmly rub the King's nose in the fact that a month had gone by since he had first told the Prime Minister that he was prepared to renounce the throne in order to marry Mrs Simpson, with the acid observation that 'There had been no need for Doctors at that time'.

Whilst the Cabinet was in session, Churchill and Beaverbrook resumed their conversation of the previous night at Churchill's flat in Morpeth Mansions. It was no more productive than the first leg of the discussion. Beaverbrook was now staking heavily on Brownlow succeeding in persuading Mrs Simpson to withdraw. Just after Churchill left Stornoway House early that morning, his hopes had been fed by a message that had arrived for onward transmission to the King in the infantile code they had devised:

W. M. Janet [Mrs Simpson] strongly advising the James Company [the King] to postpone purchase of Chester shares to next autumn and to announce decision by verbal methods, thereby increasing popularity, maintaining prestige, but also the right to re-open negotiations by the autumn.[29]

Beaverbrook claimed that this meant that Mrs Simpson was offering to withdraw completely rather than trying to persuade the King not to abdicate before his coronation, and leaving the matter open until later in 1937, rather as Duff Cooper had advised the King to do in mid-November. It was a weak straw to cling to and Beaverbrook might merely have talked it up to disguise the extent to which he was double-crossing Churchill. In his later accounts of the conversation, Beaverbrook emphasised his continuing disagreement with Churchill over the right tactics to adopt and implied that he argued the case to Churchill in terms of the King's determination to avoid a conflict with the government: 'Our cock won't fight.' He concluded with a final and seemingly hopeless, 'No dice.' He did not disclose to Churchill what he had learned from Simon earlier that morning. Beaverbrook contented himself with the bland statement: 'Unfortunately the same information was not conveyed to Churchill. Like myself, he had thought on Friday the King had decided to resist abdication after all. But, unlike myself he still thought the same on Saturday.'[30] Why did Beaverbrook leave his old crony and ally under such a damaging misapprehension? Simon might have told him that the information was entirely confidential, although it is hard to believe that this would have counted for much to Beaverbrook. More likely he was following the same apparent ruthless logic as the King: keeping Churchill warm for a fight with the government that was looking ever less likely. He might simply have been taking twisted revenge for Churchill having displaced him in the King's counsels. Beaverbrook is one of the few figures in British history who relished mischief for its own sake, making this explanation credible.

In his later account of the crisis, this was the point at which Beaverbrook claimed to have washed his hands of the whole affair. After a week of banging his head against the brick wall of the King's refusal to sanction an all-out press campaign, Beaverbrook decided to cut his losses. He retreated to his country house at Cherkley: 'I considered myself well out of it.'[31] He had been defeated by his old nemesis: 'Baldwin had triumphed. He had dethroned his King just as easily as he had jettisoned Empire Free Trade.'[32] Even the hope that Brownlow would persuade Mrs Simpson to withdraw also appears to have faded away. He did not follow up the coded message that he claimed had fired his hopes on the night of Friday with anything more than a single, tentative phone call to Brownlow at Cannes. A telephone call from the King on the Saturday night confirming that he had decided to abdicate was the final nail in the coffin. It was the end of Beaverbrook's active involvement in the King's Party, and for the remainder of the crisis he 'lived as a mere spectator of the drama'.[33] It is fitting that Beaverbrook himself delivered the most apt epitaph for the King's Party, writing to the Duke of Windsor's ghost writer as he was setting down to his work years later: 'We were indeed a King's Party. Unfortunately the King was not a member of it.'[34] The King held back from the fight because Mrs Simpson was afraid of the newspaper publicity. Above all he wanted to marry her, if necessary sacrificing the throne to do so; he never for an instant shared Beaverbrook's obsessive goal of getting rid of Baldwin.

This still left Churchill as a determined champion of the King's cause, or at least his own understanding of it. Whatever the King or Beaverbrook actually said to Churchill, it signally failed to deter him from launching a frenetic one man campaign. He followed up his letter to Baldwin with a lengthy press release in roughly the same terms, which trotted out in detail the argument that marrying Mrs Simpson was only a hypothetical possibility and it would be five months before it became a real one. In the face of the momentum that the crisis had developed, it was decidedly feeble, but it was inevitably mentioned in the following day's newspapers.

Churchill rounded off the day's damage to his reputation with a letter that was barely coherent and so unbalanced that Roy Jenkins asserted in his biography of Churchill that he must have been quite drunk to write it.[35] It is tempting to agree.

> SIR,
>
> News from all fronts!
>
> 1. No pistol to be held at the King's head. No doubt that his request for time will be granted. Therefore – no final decision or Bill till after Christmas – probably February or March
>
> 2. On no account must the King leave the country. Windsor Castle is his battle station (poste de commandement). When so much is at stake, no minor inclinations can be indulged. It would be far better for Mrs. Simpson to return to England for a day or two, than for the King to go abroad now. Please let me talk to you about this, if there is any doubt.

(This would anyhow show that she had not been driven out of the country.) But of course better still if she preferred to remain where she is for this critical time.

3. Lord Craigavon, Prime Minister of Northern Ireland, is deeply moved by loyalty to the King, & (is) all for Time. Could not he be invited to luncheon tomorrow? He has a constitutional right of access (I think) & anyhow there could be no objection. His visit should be made public. He shares my hopes such as they are of an ultimately happy ending. It's a long way to Tipperary.

4. Max. The King brought him across the world. He is a tiger to fight. I gave him the King's message – but please telephone or write – better telephone. I cannot see it would do harm to see him if it could be arranged. Important, however, to make contact with him. A devoted tiger – very scarce breed.

5. For real wit, Bernard Shaw's article in tonight's Evening Standard shd. be read … It is joyous.

Summary. Good advances on all fronts giving prospects of gaining good positions & assembling large forces behind them.

Your Majesty's faithful, devoted Servant & Subject

(signed) WINSTON S. CHURCHILL[36]

It is hard to know where to start with an analysis of the flaws in the letter. It was utterly wrong in predicting that the government would give more time. Churchill had failed to detect the growing ambiguity of Beaverbrook's position and hoped still to mount a joint campaign. Referring to Mrs Simpson as a 'minor inclination' was almost perfectly calculated to enrage the King. There is no sign that the King replied and Churchill was left in his mood of hyperactive and self-destructive exaltation.

Churchill's mood of exaltation and bellicosity abated as the weekend went on. On the Sunday two of his old friends and allies, Sir Archibald Sinclair and Bob Boothby, came to Chartwell, his country home, and talked some sense into him. Together they formulated a more constructive programme to keep the King on the throne than the unadorned stonewalling that Churchill had been proposing up till then. Churchill was to advise the King that his only chance of keeping the throne was to make a public declaration that he would not marry 'contrary to the advice of his Ministers'.[37] A letter proposing this was taken to Fort Belvedere on the Monday morning, but it came far too late to have even a chance of changing what he had decided to do. Monckton expressed polite enthusiasm when he read it, but that is as far as it ever got.

CHAPTER 14

THE LONG AND SINISTER SHADOW

The King's Proctor ... throws a long and sinister shadow. In the lonely months that lay across the abyss of abdication she and I would both be vulnerable to possible intervention in the courts, which might cost W her freedom and I the marriage for which I had given up my throne.

DUKE OF WINDSOR, DRAFT MEMOIRS[1]

I T IS OFTEN said that that Mrs Simpson was unacceptable as a wife for the King because she was 'twice divorced'. This is a convenient shorthand but it is inaccurate. Even the alternative euphemistic circumlocutions 'with two husbands living' or 'had twice been in the divorce courts' miss a very fundamental point. Because her decree absolute was not granted until May 1937, she was still married in the eyes of the law and of many ordinary people during the crisis. This made the King's desire to marry her doubly scandalous as well as being downright preposterous. He wanted to marry a woman who was someone else's wife. It also threw up a series of practical questions, which deeply influenced the course of the crisis. The most important of these was that, as in any divorce case under English law of the time, there had been a possibility that the King's Proctor might intervene in

Mrs Simpson's divorce from the day that the decree nisi was granted at Ipswich. Interventions by the King's Proctor were almost invariably successful and this had the effect of cancelling the decree nisi and leaving the couple still married to each other.[2] This danger hung over the entire period of the crisis. It remained a significant factor until well after the King had abdicated. The risk never went away, but there were constant changes in how the risk was analysed by the various individuals in the government, in part because it would have brought such huge additional uncertainty to an already complex series of problems. With bewildering rapidity, intervention switched between being a threat and being an opportunity.

At the start the hardliners had been happy to deploy intervention as one of the weapons in their arsenal. It had served as a panic factor to stampede Hardinge into writing his letter, when the publicity it would have caused was anathema to court and government. It had also offered the illusion of a quick and brutal solution to the whole affair as a way of keeping Mrs Simpson married to Ernest for good and thus unable to marry the King. This idea had a sufficient head of steam for Baldwin to mention it to Stanley Bruce, the Australian High Commissioner and one of the most influential voices in the Prime Minister's ear, in the course of a long discussion of the tactics of handling the affair at Chequers on 15 November: just before his crucial audience with the King after the Hardinge letter, 'The Prime Minister also indicated that certain people are distinctly active with regard to the divorce and are determined to oppose the granting of the decree absolute'.[3] Frustratingly, it is not spelled out who these 'certain people' are, but the fact that the Attorney General Sir Donald Somervell was required to advise on the possibility as a potential 'solution of the problem' suggests that it was being touted as an option at the highest level of government.[4] Bruce himself believed that the decree absolute would have to be blocked if the King claimed to the Prime Minister that he did not intend to marry Mrs Simpson as this was the only sure way of preventing a marriage; clearly the King's word counted for little. Ramsay MacDonald, who had immediately been suspicious of Mrs Simpson's divorce, appears to have lobbied for the King's Proctor to be consulted, if nothing more, two days before.[5]

If it had been simply a question of handling the two stray members of the public who had written to the King's Proctor at that stage it would not have had to be dealt with at this level. Whoever the 'certain people' might have been, they were not deterred by a risk that was instantly obvious to Bruce: 'It is almost impossible to visualise the scandal that this would involve as the King's name would inevitably be dragged in.'[6]

At this stage Wilson certainly looked on the possibility of intervention as a significant factor. It was a point on which the King appeared vulnerable and Wilson probably felt he should be reminded of it. When Baldwin had the fateful audience with the King in the wake of the Hardinge letter, Wilson reported that the Prime Minister had used the subtle constitutional question of whether the King could appear in his own courts as a way of questioning the validity of the divorce.[7] Here Baldwin was probably telling Wilson a white lie. The constitutional point was a complex and hypothetical argument, which also implied that the King was open to being accused of adultery with Mrs Simpson. On neither count would it have been a wise question to raise. Like most people, he would have struggled to grasp the relevance of the fact that he was 'not justiciable in his own courts' (or what this meant) and would have been infuriated by the insinuation of guilty conduct with Mrs Simpson. Neither of the participants in the conversation ever mentioned anything like it. It is far more likely that Baldwin mentioned doubts over the divorce only in vague and general terms after Wilson had fed him the constitutional idea.

Somervell's advice had been enough to kill the thought of promoting intervention in the days before the confrontation triggered by Hardinge's letter, but it had not gone away. It resurfaced a little less than three weeks later, just after the story had broken in the newspapers, lending an aspect of emergency and time pressure to the crisis. Yet again intervention shifted shape into something that suited the hardliners' agenda at that particular moment. By a piece of convoluted logic it had become a reason for the King to abdicate quickly. When the inner group of ministers were called to Downing Street at 9 p.m. on Wednesday 2 December for Baldwin to brief them on his fraught audience with the King, Chamberlain argued:

Here I put in that one effect [of a broadcast] might well be to stir up persons who would take particularly violent views as to the impropriety of the marriage to intervene with affidavits in the divorce proceedings and thus bring about the very result against which the K. had asked for a guarantee.[8]

The next day Simon followed up what Chamberlain had said with a letter to Baldwin. Ostensibly, it set out Simon's analysis of the legal situation but, in reality, it presented intervention as a tool to push the King toward abdication.

One of the foremost preoccupations in the King's mind in reaching his decision is whether anything might occur which would prevent the divorce decree from being made absolute ... I would first point out that any risk there may be of an attempt by a member of the public to intervene in the proceedings for the purpose of preventing the decree being made absolute would be greatly reduced if the interest of the King in this matter was that of a private person. It is always possible that some zealous citizen may try to block the divorce on 'patriotic' grounds in order to prevent the King's marriage. But if the King became a private citizen this motive would disappear and I should regard the risk as quite negligible.[9]

Put simply, if the King behaved himself and abdicated, Mrs Simpson was practically certain of her divorce, otherwise someone would probably interfere. Simon ruled out the possibility that the King's Proctor might intervene in her divorce on the basis of the evidence then available. Weirdly he then undermined his argument of the threat from a 'zealous' citizen when he admitted that such things were almost unheard of: 'This method is exceedingly rare – in my own professional experience I have never come across such a case.' And yet he had just made something that could be read as a definite prediction on behalf of all the cranks of Britain. One is left with the suspicion that what Simon was really writing about, but at which he could only hint, was the possibility that a suitable crank might be found to perform the King's Proctor's task for him.

It is a moot point whether Chamberlain and Simon were trying to send a disguised threat to the King or merely trying to push a weak argument for his leaving the throne. Whichever it was, it was important enough for Chamberlain to ask Baldwin at the start of the discussion at the following morning's Cabinet meeting whether he had, in fact, put the point to the King. Baldwin did claim that he had, although this cannot have been in a sufficiently direct or emphatic form to get the full message over.[10] Chamberlain was probably right to suspect Baldwin of shirking the task. Most likely the Prime Minister simply did not think the argument would be effective. It seems to have been a rerun of Wilson's ambitious attempt to get Baldwin to persuade the King that Mrs Simpson's divorce was flawed because he was immune to a legal accusation of adultery with her.

Simon treated the entire Cabinet to an even more menacing version of the argument just after Churchill's letter had been read out. Even in Sir Maurice Hankey's restrained prose the snarl is almost audible as Simon came wafer-close to a direct threat to torpedo Mrs Simpson's divorce if the King played for time:

> The Home Secretary pointed out that if the King were to adopt a 'stone-walling' attitude the result would probably be to render the grant of a Decree Absolute to Mrs. Simpson's divorce more doubtful. He thought His Majesty ought to be warned of this risk by whoever was the proper authority … But now, after the Prime Minister had announced that if the King married Mrs. Simpson she must be Queen, strong efforts were likely to be made to challenge the divorce in the Courts … the King ought to be told, and warned that if his aim was to be able to marry Mrs. Simpson 'stone-walling' would not be a good way of attaining that object.[11]

Nowhere in any of the analysis of whether the King's Proctor might intervene did Mrs Simpson's interests get a mention. Intervention was treated solely as a possible move on the politico-legal chessboard. The only hint that human emotions might be involved was speculation as to what patriotically motivated cranks might do. It was taken for granted that the press and other politicians would meekly accept what the courts might do as an unalterable fact of life. Mrs Simpson had blundered into high politics through her affair with the King. As far as the politicians and bureaucrats were concerned, neither she nor anyone else could expect any consideration to be given to the human aspect of her divorce. This reflects not merely contemporary attitudes to such matters but shows again the same blind-spot in the government's analysis of the situation that had vitiated Fisher's scheme to get Mrs Simpson out of the country. It showed not only callousness, but the lack of a pragmatic ability to investigate all the possible avenues to a solution. The government never reflected on the detail of the relationship between the King and Mrs Simpson, entirely missing the fact that she was far less committed to the relationship than he was. Her divorce was assumed to be a project that both were bent on. The government was looking at destroying it from the outside and ignored the fact that it was vulnerable from the inside as well.

The King found himself facing two unpleasant interrelated facts as the tempo of the crisis accelerated. Struggle as he might to avoid recognising it, it was impossible to marry Mrs Simpson and remain on the throne. He would have to make a choice, but the risk of intervention further complicated what would never have been an easy or simple decision. It meant that even if he left the throne it was still far from certain that he would be able to marry Mrs Simpson under any circumstances. It had already been on his mind at the traumatic audience on Wednesday 2nd when he made the impossible request of the Prime Minister simply to guarantee that Mrs Simpson would get her decree absolute. Baldwin gave these fears a very large boost the following day when, almost at the end of the audience, he slipped in a vastly softened version of the warning from Chamberlain and Simon. The 'zealous' citizen motivated by 'patriotism' was diluted to some 'muddle-headed busybody' who might try to delay proceedings by mounting an intervention falsely alleging collusion.[12]

From then on the King was increasingly preoccupied. His concern was fuelled from within his own camp by Monckton, who had long understood the danger: 'I was always desperate lest you should fall between two stools

– i.e. abdicate and then find that [Mrs Simpson] was not free.'[13] In part, Monckton was motivated by the lawyer's natural instinct to nail possible legal problems, but it must have been clear to him that his principal was vulnerable to hostile action. Monckton presents the decision to begin to investigate coping with the danger of the King's Proctor as though it were an abstract legal one, but, as he was almost constantly in Downing Street, it is hard to believe that some of the government's thinking on the possibility of intervention did not feed through to him.

From an early stage the King had spotted that the government was alert to the possibility of intervention and sensed that it was being exploited against him. In typical style, he contrived to ignore the fact that the risk was an elementary legal aspect that he himself should have had in mind when making his plans. He also presented Mrs Simpson as the immediate victim of the government's machinations:

> Always in the background there was pressure of another kind, and of this Mr. Baldwin made full use. It is a commonplace of the human character that a man who is quite indifferent to threats against himself may feel very differently if the threats are directed against those he holds dear. In the Government's war of nerves, this peculiarly demoralising weapon was not neglected. Always in the background, I was aware of an ugly threat to Wallis. At first, this threat took the form of vague hints and obscure allusions. There were frequent references, more or less direct, to the possibility of intervention in Wallis's divorce case.[14]

The King felt that he, as well as Mrs Simpson, was being coerced. This rankled with him long afterwards, particularly in the light of the claim from the government side that no pressure had been applied to him, and he complained in one draft of his memoirs:

> Several days later, as the crisis ebbed, the Times rejected with outraged sanctimoniousness the 'abominable and malignant insinuations that pressure had been brought to bear upon the King by his Ministers'. And to the

extent that no active pressure was ever applied the statement is technically true. But pressure of a sort was certainly there – the passive yet implacable grip of a vize which, having fastened upon its victim, never relaxes.[15]

Isolated and constricted in the oppressive atmosphere of Fort Belvedere, the King was increasingly vulnerable to his own sense of pressure. By the time that talks began on the Saturday morning, the threat of intervention was beginning to tell on the King. Monckton told Downing Street that the King was increasingly agitated to the extent of 'threatening to do some violence to himself'.[16] He had threatened suicide when Mrs Simpson briefly tried to leave him at the end of the *Nahlin* trip and the danger that the King's Proctor might wreck Mrs Simpson's divorce and prevent him from marrying her had pushed his thoughts in the same direction.

When the King finally faced reality sufficiently for him to allow Monckton to begin discussing with the government the ways and means of abdication, the question of intervention took centre stage. Wilson performs one of the many reversals of straight-line chronology in his notes when he comes to the episode and tries to disguise the fact that the King's decision to open negotiations had not come through official channels. It was, however, clear from the start that the King's willingness to abdicate was closely linked to – in practice depended on – removing the threat of the King's Proctor. 'It appeared that at that time the plan in the King's mind was that he should abdicate, but that, through the acceleration of the divorce proceedings, he would be assured that it would be possible for him, after abdication, to marry Mrs. Simpson.'[17]

The negotiations on the details of abdication began almost as soon as the King had made his decision on the Saturday morning. Monckton and Allen travelled up from Fort Belvedere with a formal remit to tell the Prime Minister that the King had decided to go, and an informal one to lay the risk of intervention. The King's fragile state added another layer of urgency to the discussions that began with a long session at Downing Street and continued over lunch in a private room in Windham's Club in St James's Square, which Monckton had established as his London base. At that stage

it was a highly confidential affair involving just four individuals: Monckton and George Allen, the King's lawyers, and two of Baldwin's closest
confidants, his parliamentary private secretary Tommy Dugdale, and Sir
Horace Wilson. The only senior minister who appears to have been given
an inkling of what was afoot was Sir John Simon, who knew enough to
assure Beaverbrook that the question of the divorce was being settled by
legislation. Even Chamberlain, who had been closely involved in all the
major steps up till then, does not appear to have known, and the Cabinet
as a whole was given only the sketchiest indication that something was in
hand to neutralise the threat of intervention.

The possibility that the government might somehow instruct the divorce
court to speed up the process of Mrs Simpson's divorce was rapidly dis-
carded. Monckton then proposed a radical but straightforward method of
dealing with the linked questions of abdication and Mrs Simpson's divorce.
He suggested that two bills should be introduced simultaneously to Parliament: one was the legislation that would have been needed in any case
to effect the abdication and the other one would grant Mrs Simpson an
immediate decree absolute. This was not quite as outlandish as it might
seem today. Up to 1857 the only way to obtain a divorce had been through
a private Act of Parliament for the individuals concerned. Monckton was
proposing no more than a once-off revival of the practice. Moreover, no vital
principle of British law was at stake either; Scotland and certain Dominion
territories also got along perfectly well without the long interval between
the two steps in the divorce process. By coincidence, a Private Member's
Bill was working its way through Parliament that would have disposed
of the difficulty. Elected to Parliament in 1935 as an independent MP, the
author and barrister A. P. Herbert had been leading a high-profile campaign
against the absurdities of the then current divorce law, first in a humorous
novel *Holy Deadlock* and then in Parliament. His Bill would bring the gap
between decree nisi and decree absolute down to six weeks from the six
months that were causing so much uncertainty. It was passed the following year with tacit government support.

Monckton's Two Bills plan was a superficially elegant solution and it was decided that it should be put to the King by the Prime Minister at the audience that had been arranged for that afternoon, ostensibly to discuss Baldwin's planned message to Parliament on the Monday. It is perhaps an indication of how much Baldwin was operating on his own politically in handling the crisis that he now made what in retrospect was a bad tactical mistake. He had not discussed the Two Bills idea with any of the Cabinet, and its greatest flaws were political. No senior politician had had a hand in designing it and it was essentially a piece of lawyerly cleverness that would have to be subjected to the bruising process of political debate before it would have a chance of working. Perhaps Baldwin's sense of proprieties dictated that the plan should be agreed with the King before the other politicians. No Prime Minister had negotiated an abdication before and there was no rule book.

Baldwin and Dugdale set off on the increasingly familiar road to Fort Belvedere at the maddeningly slow speed that the Prime Minister dictated. The agony of the journey was soothed by Baldwin's obvious concern that the crisis was placing strain on Dugdale's home life and his delight in learning that Dugdale's wife had just discovered that she was expecting her first baby.[18] Even in the midst of the crisis, Baldwin did not lose the human touch that made him such an effective politician. Once again they missed the unobvious turning into Fort Belvedere and had to reverse course.

The audience was one of the briefest of the whole affair, but it went on to become the source of much bitterness on the part of the Duke of Windsor. It was artificially prolonged by a small charade in which Monckton spared the two principals in the conversation the ticklish responsibility of introducing the Two Bills.[19] To some extent the whole audience was a charade; the main issue had been agreed between the King's lawyers and the men from Downing Street at Windham's Club beforehand, but the form of negotiation was maintained. The King told the Prime Minister that he was prepared to sign his abdication to allow the legislation to go through Parliament on the Tuesday '...but – There was a but.'[20] This was the qualification that the second Bill would dispose of the risk of intervention by expediting Mrs Simpson's divorce. The King was happy with the solution that it offered, but Baldwin made what turned out to be another error. He failed to warn the King that there was no absolute certainty that the second Bill would pass. According to the Cabinet minutes he told the King that it was a matter he 'thought could be got through the House of Commons'.[21] In the then Duke of Windsor's later account, he claimed that Baldwin had promised to resign if the Cabinet refused the second Bill.[22] It is improbable that Baldwin would have made such a hazardous commitment, and the credibility of this claim is severely if not fatally undermined by the context in which it is placed. In the Duke of Windsor's account, Baldwin's supposed promise follows on from Baldwin telling him that he had fixed a meeting of the hardline ministers most likely to oppose the second Bill for the following morning, at which he would overcome their opposition. In fact, this meeting was not arranged until later that night, well after Baldwin had left Fort Belvedere. Wrong though this later account may be, the King was left with little doubt that the Two Bills solution was going to happen and that he could be sure of marrying Mrs Simpson. The spectre of the King's Proctor was banished. The King authorised Baldwin to tell his mother, Queen Mary, that he would definitely abdicate the following morning.[23] As far as the King and the Prime Minister could tell, the affair had been settled.

CHAPTER 15

SUNDAY MORNING AT HENDON AERODROME

Tom went in to Ulick Alexander.
'You fellows are pretty cool; and what about these
aeroplanes at Hendon?' he said.
'How did you know about them?' said Alexander, who was evidently surprised.
'Will you go and cancel them now?'
'I can't do that. They are under the King's orders,' said Ulick Alexander.
'Never mind that, it must be done.' ... And it was done.
NANCY DUGDALE, DIARY

SINCE THE WEDNESDAY that the crisis became public property the government had had to cope with a nightly succession of new and unexpected initiatives from the King. The government had dealt with each in turn: blocked, in the case of the broadcast and an instant guarantee of a decree absolute for Mrs Simpson; acceded to, in the case of consulting Churchill or getting serious consideration for the Two Bills. To the King, though, it seemed that the government had refused everything he proposed from the morganatic plan onwards. He was less and less inclined to give the Prime Minister the opportunity to do so again. The way in which he had bounced Baldwin into authorising his conversation with Churchill was a long step in this direction, but he had further to go. There was one more shock that he had in store for the government – and the country.

When the King had worked on the original idea for a broadcast plan that Mrs Simpson had sold to him, he had added a refinement of his own: leaving the country whilst the public made up its mind as to whether to allow him to have his way. The broadcast remained by far the more important part of the scheme and it was the only one to which the government gave any consideration. In the excitement over the broadcast itself, no one in government had paid any serious attention to the plan for the King to absent himself from the country. It had been introduced in only the vaguest terms and barely discussed, if it had been discussed at all, between the King and the Prime Minister. When the broadcast idea was formally killed off by the Cabinet meeting on the Friday morning, the plan for the King to leave Britain slipped from government attention and no further notice at all was paid to it. Perhaps it was assumed that it had never been anything more than an integral and minor part of the broadcast scheme. Perversely enough, the one man who recognised the danger of the scheme was Churchill, who immediately saw that it would be disastrous. In the King's mind, however, it had taken on a life of its own. After the stress of the preceding weeks the attraction of a couple of weeks' undisturbed relaxation in the mountains was a powerful force in itself, probably more powerful than whatever part the King's absence from Britain was supposed to play in the unique constitutional experiment that Mrs Simpson and he had dreamed up. It would also be a lot easier to implement. In contrast to the broadcast, which would have required the services of the BBC, a major arm of the state which had shown itself fully obedient to the government, the journey to Switzerland required far smaller resources – resources that were already available in the royal household.

The practical preparations for the broadcast had lain in the hands of Sir John Reith and were never initiated as the government never gave its authorisation, but Fort Belvedere could make the arrrangements for the flight to the Alps undisturbed. Rooms were booked at the Dolder Grand

Hotel in Zurich and a letter of credit for £5,000 was obtained from Coutts Bank.[1] Very little thought had gone into the preparations, notably in regard to security or privacy. The King did not even know the Dolder, which had been chosen on no more than the recommendation of Godfrey Thomas. It stood on a hilltop just outside the centre of Zurich served by a public funicular railway and a short tram ride, but its grounds were relatively small. Fort Belvedere's extensive park shielded the King from the vast press pack camped outside, but the Dolder would have offered no such protection. Moreover, the King would not have been the only guest. A stay there would have been anything but the oasis of tranquillity and seclusion for which he yearned, but the Dolder was the place on which unthinkingly he had set his heart.

How the King would get to Switzerland presented no major difficulties. One facet of the King's modernity was his fascination with aviation, then a glamorous and innovative development. In those days, to be 'airminded' was a badge of forward-thinking. As Prince of Wales, Edward had learned to fly himself, taking risks with as little fear or reflection as he had when riding his horses. He had bought the first aeroplanes for the royal household, creating the embryo of the royal flight of the RAF, which he used routinely. He flew from Sandringham to London on the day of his accession in January. He had taken on a reserve officer of the RAF, Edward 'Mouse' Fielden, as his personal pilot and, in 1933, chief air pilot and extra equerry. By 1936 the King had acquired a de Havilland Dragon Rapide as his personal aeroplane with the registration, G-ADDD. It was jauntily painted in the colours of the King's beloved Brigade of Guards, but it was a curiously conservative choice of machine. It was a biplane with a fixed undercarriage unlike its main British competitor, the far more modern Airspeed Envoy, which had better performance in every respect and was chosen for royal service the following year. G-ADDD remained in the possession of the then Duke of Windsor.[2] It was based at Hendon aerodrome, the principal RAF station for the London area, and could have managed the trip to Zurich comfortably in a day.

By the weekend the King was looking at the broadcast and Switzerland as unconnnected ideas. Even after Baldwin had killed off the idea of a broadcast the King craved escape from Fort Belvedere and the trap he had created for himself in Britain. Over dinner on the Friday evening he told Churchill that

> he wanted a fortnight to weigh the whole matter. He felt himself a pris-
> oner in the Fort. If he could go to Switzerland with a couple of equerries
> he would be able to think out his decision without undue pressure …
> [W]hat would happen if he made this request to Mr. Baldwin when he
> saw him the next day?[3]

Any thought that his absence from the country would allow his subjects to decide his fate had been quietly dropped. The King just needed a holiday. Churchill did not offer a direct prediction of what the Prime Minister's respsonse might be, but his view is implied in the strong advice against the idea that he gave the King on the grounds that everyone would think that he had simply left the country to be with Mrs Simpson in Cannes. It was advice that Churchill repeated urgently when he wrote to the King the following day. Leaving the country also had the flavour of deserting a battle station. As usual with unwelcome advice, the King made no response and passed on to other matters. His mind was made up.

When the King saw Baldwin the following day to discuss the Two Bills plan, he did not ask him about the idea of leaving the country to reflect, but this did not mean that the idea was dead. The King had probably drawn the conclusion from what Churchill had advised him that the Prime Min-ister would have taken a similar line and would have blocked the idea of the King leaving the country. He would not have been wrong. Rather than risk yet another rebuff by Baldwin, the King simply went ahead with the preparations in secrecy. That afternoon, Fielden was instructed to be ready to leave for Zurich at 9.30 the following morning. An extra aeroplane had also been arranged to transport the luggage of the King and his entourage, which was set to leave at the same time. This meant that the King would leave for Zurich before the government had a chance of even considering

Stanley Baldwin (*right*) had come to know Edward's personality well when he was Prince of Wales during the 1920s. He viewed the prospect of being Prime Minister when Edward succeeded to the throne with deep foreboding.

© Hulton Archive / Stringer via Getty Images

The widely reproduced photograph of Edward as Prince of Wales captures the charm and glamour that inspired high hopes for his reign – hopes that were to be dashed by bitter disappointment.

© Print Collector / Contributor via Getty Images

Most readers of the *The Sketch* in 1935 were not to know why Mrs Simpson had been singled out for the front cover. Only a tiny handful would have understood that Slipper, the Cairn terrier, was a symbol of the Prince of Wales's commitment to her.
© Hilary Morgan / Alamy Stock Photo

As Prince of Wales, Edward was a keen skier and took Mrs Simpson to Kitzbühel in 1935. She did not do well on skis. In his first, solitary months of exile after the abdication, skiing provided him with a welcome distraction, but it does not seem to have featured in their married life.

When Neville Chamberlain (*right*) became Prime Minister soon after the crisis, Sir Horace Wilson (*left*) remained as chief civil service adviser. Wilson supported Chamberlain's appeasement of the fascist powers as enthusiastically as he had supported his hard line towards the King.

© Popperfoto / Contributor via Getty Images

Sir Warren Fisher combined a gushy, Edwardian style with vaulting ambitions for the civil service and a steely resolve not to allow anything to get in the way of doing what was right for the Empire.

George Grantham Bain Collection, Library of Congress, Wikimedia Commons / Public Domain

LEFT The King paid his respects at the memorial to the dead of the Gallipoli campaign. His affinity with war veterans was entirely genuine, but the visit rebounded against him during the crisis when Mrs Simpson's presence was taken as a desecration.

© AP / Press Association Images

BELOW The global press told the world of the intimacy between the King and Mrs Simpson during the cruise of the *Nahlin*, but the British newspapers kept silent.

© Keystone / Stringer via Getty Images

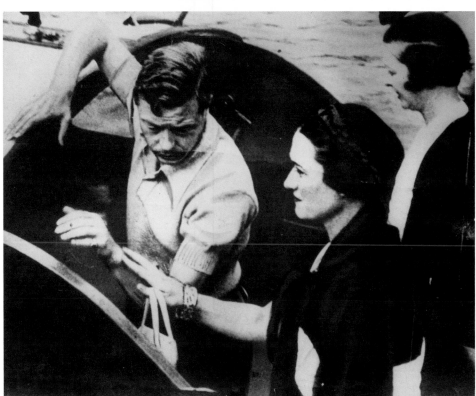

Sir Samuel ('Slippery Sam') Hoare was close to Beaverbrook, and the King thought that he might support him in the crisis, but he remained loyal to Baldwin. His enthusiasm for winter sports was a gift to satirists.

© Imagno / Contributor via Getty Images

Sir John Simon ('Sir John Snake') was a highly successful barrister, but, like Hoare, he was unpopular and mistrusted. It was said there would be 'no moaning at the Bar when he puts out to sea'. He and Hoare became the mainstays of the Cabinet when Neville Chamberlain took over as Prime Minister in May 1937.

Wikimedia Commons / Public Domain

LEFT The 'King's Party' at war. Winston Churchill (*right*) and Lord Beaverbrook (*left*) were cronies of long standing, but they pursued different goals during the crisis: Beaverbrook wanted, above all, to unseat Baldwin, and Churchill wanted to keep the King on the throne.

© Keystone / Stringer via Getty Images

BELOW The King's visit to the abandoned Dowlais steel works in depressed south Wales sparked his heartfelt call that 'something must be done'. The government saw how his words were being exploited in the burgeoning crisis over his relationship with Mrs Simpson.

© AP / Press Association Images

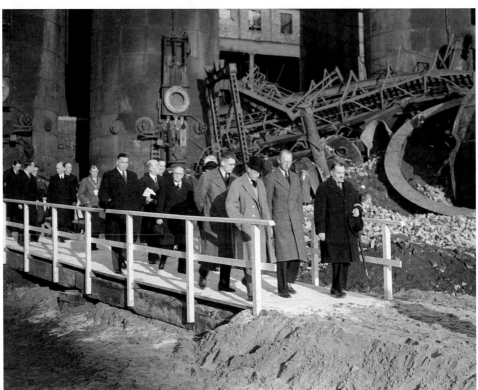

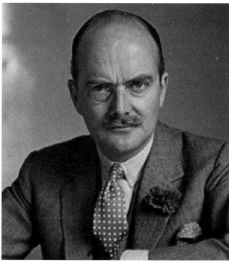

Fort Belvedere was Edward's private sanctuary and refuge from his royal duties, the emblem of his desire to compartmentalise his life. He spent the last days of his reign there, but it had become a claustrophobic bunker by then.

Wikimedia Commons / Public Domain

Bernard Rickatson-Hatt, chief editor of the Reuters news agency, was a friend to both the King and Ernest Simpson, though he may have had additional, conflicting loyalties. His early career was decidedly colourful.

Walter Monckton was a good friend of the King's from their days together at Oxford, but he despised Mrs Simpson. By the time he became the link between the King and the government, abdication was by far the most likely outcome, and his work of helping arrange terms was far easier than Hardinge's near-impossible task.

© Hulton Archive / Stringer via Getty Images

Mrs Simpson's Buick makes its way through the press pack besieging the Villa Lou Viei in Cannes. Even without its conspicuous registration, it was unmistakable on French roads and another example of how the King's attempts to keep secret the movements by the central figures in the crisis usually failed.

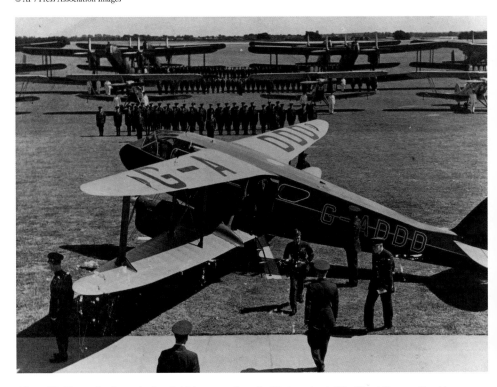

Edward VIII was the first reigning British monarch to fly. He bought de Havilland Dragon Rapide G-ADDD personally and had it painted in the colours of the Brigade of Guards. It would have taken him to Zurich if his plan to bolt the country had succeeded.

the Two Bills scheme and still less of beginning to implement it. The King treated the plan with his established style of noisy and ineffectual secretiveness. The stage was set for a fantastically irresponsible and cavalier act. When Maurice Gwyer, the government lawyer, had analysed the options available he had concluded his review of possibile scenarios with what must have seemed like the unlikeliest of possibilities: that Edward VIII would imitate James II and simply flee the country with nothing settled. He was now planning to do exactly that.

The King and the country escaped the consequences of this folly because of a combination of Fielden's sense of discipline and the government's intelligence operations. Some time on the Saturday, Fielden had sought Air Ministry approval for leaving the country. The only account of what happened in any detail is Wilson's, who described this move as merely 'the usual application ... to take the aeroplane out of the country', but the way in which it was handled was anything but routine.[4] The request was passed up the hierarchy of the Ministry until it reached the Air Minister himself, Lord Swinton. Presumably the lower echelons of the Ministry had been put on alert to apply special treatment to such a request. There was good reason for the authorities to be on their guard. The government had been alerted to the likelihood that the King would fly to Zurich by cables between journalists, who had got wind of the story, and which had been passed on by Cable & Wireless Ltd., which had already betrayed the Simpsons' dealings with the Hearst press.[5] Equally, Fielden himself must have recognised the implications of the proposed flight and made a point of ensuring that it received appropriate consideration. Fielden had been placed in a very difficult position by the King's orders and few would blame him for breaching confidence.

In turn, Swinton alerted Downing Street in the person of Chamberlain, who spotted major trouble brewing and went to No. 10. There he found Wilson busy in conference with the laywers preparing the Two Bills, but the Prime Minister absent at Fort Belvedere. After a brief discussion with Wilson, Chamberlain telephoned Dugdale at the Fort in a state of great agitation to attempt to get the arrangements at Hendon cancelled.

The combination of a poor telephone line and Chamberlain's state of excited stress meant it took some time for him to make himself clear to Dugdale.[6] Dugdale was highly amused at Chamberlain's departure from his usual Brummie phlegm, but fully understood the importance of what he had to do once the situation was clear to him, and he did not hesitate to tackle the problem. Whilst the men at Downing Street waited to hear back from Dugdale, they began to prepare for the worst. Wilson judged that things might move so fast that drastic action might be required. He told the lawyers to get an Instrument of Abdication ready for the King's signature.[7] Had the King persisted with the plan of flying to Zurich this would have meant that he could be confronted by the government at Hendon aerodrome and told that he would have to abdicate before he was allowed on the plane. It is a moot point as to whether Wilson saw this possiblity as a satisfactorily speedy and emphatic conclusion to the crisis or, as it would almost certainly have appeared, a humiliating and shameful combination of royal caprice and government ruthlessness.

Fortunately for everyone, Dugdale was able to defuse the situation. He recognised that the time for the traditional courtesies had passed and forcefully told Ulick Alexander to stand the machines down, in spite of Alexander's protestations that he was acting on royal command.[8] Alexander had placed himself on the back foot by showing his surprise that the government should have learned about the machines, which was tantamount to an admission that the explanation for the arrangements was not innocent. After his token resistance, Alexander complied with Dugdale's instructions.

The moment of greatest danger had passed, but Wilson was not going to let the opportunity slip past to ratchet up the measures that he thought were necessary to keep a check on the King. That morning he had already tried to persuade Chamberlain and Simon that the King's telephones should be tapped, as he later put it with breathtaking hypocrisy '… in the interests of the King as head of the State'.[9] The risk that there might be some repetition of the scheme to fly to Zurich offered a perfect pretext for Wilson to return to the charge, and this time Chamberlain agreed. All that was necessary for Wilson to implement the move was to obtain formal endorsement of the wiretap from Sir John Simon as Home Secretary. In his quasi-judicial capacity, the Home Secretary's approval was required for all phone taps in Britain. Whilst Chamberlain went out to dinner, Wilson called Simon to Downing Street, where he rubber-stamped the decision that had already been taken.[10] The phone lines between the King's addresses in the UK, Buckingham Palace and Fort Belvedere, and the Villa Lou Viei – the villa where Mrs Simpson was staying – were tapped. With MI5 and the Metropolitan Police Special Branch already on the job, the King was now the target of almost the full range of security organisations that the British state could deploy against him. There is no sign that the Prime Minister was asked or even told about this final piece in the jigsaw of surveillance around the King even though he was at Downing Street, albeit probably sound asleep.

Unnoticed at the time, Downing Street's reading of the King's intentions was wrong on one point. It was insignificant on the Saturday night, but by the Wednesday morning it had acquired an unexpected importance. As Churchill had warned the King, Downing Street jumped to the conclusion that the King intended to use the aeroplanes to join Mrs Simpson at Cannes. If the King's yearning for a quiet break in the mountains had registered at all in Downing Street, it had not been believed. A flight to Cannes would have been a bit more scandalous than a flight to Zurich, but either would have been intolerable. Dugdale did not know exactly what he was stopping, but he knew that it had to be stopped.

In their subsequent accounts of the Zurich episode, both Wilson and the Duke of Windsor were notably dishonest. It could have had horrible consequences and so was best buried, but each side wanted something on record to give their preferred version of the story if the facts should leak out. Almost in passing, the Duke implied that arrangements had got no further than identifying somewhere to stay at Zurich.[11] His claim that 'if nothing came of Walter Monckton's Two Bills, I would repair there to wait' is self-evidently false as the process of realising the scheme would not even have begun at 9.30 on the Sunday morning. Wilson too links the flight to Zurich to the Two Bills scheme, albeit in the shape that it was originally conceived, as something that would follow the King's proposed broadcast.[12] He appears to have been motivated by a desire to present things in the kindest light possible by asserting that it was all due to mere oversight. He claims that Alexander told Dugdale that it had simply been omitted to cancel the arrangements for the planes once the King had been told that the broadcast had been blocked. This is not remotely supported by Dugdale's own account.

CHAPTER 16

A MICROCOSM OF THE CABINET

We settled to postpone the P.M.'s visit to the Queen and to summon Halifax,
Inskip, S. Hoare, M. Macdonald [sic] Runciman K. Wood & O. Stanley
as a sort of microcosm of the Cabinet to give further
consideration to this proposal tomorrow at 10.

NEVILLE CHAMBERLAIN, DIARY,

5 DECEMBER 1936

HAVING THRASHED OUT an agreement in principle on the idea of the Two Bills with Monckton as the King's representative, Wilson moved onto the next stage in the process. Time was short and there was no harm in working on the assumption that the principals – the King and the Prime Minister – would endorse the terms that they had concluded. The government would need two separate pieces of legislation that would need to be prepared in far less time than was normally available. Whilst Baldwin and Dugdale were at Fort Belvedere, Sir Horace Wilson had begun to transform the idea of Two Bills into a practical proposition. He called the government's two top lawyers, Sir Maurice Gwyer and Granville Ram, to Downing Street to begin the process of drawing up the necessary legislation. They faced an epic task to prepare the legislation for Parliament possibly as soon as the Monday.

That Saturday night in Downing Street was the most crowded few hours of the crisis. Wilson had been toiling through the day, but his efforts were interrupted at about 7 p.m. when Chamberlain came to see him with the news of the aeroplanes waiting at Hendon. This led to the lawyers briefly being taken off their work on the Two Bills to prepare an instrument of abdication for immediate use. Dugdale's resolute action at Fort Belvedere meant that this was not needed and Chamberlain was able to set off for a dinner party still in ignorance of the Two Bills plan.[1] On his way out he told Wilson to put into action his plan for tapping the King's phones.[2]

At around 8.30 p.m. Baldwin returned from Fort Belvedere with the news that the King had made up his mind to abdicate. Baldwin was sure that the Two Bills solution would be implemented, and things were put in hand to smooth the way for an announcement on the Monday. The full Cabinet would need to approve the scheme and a meeting was summoned for 5.30 p.m. on the Sunday, which would give the lawyers time to prepare legislation for the ministers to rule on. An audience with Queen Mary was fixed for 10.30 a.m., at which the Prime Minister could tell her of her son's decision to abdicate.[3] Cosmo Gordon Lang, the Archbishop of Canterbury, was bidden to Downing Street; the Two Bills construction involved a ticklish question of ethics and, whilst it was not essential, his approval would be another important part of the drive to implement the deal. The Bills would have to be passed by Parliament, so meetings were fixed with Clement Attlee and Archibald Sinclair. They had backed the government at every step so far, but their approval was still needed. With all this under his belt, Baldwin seems to have gone straight to bed; there is no record that he played any part in the remainder of the night's events. This was doubtless one of the occasions about which Chamberlain complained boastingly to his sister that he had 'been up night after night till one o'clock or after long after S.B. has gone to bed'.[4]

But for the Hendon aeroplanes episode, that is where things would have rested until the Sunday. As was discussed in the previous chapter, it was not enough for Chamberlain to agree to the phone taps; Sir John Simon had to give them some formal approval in his capacity as Home Secretary and Wilson called him into Downing Street to do this where he arrived at about 9.30 p.m. At this point Wilson put Simon fully into the picture about the Two Bills. Simon had already been told enough to assure Beaverbrook on the Saturday morning that the threat of intervention by the King's Proctor was being removed by legislation, but when he was presented with the Two Bills scheme in detail, he was appalled. His fellow hardliner Chamberlain was called back to Downing Street to provide assistance and, in his turn, briefed on the Two Bills scheme and on the conversation between the King and Baldwin at Fort Belvedere. It was thus the hard core of the hardliners, Chamberlain, Simon and Wilson, who sat down to deal with what they saw as the flaws in the Two Bills deal; problems that Baldwin had not considered in the press of events. Right from the start none of them showed much enthusiasm for the concept itself; all had 'misgivings'.[5] It is tempting to suppose that Wilson had first worked on the plan when the Prime Minister told him to, but when he came to discuss it with the man for whom he would probably be working in a few months, he could let his instinctive concern rip. At the start, it was Simon who was the most hostile to the idea, but Chamberlain endorsed his stance.

> Simon thought this a shocking precedent. He realised that in the surge of sympathy with the K. which the abdication would evoke the bill might be carried but afterwards it would be a terrible argument against the monarchy that this special favour had been given to an ex King because he had been K.. What would the non conformists say? I felt the same scruples. It wd. be considered as an unholy bargain to get the K. to abdicate. I doubted if the Labour Party wd. support it.[6]

The three men around the table disliked the Two Bills both from a moral perspective and one of practical politics, but they knew that an accommodation would remove the one remaining obstacle to a swift end to the crisis. There was also an element of fairness. Chamberlain saw that the King was

making 'an unparalleled sacrifice … all the more poignant because in making it he had no security that the purpose for which it was made could be
achieved' and admitted the 'cruelty' of his position.[7] Simon had already
spotted the more pragmatic argument for the deal: that keeping the ex-King
in limbo would leave him '"knocking about Europe for four months" with
all the consequential possibilities of mischief-making on the Continent and
here'.[8] There was no need to go further into the potential for trouble that
Edward might cause. The lawyers were called from upstairs in case they
might be able to offer some guidance on how the divorce proceedings might
be expedited. They had already looked at this possibility themselves and
poured cold water on the idea. Somervell was firmly against the idea that
the government might approach the President of the Divorce Court directly
and, even less helpfully, was no more enthusiastic about the Two Bills than
the hardliners. Other possible solutions were floated, but every time the
discussion returned to the ugly fact that almost any construction would
be a deal or look like a deal. Accelerating the passage of A. P. Herbert's
Private Member's divorce law reform Bill briefly offered an elegant solution, but the government would have had to sponsor at least part of such
a move, which brought things back to a dubious bargain.

The best that they could come up with was a suggestion from Chamberlain that the matter be fudged, with the government making a vague
commitment to help on the point of Mrs Simpson's divorce bundled into a
package of measures designed to smooth the transition between two Kings.
This was enough to wear down Simon's initial visceral dislike of the plan
and he came to accept that 'bearing in mind the need to give the new King
the best possible start off … the scheme had more advantages than he had
at first been inclined to think it had'.[9] It was hardly a ringing endorsement
for a proposal that arose from near desperation.

The quartet talked around the subject for more than two hours, but
sometime after midnight they abandoned the effort to come up with a hard
and fast plan. Chamberlain's fudge was not enough on its own and they
knew that more would have to be done. It was Wilson who called time
on the proceedings with the suggestion that the question be referred to

a larger group of ministers the following morning, and this was accepted without demur. Knowingly or unknowingly, this step was the death knell for the Two Bills plan. The Sunday morning meeting would make the real decision, which the full Cabinet would rubber-stamp in the afternoon. In Wilson's silky prose:

> It would be unwise to confront the whole Cabinet with this very difficult problem unless it had been carefully examined beforehand by some Ministers so that the Cabinet would have the advantage of some lead, or at least a clear exposition of the proposal, its advantages and its disadvantages.[10]

The key choice would be which ministers to have at the morning meeting. Inevitably, seniority within the government was a major factor, but they were also picked on the basis of their sympathy for the hardliners' stance. Halifax was senior in the government, a High Churchman and thus reliably conservative, as had been demonstrated by his membership of the cabal Chamberlain had organised three weeks before to attempt to railroad Baldwin into sending the King a peremptory ultimatum. Hoare was also senior and had proven faithful to the government line despite his foot in the enemy camp. Walter Runciman was another of the cabal, albeit freighted with nonconformist morality rather than the Anglican flavour of Christianity. The others were chosen on the basis of their likely opposition to a deal: the 'noted Churchm[e]n' Thomas Inskip and Kingsley Wood, another noncomformist, and a younger more secular hawk Oliver Stanley.[11] Quite who chose the ministers is a mystery, but their names were on a note that Wilson wrote for Baldwin, which served as a list of men to summon.

When the ministers gathered at 10 a.m. the following day, it was soon clear that the Two Bills proposal was in deep trouble. Baldwin's description of the King's dilemma attracted as good as no sympathy. Simon endorsed the idea of the Two Bills ineffectively, deploying his uniquely personal combination of legalism, tepidity and ambiguity. His argument in favour of making an exception for the King because he supposedly did not have the option of lying low until he was free unlike 'a prominent Civil servant,

who would have to give up his job in the event of a divorce' has the flavour of an advocate pleading a truly hopeless case.[12] It opened a wide
flank for Sir Thomas Inskip, Scottish lawyer and Anglican evangelical, to
slip in a damning comment on the King's moral fitness for the job. Inskip
was one of the most junior and unimportant members of the Cabinet, but
the accident of fate gave him a key albeit walk-on part in the crisis. His
appointment to the Cabinet in March had excited widespread derision
and predictable comparisons with Caligula elevating his horse Incitatus to
the consulate. To ease political pressure to accelerate rearmament (notably
from Churchill) Baldwin had decided to appoint a minister for the Coordination of Defence but had exposed the move as a piece of empty tokenism
by choosing Inskip, an ineffectual safe pair of hands. Inskip had made his
name in Parliament with magnificent speeches against the modernisation
of the Church of England's prayer book and was firmly in his element on
a question of morality. He took up Simon's comparison of the King and
another public servant with the equally dubious but infinitely more telling assertion that 'if a prominent Civil Servant was publicly known to be
engaged in an affair of this kind (like Mr. Parnell, for example), he would
have to go'.[13] Charles Stewart Parnell MP had led the Irish Home Rule
movement until 1889, when his mistress's husband sued her for divorce,
creating a scandal which drove Parnell out of politics. Inskip's allusion was
historical, but it was also thoroughly topical. Elsie Schauffler's play on the
subject had just premiered in London after a prolonged battle to force it
past the censorship of the Lord Chamberlain.

Inskip's intervention was the turning point in the discussion. Chamberlain began by distancing himself from the proposal by announcing that it
had been sprung on him only the previous evening, but his most telling
argument against the Two Bills proposal and ultimately its fatal flaw was
that it constituted an unholy bargain. No one disagreed and it became rather
the leitmotif of the meeting to castigate any such bargain as unacceptable.
No one attached any moral or practical importance to the six-month gap
between the two stages of divorce; it was shortening it for one individual
that stuck in the ministers' craw. Ever alert to wider consequences, Inskip

warned that manipulating one divorce would corrupt any change to divorce law and deliver 'a blow to the sanctity of marriage'. One minister came up with the ugly, but compelling argument that accelerating Mrs Simpson's divorce by legislation would create the impression that the divorce was flawed – either because the couple had colluded or because Mrs Simpson herself had also committed adultery – so could and should not be legally finalised. The government would thus appear to be colluding in an abuse of the judicial process. The nearest that the discussion got to pragmatism was an argument that such a bargain would weaken the government's moral authority, internationally above all. None of the ministers, not even Baldwin, raised the danger that the King might back away from his half-commitment to abdicate if he could not be certain of marrying Mrs Simpson. The Two Bills were dead.

Monckton had spent the two hours whilst the ministers deliberated, awkwardly sitting in Wilson's office whilst the civil servant waded through his paperwork. He was summoned into the Cabinet room by the Prime Minister in person, but it was Chamberlain who explained to him why the Two Bills had been turned down: because the appearance of 'a bargain where there ought to be none' could not be condoned.[14] It was only at this point that ministers developed an interest in how the King would react to the verdict and the question was put to Monckton. With some courage Monckton told the hostile figures around that table that in his own opinion the King would want more time to consider the question of abdication and also 'advice from other quarters' including Churchill.[15] Monckton pointedly explained the King's likely need for advice by the 'divergence of view' amongst ministers that he would detect, in other words because the government had gone back on what the Prime Minister had offered the King. He thought the refusal of the Two Bills plan 'would materially alter the position'. Monckton received a decidedly hostile reception beginning with a diatribe by Chamberlain on the urgency of the question and how the uncertainty was damaging the pre-Christmas trade. When Ramsay MacDonald asked Monckton how much more time the King would want, he asked for a fortnight. It was a forlorn hope.

Baldwin began by attacking Monckton's ideas of where the King might find alternative advice. He was firmly warned off seeking advice solely from the men who had advised him so far; Baldwin suggested he might also wish to try the far more respectable press baron, Lord Camrose of the *Daily Telegraph*. In Baldwin's view, anything that smacked of a 'King's Party' ought to be anathema to the King. As to timing, Baldwin in practice set the King one deadline. He should be told of the decision by the meeting of ministers before the full Cabinet meeting at 5.30 p.m. and, by clear implication, make some response. In practice, the King was being left with only a couple of hours to ask for the extra breathing space that Monckton had tried to keep open and, if need be, to fight on. Pressure was piled on the King. The presence of Monckton provided ministers for the first time with a channel through which they could send their message directly to the King without having to go through the Prime Minister. To speed the King towards a decision, one of the ministers pointed to the 'dangers of delay', in particular the threat of intervention 'from those who wanted him to remain King' and, more menacingly, 'the risks to the lady herself'.[16]

Baldwin was so abashed at his failure to convince the hardline ministers to accept the Two Bills that he told Monckton after the meeting that he would have to resign.[17] As the Prime Minister doubtless intended him to, Monckton talked him out of this thought with the claim that the King would not accept the resignation. When Monckton told the King about this conversation immediately afterwards he confirmed that he would not have accepted Baldwin's resignation.[18] This little piece of theatre did, though, help feed the legend later promoted by the Duke of Windsor and Beaverbrook that Baldwin had placed his premiership on the line in advance of the meeting of ministers. In their accounts of the crisis, both the Duke and Beaverbrook asserted that Baldwin had promised in advance to resign if the Two Bills plan was rejected, and the Duke simply did not mention that he had approved of Monckton turning down Baldwin's idea of resignation on his behalf.

The rough treatment handed out to Monckton's attempts at temporising on the King's behalf appear to have convinced ministers that the King would have to accept the meeting's verdict in a docile fashion and the remainder of the day was spent in occasionally farcical anti-climax. Wilson was set to unwinding the plans made the night before to transform Two Bills into a reality. The opposition leaders could be stood down from their appointments with the Prime Minister, although it was too late to reach Sir Archibald Sinclair, so Baldwin took the opportunity to sound him out on Churchill's attitude; he and Churchill were personal friends of long standing and he had been Churchill's battalion adjutant on the Western Front. It was rather different with the Archbishop of Canterbury, on whom it was clearly unacceptable to inflict the indignities that political leaders have to bear. In his honour, the Prime Minister maintained the charade that the Two Bills proposal was still a live one and sought his opinion on so grave a moral issue. It was the only time during the crisis that we can be certain that the government asked for his views – even if they did not matter as the question had been settled – and he emerges as anything but the furious scourge of loose behaviour that the Duke of Windsor later depicted. In fact, he had no perceptible influence on Baldwin's handling of the crisis.[19] Moreover, Lang appears as a ditherer, capable of rivalling Simon at his least decisive. The intrusion of the Church of England into the deliberations offered Baldwin rare light relief and allowed Wilson one of the occasional moments of understated irony in his notes, when he described what Baldwin told him of the conversation:

> The Archbishop had begun by thinking that the proposal would not do; but had then seen its possible advantages and had been disposed to favour it; after further consideration he was inclined to come back to his first view. The Prime Minister seemed to think that, on the whole, he had not got very much guidance.[20]

After this moment of badinage, Wilson pushed the Prime Minister's nose firmly back to the grindstone with the hardest of hardline arguments. The House of Commons would expect some statement the following day and it was up to the Cabinet, when it met later that afternoon, to do more in this

direction than merely rubber-stamping the decision taken by the morning's meeting of ministers. 'It would be a good thing if the discussion could
then turn upon what other alternatives were available for the King's consideration.'[21] In simple terms, the Cabinet should decide on a statement to
Parliament that made plain that the King could either renounce Mrs Simpson or abdicate. After the Prime Minister had ruled out the morganatic
option on the Friday afternoon, he was to go to the next stage and state
directly that the King had to choose between Mrs Simpson and the throne.

When the Cabinet met at 5.30 p.m. the Two Bills proposal was disposed of even more rapidly than at the meeting of ministers. The mass of
the Cabinet had no greater appetite than the hardliners. Lord Swinton, the
Air Minister, was the only one who spoke in favour of it and then only
because he judged it was in the national interest. He was firmly told not
to worry about the King's Proctor and the discussion moved on. It was a
meeting of surprising reversals of stance. The most vehement criticism of
the proposal came from the only minister who had spoken out in the King's
favour at earlier Cabinet meetings. Duff Cooper had been appalled when
he found out about the Two Bills scheme from Walter Elliott after lunch
and he identified yet another flaw with the plan; this time one that took a
more charitable view of the King's position:

> I thought this was a disastrous proposal. It would obviously be said
> that the Government must want to get rid of him [the King], as they had
> refused to introduce legislation for a morganatic marriage in order to
> keep him, but were willing to introduce legislation, which according to
> existing law, would legalise adultery, in order to expedite his departure.[22]

Duff Cooper was even more forthright with the Cabinet to whom he
described the second bill as 'a Special Act to allow the King to commit
adultery'.[23] The other minister to shift tack radically was Neville Chamberlain, who pulled back from being the persistent advocate of bludgeoning
the King into giving his decision as soon as possible. Instead – somehow
– he had concluded that public opinion on its own would force the King to

choose: 'Moreover if we sat back the public wd. presently realise that the only choice lay between renunciation of marriage & abdication & if the K. persisted in refusing the first all opposition to the 2nd would fade away.'[24]

Opposition was so strong that there was no need to debate the specifics of the Two Bills plan, so the meeting switched into a general discussion of what the next steps should be. Enthusiasm for pushing the King for a quick choice had ebbed amongst the other members as well and the Cabinet finally moved to the position that Baldwin had championed all along, of allowing the King to choose in his own time, albeit in the knowledge that he would find it very hard to delay any length of time. Chamberlain had drafted a statement for the Prime Minister to make on the Monday afternoon, which read suspiciously like the kind of thing that Wilson had been pressing on Baldwin before the meeting. It urged a speedy decision and ominously referred to the 'strictly limited' alternatives available to the King unless he gave up Mrs Simpson.[25] It was decided to redraft it into a considerably more emollient form.

Ministers had spent the afternoon in the apparent expectation that the King would not create too great a fuss that the Two Bills had been refused, but the risk was still there. When Monckton arrived at Downing Street from Fort Belvedere, Baldwin left the Cabinet meeting to find out how the King had actually reacted to the death of the Two Bills plan. The news was good and it looked as though the moment of greatest danger had passed: 'The King was, of course, disappointed at the first reaction of Ministers but had not expressed himself strongly on the subject. Mr. Monckton thought that the Cabinet should wait and that the King would not take long to reach his decision.'[26] Monckton had found the King in low spirits already and even his anger at Chamberlain's gratingly materialistic argument for an early decision inspired no more than the acerbic thought that the Chancellor of the Exchequer 'was being a trifle more mercenary than his office demanded'.[27] The King was a beaten man. Everything for which he had asked, save the conversation with Churchill, had been refused by the government. He was left grumbling impotently at the imbalance of force between a constitutional monarch and a democratic government. Even supposing that he actually believed that Baldwin had offered to resign if he could not secure the Two Bills, the King did not challenge Baldwin to deliver on the promise. He was ready to abdicate, taking the chance that Mrs Simpson's divorce might yet be blocked.

The sequence of events leading to the demise of the Two Bills plan was another episode that Wilson was at pains to conceal in his notes. This time his personal reputation was at stake. Not only had he played a large part himself in formulating a plan that proved to be severely flawed, but he had also played a major part in killing it off against the wishes of the Prime Minister when these flaws became too apparent.

Wilson's account of the episode begins with a straightforward description of how he and Monckton devised the plan together with Dugdale and Allen, which is amply borne out by other testimony. It is when he moves on to the events at Downing Street on the Saturday night when the action becomes more confused and the number of disinterested witnesses dwindles, that it becomes hard to disentangle what actually happened from what Wilson wants to hide. The key moment in the proceedings is the arrival of Simon at Downing Street. In Wilson's draft version, it is possible to make out that he had been called in to sign the warrant for the phone trap, albeit only by identifying the connection between two passages in widely separated parts of the text. In the passage that says when Simon arrived at Downing Street, Wilson attempted to kill two birds with one stone of elegant false suggestion: 'At about 9.30 p.m. the Home Secretary came to see me. I ... told him of the proposition that was under examination...' It reads as though Simon was called in specifically to be told of the Two Bills, rather than having come on the quite different and unrelated errand of signing off the wiretap. Wilson does not explain at all why Chamberlain returned to Downing Street.

When he came to prepare the final version he probably spotted that too much was revealed in the draft or that it did not hang together. He opted for a more radical solution. In the final version, all references to the aeroplanes at Hendon and the upshot of this episode are omitted, and all we are told is that 'later in the day it [the Two Bills plan] was discussed with the Home Secretary and the Chancellor of the Exchequer'. He does, though, still slip in a significant obfuscation of the record. To mask the fact that the two hardliners and Wilson himself were worrying the question of the Two Bills to death whilst Baldwin slept upstairs, Wilson introduces his favourite device of jumbling chronology. In the midst of his account of the agonised discussion at Downing Street, he inserts a paragraph saying that 'The Prime Minister had in meantime gone to Fort Belvedere'. Read closely it is not an untruth in the strictest sense, but it creates the entirely misleading impression that Baldwin's visit to Fort Belvedere was taking place at the same time as the three-way discussion.

Wilson erased his own part in the decision to summon the hardline ministers on the Sunday morning, but this may be no more than a civil serv-ant's self-effacement. When he revised the draft he struck out not only the statement that he had suggested the meeting and replaced it with a bland 'it was thought', but also the reference to his note to Baldwin giving the names of ministers summoned. He also tries lamely to trivialise the impor-tance of the morning meeting. He practically contradicts himself on the role he set out on the Sunday night for the meeting of ministers when he refers to the possibility that the full Cabinet might 'endorse – if they did endorse – the conclusions tentatively arrived at by Ministers in the morning'. It is harder to think of a less tentative conclusion from a meeting than the rejection of the Two Bills in the morning. Wilson trapped himself further in self-contradiction by stating that the full Cabinet was genuinely taking the decision even though he had just written that the morning meeting meant that 'it was found no useful purpose would be served by seeing the Opposition Leaders'.

Somebody, most probably Wilson himself, was also feeding a far more blatant fiction into the record. Both Monckton and, through him, the Duke of Windsor himself, were led to believe that the meeting of ministers had been fixed before Baldwin came to Fort Belvedere on the Saturday afternoon and that it had been designed to tackle in advance potential resistance from hardliners.[28] Nothing else supports this timing. Both Chamberlain's diary and Wilson's own notes are quite unambiguous that the meeting was called by the threesome late on the Saturday night. The similarities between this distortion and what happened over Hardinge's letter are too strong to ignore. In the same way that Monckton was told with literal accuracy, but quite misleadingly, that the Cabinet had not discussed the issue before the letter was written, someone had told Monckton that the Sunday meeting had been summoned by the Prime Minister himself. Jumbling the sequence of events leading to the meeting of ministers had a further, unintended consequence by contributing to the Duke of Windsor's belief that Baldwin had staked his premiership on the outcome of the meeting rather than merely issuing an almost certainly insincere offer of resignation afterwards.

OVER THE
EDGE

CHAPTER 17

RATHER A FACER

*After some further talk, I discovered that what Mr. Goddard was
really saying to me was, in effect, what price could be paid to Mrs. Simpson for
clearing out? This was rather a facer for me as the point had not occurred to me
before and nowhere in my experience could I find any help. We discussed this
point for a little while and agreed that Mr. Goddard's proper course ...
was to remind himself that he would be talking to Mrs. Simpson
as her solicitor and therefore that ... his best line would be
to try to find out what was in her own mind.*

SIR HORACE WILSON, ABDICATION NOTES[1]

B Y T H E S U N D A Y night it seemed that the crisis was close to being
settled. The King had decided to abdicate and to take the risk of
intervention in Mrs Simpson's divorce. But hopes of an easy conclusion were overtaken by a series of events that brought fresh complications
and added new twists to old ones. New uncertainties and doubts arose during the course of Monday, which was crowded with developments both
private and public. The episode that stands out in this day of confusion is
the decision to send Theodore Goddard, Mrs Simpson's solicitor, to see
her in Cannes by plane. It bore on almost all the day's other occurrences

in a bewildering and tangled pattern of motivations that added time and complexity to the crisis.

The day's biggest change was that the government started to pay some attention to Mrs Simpson as an individual. With hindsight it is only surprising that this had not happened sooner. One of the curiosities of the abdication crisis is how little interest the government had paid to Mrs Simpson herself up to that point. Perhaps it reflected the prevailing attitude of society in those days that women were strictly an accessory element in life, that vast amounts of effort were devoted to trying to change the King's behaviour, but very little to trying to influence Mrs Simpson's. Mrs Simpson was not just a woman, but a woman with a deeply tarnished reputation, especially to the handful of men who knew of the Special Branch dossier on her and her husband. It is a moot point whether the government would have tried anything but for the fact that she had fled for Cannes and could thus now be approached separately from the King.

The ball was set rolling on the Sunday evening as the politicians weighed the outcome of the afternoon's Cabinet meeting. The guests at a large dinner party given by the Channons included Duff Cooper, the Chief Whip Margesson and Leslie Hore-Belisha, who talked the question over once the meal was over. Honor Channon, more mindful of the King's interest than her husband was, begged Margesson to try to work on Mrs Simpson.[2] In what might be considered something of an understatement, they agreed that 'not sufficient effort had been made hitherto' to prevent abdication. They also admitted amongst themselves the frightening truth that 'the only person who could change the King's mind was Wallis'.[3] They concluded that 'somebody having authority' should persuade her to give up the marriage by telling her directly that she was doing harm and her future was hopeless. Duff Cooper had spoken to Brownlow at the Villa Lou Viei that afternoon and learned that Mrs Simpson's morale had fallen to the point that she was near despair. An appeal to her might thus find fertile ground. Margesson was willing to undertake the mission to Cannes and promised the others that he would try to get approval the following morning. He was as good as his word and saw Chamberlain just after breakfast the next day with a report of what Brownlow had told Duff Cooper from Cannes: 'She realised the game was up and was ready to agree to renunciation.'4

Margesson found himself pushing at an open door. After having changed his mind the previous afternoon on the need to push the King into a quick decision – in practice to commit himself to abdication – Chamberlain now began to wobble seriously on how to end the crisis and started to see the attractions of Mrs Simpson solving the problem by giving up the King. Having spent the best part of a month arguing and intriguing for the government to make moves that would almost certainly have driven the King towards abdication, Chamberlain had finally recognised just how extreme this was as an outcome. In addition to whatever Margesson told him, Chamberlain had seen that most newspapers were taking the line that renunciation would be the best solution. It was anything but a wholehearted volte-face. Chamberlain was positively grudging and grumbled that 'although I have felt all through that we should never be safe with this K.[ing] I did not feel we ought to discourage any chance of this solution'.5 Moreover, he had his own preferred candidate for the job and one quite different to the political heavyweight whom the group at the Channons' dinner party had wanted. In fact, it was someone with a proven track record in failing to make Mrs Simpson do what he or the government wanted. It was Theodore Goddard, her solicitor for the divorce cases and the hardliners' intermediary in Fisher's unavailing attempt to remove her from the scene after the Ipswich hearing. The choice of Goddard as a go-between reflected the fact that another, quite different set of considerations were at work, and it severely compromised the attempt to make Mrs Simpson abandon the King. There is no sign that anyone gave serious thought to sending anyone other than Goddard to Cannes. Goddard was the hardliners' man and they were firmly in the driving seat.

Goddard's qualifications to act as an intermediary with Mrs Simpson had not improved since his first failure. He had not seen her since the divorce case and there is little sign of any other communication. It was only by a ludicrous coincidence he had found himself briefing the government again just after the press silence broke. He also acted as solicitor to a former national Labour minister, Jim Thomas, who had been forced to resign in May 1936

over the leakage of Budget secrets. In December, Thomas was contemplat-
ing an attempt to make a return and Ramsay MacDonald, notionally his
party leader, took Goddard to lunch at the House of Commons to try to
head him off, entirely unaware of the connection between Mrs Simpson
and Goddard, still less the dubious purposes to which it had been put.

> 'You know, surely, that I should like to talk with you about the position
> of our friend.'
> 'Yes, I know you are interested in her.'
> 'Her? What do you mean?'
> 'Mrs. Simpson. She is a friend of yours.'
> 'No! … And why did you think I wanted to talk about Mrs. Simpson?'[6]

After MacDonald recovered from the shock of being labelled a friend of
Mrs Simpson, the two discussed the case. Once again Goddard showed the
ambiguity of his loyalty towards his client. He admitted that he thought
the proceedings had not been 'usual' and that he expected the King's Proctor would be called on to act. By the Monday his predictions were looking
increasingly accurate. Whether Goddard actually believed MacDonald's
claim of ignorance hardly matters; wheels were turning that would soon
bring him back into action on behalf of the government.

Having spent months in trying to get Mrs Simpson out of the country
and finally succeeding, Wilson wanted to keep her there and had already
started fretting at the possibility that she might want to return to the UK.
As the wiretaps on Fort Belvedere that he had successfully lobbied for on
the Saturday revealed, Mrs Simpson was insisting stridently to the King that
he should not abdicate, in the course of fraught telephone conversations
between Cannes and Sunningdale. The poor quality of the international
phone lines of the era gave them an agonising edge of technical imperfec-
tions. The King sometimes had to shout so loud to make himself heard that
almost everyone in Fort Belvedere could hear his end of the dialogue; the
wiretaps were hardly necessary.[7] It was bad enough that Mrs Simpson was
trying to persuade the King to stay on the throne by phone, but it would
be even worse if she were in a position to do so face-to-face. According to

Wilson's account, Monckton and Allen had already considered how to deal with the threat of Mrs Simpson returning to the UK over the weekend.[8] Monckton had already put Goddard on standby for a journey to Cannes, 'in the hope that, as her solicitor, he might be able to put before her considerations which would induce her to stay away'.

There was another message that Wilson wanted to be sent to Mrs Simpson – one that showed that he was taking a different view of the crisis to the politicians'. Unlike Chamberlain, there is no sign that Wilson himself had developed any doubts that it would be a good thing if the King abdicated. As far as he was concerned, the consensus was that the King should go. As well as warding off any threat that Mrs Simpson might come back to Britain, Goddard could also head Mrs Simpson off from further efforts to persuade the King to stay: '[I]t appeared evident that she was out of touch with opinion here and that on that, and on other points, there might be occasions when it would be a good thing if a man of Mr. Goddard's experience was at her side.'[9] Wilson was clearly aware that Mrs Simpson was trying to persuade the King that his popularity was great enough to keep him on the throne and was insisting that he did not abdicate. The combination of the wiretaps and the audibility of the King's side of telephone conversations at Fort Belvedere meant that their conversations were almost an open book.[10] In Wilson's eyes, what mattered was to stop Mrs Simpson's efforts to talk the King out of abdication – or, worse, to fight the government – and not to make her renounce him.

As if this were not enough, the question of intervention in Mrs Simpson's divorce reared its ugly head again. Chamberlain had hardly gone in to see the Prime Minister with the plan to send Goddard to Cannes, when the lawyers arrived with word that the King was still hoping that the government might give him some certainty that Mrs Simpson's divorce would go through. This was enough to bring Chamberlain back to his old mantra that the best way for Mrs Simpson to get her divorce was for the King to abdicate, thus removing the temptation for muddle-headed or excessively patriotic individuals to lodge an intervention. This was the last hurrah for this piece of wishful thinking, which had once been so potent amongst the hardliners, and within minutes it was overtaken by a new and far more pressing iteration of the intervention danger. Chamberlain was called out of the room by Wilson, who told him that after weeks of being no more than a hypothetical possibility, intervention was now imminent. Worse, it was coming from two directions and would attack the divorce on both the grounds available. The King's Proctor had heard from

> a reputable firm of solicitors that they were going to put in an affidavit on collusion and from a less reputable individual who said he had in his employ a servant of Mrs. S. who was prepared to give evidence of her misconduct at her flat, in Cornwall & elsewhere.[11]

It was looking as though Monckton's worst fears were being realised and that Mrs Simpson would find herself permanently imprisoned in her marriage to Ernest.

Here Baldwin saw a silver lining to the cloud as intervention offered an opportunity to save the King from marrying 'a woman who could only make him miserable'.[12] Chamberlain performed his third volte-face in little more than an hour and, in an unaccustomed concession to humanity, endorsed this view. As before, Goddard was to be the messenger and an uncompromising message was agreed upon. Goddard would

> tell her plainly that all chance of her marriage to the K. as K. was at an end as the country & the Dominions would not have her at any price. Moreover that she would not get her divorce & her best chance was now to withdraw her petition & get what kudos she could from a renunciation.[13]

Baldwin and Chamberlain were behaving as though successful intervention was a practical certainty, but once again there must be some suspicion that the risks of intervention were being manipulated. Chamberlain's belief that a private intervention was about to be launched might simply have been a misunderstanding, but there is some similarity here with the way in which Fisher had claimed inaccurately to Hardinge that two affidavits had been filed when the civil servants were trying to panic him into action almost a month before. In fact, Sir Thomas Barnes, the King's Proctor, had told Wilson that the 'reputable' solicitors had formally requested his intervention rather than launching intervention on their own or anyone else's behalf.[14] None of the growing number of letters that the King's Proctor had received since the press broke its silence questioning the circumstances of Mrs Simpson's divorce had even mentioned the possibility that the writer would intervene as a member of the public. None of the letters to the King's Proctor, including the 'reputable' firm's, offered substantial new evidence or accusations.

None of the outside solicitors who were interesting themselves in the case had new evidence, but the government had just been confronted by what looked like potentially new important testimony. This provided a far stronger reason for the civil servants to anticipate that intervention might succeed and this, rather than what was coming into Barnes's office, might explain what they had done. On that same Monday morning, as the idea of Goddard going to Cannes had taken shape, Ernest Simpson, who had been practically absent from the story since Sir Maurice Jenks had told the government in January that he was willing to give his wife up to the King, had now begun to harry Downing Street with telephone calls, offering whatever help he could. As the government's harassed law officers concluded instantly, the most likely form that this proffered assistance would take was testimony that he had colluded with his wife in the divorce case. The law officers knew that this would be fatal to her chances of a decree absolute, throwing the situation irredeemably out of control. Unlike adultery, where the courts had the option of granting a 'discretion' to the petitioner, 'collusion is an absolute bar to a divorce'.[15] The evidence of one of the spouses that the couple had colluded would have been enough to destroy the case, but the fact that Mrs Simpson was paying her husband's costs (unknown, of course, to the government's lawyers) would have made the accusation of collusion almost impossible to refute. Worse, Ernest Simpson again wanted to speak to the Prime Minister personally – presumably to negotiate some adequate reward for his assistance. It was hard to imagine any more squalid and compromising conversation and the law officers were at pains that Ernest should be held at the greatest distance possible. A successful intervention might leave the King on the throne, but the scandal of an apparent deal between the Prime Minister and a near pimp was beyond any price that could be contemplated. Sir Maurice Gwyer's assessment of what Ernest Simpson was up to was correct. That day Ernest had also sent a message to Clive Wigram, Hardinge's predecessor as private secretary to the King, offering to wreck the divorce by giving evidence that the divorce was a collusion between the couple and the King.[16] Wigram was just as horrified as the government law officers, but for a rather different reason. He knew his former master well enough to predict that if the divorce collapsed, the King or ex-King would simply cohabit with Mrs Simpson.

Once the decision had been taken to send Goddard to Cannes as an informal agent of the government, he was taken to lunch at Windham's Club by Monckton in order to meet Wilson. This seems to have been the first time that Wilson and Goddard met in person; Fisher, who had handled the earlier contact directly, was ill. Wilson was suitably impressed by the strength of Goddard's dislike of his client. Wilson shared Fisher's resentment that she had failed to 'fade away' after the decree nisi. He was a man whom Wilson was prepared to trust, but he was also enough of a negotiator to have spotted a way in which his client's material interests and the government's aims might coincide. At this stage in the proceedings it was common ground between Goddard and Wilson that he was going to Cannes to find an opportunity to 'induce her to give up the King'.[17] Wilson was unused to the workings of the rougher end of such negotiations and it took him some time to understand that Goddard was asking him 'what price could be paid to Mrs. Simpson for clearing out?'[18] It was certainly not the kind of question with which senior civil servants often find themselves dealing: 'This was rather a facer for me as the point had not occurred to me before and nowhere in my experience could I find any help.' After a brief reflection, Wilson recovered his poise with the decision that the gravity of the crisis merited all-out pragmatism, that this was not the moment for extreme civil service fastidiousness. He told Goddard that he could open negotiations by asking her price. Wilson left Goddard with discretion to tell her if she was opening her mouth too wide, 'to say anything that he thought proper as to the reasonableness or otherwise of what she thought might be done'. If the terms were not too stiff Goddard should identify and approach the 'proper part[y]' with whom to discuss any demands that she might come up with. Wilson had gone far enough by accepting the idea that Mrs Simpson might be bribed and did not want to get involved in actually paying the bribe. Whether Mrs Simpson could be paid off was not a question of ethics but one of practicalities, notably finding a suitably indirect and totally deniable conduit.

Had Goddard simply set off for Cannes after lunch with Wilson, the job would have been complicated enough, but for reasons that remain obscure he went on to Fort Belvedere with Monckton to see the King. According to Wilson's notes, this had already been planned before the lunch, but according to the Duke of Windsor's published memoirs, Goddard arrived unheralded with 'a vague plan for going to Cannes to talk to her'.[19] In one draft of the memoir, though, the Duke of Windsor claimed to have found out about the plan somehow and had summoned Goddard to Fort Belvedere to forbid him from going.[20] Goddard did not mention that he had been talking to the government. The most likely reason that Goddard saw the King was to find out what he was thinking, both in his capacity as Mrs Simpson's solicitor and information-gatherer for the government. All that has survived of their conversation is that he told the King of his plan and that the King told him directly that he would not allow it. The King, of course, had no legal authority whatsoever for this, but Goddard felt, or claimed to have felt, that this placed him in a quandary. As well as whatever task that he was to perform on the government's behalf, he was beginning to feel that he ought to advise his client on the comparatively mundane question of her divorce proceedings. He had already picked up rumours of imminent intervention and Wilson had hinted to him that these were accurate. As her solicitor, it would unarguably be his professional duty to advise her on what to do if intervention were made or a very strong probability, although it is debatable whether this would have required a face-to-face conversation.

Goddard and Monckton were still at Fort Belvedere when a phone call from Cannes added yet another and entirely unexpected ball for everyone to juggle with. Mrs Simpson told the King that she was just about to release a statement to the press and wanted the King's approval. It was carefully phrased and ambiguous, but most readers would have taken it to mean that she was willing to give up the King:

> Mrs. Simpson throughout the last few weeks, has invariably wished to avoid any action or proposal which would hurt or damage His Majesty or the Throne.
>
> To-day her attitude is unchanged and she is willing, if such action would solve the problem, to withdraw forthwith from a situation that has been rendered both unhappy and untenable.

The statement came as a surprise to almost everyone, but it was the outcome of two separate and potent forces. Brownlow had been trying to persuade Mrs Simpson to renounce the King from the start of their journey and he had continued to do so as their friendship deepened over the course of their adventures in France. By the Saturday night he had made enough progress to send the telegram to Beaverbrook that briefly spurred his optimism. In Brownlow's eyes, the statement was a step in the right direction, albeit far from decisive.[21] He was motivated by genuine loyalty to the King, by what he had promised Beaverbrook and, possibly, because he believed that Mrs Simpson did not want to marry the King. On her side, Mrs Simpson was trapped between conflicting forces and under such stress that she was barely thinking. She repeatedly tried to prevent the King from abdicating. She feared that she would be blamed publicly if the King actually abdicated.[22] She had already recoiled from press coverage of her relationship with him and she knew that this would intensify massively if he gave up the throne to marry her. Everything suggests that Mrs Simpson would in fact have been willing to forsake the King. Her dominant motive was self-interest. She was alert to the material and prestige advantages of being a King's mistress, but it was far from clear how many of these would be available to an ex-King's wife. Marriage to an unstable, possessive obsessive – whom she did not love – might also have been an unappealing proposition, and there is no evidence that she would have been emotionally distressed if he had abandoned her.

She may also have predicted, however dimly, something that was to nag her through their marriage, 'that by marrying her he had become a less important person'.[23] Getting him to focus on the advantages of remaining King would have offered an elegant solution to this conundrum, but to a far greater extent than anyone else she knew how reluctant the King would be to give her up.

Mrs Simpson read the statement to the King, who recognised its true purpose: publicly to place responsibility for events onto the King's shoulders.[24] He entirely approved of this. It was true and it would be a relief to Mrs Simpson. However, he was naive in thinking that anyone else would believe this and blind not to understand that Mrs Simpson might actually be happy to withdraw. His approval of the statement was evident to everyone at the Fort, although it is not clear whether this was because he was having to shout so loud that it was practically impossible not to overhear him. The combination of Mrs Simpson's statement with the King's attempt to block Goddard's journey to Cannes offered ample material to be discussed at the highest level, and the three lawyers – Allen had joined the group – set off for Downing Street.

The crisis was still in full swing in Downing Street, Fort Belvedere, Villa Lou Viei, the lawyers' offices and in the inmost thoughts of the King and Mrs Simpson, but whilst Goddard had been at Fort Belvedere, the threat of an imminent constitutional crisis had practically vanished. Baldwin's statement to the House of Commons at 4 p.m. had been received with vigorous cheers. The Prime Minister had read the situation correctly and Parliament was very happy to endorse the conclusions he had drawn. The public mood had swung against the King. MPs, especially those who had returned to rural constituencies for the weekend, would have been exposed to the conservative instincts of people outside London. By contrast, Churchill had totally misread the mood of the House. He had not been talking to country station-masters or tenant farmers but to a Tory 'die-hard'. The die-hards had fought bitterly against Dominion status for India, with Churchill as their ally. More out of dislike of Baldwin than love of Edward VIII, they had decided to fight to keep him on the throne. They had lobbied Churchill for his support and Boothby suspected that one of them had egged Churchill on to a disastrous intervention in the House of Commons.[25] Churchill figuratively tore up the vaguely statesmanlike scheme decided at Chartwell the previous day, and once Baldwin had resumed his seat, he rose to repeat his demand of the previous week that no 'irrevocable action' should be taken. Neither the King nor Beaverbrook had seen fit to tell him the truth and he was still wrapped up in some romantic vision of defending his sovereign to the last. And it proved to be almost the last for Churchill. Yet again he fell victim to his own headstrong and unreflecting approach. He persisted in the face of a hostile House and was shouted down when he tried to follow up his initial question. MPs from both sides of the House yelled 'twister' at him, a legacy of the distrust he had earned by crossing the floor twice. He was called to order by the Speaker for attempting to make a speech at Question Time, a poignant blow for a politician who respected Parliament and its traditions deeply. Bitterness and frustration overwhelmed him and he shouted at Baldwin, 'You won't be satisfied until you've broken him.'[26]

The vast bulk of MPs were happy to see Churchill humiliated, but even Bob Boothby, one of the tiny band who kept their loyalty to him through thick and thin, was struck by bitterness that Churchill had casually tossed aside the approach that he and Sinclair had agreed with him the day before. Boothby could not resist a venomous but telling analysis:

> Now when a dog does that [glance around furtively], you know that he is about to be sick on the carpet. It is the same with Winston. He managed to hold it for three days, and then comes up to the House and is sick right across the floor.[27]

The King's Party was dead and buried, and with it, almost, Churchill's political career. Churchill had suffered many rebuffs at the hands of the House of Commons in the course of a long and bruising career, but this has a strong claim to having been his worst. Immediately afterwards, J. C. C. Davidson was reading the ticker tape in one of the corridors when Churchill joined him and said that his political career was finished. Days later he was still profoundly depressed by what had happened.[28] All the effort that he had devoted to rebuilding his credibility around the 'Arms and the Covenant' campaign to counter Nazi rearmament had been destroyed: he had 'undone in five minutes the patient reconstruction work of two years'.[29] Curiously, it was one of his most dedicated critics through the crisis, Nancy Dugdale, who saw through the immediate setback and recognised his resilience, observing shrewdly, but not necessarily charitably, that he had received 'a rebuff from which only a ferro-concrete man would recover' and that 'It is astounding you cannot kill Winston with any known political axe'.[30]

In their sudden enthusiasm for persuading Mrs Simpson to renounce the King, the men at Downing Street might be forgiven for not spotting the significance of something else that Monday. By perverse coincidence they had started thinking about persuading the King not to abdicate just at the moment when he was finally sending a signal that he had reached a firm decision to go. The King's side had begun to talk about money, which had barely been mentioned before. The King had raised the question with his personal banker, Sir Edward Peacock, that morning, having told him that he would abdicate the evening before. He was 'anxious as to financial arrangements' and it was this, as much as getting certainty for Mrs Simpson's divorce, which Peacock and Monckton came to Downing Street to discuss. Here the ministers were able to give the King's emissaries much more comfort than on the question of divorce, although a sceptic might observe that politicians are always happy to offer money in principle, but become rather more elusive on precise terms. 'Both cordially agreed to the principle of making provision for the King but they could not name a figure.'[31] Even Chamberlain was prepared to be as generous as he ever got: 'we would certainly do what we could.'[32] Even to a Chancellor of the Exchequer almost obsessed with keeping a tight control on public finances, it might have seemed an acceptable price to pay for removing so unsuitable a monarch.

The money question had retreated into the background when the little convoy of lawyers arrived at Downing Street that afternoon at almost the same moment that Mrs Simpson's statement appeared on the newswires.

Goddard told Wilson what had happened between him and the King and explained how this placed him in the dilemma of reconciling his professional duty with royal command. Wilson went upstairs to pass this onto to the Prime Minister together with the text of Mrs Simpson's statement. Whilst Wilson was away, Goddard got on the phone to his legal colleagues, who confirmed to him that intervention was a near certainty which made it all the more urgent that he advise Mrs Simpson. After talking to Wilson, Baldwin decided that he should take the unprecedented step of speaking directly to Mrs Simpson's representative, and Goddard was thus shown upstairs. Baldwin was especially anxious to get an explanation for Mrs Simpson's statement, which seemed to be quite at variance with the King's continued commitment to marrying Mrs Simpson. Baldwin faced another layer of uncertainty created by the growing threat to the Simpson divorce, not knowing how she and the King would react if the case were blocked. Goddard might be able to help the government here.

Goddard's interview with the Prime Minister features as one of the comic moments of the crisis in both the recollections of Dugdale and the more or less light-hearted account that Baldwin gave to his niece a year later. Both accounts emphasised how out of place Goddard not only felt himself to be, and was perceived to be in such august surroundings and company. Baldwin described him as 'a big, burly chap with a large face, "plain and pale like a ham" ... And he looked more like a ham than anything that I have seen that was <u>not</u> a ham.'[33] It was the epitome of the small tenant farmer interviewed by the lord of the manor, nervously twisting the brim of his hat in his hands. Beneath the Wodehousian drollery lay a deeper truth: in social terms both Goddard and his client had come from another world. Snobbism was as potent a reason for looking down on Mrs Simpson as moral disapproval. Goddard's opening remark was painfully class-conscious: 'I hope you won't think me a Bolshie, Sir.'[34] This threw Baldwin and he spent the rest of the conversation working out what it meant. Goddard was afraid to be seen as having spoken out of turn and he was also keen not to be tarred with the same brush as his client, whose untrustworthiness was tantamount to outright sedition. It was much easier to deal with Goddard's reluctance to disobey royal command than to help him cross the social minefield. Baldwin told him directly that his own duty as a solicitor took precedence over his sovereign's wishes. It was the same advice that Goddard would have been given by anyone familiar with professional ethics, but in practice Baldwin's approval lent an aura of official sanction to the mission.

Wilson and Dugdale set to the task of finding an aeroplane for Goddard to make the flight to Cannes. At that time of night, this proved to be difficult and the chief civil servant at the Air Ministry was brought in to help. Reading between the lines, Downing Street hoped that it would be possible to use a commercial charter, which would have implicated the government far less in the arrangements. Exactly which aeroplane was used remains one of the minor mysteries of the crisis. Dugdale specified that it was a private aeroplane, but Goddard later described it as 'a small Government machine'. Perhaps he was anxious to emphasise the official aspect to his journey, but he might merely have assumed that because the government had made the arrangement, it was one of their own machines.[35] Beaverbrook also referred to it as a government plane and he too had personal motives for presenting Goddard as the Prime Minister's envoy.[36] However, apart from RAF military machines, there is no evidence that the British government had any aircraft at its disposal at the time. Downing Street signed off one feature of Goddard's mission, which soon acquired an equivocal but farcical element: Goddard was to be accompanied by his personal doctor. Supposedly, Goddard, who like many people in those days had never flown before, was sufficiently concerned at the medical consequences of a flight. Unknown to Downing Street, Dr Kirkwood also had something of a reputation as an obstetrician, which was soon to be the source of much comment. One of Goddard's legal clerks completed the party. Early the following morning – Tuesday 8 December – Goddard set off for Cannes with an ample stock of things to do and discuss with his client.

Downing Street were happy to see Goddard on his way, but it is far harder to reconstruct what precisely they hoped that his mission would bring. Everyone seemed to have a rather different view of the affair. Perhaps the simplest motivation was the strongest: to find out what Mrs Simpson was up to in Cannes. Wilson and Dugdale 'were anxious to find out the latest game which Mrs. Simpson was playing'.[37] The planes scare of Saturday night was fresh in everyone's mind and Downing Street would have wanted advance warning of any repetition. Since then Mrs Simpson had been putting pressure on the King not to abdicate, which increased the risk that he might simply leave the country. It was certainly Goddard's intelligence-gathering task that stuck most firmly in the mind of Perry Brownlow, who had to handle him when he arrived in Cannes: 'I have always understood and still believe that he was sent by Horace Wilson or Baldwin as a "Cloak and Dagger agent" to find out what [Mrs Simpson's] statement of Monday night to the press really meant.'[38] Moreover, the Downing Street staffers do not seem to have entertained very great hopes that any of Goddard's other objectives would be realised. The idea that Mrs Simpson might renounce the King features in Wilson's accounts solely in the context of Goddard's thought that she might be bribed to do so. To Dugdale, the questions of intervention and the Cannes statement were merely pretexts that could be fed to the King to explain why his wishes had been disregarded.[39] By contrast, Monckton believed that 'it was agreed that he should fly out and pressure his client, Mrs. S., in that direction [to give up the King]'.[40] Goddard felt that he had been working as much for the government as Mrs Simpson and actually proposed to charge the Treasury 500 guineas for his work, although the payment seems to have been laundered through Allen's firm.[41] This provides an interesting sidelight on the professed patriotism of Goddard's conduct and on his loyalty to his original client.

As if all this does not leave sufficient confusion over the origins and motives of Goddard's journey to Cannes, other accounts supplied even less reliable versions. Baldwin told his niece that Goddard was concerned that Mrs Simpson was talking to the press without reference to him, for which no other evidence exists.[42] Beaverbrook supported the explanation that Goddard tried to persuade Mrs Simpson to renounce the King, but managed to confect an explanation for this that was discreditable to Baldwin: if Mrs Simpson renounced the King, this would get Baldwin off the hook of his (supposed) promise to resign if the Two Bills scheme were rejected.[43]

CHAPTER 18

MISSION TO A MADHOUSE

*S.B. went to the Fort this afternoon and returned about 11. As he went
straight to bed I have not seen him (I was at the House until after 11) but
J. Simon came into my room at No 11 about 11.30 and told me that he
had had a very hard time saying that he had been in a madhouse.*

NEVILLE CHAMBERLAIN, DIARY, 8 DECEMBER 1936

THE DECISION TO endorse Goddard's mission to Cannes presented the government with ticklish problems, not so much about
the basic principle but about the potential ramifications. All manner
of unwelcome constructions might be placed on what Goddard was up to;
in particular, it might be argued that a royal command had been breached.
Admittedly, the King had had no legal right to tell Goddard that he should
not go to Cannes. As a solicitor, it was Goddard's duty to advise his client
on an important development in a legal action in which he was representing her. There was no legal or ethical reason why the government should
not approach Mrs Simpson and reason or negotiate with her directly. To
this extent, Downing Street could approach things with an entirely clear
conscience, but after his conversation with the Prime Minister and the
logistical help from the Air Ministry, Goddard was undeniably linked to

the government. It was, of course, inevitable that the King would learn that his wishes had been defied with the government's approval. He would have to be told, although it is unclear whether Downing Street recognised this rather obvious fact as soon as they despatched Goddard. No one imagined that he would be happy to learn about Goddard, but he would be even more aggrieved to hear about it from Mrs Simpson in Cannes.

Downing Street's first idea had been to tell the King about Goddard's journey at the very last moment, but this was changed.[1] It was only when Wilson together with the government's top law officers, Somervell and Gwyer, were reviewing legal points with Peacock on the Tuesday morning that a definite decision was taken as to how and what the King should be told. A short conclave of Baldwin, Chamberlain and Simon decided that Goddard was to be given discretion to disclose to Mrs Simpson that he had discussed his mission to Cannes with the Prime Minister before leaving, that in practice the Prime Minister had authorised him to ignore the King's wishes.[2] He could explain that the news of impending intervention imposed a professional duty on him to advise her and, for less obvious reasons, that her statement to the press made the matter urgent. What Downing Street was keen to avoid was any suggestion that Goddard might have been sent to Cannes with some message directly from the government. A telegram was duly despatched to reach Goddard en route giving him these extra instructions.[3]

The man who was deputed to perform the job of telling the King about Goddard's journey was George Allen, the King's personal solicitor. Allen is a far less prominent figure in the various accounts of the crisis than Monckton, but he was also a key adviser to the King. In the final phase of the crisis, Allen and the King's banker, Sir Edward Peacock, came to the fore as the dialogue shifted to the negotiation of terms. Dugdale's snapshot of Allen's persona gives another small hint as to why Allen should have been chosen to bear the message rather than Monckton. He was 'Tough No. 1' in a group of hard men who had foregathered at Downing Street the previous evening to handle the affair, 'Tough No. 2' being Peacock and 'Tough No. 3' Goddard.[4] Allen was a hard-nosed City lawyer who was in the process of building one of London's most successful and high-profile firms of solicitors. The emollient Monckton was almost universally liked, whereas Allen was a man to respect, if not to fear.

Allen also had a far more sensitive message to take to the King. It was at least as important as the news of Goddard's journey and probably far more. It was also much more delicate and potentially immensely compromising to the government. By some measures it could be read as applying pressure on the King. He was taking to the King a copy of a letter explaining a radical change in the way the government assessed the risk of intervention in Mrs Simpson's divorce. The week before, it had been an abstract and unquantifiable possibility, albeit with a heavily veiled threat that it lay within the government's power to make it happen. The previous Thursday, Sir John Simon, who as a distinguished lawyer had rather hijacked the role of giving the Prime Minister legal advice from any of the government's formal law officers, had taken a sanguine view on both the risk from the official and the private legal fronts. He was 'as an old Attorney General ... quite satisfied that intervention by the Attorney General in the present circumstance would not take place at any rate unless some new and glaring evidence of collusion was forthcoming hereafter'.[5] As to the risk of one of the Prime Minister's hypothetical busybodies: 'I do not think that it is likely that anybody would undertake such a burden or that he would succeed if he tried, but, as I have said, the risk is immensely reduced if the King became a private person.' If the King abdicated, the risk was 'negligible'.

By the Tuesday, Simon had changed his opinion on every point. Intervention had become not only a near certainty, but was also seen as almost sure of succeeding.

> I have now reason to believe that intervention with a view to stopping the divorce, prompted by private persons whose action cannot be controlled, is far from being unlikely. This would be independent of the King's Proctor, but it seems to me that if this material [new evidence of collusion] was brought by these informants to the notice of the King's

Proctor, he might well find it necessary to intervene for the purpose of preventing Mrs. Simpson from getting her divorce.

<u>And I wish most particularly to point out that this intervention would not be avoided by the summary abdication of the King</u>. Indeed, so far as the King's Proctor is concerned, he might well feel that his duty to intervene would be strengthened if the only matter to be considered was collusion between Mr. & Mrs. Simpson and that the Throne had passed to a new occupant.[6]

The previous week, Simon had addressed only the risk that the King might be accused of adultery with Mrs Simpson, but now he had to accept that the divorce might also be challenged on the grounds of collusion. Even more radically, Simon had abandoned the cosy and never very convincing fantasy that abdication would eliminate the risk that some 'busybody' would intervene.

Simon did not explain his volte-face in his letter. The only explanation in the record comes from Wilson and it is minimal and heavily understated: '...further information reached him that the position had somewhat changed.'[7] The 'further information' was probably a combination of the letters to the King's Proctor, notably the one offering evidence of collusion, and the appearance of Ernest Simpson, who could probably supply unarguable testimony that there had been collusion. Simon had also misread the dynamics working on the government's law officers. His blithe confidence of the week before that no Attorney General would rock the boat by now appeared to have been misplaced. His current successor in that office, Sir Donald Somervell, whom Barnes and Gwyer had briefed on the letters demanding action from the King's Proctor, 'disclosed great anxiety as to intervention' on the Tuesday morning.[8] The legal calculus was different. When the possibility of intervention had first been mooted weeks before, Somervell had accepted that accusations against the King could not be heard in court, although he had qualified this as a 'debatable point'.[9] More important, 'at that time the only suggestion [as grounds for intervention] was of possible adultery between the King and Mrs. Simpson'.

This point was irrelevant to any accusation of collusion between Ernest and Wallis Simpson, which would be admissible in court as with any other divorcing couple, and this was precisely what the 'reputable' solicitors were claiming. Finally, Somervell was a relatively late entrant to politics and remained far more of a lawyer than Simon. He resented the fact that Simon had supplanted him as the government's legal adviser and may have decided that it was safer for him to adopt the most conservative position possible. He showed great sympathy when his subordinate, the King's Proctor Sir Thomas Barnes, found his professional conscience impelling him to investigate the Simpson divorce.

This climb-down was too embarrassing to be labelled as a cynical manoeuvre, but it did serve the government's interests by keeping alive the threat of intervention to use as a lever to work on the King. Simon could already see how this threat might be deployed. The King had to accept the possibility that he might be abdicating for nothing: 'His Majesty in my judgement must face the fact that whatever may be his decision as to abdication this course does not hold out any increasing prospect of his being able to marry the lady.' On the face of it this was direct advice (though not in the formal constitutional sense) to remain on the throne and abandon hope of marriage. Simon's letter was the springboard for one last attempt to head the King away from abdication.

The message that Allen took with him to Fort Belvedere was simple and brutal. The threat of intervention was now so strong that it could not be ignored and it was likely to change the entire situation. It explained why Goddard had set off for Cannes in spite of the King's express wishes. In practice, Goddard was bearing the same message to Mrs Simpson that Allen was bringing to the King. The King himself had to be aware that he would be deprived of the possibility of marrying Mrs Simpson. Both were being told indirectly to abandon the idea of marriage. If Downing Street expected this to produce an instant change of heart in the King, it was sadly mistaken. Just as he had recognised that Hardinge's letter had come ultimately from the Prime Minister, the King understood that Allen's message came from Downing Street, and he reacted with similar fury. He paid no attention to the hard, practical question of intervention. All he saw was that Mrs Simpson was being pressured to abandon him and this had to stop. His immediate reaction was to call the Villa Lou Viei and to tell Mrs Simpson to pay a minimum of attention to Goddard, if she saw him at all. Neither on his own nor on Mrs Simpson's behalf did he go into the question of intervention in any detail.

The threat of intervention drove Baldwin to make a final, last-ditch attempt to persuade the King not to abdicate. Almost alone of the men in Downing Street, he understood the depth of the King's desire to marry Mrs Simpson and feared that he would be utterly thrown if her divorce collapsed. Baldwin decided to go to Fort Belvedere with a dramatic vision of having to reason with a King who was 'sadly upset' or 'in an excited state' and was willing to spend the night in the effort.[10] Baldwin relished the drama of his mission: 'Have my bag packed quickly. The King will be going through hell tonight, and I am going with him.'[11] The agonising debate with the King imagined by Baldwin never took place, although something weirder and arguably more unsettling occurred. The evening at Fort Belvedere that followed had the feel of a drawing-room comedy, but comedy haunted by irresponsibility that verged on madness, and foreboding at what it would bring.

Baldwin's moment of doomed self-dramatisation sparked the evening's first moment of farce. When they arrived at Fort Belvedere, Dugdale, who had accompanied the Prime Minister, brought the overnight bag straight in from their car and left it, rather tactlessly, in the middle of the hallway to the horror of the King, who recognised what it implied. Even at the best of times he found talking to Baldwin irksome and his habit of cracking his finger joints grated on his nerves. The prospect of his Prime Minister as a self-invited house-guest was appalling. He was near exhaustion from stress as well and not in the mood for company of any kind. He had only agreed to Baldwin coming out of courtesy as he had decided firmly to abdicate come what may and saw no point in talking about it anymore.[12] He also detected some of the self-dramatisation that was working in Baldwin, to which he ascribed a venomously cynical explanation: his Prime Minister was already preparing the speech that he would have to make in Parliament to explain the King's abdication and was calculating that the image of him pleading through the night with his sovereign to reconsider would be a suitably colourful and moving adornment.[13] The King quietly took Peacock aside and confirmed his suspicion that Baldwin did indeed propose to stay the night. The banker offered to get rid of the Prime Minister, but the King remembered his royal manners: 'I could not do that. The Prime Minister has been so kind as to come here to help me, I could not let him leave without giving him dinner. He must stay.'[14] It was agreed that he should have dinner and then return to Downing Street.

Baldwin knew quickly that his mission to Fort Belvedere was doomed. The King was utterly committed to marrying Mrs Simpson. Just as he had arrived, the King had come off the phone to Mrs Simpson. He entered the room

> gesticulating with his arms above his head. 'She is the most wonderful woman, I have the most wonderful woman in the world behind me in this, she does not mind, it will simply draw us nearer together. I mean to go & leave the way clear for my brother.'[15]

According to Baldwin's later account, the King 'had the most beautiful look I have ever seen on his face, like a young knight who has just seen the Holy Grail … It was hopeless to reason with him.'[16] All that was left was to go through the motions. Both men were in a state of near exhaustion during their final audience at which Monckton was also present. Baldwin delivered yet again his plea to the King to reconsider his decision, but the King refused and told him bluntly to stop trying. Baldwin's tiredness exacerbated his deafness so he did not hear what the King told him and repeated his plea with even greater vigour and eloquence.[17] It had no effect. The King told Baldwin directly that if Mrs Simpson's divorce was blocked, he would go and that they were closer together as a couple than ever before.[18]

Baldwin had one other task to perform at Fort Belvedere, although he might not have been aware of it when he set off. It arose from a question that was looming large in Downing Street. The King's resilience to the threat of intervention created a horrible possibility: that he might simply ignore all convention and decency by abdicating and simply cohabiting with Mrs Simpson. It would have been immensely scandalous, and to try to stop it happening, Downing Street deployed the oldest tool in the book: money. The hardliners saw that the threat of withholding money from the ex-King offered a lever to prevent this and felt no qualms about using it. Before he left Downing Street, Dugdale had been briefed by Wilson that the King should not be promised any money if he decided to abdicate.[19] This would keep open the possibility of using money as a lever to prevent him cohabiting with Mrs Simpson. Getting the Prime Minister to deliver this message made for the next episode of farce. Immediately after the audience, he and the King re-joined the Duke of Kent and Dugdale for a brief conversation before dinner. The Duke had been entertaining Dugdale to a sustained rant against the iniquities of Mrs Simpson, prefaced by his amazement that none of his brother's forty-five million subjects had killed her.[20] Dugdale tried to manoeuvre the Prime Minister to one side to pass on quietly what Wilson had told him before leaving Downing Street, that he was not to promise the King any money. If he did, the government would have little left to force the ex-King to respect the decencies. Here again Baldwin's deafness sabotaged the plan and Dugdale practically had to shout to make himself understood, but finally Baldwin heard. His immediate reaction was an affronted – 'But you can't let him starve' – but he did not, in the event, make any commitment.[21]

None of the men around the table that night would ever forget the dinner that ensued. It began in an atmosphere of impending doom. Before sitting down, Baldwin had talked to the Dukes of York and Kent. Both were convinced that their brother was making a catastrophic mistake, 'that this affair could end in nothing but misery and disaster', but they knew they were powerless to stop him.[22] It was only through a last, almost superhuman effort by the King that the dinner did not degenerate into a wake. Monckton had seen just how exhausted the King was and tried to persuade him to eat alone in his room, but the King insisted that he would be the host.[23] He displayed thespian talents fully the equal of his Prime Minister, making

his entry in the persona of an ageing juvenile lead with a breezy apology
for having taken so long for his bath: 'Just a tub. Sorry to be so long. Have
a drink. I'm afraid I'm not much of a host tonight.'[24] Whilst everyone else
at table was weighed down by the gravity of the events, the King acted the
life and soul of the party, talking as though it was merely the most ordinary
of social events. He talked about his travels as Prince of Wales, in particular
his visit to Latin America.[25] He succeeded in avoiding any reference to the
reason why they were all at Fort Belvedere. It was probably the only heavyweight dinner party anywhere in Britain that evening at which the crisis
was not mentioned. It was a bravura performance and deeply impressed the
Duke of York, who was in despair at what was happening and oppressed
by fears of his own inadequacy to succeed his brother. Half in admiration,
half in despairing hope that he himself would be saved from the test, he
repeated 'isn't my brother wonderful, isn't he wonderful?' and whispered to
Monckton 'Look at him. We simply cannot let him go.'[26]

But the hope was futile as everyone knew, and the King's effort was show-
manship and nothing more. Like an actor seeking confirmation that he had
delivered what he already knew to be a triumph, the King asked Peacock
when the others had gone, 'How was that?' Peacock assured him, 'Grand,
Sir. An amazing effort...' and told him to go to bed.[27] Ever afterwards the
Duke of Windsor was happy at the effect that he thought he had made on
his Prime Minister as an 'unbowed, unresentful if somewhat whimsical Sovereign'.[28] He imagined that this was confirmed by Baldwin's description of
him to the following morning's Cabinet as like a young man happily looking
forward to his wedding and honeymoon. He was deluding himself entirely.
In trying to convince the Prime Minister that he did not care about what was
happening, he had created the impression that he was not even aware of it.
The first thing that Baldwin said to his wife when he returned to Downing
Street was, 'Well I feel as though I have been in Bedlam, the King doesn't
seem in the least put out, he just wants Mrs. Simpson & doesn't seem to
grasp the gravity of the whole affair'.[29] He told Simon the same thing.[30]

The dinner was all the more unsettling because of the contrast between
the departing King and his successor. Dugdale was depressed by what he

saw as the dullness of the Duke of York, which appeared in stark contrast to the effervescence of his older brother. He failed to grasp the depression into which the whole affair had thrust the younger brother, and his apprehension of what awaited him. Baldwin could see through the superficial discrepancy between the King's meretricious skills and his brother's more solid but unspectacular talents. It was a perception that he had already shared with Duff Cooper three weeks before when abdication had first appeared as the most likely outcome. Baldwin drew the comparison between the Duke of York and his father who was 'most uninspired and dull, only by perseverance, reliability, example to his people, and a sense of duty did he gain for himself the much loved position he held when he died.'[31] History was to prove Baldwin quite right, but others shared Dugdale's initial pessimism. Baldwin's perception of the true abilities of the man who would succeed Edward was one of the many factors that he had to balance through the crisis, in this case a positive one. His certainty that Edward VIII's successor would be up to the task was a deeply hidden aspect of his calculation of what abdication might mean for the country. Beaverbrook's claim that Baldwin conspired to replace Edward with his brother from the start is absurd and tells us more about Beaverbrook's twisted mind than anything, but the prospect of the Duke of York succeeding was the silver lining in a dark cloud. His success as George VI was the consolation prize for the crisis.

By the end of dinner, Baldwin knew that further discussion was futile and got ready to return to Downing Street. His hastily packed suitcase was retrieved from behind the front door, unneeded. He took the King aside for final, definitive confirmation that his decision to abdicate was irrevocable in terms that suggested that the strain of the dinner had not weakened his sense of the dramatic: 'I suppose if an Archangel asked you to give up Mrs. Simpson it would have no effect?'[32] The King's reply, 'Not in the least', put an end to any possible doubt in Baldwin's mind that he was entirely determined to go. It was the moment that he knew for certain that he had steered the affair to the happiest outcome it might have had. The sense of drama and of his own contribution to great events with which he had begun the journey to Fort Belvedere had not left him. As they were setting off, he told

Dugdale: 'This is making history. This is what I like.'[33] Baldwin knew that he could end his political career on a high note. Baldwin knew that the point of no return had been reached and that he had done all that he could have done. The only important decision that there had ever been to be taken, had been taken. Baldwin had patiently shepherded the King to the point, fending off his colleagues' attempts to hurry the process along. The King was utterly determined to go and his Prime Minister knew it. He knew better than his colleagues and the woman for whom the King was leaving the throne. At the other end of Europe, Mrs Simpson had yet to travel the final few inches to recognising that there could be no going back whatever. The combined accidents of poor communications and the redundant determination of two men with quite different motives to fight to the last were to keep the public appearance of crisis alive for another day.

CHAPTER 19

BEYOND RECOVERY

He [Stanley Baldwin] himself ... had now the gravest doubts as to whether in any circumstances, even if the King threw the lady over and whatever steps were taken, such as an interval for a rest-cure to restore his perspective on the matter, the King could recover his position or whether his own successor as Prime Minister would not later be confronted with equally difficult situations. He deeply regretted this. He knew and admired the King's fine qualities, but doubted if, even so, he could recover his position.

MINUTES OF CABINET MEETING ON 9 DECEMBER 1936

G ODDARD'S MISSION TO Cannes had an inauspicious beginning. The party experienced a nightmare journey and was lucky
to arrive safely at all. The weather was atrocious. Another British plane crashed in the area and Downing Street thought at first that their
emissary had gone with it.[1] Goddard's plane suffered an engine failure and
had to land at Marseilles from where he continued to Cannes by road. If he
had genuinely brought Kirkwood along with him for medical assistance, he
would not have regretted his decision. By the time he arrived, it was late at
night and he checked into his hotel in the hope of a night's rest before he

saw his client the following morning, but his arrival in the south of France had an almost instant impact.

Somewhere along the way the news of the mission had leaked out and had done so in a way that might have been calculated to draw the maximum attention to it. Much points to Goddard having been intentionally responsible. After a frantic evening of discussions and phone calls, Brownlow was about to go to bed at 2.30 a.m. when one of the accompanying detectives brought him a message from four of the British journalists amongst the vast press pack besieging the Villa Lou Viei. It told Brownlow that Goddard had arrived and, far worse, said that he was accompanied by 'Dr. Kirkwood, the well-known gynaecologist and his Anaesthetist'.[2] The American papers had received the same information, but the British journalists wanted a comment before they filed the story. To add to all their other problems, it now looked as though Mrs Simpson's party would find themselves fending off a story that she was pregnant. Goddard himself was probably the source of the story, given the detail that the journalists had. Goddard's landing at Marseilles was not scheduled but the journalists knew that it was where he had arrived. Moreover, it stretches credulity that any stray press informant, even at a prestigious Côte d'Azur hotel, would have recognised Goddard and, still less, Kirkwood, or known of the latter's professional specialisation. The whole episode very soon sparked the suspicion that it had been stage-managed by Goddard. At Downing Street, Dugdale surmised that Goddard had chosen Dr Kirkwood as his travelling companion with the intention of creating the rumours.[3] In Cannes, Brownlow stopped short of accusing Goddard directly of intentional manipulation, but his furious reaction implies that he thought this or something near to it. Brownlow labelled Goddard's conduct as grounds for 'indignation and mortification'. At its kindest, he saw Goddard as guilty of foolish indiscretion. He labelled the episode as the 'last straw' and felt that it threatened to undo everything that he and Herman Rogers, Mrs Simpson's friend and owner of the villa in Cannes, had done 'to protect [Mrs Simpson's] dignity, good name and peace of mind, and obviously the prestige of the King'.[4]

Brownlow instantly issued a denial of the journalists' story with the improbable fiction that Goddard had come out merely to deal with mundane topics such as the lease on her house in London. He was still furious when he telephoned Goddard at the hotel the following morning. He was determined to kill any idea that there was any medical reason for his visit at all and was not troubled to impose draconian conditions on Goddard to achieve this. He seems to have positively relished dictating these to Goddard. He was to come to the Villa Lou Viei by taxi on his own and to walk the last 100 yards to the gates carrying nothing in his hands, thus walking the gauntlet of the journalists who could verify his identity and that he was merely a solicitor, unequipped for any surgical purposes.

Even if charity dictates that Goddard is exonerated of manufacturing the rumour of Mrs Simpson's pregnancy, his mission was complex enough when he set off and it was about to become more complex still. Whilst Brownlow was taking steps to prevent anyone from imagining that Goddard and his party had arrived in Cannes to deal with a pregnant Mrs Simpson, ministers in London had come up with yet another task for him to accomplish. Simon had been appalled at the prospect that the King might simply ignore the consequences of intervention and cohabit with Mrs Simpson if the divorce were blocked, and he persuaded Chamberlain late on the Tuesday night that a message should be sent to both threatening not to give the King any money from the Civil List if they did.[5] It was the same message that Dugdale had tried to make Baldwin give the King at Fort Belvedere that evening. They believed that her sole interest in the affair was what money she could make from it and thought that her influence would thus be sufficient to prevent this happening. A telegram was sent to Goddard at Cannes instructing him not to leave until he had spoken to Wilson, who was to pass on the message from Chamberlain and Simon.[6] Perhaps fortunately it arrived after Goddard had set off for the Villa Lou Viei. He had already been given a bewildering array of jobs.

When Goddard finally began his conversation with Mrs Simpson she was under severe stress and barely taking things in.[7] On top of all the agony of the journey and the press siege, she had been told by the King and by

George Allen that Goddard was coming out to speak to her because of the risk of intervention and 'this had caused her considerable doubts as to the future'.[8] Rather than try to belabour her with the full array of questions and advice with which he was freighted, Goddard focused on the most important message that he had brought. He told her what the mood was in Britain and advised her directly to abandon her divorce.[9] He thought that he succeeded. According to his later account she told him that she 'was willing to do anything that eased the situation' or, in more concrete terms, 'was quite prepared to give him up'.[10] Goddard even wrote out a short statement on Miramar Hotel notepaper in which he said on her behalf that 'she was willing and still is perfectly willing to instruct me to withdraw her petition for divorce and indeed willing to do anything to prevent the King from abdicating' in the belief that she approved of what it said.[11] Goddard was at great pains to persuade Wilson of the importance of the Miramar memorandum, but it was no more substantial than Mrs Simpson's statement of Monday night. Brownlow did not even countersign it. At one level it served again to thrust the apparent responsibility on the King; at another it certified to Downing Street that Goddard had done his utmost and that was probably why he thought it was so important. In reality, his mission had failed on almost every level.

Goddard was guilty of over-optimism, if not worse. Mrs Simpson was not in a state to make a rational decision. Moreover, all that really counted was what the King wanted. Goddard should have understood that she was telling him the absolute truth when she told him, 'Wherever she went the King would follow her'.[12] The matter was settled by a telephone call to Fort Belvedere, which put an end to Goddard's efforts. Just as he had told the Prime Minister the previous night, the King made it clear that he was determined to marry Mrs Simpson and to abdicate. It was enough for Goddard and he decided to come home, but when he called Wilson, having finally received the phone message sent on behalf of Chamberlain and Simon, he was urged to make one last effort. Wilson wanted to be certain that Mrs Simpson was aware of 'all the consequences of a certain decision, including the worst...' and told Goddard that George Allen was trying to reach him to pass on the same message.[13] Wilson appeared to hope that the prospect of the King abdicating and finding Mrs Simpson unable to marry him, might be enough to turn the scales. Goddard did agree to talk to Allen, but whatever they said, it was not enough to alter his assessment of the chances, and he returned to London. The threat of intervention thus vanished from the scene as a factor in deciding whether the King would abdicate or not, but it was far from dead.

At the same time as Goddard was talking to Mrs Simpson in Cannes, the Cabinet met for what was to be its last substantial discussion of the crisis. After his evening at Fort Belvedere with the King, Baldwin knew what was going to happen and that it was just a matter of shepherding his ministers to the obvious and inevitable conclusion. Even if Goddard had succeeded in obtaining Mrs Simpson's instructions to abandon the divorce case and to give up the King, Baldwin knew that it would not have ended the affair. Indeed, as Baldwin saw things, it would probably have made things worse: 'If that meeting would by any chance result in a decision to give the King up, there was every risk that the King would proceed to Cannes by air if he could obtain an aeroplane.'[14] The King's hare-brained scheme for an Alpine holiday now rebounded on him to his double discredit. In Baldwin's eyes, he had now burned all his bridges and was beyond redemption. What the Prime Minister now said to the Cabinet about the King went even further than the hardline position that the Australian Prime Minister Lyons had set out in his message responding to the question of the morganatic proposal. Baldwin told the Cabinet, he

> had the gravest doubts as to whether in any circumstances, even if the King threw the lady over and whatever steps were taken, such as an interval for a rest-cure to restore his perspective on this matter, the King could recover his position or whether his own successor as Prime Minister would not later be confronted with equally difficult situations.[15]

The King could simply no longer be trusted; he had to go and the sooner
the better. It was the closest Baldwin ever got to a verdict on the King as
a man, and it does suggest that nothing had happened to change his view
from the one he had shared with Lascelles in Ottawa almost a decade
before. He had done his utmost to save the King from himself, but finally
the King's own flaws were too great.

As the weeks had worn on, Baldwin had needed to become ever more
careful in his handling of the King. To begin with, Dugdale saw him as a
father dealing with a wayward son, but towards the end it was the analogy
of a doctor with a mental patient that appeared more appropriate.[16] In
the final days, Baldwin did not trouble to conceal his view of the King's
capriciousness and instability, telling a peer that 'It seems to me that I've
got a film star to deal with these days'.[17] To the end he pitied the King
but reserved his hatred for Mrs Simpson, 'who goaded him on to fight'.[18]
He railed against her 'evils'.[19] Downing Street blamed Mrs Simpson for
using her dominance of the King in her own interests:

> It seems clearly to have been her brain that evolved the lines of the cam-
> paign for the marriage and when she retreated to Cannes and was forced
> to realise that public opinion would not stand it, she nevertheless with
> great persistency urged the King to ensure, before his departure, the
> grant of the conditions which – she clearly realised – were essential to
> her eventual return ... to set up a rival Court, to exercise influence...[20]

Baldwin had washed his hands of the King, but he was still acutely aware
of the perils of the situation, in particular the risk of intervention and how
badly it might affect the King: 'he expressed serious apprehensions as to
the effect on the King'.[21] But the time had come to make a hard decision
and Baldwin was prepared to take the risk of the King abdicating and being
unable to make the marriage for which he had left the throne. For all the
abuse that his detractors heaped on Baldwin's willingness to temporise,
he showed here that he could cut the Gordian knot. In a neat reversal of
the internal debates on the crisis, it was Chamberlain who was fixated on

the risks. Chamberlain had an ugly premonition of successful intervention and scandalous cohabitation. Worse, Mrs Simpson might turn up
her nose at whatever payoff the King might be offered and persuade him
to stay on the throne. He was haunted by the same fears of civil unrest
that had dogged Wilson. Having decided that the British public actually
wanted renunciation, he feared it might react with an 'outburst' if it did
not get one. Sir John Simon added another touch of panic when he found
a way of trivialising the risk of intervention that only served to pour oil on
the flames. He let his imagination run riot with the image of Mrs Simpson
obtaining a Reno divorce if she abandoned the British case. Baldwin cut
through all this with the simple statement that 'the King had been most
anxious to sign his Abdication that very day and get it all over'.[22] As he
was leaving Fort Belvedere he had discussed a timetable with the King as
well as hypothesising about celestial intervention.

All that was left was to put things into proper constitutional form. Baldwin went through the motions of asking his colleagues' opinion, but he
knew what he was going to do. They obliged with a welter of abstruse
constitutional points and recondite practicalities. Predictably, Malcolm
MacDonald was well to the fore with a long exploration of how the process was to be synchronised with the Dominions, concluding that matters
would be better kept on an informal basis for the time being. This gave
Baldwin his opportunity to tell the Cabinet firmly that there was now time
pressure and, moreover, that 'he was anxious to avoid another journey to
Fort Belvedere that day, if possible'. After his conversations with the King
the night before, Baldwin had no doubts, but he was also heartily sick of
the road to Sunningdale. Instead, it would be possible to cast 'a written
communication' to the King in a way that avoided upsetting the Dominions. This was the cue for Simon to whip out a letter that he had already
drafted. The lines that mattered had already been scripted, but the ministers were being allowed to adlib for the others. Gently, the Prime Minister
also led the Cabinet to endorse him making a statement to Parliament the
following day. MacDonald had fixed 10 p.m. as the best time to do this,
as it would allow simultaneous announcements throughout the Empire.

The last thing that Baldwin wanted was to be kept up late into the night by a debate in the House of Commons following a statement at that time. He even turned down Halifax's counterproposal of 7 p.m., which for some unexplained reasons would have suited his fellow peers, but did not demur at Duff Cooper's idea of 4 p.m. He knew he could put an end to the undignified Dutch auction by leaving the final choice to Chamberlain's Cabinet Committee.

At the very end of the meeting, Halifax made his second contribution to the discussion by feeding a line to Baldwin that allowed him to encapsulate the whole crisis in a brisk putdown. Halifax appears not to have been paying much attention and felt that he and his colleagues needed a lead from the Prime Minister, whom he asked 'what steps he contemplated in order to enable the Cabinet to reach a decision that night'. In one of his rare and well-disguised moments of irony, Hankey minuted the dryness of Baldwin's reply that 'The PRIME MINISTER supposed that an answer would come from the King'.[23] Baldwin had no doubt how the King would respond to the Cabinet's message when it reached Fort Belvedere. The choice had always been the King's to make. Baldwin had never expected that it would be the right one, but he had understood that his job as Prime Minister was not to force any choice on him. Baldwin knew that it had never been the Cabinet's decision to make. The politicians had merely been spectators throughout the affair. They could only react and could not hope to influence the outcome.

The Cabinet's formal message was duly despatched to Fort Belvedere, but Baldwin did not even wait for the King's written reply to call the next meeting to set the final seal on procedure. A telephone call from Monckton confirming that the King was adamant in his decision to abdicate was enough. In contrast to the morning's meeting, the Cabinet that met just before 8 p.m. merely rubber-stamped the logistical arrangements for the legislation and announcements required to accomplish the only voluntary end to the reign of a British monarch in modern times. Baldwin wanted the abdication completed by the Friday night.[24] Another weekend of uncertainty of any kind was the last thing that the country needed. It was Simon whom the Prime Minister put in charge of the arrangements, and he had chosen his man well. Simon is best known to history as an advocate who always saw two sides to a question and as a result was an indecisive politician, but for the second half of the First World War he had taken a break from politics and learned the trade of a senior staff officer for Hugh Trenchard, commander of the Royal Flying Corps and the founder of the Royal Air Force. Trenchard was entirely unimpressed by Simon's status in Westminster and had demanded the same standard of excellence he sought from his other officers. That evening it was the clear, incisive brain of the military planner that dominated. Simon's performance stamped itself on the memory of the group of five men who were called together to make the arrangements, of whom three were former combat soldiers:

> Sir John gave us complete orders to ensure that the Instrument of Abdi-
> cation and the Messages should be distributed at the right time and place
> throughout the Empire and that there should be no breakdown in the
> machinery. I have seen many Staff Officers but none so competent.[25]

After weeks of temporising and uncertainty, the crispness and clarity of the briefing signalled that once the decision had been taken, the agony would be brought to a close as efficiently as possible. To 'Tommy' Lascelles, the royal secretary, it seemed a moment worth preserving and years later he

> got from Simon a promise to send me a copy of the masterly opera-
> tion-order which he dictated to a midnight meeting that I attended in
> Downing Street on the eve of the Abdication ... [which] should cer-
> tainly be in the archives at Windsor for the guidance of any who may be
> so unfortunate as to conduct another abdication in the future.[26]

The government was leaving nothing to chance as abdication moved from a dreaded eventuality to a firm administrative project, and it did not scruple to attack Mrs Simpson's reputation if it detected a potential obstacle. With the Prime Minister due to make a substantive statement to Parliament, which would be followed by the actual legislation to effect abdication, the time had come to study the likely impact on MPs and the risk of any upset. The official opposition parties had been behind the government's line from an early stage and Churchill had suffered a savage mauling on the Monday afternoon, but this was no guarantee that hostile comment or even votes against the government might not come from elsewhere. One possible source of difficulty was the 'die-hard' right wing of the Conservative Party. A group of MPs chose to adopt the King's cause and wrote to him assuring him of their support if he tried to assert his rights under the constitution.[27] They appear to have been grouped around the Imperial Policy Group, founded in 1934, with a vocal policy of strengthening the Empire and maintaining British rule in India.[28] The battle over granting a measure of autonomy in India had been lost by 1936, but the group still counted a number of Tory peers and MPs. Its leaders saw an opportunity to express openly 'acute and growing anxiety at the Government's action and procedure'.[29] At least one of the group's MPs was appalled at this attempt to hijack the affairs of the monarchy for political reasons and Baldwin later dismissed it as an 'insignificant group', but Downing Street took steps to neutralise it nonetheless.[30] On the Wednesday afternoon, Dugdale saw two of the Imperial Policy Group's leaders – Lord Mansfield, a Scottish grandee, and Kenneth de Courcy, its secretary and 'intelligence officer' – and 'enlightened them upon one or two things they did not know'.[31] They left 'somewhat chastised'.[32] Exactly what Dugdale told Mansfield and de Courcy is unknown, but it almost certainly included some version of the Special Branch reports about Mrs Simpson's relationship with Guy Trundle, which were definitely used to discredit her soon after the abdication. In 1938, the Trundle story was relayed to the incoming US ambassador, Joseph Kennedy, by Sir Edward Peacock, to whom Baldwin had referred him when he asked for information on the financial side of the abdication.[33] It was couched in sufficiently lurid terms for Kennedy to be willing to describe her publicly as a 'tart'.[34] Peacock passed off the information as common knowledge, but the leak was clearly designed to ensure that Kennedy did not become too sympathetic to his countrywoman.

De Courcy claimed to have heard years later practically the same allegations as he received from Dugdale from a courtier that 'her personal record is so shocking that no English gentleman could properly advise Queen Mary to receive her or in any way relent'.[35]

This provided the kernel of fact around which has grown the legend of the 'China dossier' on Mrs Simpson compiled by the secret services, which has inspired so much speculation and fruitless searching as well as providing a pretext for near-pornographic tales of Mrs Simpson's life. Caution is called for throughout. The description rings more evocatively to a modern listener than to someone of the era. The word 'dossier' had no stronger meaning than the word 'file' has now. The Police Special Branch was also classed as one of the secret services so it is possible that the only allegations made against Mrs Simpson were those in the 1935 reports.[36] The term was used by de Courcy only long after the event as a shorthand for the allegations against Mrs Simpson, although this was in the context of asserting 'no such authentic dossier ever existed'.[37] He reported that these allegations included one that 'Mrs. Simpson's private life in China left much to be desired'.[38] De Courcy was a noted fantasist, who later served a prison sentence for company fraud. He claimed to hold a – completely imaginary – dukedom and boasted that he was a friend of Sir Stewart Menzies, Head of MI6, and that Menzies had told him that he had a hand in the killing of Lavrenti Beria, Head of the KGB.[39] The only supporting evidence that rumours about Mrs Simpson's time in China were even current is a story picked up by the high Society littérateur Osbert Sitwell that she had taken a Chinese lover when she was in Shanghai, which would have been deeply shocking.[40]

The drive to bring a swift and clean end to the crisis meant that important questions were left open. Had the King accepted the inevitability of abdication earlier there could have been time to settle them in calm conditions, but he was now paying the price for delay, which had eliminated any leverage he might have held over the politicians. It is easy now to see the seeds of the crop of bitterness being sown that grew strong in the aftermath of the abdication, but the government had decided to draw a line. The question of the King's financial arrangements was left unresolved deliberately

when Peacock spoke to Baldwin and Chamberlain at 6.15 p.m. shortly
before the second Cabinet meeting of the day.[41] The politicians repeated
their earlier willingness to grant him money in principle, but refused to
make any commitment. They could not bind the House of Commons to
approve any agreement and the memory of the fiasco over the Two Bills
plan was an awful warning of what might happen if political approval for
anything was taken too readily for granted. More important, the threat of
withholding government money remained the best lever to prevent the
King from cohabiting with Mrs Simpson before she was divorced and they
could be married. Baldwin and Chamberlain maintained their outwardly
benevolent attitude to money when the discussion with Peacock turned
to the question of what the King should do once he had abdicated. It is a
telling register of just how much the single, vital question had dominated
the preceding weeks of frantic debate that this point had been ignored up
to the last moment. From an early stage it had been taken for granted that
the King would go abroad, but no one had considered how long he should
spend out of Britain or any other details. When the matter arose, Peacock
suggested an absence of two years which Baldwin thought 'would help
very much'.[42] When Peacock put the figure to the King later that night, he
did not demur. It was left entirely open as to whether his return would be
subject to any conditions. The politicians were similarly non-committal but
ostensibly friendly when Peacock raised for the last time the possibility of
legislation to finalise Mrs Simpson's divorce immediately. Baldwin's reply
that Peacock should 'Leave this thought with me' would have rung warning
bells in the ears of anyone attuned to politicians' non-promises, but the King
had run out of bargaining chips and soft-soap was all he could expect.[43]

One question of the King's future was settled on the Wednesday morning, but in a way that, probably accidentally, made a very large contribution
to the abdication's legacy of bitterness. The Duke of York agreed that his
brother should retain royal status after his abdication, which meant that
he would be a Royal Highness.[44] The Duke was partly motivated by an
inexplicable fear that his brother would become politically active as a non-
royal peer or even stand as an MP, but in isolation the decision was quite

uncontroversial and to all appearances a warm-hearted fraternal gesture. It was agreed informally between the brothers with no advice from politicians or lawyers. Only later when its full implications had to be faced did great difficulties arise. The King appears to have taken his brother's promise to apply to Mrs Simpson when he married her and was furious when the title was withheld.[45]

Baldwin was taking a risk in pushing ahead with abdication with, on the one hand, Mrs Simpson uncommitted to marriage and, on the other, the danger that intervention might create a devastating scandal in which the government could be accused of having provoked the abdication of the King to prevent him marrying a woman who was now unable to divorce her current husband. Both were serious risks and beyond his control. Indeed, before the day was out Mrs Simpson denied, or at least went through the motions of denying, the King a third time. It would not have stopped the abdication if it had been followed through, but it would have meant a different, and probably much worse, outcome to the crisis. It is little wonder that when they met in the aftermath of the abdication, Baldwin joked to Brownlow, the man who had pushed Mrs Simpson the hardest to renounce the King, that, had he succeeded, he would have been thrown into the Tower for the rest of his life.[46] History would have viewed Baldwin's performance in a quite different light.

Mrs Simpson and Brownlow had briefly escaped from the prison of the Villa Lou Viei to see Esmond Harmsworth at his mother's villa nearby, where he had come with a last-ditch scheme to keep his friend on the throne. He broached a nebulous and devious plan involving the King leaving the country, which would be entrusted to a Council of State, publicly renouncing Mrs Simpson and then reneging on the promise once he had been crowned.[47] Neither Mrs Simpson nor Brownlow saw anything in this and, when he learned of it, the King quite rightly said that he and Mrs Simpson would have deserved to be hanged if they had followed it.[48]

On the way back to the Villa Lou Viei, Mrs Simpson was sufficiently unsettled by this lunacy and everything that had gone before for Brownlow to have a final try at making her save his master.

Brownlow played on Mrs Simpson's fears of how she would appear to the world if the King did abdicate and warned her 'as kindly and gently as [he knew] how' of the 'appalling position' in which she would find herself.[49] It was not the moment for a hard approach and even this was enough to make her break into tears and ask him what he would do in her place. Brownlow sensed that the moment was ripe and told her 'although it is very late and the mills of God are grinding fast and all too surely, if I were you I would leave Europe and perhaps we could still save the position'. She agreed at once to what Brownlow described with some understatement as a 'wild' suggestion. The plan got as far as Brownlow sending one of the Scotland Yard detectives to the railway station to book a private carriage to Genoa from where the next liner was sailing away from Europe, to the Far East. Brownlow even proposed to accompany her on the journey. He drafted the second statement of the day to be fed to the press, which said simply, 'Mrs. Simpson has abandoned the project for marriage with his Majesty & is leaving Europe tonight – for an indefinite period'.[50] Unlike its predecessors it did not aim to load the responsibility onto the King's shoulders, but it was to prove to be just as much of a blind alley.

Just as had happened when Mrs Simpson had agreed to follow Goddard's advice, the plan did not survive the ensuing telephone call to Fort Belvedere to tell the King that she now planned to leave him. The King, in Brownlow's words, 'raised Hell' and finally resorted to the service of Allen to draw up a chilling statement of the only available alternative: 'The only conditions on which I can stay here, are if I renounce you for all time.'[51] To make absolutely sure that she understood, he added that he would not renounce her and had given his final word to the Cabinet. For good measure he got Allen to read the sentence to her again. The cruise from Genoa was consigned to oblivion. It is a moot point whether it would even have been effective. The King, she had been sure earlier in the day, would follow her to the ends of the earth.

In the face of the King's iron resolve, it is barely relevant to the analysis of the crisis how seriously Mrs Simpson wanted to withdraw, but it mattered for her reputation. The statement made in her name entirely failed to save her from blame for the crisis; in fact it hurt her reputation as it was seen as a piece of self-serving humbug. In Nancy Dugdale's words: 'After having done her utmost to split the country ... she now played the part of the gilded angel who, having failed to accomplish this, only wanted to act for the best.'[52] 'I despise her for making it at the eleventh hour, running away when she knows she is beaten.'[53] Tommy Dugdale's was, if anything, more damning: Mrs Simpson made the Cannes statement out of 'fear for her own safety'; her claim to Goddard that she was willing to withdraw was 'not in substance differ[ent] from similar declarations by the schemers in a hundred penny novelettes.'[54] Walter Monckton claimed contemptuously, 'she would periodically offer to clear out but always being quite sure that the King wouldn't agree'.[55] Monckton was almost certainly influenced by Wilson's scepticism of Mrs Simpson's sincerity, which would have been shaped by his access to the transcripts of her phone calls.[56]

CHAPTER 20

LYING LIKE A GENTLEMAN

He did more than justice to the King but lied like a gentleman about the
King's behaviour. He gave the impression of the King as a grave and
composed man regretfully insisting upon either Mrs. Simpson as wife
or abdication – whereas the king's friends and Baldwin's friends know
that the king on many occasions was 'impossible' as the idiom goes.
COLLIN BROOKS, JOURNAL, ON BALDWIN'S SPEECH ON 10 DECEMBER

SIR JOHN SIMON'S late-night briefing session set the machinery in motion to handle every necessary formal aspect of the King's abdication. First and foremost, came the production of the documents that the King would have to sign himself to attest that he wanted to leave the throne. They were a message to Parliament announcing his intention and a formal Act of Abdication. Separate examples were required for the Prime Minister, the Houses of Parliament and each major part of the Empire. By a quirk of constitutional procedure, the House of Lords and the House of Commons shared one Act of Abdication between them, so this made a total of fifteen pieces of paper. They were ready by about midnight and it fell to Monckton to take them to Fort Belvedere. At 10 a.m. the following morning, the King and all three of his surviving brothers met in the octagonal drawing room of the Fort, where the King had held his final audience with Baldwin on the Tuesday evening. With only the four members of the King's entourage who had worked most closely with him through the crisis – Monckton, Allen, Peacock and Alexander – as witnesses, the four brothers in turn took their place at the table to sign the papers. It took some time to produce thirty-six calm and deliberate signatures fitted to the solemnity of the occasion.[1]

Simon had composed the Message to Parliament, and it was as dry and legalistic as could be expected. The closest it came to a human touch was a very indirect admission that the King as a bachelor could 'no longer discharge this heavy task with efficiency or with satisfaction to Myself'.[2] He simply 'appreciated' the appeals that had been made to him to take a different course. It was very far from what the King wanted to say in explanation for his departure and he had no intention of letting a bloodless government lawyer issue the final word on his reign and the reasons for it ending. There were two ways in which he was going to do this. Once he had abdicated, he would broadcast to his people by radio to explain his choice. He would no longer be King and thus held in check by the constitutional rule that reduced him to the status of a mouthpiece for his ministers, which had been used to prevent him appealing directly for a popular verdict in favour of his marriage the previous week. The King gave the government as good as no choice as to whether he would broadcast, but he did say that 'out of courtesy' he would let the Cabinet see the text in advance.[3] The King also wanted Baldwin to make two specific points in his statement to Parliament that afternoon. According to the King's account, Baldwin had asked him for suggestions through Monckton, although Monckton's narrative is silent on this point.[4] The King gave Monckton two scribbled slips of paper. One was entirely uncontroversial and said that he and his brother and successor had always been on the best of terms and that he was 'confident that the Duke deserves and will receive the support of the whole Empire'.[5] The other was far more delicate and went to the heart of the question of who might be blamed for the crisis: 'Mrs. Simpson – Has consistently attempted to withdraw and even yesterday made a final attempt to dissuade the King from the course he has resolved to take.'[6]

Not merely did the King want to take full public responsibility for his act, but he specifically wanted it to be taken off the shoulders of Mrs Simpson. He wanted the Prime Minister to make the same statement that Mrs Simpson had issued from Cannes on the Monday evening.

Even before he could find out whether Baldwin would oblige him on this score, the King received a brief foretaste of the colder, less deferential world that awaited him once he had stepped down and joined the small and unhappy band of Europe's ex-monarchs. The message was delivered to the King in person at Fort Belvedere by Simon, this time wearing his hat as Home Secretary, the minister with departmental responsibility for the police. Now that the King was abdicating, the police detectives guarding Mrs Simpson at Cannes would be withdrawn. It was a singularly mean-spirited and petty move, which inevitably 'distressed the King greatly as he was most nervous for Mrs. Simpson's safety'.[7] The step had been triggered by an argument between Lord Brownlow and Inspector Evans, but the King was unaware of this and he was focused on the police's job of protecting Mrs Simpson.[8] By any standard there was some threat to her safety even if Wilson's panicky fears of mob violence are discounted. The scale of public funds involved was trivial and Mrs Simpson's unpopularity was the only reason why Simon might have faced parliamentary criticism for keeping the detectives in place. Simon was letting vindictive instinct drive his natural political gutlessness. It is unclear whether Simon had had the decision approved by the Prime Minister, but it was rescinded, albeit in extremely grudging terms, the following morning. Withdrawing the police would have been tantamount to a public declaration that the ex-King and his entourage deserved no greater protection from the British state than any other citizen. Wilson may also have appreciated the availability of police at the Villa Lou Viei as a source of intelligence when they became aware of talk that Mrs Simpson might leave secretly for Germany.[9]

Downing Street does not seem to have told the King in advance whether either of the points he had asked for would be included in Baldwin's speech, so he had to wait for it to be reported to find out whether they had been. Here, too, he was disappointed and bitterly so. Baldwin did refer to his

message about the Duke of York to great effect in his speech, but the only
time he mentioned Mrs Simpson was to quote what the King had said to
him at the fateful audience after the Hardinge letter when he announced
that he was going to marry her. There was no reference to her willingness
to renounce the King at all. Admittedly it would have been difficult to persuade the House of Commons of the literal truth of the King's note in light
of the brutal fact that Mrs Simpson had not followed through her public
statement from Cannes on the Monday night, but it was a harsh omission nonetheless. Monckton, who was the only person aware of the note's
existence other than the King and the Prime Minister, did find it 'a little
hard on Mrs. Simpson that no reference was made to it'.[10] As he neither
liked Mrs Simpson nor believed she was sincere in her offers to withdraw,
it is a telling verdict. The King was deeply upset and labelled Baldwin's
entire speech 'an autobiographical triumph disguised as a homily on the
errors of a King'.[11] The omission was doubtless an 'allowance for the prejudices of [Baldwin's] less forgiving followers, even at the risk of deliberate
historical gloss'. He accused Baldwin of unwillingness to render 'simple
courtesies' because he was a politician and obliged to run for office. His
contempt for Baldwin ignored the fact that he would never run for office
again, and he contrived to overlook the string of laudatory comments that
Baldwin made about him. Baldwin certainly held a very low opinion of
Mrs Simpson and would have had no qualms about casting her as the vil-
lainess of the piece.

Not, of course, that strict historical accuracy played much part in
Baldwin's speech. It was widely praised for its effectiveness, but no one
in the know said that it actually revealed anything or was even truthful.
It is worth quoting the opinion of Lord Rothermere's friend and assistant, Collin Brooks, who had been at the outer edges of the crisis and
was a journalist of long experience. Even though he could notionally be
counted as part of the King's Party camp, he had a low opinion of the King
personally and unmitigated contempt for Baldwin as a politician. Brooks
saluted Baldwin for his effrontery in claiming that he was talking almost
impromptu:

He is a veritable Bagstock* of a fellow – 'deep and devilish sly, is tough old Joe, Sir…' for having brooded over this inevitable announcement since November 16 he began, Anthony-like by remarking that he had no time to prepare a speech and proceeded to deliver a plain tale of great effective skill.[12]

Brooks recognised that the picture of the King was idealised to the point of dishonesty but condoned the device:

He did more than justice to the King but lied like a gentleman about the King's behaviour. He gave the impression of the King as a grave and composed man regretfully insisting upon either Mrs. Simpson as wife or abdication – whereas the king's friends and Baldwin's friends know that the king on many occasions was 'impossible' as the idiom has it.

Roughly the same view came from the other end of the political spectrum and it was delivered openly in the House of Commons. At the very end of the debate a handful of MPs from the far-left Independent Labour Party or the Communist Party spoke against the government. One of them accused Baldwin and his colleagues of outright hypocrisy in praising a man whom they had decided to remove, in tones that still read blisteringly in Hansard:

I should not be honest if I did not do so. I have listened to more cant and humbug than I have ever listened to in my life. I have heard praise of the King which was not felt sincerely in any quarter of the House. I go further. Who has not heard the tittle-tattle and gossip that is going about? If he had not voluntarily stepped from the Throne, everyone knows that the same people in the House who pay lip service to him would have poured out scorn, abuse and filth. Some months ago we opposed the Civil List. To-morrow we shall take the same line. I have no doubt that you will go on praising the next King as you have praised this one.

---

* A hard-nosed and manipulative character from Dickens's *Dombey and Son*

> You will go on telling about his wonderful qualities. If he is a tenth as good as you say, why are you not keeping him? Why is everyone wanting to unload him? Because you know he is a weak creature. You want to get rid of him and you are taking the step to-day.

The only widespread criticism of Baldwin's speech was that he spoke too much about himself. Apart from the King and Monckton no one appears to have noticed, still less objected to, his silence on Mrs Simpson, even her uncritical admirer and supporter, Chips Channon. Baldwin's true opinion of the personalities involved is also suggested by the letter of warm congratulation and support that he wrote to Cosmo Gordon Lang, the Archbishop of Canterbury, on Lang's broadcast about the crisis two days after the abdication.[13] Lang savaged Edward for abandoning his duty because of his craving for private happiness and 'Even more strange and sad it is that he should have sought his happiness in a manner inconsistent with the Christian principles of marriage, and within a social circle whose standards and ways of life are alien to all the best instincts and traditions of his people'.[14] Many people found Lang's words offensive and unnecessary, but there is little doubt that he was expressing what the higher levels of the Establishment thought of Mrs Simpson and her friends. At an early stage in the crisis, Baldwin told his confidant Tom Jones, 'I have grown to hate that woman. She has done more in nine months to damage the monarchy than Victoria and George the Fifth did to repair it in half a century.'[15] Soon after the abdication Tommy Dugdale, Baldwin's parliamentary private secretary, wrote a savagely critical assessment of Mrs Simpson, which concluded that she was 'selfish, self-seeking, hard, calculating, ambitious, scheming, dangerous'.[16]

The government's reluctance to commit itself to any financial settlement threw the question onto the soon-to-be ex-King and his family. This opened one of the richest veins of bitterness in the whole affair, to a great extent because of the King's flagrant dishonesty. In the words of his biographer Philip Ziegler: 'He told a lie for reasons of self-interest, and this cannot be condoned. It was a foolish lie ... It was a suicidal lie.'[17] The brothers together with legal and financial advisers had gathered at Fort Belvedere on the Thursday evening to discuss the financial arrangements that abdication would make necessary. The King opened proceedings with an impassioned speech in which he claimed that he would be hard pressed financially once he left the throne if the government did not grant him a Civil List pension. By one account he claimed he would have less than £5,000 per year on which to live.[18] His strongest bargaining chips were the ambiguous legal position of the palaces at Sandringham and Balmoral created by his father's will. He insisted on getting the fullest monetary value possible for his interest in the palaces. An agreement was signed under which the Duke of York promised him £25,000 per year unless the government granted him a pension of that amount under the Civil List. What the King failed to disclose to his brothers was that he had accumulated a large private fortune stemming from the revenues of the Duchy of Cornwall during his time as Prince of Wales, which had been shrewdly invested by Peacock. It was probably in excess of £1 million, which, even though it had been conservatively invested in gilt-edged bonds, would have brought in £30,000 a year.[19]

The abdication bills passed through both Houses of Parliament smoothly, with no opposition. The Imperial Policy Group had been silenced by Dugdale's briefing. In his final act as sovereign, the King had given the Royal Assent to the Act, and at 1.52 p.m. on Friday 11 December he ceased to be King. The British constitution does not recognise any such thing as an interregnum so, until he had abdicated and been succeeded by his brother, he was still King and the only person who could give the Royal Assent. By this quirk he thus had to approve his own departure. Edward's abdication also opened the question of what he should be called as the ex-King. It had already been decided that he would retain royal rank and thus the style of Royal Highness, but no further thought had been given to a title.[20] As he was to broadcast on the BBC that night, the question became an urgent one. He would have to be announced by name and title. Sir John Reith was the man who needed to know the most. At one point, Reith suggested to the Duke of York that he should refer to him as 'Mr. Edward Windsor'.[21] The Duke of York disposed of this offensive and demeaning notion with the common-sense statement that, as the son of a peer, the least that his brother rated would be 'Lord Edward Windsor'. He also dropped in the suggestion that he could stand for Parliament. This terrifying prospect was an unsubtle but completely effective way of ensuring that the ex-King would be given a peerage in his own right as soon as possible. The brothers settled on the title Duke of Windsor. Quite how seriously Reith intended his suggestion is open to question, but the episode gives a further flavour of how the ex-King was starting to feel the chill now that he was no longer protected by the deferential aura surrounding a monarch. Graciousness was not noted as one of Reith's strong points and he was unarguably aligned with the Establishment hardliners.

Churchill was a noted foul-weather friend, whose loyalty to his friends usually rode out their problems. Even though he had been badly shaken by the reaction of his fellow MPs to his intervention on the Monday, he was not deterred by the risk to his reputation of associating further with someone who was set fair to become Britain's highest-profile social pariah, and came to Fort Belvedere for lunch on the Friday to give a final show of support to the King, and to take his leave. They were together at table the very moment that Edward VIII formally ceased to be King.[22] Churchill could claim to have been the one subject of King Edward VIII who stayed with him to the very last. Churchill made sure that the King felt he had been given adequate time for reflection by Baldwin.[23] He finally understood that it had been Edward's own decision not to accept Churchill's advice to stonewall and play for time. They do not seem to have discussed how this could be squared with the King's opening words at their dinner on the previous Friday night, which implied that he had not agreed to abdicate. Now that he had abdicated, he no longer required Churchill's support on the question of his marriage, but he did want it for something else. The ex-King was looking to the future and treated Churchill to a similarly specious plea of impending poverty to the one to which he had treated his brothers.[24] It is unclear from publicly available evidence whether the ex-King told Churchill about the agreement between Edward and his brothers which underwrote him against a failure to grant the ex-King a pension from the Civil List, but over the next few months Churchill vigorously championed granting him one. Churchill also advised Edward on the draft of the broadcast he was to make that night. It was in essence the text that the King and Monckton had prepared together, but Churchill added a few almost unmistakable touches of his own, notably a contrast between the ex-King's solitary state and that of his brother and successor, who had 'one matchless blessing, enjoyed by so many of you and not bestowed on me – a happy home with his wife and children'. Churchill drew immense strength and support from his own marriage, so this comment was genuine and heartfelt. He left Fort Belvedere in tears, quoting a couplet of Marvell's:

> *He nothing common did or mean*
> *Upon that memorable Scene*[25]

It was doubtless done with an eye to posterity and the image that he hoped it would hold of the former King, who quoted it approvingly in his memoirs. It was just as much a part of the manipulation of the historical record as Baldwin's speech the previous day. It would be some time before Churchill discovered that the King had lied to him as he had lied to his brothers about his finances.

Whilst Churchill stayed loyal to Edward to the last, it was otherwise with his domestic servants, who gave him another lesson in the realities of power and status. One by one they declined his instructions and invitations to join him in exile. He complained bitterly of 'their amazing disloyalty', but this tells us more about his egocentricity and foolishness than anything else.[26] A precarious existence in the household of an ex-monarch was not an enticing prospect in its own right, even before taking into account his close-fistedness. Edward did not seem aware of how little he had done to earn their personal loyalty and certainly had no idea that the thought of working for his intended wife was actively unpleasant. It was an easy decision to shift allegiance to the new regime.

After lunch, Monckton had driven up to Downing Street with the draft of the ex-King's broadcast, which was then shown to Simon. The government had not been invited to comment on the draft, but in practice held a power of veto. No longer King, the constitution allowed Edward to speak in his own right, but Reith was a servant of the government, and the BBC would not have broadcasted anything with which it was unhappy. In the event, the government found nothing to object to. The ex-King was allowed to say what Baldwin had declined to say in his speech to Parliament, that Mrs Simpson had repeatedly tried to alter his decision. It is perhaps revealing that Edward did not give her name and referred to her as 'the other person most nearly concerned'. In the days before near-universal use of given names, to have done otherwise would have reminded his listeners that the woman he loved and intended to marry was still someone else's wife. He may also have understood the resentment that her name might have provoked. For the rest, its restrained understatement chimed with Baldwin's more histrionic but equally sugar-coated speech the day before. Much to his later chagrin, Edward had taken up a heavy hint from Baldwin that he should 'stress that he had at all times shown me every possible form of consideration', and thanked his ministers.[27] Baldwin wanted to 'preserve the unity of the realm' by making it clear that there were no hard feelings between him and the King.[28] He competed with Baldwin in playing down how close the country had come to an all-out constitutional crisis: 'There never has been any constitutional difference between me and [Ministers] and Parliament. Bred in the constitutional tradition by my Father [another Churchill touch], I should never have allowed any such issue to arise.'[29]

Sir John Reith came to Windsor Castle to superintend the broadcast in person and found the ex-King under the same carapace of false normality that he had been presenting to the outside world all week. Reith had been braced for a much more trying experience.[30] He began with a voice test for the ex-King, which provided a final moment of comedy. Despite Reith's best efforts to direct him away from anything in the newspaper from which he was reading that referred to him, Edward lit on a report of a tennis match in which Sir Samuel Hoare praised the Duke of York's skills as a tennis player. The broadcast was heard all over the world. At this remove it is impossible to assess how great an impact it had. Whilst it did not trigger any widespread outpouring of public emotion, it was still enough to move Reith to overcome his doubts about Edward and detect the tragedy of the moment: 'What an occasion. What that young man has thrown away – a greater opportunity than any King or any man ever had. I felt very sorry for him.'[31]

The arrangements for the ex-King's departure from his former realm were marked by a final flourish of flair, which showed that he had not lost his sense of the dramatically effective. He wanted to leave that very night by Royal Navy destroyer, and overrode the pleas of Hoare, who was organising the operation in his capacity as the First Lord of the Admiralty and wanted to 'provide a more fitting departure'.[32] Perhaps Hoare had a more imposing warship in mind for the task. By one account, Hoare's personal transport, the Admiralty yacht HMS *Enchantress*, was to have carried the ex-King until someone was alert enough to realise that her name would have provided ample fodder for dubious comment and ribaldry.[33] The destroyer HMS *Fury* was substituted in a final gesture of advance news management. The ex-King had been given another foretaste of the more humble life he was going to lead when he found himself carrying Slipper on board under his arm.[34] In an unconscious protest against his uncertain future, Slipper fouled the Captain's cabin.[35] Surgeon Commander H. E. Y. White, the senior Naval doctor from the crew of the royal yacht *Victoria and Albert*, was added to *Fury*'s complement at the insistence of the ex-King's equerry Piers 'Joey' Legh, who accompanied him on this final journey together with Ulick Alexander, 'in case the ex-King's state of mental stress should cause him to require medical attention while at sea'.[36] The doctor's skills were not required, although his shipmates might have felt the need of some attention for the exhaustion brought on by attempting to match the ex-King's nervous hyperactivity, which kept him awake until the early hours sending off radio messages, drinking brandy and talking.

The following morning, the ex-King was deposited on the quayside at Boulogne under the protection of squads of *Garde Mobile* riot police, who kept journalists and rubberneckers at a respectable distance. He paced the quay with Slipper whilst the private railway carriage, which was to take him into temporary exile in Austria, was prepared for him. Up to almost the last moment he had been fixated on the idea of going to the Dolder Grand in Zurich, the destination of the aborted flight on the previous Sunday morning, but Mrs Simpson had spotted the obvious drawbacks of staying in a hotel, and she had arranged for him to stay with her friend Kitty de Rothschild at her house at Enzesfeld near Vienna.[37]

CHAPTER 21

A COURT OF HER OWN

The Prime Minister not being available, I think I should refer through
you again to the point I made on Mrs. Simpson's 'plans' for the future.
It is clear to me that it is her intention not only to come back here (aided
by what she expects to be a generous provision from public funds) to set up
a 'Court' of her own and – there can be little doubt – to do her best to
make things uncomfortable for the new occupant of the Throne.
SIR HORACE WILSON TO NEVILLE CHAMBERLAIN,
10 DECEMBER 1936[1]

KING EDWARD VIII had barely disappeared as a threat to public
order and constitutional stability when Sir Horace Wilson began
to confront the next danger or, at least, what he saw as the next
danger. He was driven by a blood-chilling picture of Mrs Simpson as an
utterly unscrupulous adventuress bent on taking over the country in alliance with Nazi Germany. Wilson's vividly expressed concerns provide one
of the central planks in the image of Mrs Simpson as a Nazi sympathiser,
if not downright agent, which still endures. One of its leading advocates
has been the American writer Charles Higham, who also holds the crown
(against stiff competition) for an almost entirely imaginary and garbled

description of Wilson's functions: 'special adviser to the king and diplomatic liaison between various conflicting political groups including the Labour party, the British Union of Fascists, the Anglo-German fellowship, the Link and even the communists...'[2]

Everyone closely involved in the affair had been under great strain and none for longer than Wilson. Wilson had borne much of the pressure of handling the government end of the crisis since Baldwin left on his rest-cure in the summer, and the strain was showing. The lightning rod for his growing paranoia was Mrs Simpson. She, rather than the King, was the focus of his worry, and he saw her evil intentions as the source of problems past and yet to come. To some extent he was merely echoing the Prime Minister's own intense dislike of her, but he went far further in detecting an actual threat. On the morning of the abdication he spoke to Sir John Reith, who described him as 'suffering from violent emotion which prevented him from being as coherent as he could wish. The woman he said had been allowed to "get away with it" in a degree which ought to have been prevented.'[3] That evening, Wilson shared his fears with Neville Chamberlain. Even Chamberlain, who had been Wilson's faithful ally in the hardliner camp since the early autumn, recognised that his judgement was not entirely reliable by then: 'He is much strained and tired by all he has been through and is perhaps a little over obsessed with plans of mischief Mrs. Simpson may yet work.'[4] Wilson was not merely letting off steam with Chamberlain. He wanted urgent action and supported his case with a letter setting out the threats in detail.

> The Prime Minister not being available, I think I should refer through you again to the point I made as to Mrs Simpson's 'plans' for the future. It is clear to me that it is her intention not only to come back here but (aided by what she expects to be a generous provision from public funds) to set up a 'Court' of her own and – there can be little doubt – do her best to make things uncomfortable for the new occupant of the Throne. It must not be assumed that she has abandoned hope of becoming Queen of England. It is known that she has limitless ambition, including a desire

to interfere in politics: she has been in touch with the Nazi movement
and has definite ideas as to dictatorship.

The essentials for her plans are (a) that she secures her divorce and
(b) that she is provided with a sufficient income.

As regards (a), about which she is very anxious, it is unnecessary for
me to say anything. As regards (b) we have some means, at least, of saving the country from grave future trouble.[5]

It is clear from the last paragraph that Wilson wanted the government to
take active measures to thwart Mrs Simpson because of the threat she posed
to national stability.

Wilson was obviously in a mood to exaggerate the danger, but his fears
should not be dismissed out of hand. He was at the centre of the government's various intelligence operations against Mrs Simpson and the King,
as well as having a prime seat at 10 Downing Street, so the letter was written with access to the best information available to the government. The
phone taps on the line between Fort Belvedere and Villa Lou Viei would
have reported what the King and Mrs Simpson were saying to each other
until the Friday, and it almost certainly included remarks that would have
given Wilson a starting point for his assessment of her plans. Wilson's
vision of Mrs Simpson's 'court' is supported – albeit in unspecific terms
– by what the Duke of Windsor said to a former courtier who visited him
in Austria a couple of weeks after the abdication and found him brooding
on how he could rebuild her standing in Britain:

> He [Piers Legh] had asked the Duke how he proposed to occupy his time
> after the marriage, and the Duke had replied that his first object would
> be to re-establish his wife in the position which had been contemplated,
> (whatever that may mean).[6]

The fact that neither Legh nor Simon, to whom he reported the remark,
could make out exactly what the Duke meant does not mean that it should
be ignored. It obviously made enough of an impression on Legh for him

to repeat it. The Duke was acutely sensitive to his future wife's status, so he may well have begun to discuss how it might be restored in the course of one of the phone conversations with Mrs Simpson. In a similar vein, everyone in earshot at Fort Belvedere knew that Mrs Simpson was nagging the King to stand up for his rights. Her hazy grasp on the British constitution exaggerated what these rights amounted to. She also insisted that the Duke of Windsor should get as much money as possible. It would not have required any sinister motive for Mrs Simpson to worry about whether her divorce would go through. This was just another unknown in a confusing and oppressive sea of doubts. The reference to Mrs Simpson and Nazism could be explained by Vansittart's panicky fears at the start of the reign. The only part of Wilson's reading of Mrs Simpson's intentions and concerns for which there is no evidence elsewhere is his belief that Mrs Simpson was determined to become Queen. Otherwise, his letter to Chamberlain is founded in fact.

The phone taps were not the only source of intelligence, and it is striking that Wilson's fears of Mrs Simpson's plans should be so strong only a couple of days after an MI5 report that was savagely critical of Mrs Simpson, focusing on her greed and her relationship with the King, although it did not appear to discuss what her goals were.

> From very private information it is evident that she is an entirely unscrupulous woman who is not in love with the K. but is exploiting him for her own purposes. She has already ruined him in money regards and it is thought that she can be squared when she realises that she has lost the game.[7]

Judging whether Wilson was right to see severe danger in Mrs Simpson is a classic question of analysing the intelligence dimension of any episode, assessing the accuracy of the information on which he was working. MI5's information came from somewhere in the King's entourage and the fact that material on her was still flowing after Mrs Simpson's departure to France gives a clue as to the source. Many if not all the earlier reports seem to recycle comments made directly by the King, but this could not include the last one. With the King in almost total isolation at Fort Belvedere and Mrs Simpson at Cannes, one individual stands out as a potential source. The King was in regular contact with his friend Bernard Rickatson-Hatt throughout the crisis, which marks him as a possible MI5 source for the early material.[8] In particular, Rickatson-Hatt might have been the source for one of the most influential mistakes in the MI5 reports. He believed that Churchill was the true author of the morganatic scheme, almost certainly because the King told him so. By chance, Rickatson-Hatt confirmed the story indirectly to Downing Street through a friendly German journalist.[9] The jaundiced view of Mrs Simpson in the final MI5 report could easily have come from Rickatson-Hatt's other friend, Ernest Simpson, who, it will be remembered, had been trying to sabotage their divorce earlier in the week. The speed with which the MI5 operation against the King came on stream with information in October suggests that it was exploiting an existing contact, and there are circumstantial grounds for suspecting Rickatson-Hatt on this score.

Rickatson-Hatt's background marks him as the kind of man who might have acted as an MI5 informant. After serving alongside Ernest Simpson in the Coldstream Guards during the First World War, Rickatson-Hatt had gone on to serve in Turkey during the confused phase of Allied attempts to occupy parts of the former Ottoman Empire. Initially despatched there on the depressing duty of graves registration, he had risen to command the British detachment of the Allied Police Commission.[10] His story then reads like something from one of Eric Ambler's novels of seedy intrigue in the Balkans. He helped confiscate a large sum of money from an Armenian clerk, who had been denounced by his business rivals, which various British authorities spent much effort in trying to recover from him over the succeeding years, together with supposed overpayments in his salary.[11] He found it convenient to plead that his absence in the Balkans and Caucasus on 'special work' had disrupted his attention to administrative matters, and thereafter added intelligence work to his curriculum vitae.[12] He moved on to a civilian career with the Reuters news agency, where he rose to the rank of chief correspondent, as the right-hand man of the agency's head, the autocratic Sir Roderick Jones. Reuters has long had close links with British intelligence. There is a clear indication that Rickatson-Hatt was the object of very high-level government interest when the Bank of England wanted to hire him for a senior job in 1941. The job had to be cleared with Major Desmond Morton, Churchill's intelligence adviser, who in turn had to obtain approval from the Foreign Office, MI5 and Walter Monckton, who was then running British propaganda activities.[13] Rickatson-Hatt's post-Reuters career has given rise to the suspicion that he was the beneficiary of 'people in high places looking after a friend'.[14] It is questionable whether the Bank of England needed someone at a senior level whose only demonstrable expertise was in journalism, especially as Rickatson-Hatt himself insisted that he was not the Bank's press officer.[15] Montagu Norman, the Governor of the Bank of England, who hired him, had been a key ally of Sir Horace Wilson in pursuing Neville Chamberlain's policy of appeasement via back channels to Germany. When he retired from the Bank of England, Rickatson-Hatt slipped into a senior post at the Bank of London and South America.

Rickatson-Hatt's relationship with the King was sufficiently prominent for it to attract outside interest. When he died in 1966, the auction catalogue of his effects included 'Simpson divorce case papers', which featured correspondence between the two.[16] The letters were available for inspection in advance of the sale and contained references to managing newspaper publicity. They were withdrawn from sale and have never resurfaced, which suggests that a well-funded organisation or individual with an interest in keeping their contents private made the executors a high enough offer.

Britain's established intelligence operation against the German Embassy was keeping MI5 well informed of what was going on there in the final days of the crisis. Telephone conversations with Germany were also vulnerable because the Embassy trusted an early form of phone-scrambling, which the British were able to defeat.[17] The German Embassy was one of a number targeted by Section X of MI6, operating in close collaboration with MI5.[18] Von Ribbentrop's delusional view of Edward VIII had been one of the cornerstones on which he had built his plans for the conduct of the Embassy when he agreed to take it in the spring, but he had remained in Berlin until the autumn and did not arrive in London until the crisis was well under way. Hitler and von Ribbentrop were both fully persuaded of this nonsense, but at this remove it is difficult to understand fully the dynamics. Most likely the original idea came from von Ribbentrop and was enthusiastically taken up by Hitler, compelling von Ribbentrop to keep his faith in it long after it was exposed as an illusion. They focused almost exclusively on the King and there was little mention of Mrs Simpson. Von Ribbentrop's only recorded perceptive comment on the affair was to recognise the social snobbery that fed dislike of her, although she would probably have quibbled with his description of her as 'a girl of the people'.[19] Von Ribbentrop's wildest miscalculation was his confidence that the King would overcome Baldwin, that he was the 'certain winner'.[20] He attempted to send a message to the King assuring him of German support via a friendly peer, but fortunately it does not seem to have arrived.[21] The German press was instructed not to report the affair so as not to upset the King.

Von Ribbentrop was taken quite unawares when his assessment of the situation was proven to be inaccurate and was left struggling to rescue his credibility with Hitler. The Downing Street press officer George Steward had tipped off his German contacts in advance that abdication was imminent, but when this was passed on to von Ribbentrop he rather went into denial.[22] Having nourished Hitler's delusion that an Anglo-German rapport could be built on Edward's supposed friendship, he was loath to admit his error. When he did eventually telephone Hitler with a softened version of the story that the crisis was brewing, Hitler accused him of letting himself be taken in by a provocation staged as part of an anti-German intrigue. Almost to the end, von Ribbentrop clung to his delusion that Edward represented a significant force in British politics, imagining a violent struggle which would culminate in his restoration to the throne and Baldwin's overthrow. He shared this twaddle with J. C. C. Davidson over lunch on the day of the abdication. Von Ribbentrop announced that he had expected gunfire in the streets as the King's partisans fought back. 'Indeed, he said he had been extremely nervous at coming out to lunch on a day like this! He talked more nonsense than I have ever heard from anybody in a responsible position of the level of Ambassador.'[23] To cover up his error to Hitler, von Ribbentrop fell back on the stock reaction of fascism and blamed the abdication on sinister Bolshevist forces, who had been set in motion when the then Prince of Wales spoke in favour of friendship with Germany.[24] He gave strict instructions that no one else at the Embassy was to report to the German ministry of foreign affairs on the topic and told Hitler that Edward VIII had been forced to abdicate by Baldwin because he would not fall in with an anti-German policy.[25] Ever after Hitler remained convinced that it was the British Legion speech in 1935 which sealed Edward's fate, although he thought that it had been delivered in Berlin.[26] He also believed that Mrs Simpson would have become a good Queen.[27] The professional diplomats at the Embassy could only echo J. C. C. Davidson's verdict on von Ribbentrop's thinking, and their complaint was reported to MI5: 'We are absolutely powerless in the face of this nonsense.'[28] Edward VIII was a tool of Nazi Germany only in von Ribbentrop's fantasies, and the British were fully aware of this.

The record of von Ribbentrop's royal policy is a fine specimen of the incoherence and dilettantism of Nazi diplomacy and its disconnection from reality. All it achieved was to alert Downing Street that the King's Party was not the only grouping that aspired to manipulate the crisis to its own ends. It is unclear how fully Wilson was briefed on the intelligence available, but Mrs Simpson posed a real threat in his eyes and he was determined to thwart her. Money provided the obvious tool to frustrate her and through Chamberlain he lobbied hard for it to be used against her. The threat of withholding a Civil List pension for the King if he cohabited with Mrs Simpson had already been decided on whilst Goddard was on his way to Cannes. It does not seem to have been delivered to Mrs Simpson, but Sir Edward Peacock did tell the King of Chamberlain's threat 'if, in the meantime, he [King Edward] associated with Mrs. Simpson he could not get a penny'.[29] Wilson succeeded in part and persuaded Chamberlain to extend the threat to cover 'activities of a kind of which Parliament would disapprove' or 'other troublesome activities' as distinct from misbehaviour with Mrs Simpson.[30] This would embrace any agitation against the new King or with a foreign power. Peacock appears to have stopped short of giving the King the broader warning. Wilson could take some comfort from the fact that Peacock had advised the King to remain abroad for at least two years on behalf of Baldwin and Chamberlain.[31] The imminent threat of a rival court, if it ever existed, had receded greatly.

Far more deeply hidden is the answer to the question as to whether Wilson also tried to block the divorce, which he believed was an integral part of Mrs Simpson's scheme to make herself Queen. Chamberlain and Wilson talked about Mrs Simpson's divorce before Wilson wrote to Chamberlain on the Thursday, and there is a hint as to the direction that the conversation might have taken in a memorandum that Wilson wrote the following day about the discussion: '...the Chancellor agreed that steps should not be taken to interfere with any action which anyone might take to prevent the individual [Mrs Simpson] from obtaining the "freedom" that is desired.'[32] The possibility that the divorce might be blocked through the intervention of the King's Proctor offered a convenient sword of Damocles to hang over Mrs Simpson and, to say the least, Wilson did not find it an alarming prospect from the government's point of view. The double negative in what Chamberlain told Wilson might be code for tacit approval for some covert move to facilitate intervention. Chamberlain too wanted to prevent the marriage albeit for less specific reasons: 'I should like him to be saved from a marriage which I fear must end speedily in Disillusionment and disgust.'[33] On a more innocent reading Chamberlain's comment might mean no more than that the two had agreed that the government should not attempt to interfere with the judicial process should some 'busybody' launch an intervention, but there are arguments against this reading. The general possibility of private intervention had been chewed over for a good while, so the simple fact that it was raised suggests that there was some specific reason to do so. Any attempt by the government to pressure some genuinely private intervenor would have been risky in the extreme. Everything that had been said about the possibility assumed that the government would be powerless.

Even before Chamberlain and Wilson talked about intervention, a 'busybody' had finally gone into action. Francis Stephenson, a 73-year-old managing clerk at a City of London firm of solicitors, had made a formal court 'appearance' on the Wednesday, giving notice of intervention on the grounds that Mrs Simpson was collusive and that she had committed adultery with the King. He had gone to the court together with someone else from his office, an articled clerk called Gordon, whose 'politics are very advanced. He is of extreme Labour principles.'[34] According to Stephenson, Gordon immediately afterwards went to the offices of the left-wing *Daily Worker* newspaper and told them about Stephenson's court appearance 'without my knowledge or consent' and to his extreme annoyance. Stephenson's intervention as a formal judicial act was to prove very short-lived, although its practical repercussions lasted for months. To pursue the intervention, Stephenson would have had to file a formal affidavit within four days. He did draft one, but did not file it, and on 14 December he wrote to Goddard's office saying that he did not intend to proceed any further.

Superficially at least, Stephenson fits perfectly the image of the 'busybody' or zealously patriotic citizen mooted by the hardliners. A respectable elderly man with metal-framed spectacles living in the London suburbs, he was almost a caricature of an individual so innocuous that only a scandalous threat to national harmony would move him to action. It is only his thoroughness that invites us to look more closely. He insisted throughout that he was acting entirely of his own volition and he generally resembles many of the more literate people who wrote to the King's Proctor, who were affronted at the idea that Mrs Simpson might have obtained her divorce under irregular circumstances despite what seemed to be flagrant adultery with the King. When the King's Proctor later interviewed him, Stephenson said that he had no firm evidence and was only going on gossip at the Stock Exchange and the like. He trotted out rumours of astronomical bribes paid to Ernest Simpson for his complaisance.[35] He also said that he was motivated by precisely the same calculation that Sir John Simon had imagined: intervention would prevent abdication and an undesirable marriage. Stephenson's information might have been no more than gossip, but it drew on all the available sources: social chit-chat amongst brokers and jobbers dealing in US securities, articles in *Cavalcade* and American newspapers thoughtfully posted to Stephenson by convenient friends in America. He detected collusion in press stories that Mrs Simpson remained in contact with her husband after the decree nisi and her manifestly token residence in Felixstowe, but as a legal professional he skated over the apparent use of a professional co-respondent. In the eyes of the Ramsay MacDonalds of the world, this was evidence of collusion, but someone who knew the judicial game like Stephenson was aware that it was not genuinely a weak point. He accused the authorities of ignoring the convention that undefended divorce cases should be heard in open court because entry to the Ipswich Court had been severely restricted. This was the only point on which Stephenson admitted to being better informed than normal members of the public, having obtained direct evidence from a nephew who conveniently lived in the town. Stephenson's recitation of the places and dates of the King's supposed adultery with Mrs Simpson was circumstantial and comprehensive.

It was when Stephenson tried to explain his failure to follow through from his 'appearance' that he began to contradict himself flagrantly. He told the King's Proctor and the newspapers that it was the ex-King's broadcast that changed his mind. He provided journalists with a suitably vivid story of his reaction to hearing the radio:

> If the Duke of Windsor could say goodbye to his subjects with 'God save the king,' then he as managing clerk in a law office could forgive and forget and toast the new monarch, too ... His words made me think ... I realised that here was a man who wanted to be happy ... I thought of my own married happiness ... When I heard his words I regretted what I had done.[36]

If Stephenson had truly believed his intervention would prevent abdication, he had already failed and there would have been no need for this mawkish drivel to explain why he had gone no further. Even more tellingly, it was only after the broadcast that he sat down to draft a clear and precise affidavit setting out his grounds for intervening. The affidavit cites the ex-King's statement in the broadcast that he loved Mrs Simpson and wanted to marry her as evidence for adultery with her. For good measure he pointed the King's Proctor towards the International Press Agency, one of whose journalists had tried to get information from Stephenson and had claimed that he might provide Stephenson with 'useful' information on a reciprocal basis. This is being a sight too helpful for someone who supposedly just wanted the Duke of Windsor to have his happiness. By far the most plausible explanation for the brevity of Stephenson's intervention is that he had never intended to go further than his 'appearance' and the leak to the *Daily Worker*. The draft affidavit was written purely to lend credibility when, as he must have known would happen, the King's Proctor interviewed him.

Stephenson appears even less reliable when what he said in 1936 is compared to what he told one of Beaverbrook's journalists, a Miss O'Callaghan, who persuaded him to talk freely in 1949. By then his story had changed radically. He could have provided direct evidence of Mrs Simpson's adultery with the King. A friend had lived opposite the flat in Bryanston Court and from their windows Stephenson had seen the King regularly arriving there by car and letting himself in with his own latch-key, about half an hour after Ernest Simpson had left.[37] The explanation of Stephenson's change of mind as to whether to pursue his intervention is also different: he was 'quite confident and convinced that it was the Duke of Windsor's solicitors who caused him to be approached to withdraw his intervention...' When the King's Proctor interviewed him, Stephenson claimed that he had been offered hush money to withdraw his evidence in the form of expenses payments, which he had declined. In the interval before Mrs Simpson's divorce was finalised, Stephenson told Miss O'Callaghan that he went around armed with a knuckle-duster on the advice of friends. Tudor Jenkins, the senior journalist to whom Miss O'Callaghan reported, labelled the material as 'dynamite' but endorsed the view that not a word was publishable.[38] Even this was not Stephenson's final word on what had gone on. A few years later he was denying having given any information to a 'pretty girl' sent by one of the newspapers, despite being offered a blank cheque to do so.[39] The only common feature to the two versions is Stephenson's boast that he was immune to financial inducements. Even allowing for the fact that Stephenson was almost ninety by then, it is a remarkable change of tack.

It is thus unwise to attach too much importance to what Stephenson said about why he had acted. His true motivations remain hidden, but it is possible to assess what he achieved. The timing of his appearance was almost perfect from the point of view of someone who wanted to torpedo the divorce but not the abdication. It came just after the King had committed himself irrevocably to abdication, so there was no risk that the King might have decided to stay on learning of his intervention. Abortive though it was as a piece of judicial process in its own right, Stephenson's 'appearance' prolonged and deepened the uncertainty over whether Mrs Simpson would get her decree nisi. Under a quirk of English law – more precisely Matrimonial Causes Rule 56 – even though Stephenson had failed to file an affidavit and had even told Mrs Simpson that he did not intend to proceed, his 'appearance' remained on file and a decree absolute could not be granted unless it were shown how this had been dealt with.[40] Stephenson also provided another reason for the government's law officers to be as scrupulous as possible in handling the case. The King's Proctor had been deluged with letters of varying degrees of literacy, many of which alleged that Mrs Simpson's divorce case had been given an unfairly easy ride because of political pressure or outright corruption. The procedures of divorce law were certainly bizarre and oppressive, but a good number of people still believed that divorce should only be granted very sparingly. The report of Stephenson's 'appearance' in the *Daily Worker* made doubly certain that the King's Proctor would take it into account. Stephenson never explained why he had taken the articled clerk Gordon with him to his 'appearance' despite his political affiliations. His protestations of ignorance and annoyance ring hollow, and it is at least as likely that Gordon was there precisely to leak the story. Stephenson's 'appearance' did not just stay on file. It also prompted Sir Boyd Merriman, President of the Divorce

Court, to instruct the King's Proctor to undertake a formal investigation on 19 January 1937, and Goddard was informed accordingly.

At minimal cost and effort, Stephenson had ensured that Mrs Simpson's divorce was subject to legal uncertainty on two levels. His 'appearance' created another legal hurdle for Mrs Simpson to clear and the King's Proctor was politically, if not legally, certain to investigate thoroughly. A comprehensive dossier of points against the divorce had been fed into the system. Of course, none of this means that Stephenson was operating on anybody else's behalf, although his repeated claims to working entirely on his own volition are no more trustworthy than anything else he said. It is hard to escape the conclusion that if the government or someone under the government's influence had tried to come up with a suitable 'busybody' to do its dirty work, Stephenson would have fitted the bill nicely: a devious individual with a good grasp of legal procedure and a power of imagination worthy of a borderline fantasist.

Unknowingly, Stephenson was operating in parallel to the government's law officers. With the approval of the Attorney General his subordinate, Sir Thomas Barnes, the King's Proctor, had already begun to follow up allegations made by the more credible letter-writers on an informal basis.[41] Neither Somervell nor Barnes displayed any desire to block the divorce. From the outset, their primary motivations were professional instinct and a keen awareness of the need to pre-empt public criticism that they had failed in their duty. Moreover, Somervell doubted whether unearthing evidence of Mrs Simpson's adultery with the King would actually stop the divorce: 'Even if proved [adultery with the King] would not the Court on ordinary principles grant a discretion, particularly as Mrs. S. could plead the difficulty of informing the Court of her misconduct with the then ruling Sovereign?'[42]

Soon after the launch of the King's Proctor's formal investigation, the rumour mill, or at least its high-level section, made a sharp change in direction. The judiciary was no longer being leaned on to wave Mrs Simpson's divorce through; the Establishment was now keen that the divorce should not be finalised. The rumours were strong enough to prompt Monckton to write an extraordinary letter to Wilson:

2nd February, 1937.

CONFIDENTIAL

My dear Sir Horace,

As you know, I dined with the Prime Minister last week and yesterday I saw the King.

I am very anxious that an impression should not get abroad that the
powers that be would be glad if the decree were not made absolute. I do
not suppose that Mr. Baldwin wishes the decree not to be made absolute and I know the King hopes all will go smoothly. *I am less certain of
some of the others* [author's italics]. Personally I feel that if there was a
hitch we might well be in for a tragedy before the Coronation – certainly
for something extremely unpleasant.

The danger is that if the idea is spread in the region of the Inns of
Court that some members of the Government feel that there should be
no decree absolute, this may unconsciously affect the minds of any Judges
to whom it may be reported.

Is there anything which can properly be done to counteract the spread
of such a rumour?

Yours ever,

WALTER MONCKTON[43]

The ex-King's unofficial representative felt compelled to act as an intermediary between the King and the Prime Minister on one side, and a senior
civil servant (even though he worked directly for the Prime Minister) and
unnamed ministers on the other. Monckton's suspicion that 'some of the
others' did want to block the divorce gives the lie to the letter's ostensible purpose of merely quelling rumours. The letter expresses Monckton's
lightly coded belief that the hardliners, with Wilson to the fore, wanted
intervention to succeed, as Wilson had been advocating by implication to
Chamberlain in his panicky letter the day after the abdication. Monckton
was still in close touch with the Duke of Windsor and thus able to judge
how he would have reacted if he had found himself unable to marry Mrs
Simpson, which he thought would be disastrous. The letter also provides

an interesting sidelight on the vaunted political independence of the judiciary in the view of an experienced barrister that judges, even unconsciously, might fall in with perceived government wishes.

There is not the slightest indication that Monckton's letters led to any pressure being applied to Barnes to go gently. As far as can be seen, the government continued in its resolute respect for the principle of not interfering in the legal process. It did, though, make a significant choice in the way it dealt with Barnes's investigation, which could have led to a far less benign outcome. The government chose to withhold a piece of crucial evidence that it had already used during the crisis toward another goal. The government had deployed the accusations made against Mrs Simpson and Guy Trundle by the Special Branch (or something very similar to them) to head off the Imperial Policy Group when it threatened to cause trouble in Parliament, but the accusations remained buried when they might have been used to torpedo Mrs Simpson's divorce a few weeks later. Barnes did not know about the Trundle allegations, and it is inconceivable that he would not have pursued them if he had. Adultery by Mrs Simpson with anyone would have had to be taken into account. Moreover, they were in a different league to the supposed adultery with the King, which might not have been fatal to the divorce if proved. A squalid, doubly duplicitous and semi-commercial liaison would have been infinitely more damaging. Tacitly or otherwise, a decision was taken by the handful of individuals privy to the Trundle story not to alert Barnes. As well as the incalculable consequences of blocking the Duke of Windsor's marriage to Mrs Simpson, it would have been unimaginably scandalous.

Barnes was thus left investigating the relationship between the King and Mrs Simpson only, but he was extremely thorough in his task. He interviewed a wide range of individuals including crew of the *Nahlin*. He admitted that he had stopped short of paying the bribes that one of the letter-writers claimed would induce hotel workers from Hungary to come to England to give evidence.[44] Quite apart from the uncertainty over whether their testimony would have been useful, it would have been tainted by being purchased. He had no legal power to compel anybody

to talk to him so he could not force all of Mrs Simpson's servants to provide information. He said it was impossible to interview Mrs Simpson's
long-serving lady's maid, who would have be in a good position to detect
adultery, on the grounds that she was still employed by her and owed a duty.
He did interview Ernest Simpson and asked him why he had contacted
Downing Street on the Tuesday before the abdication.[45] He claimed that he
had merely thought he 'might assist on what he called the "psychological
aspect of the matter."' He thought she was less in love with the King than
he with her and might be persuaded to give him up. There was no connection with the divorce case. At that point Ernest Simpson was engaged
in a lucrative lawsuit for defamation against an army officer's wife who had
accused him of collusion, so it is barely surprising that he had changed his
story from the one he told Wigram before the abdication and would probably have told Downing Street. Ernest Simpson blamed the breakdown
in his marriage on his wife's attachment to the King, but stopped well
short of a definite accusation of adultery. Nowhere did Barnes unearth any
hard evidence of adultery between the King and Mrs Simpson and there
was genuine disagreement amongst those close to the case as to whether
they personally believed it had even occurred.[46] The couple had certainly
behaved sufficiently discreetly in this respect. Had the same level of discretion been applied to the relationship as a whole, the affair would have taken
a very different turning. None of the letter-writers offered even a coherent
explanation of why they thought the divorce was collusive.

With hindsight it is clear that Mrs Simpson's divorce was not in doubt
once the decision had been taken not to disclose the Trundle story. The
only practical effect of Stephenson's activities and the King's Proctor's
investigation was to prolong and reinforce the uncertainty. This was all
that the government really needed as it prepared for the coronation of King
George VI in May, with half an eye on the danger of disruption from either
Cannes or Austria. Stephenson's appearance was easily laid to rest at a
court hearing on 19 March 1937, albeit after a largely ritual examination of
Mrs Simpson's residence of convenience in Felixstowe and the identity
of Ernest Simpson's lover. It was again Norman Birkett who conducted

the case for Mrs Simpson, although this time he had to work rather harder for a fee so large that Mrs Simpson complained it would ruin her.[47] That still left almost six weeks before Mrs Simpson could file the formal application for the decree absolute on 27 April, which would have given ample time either for the King's Proctor to be presented with new evidence or for anyone else to intervene. It would have raised false expectations of a smooth outcome to have disclosed that the King's Proctor had completed his enquiries completely and drawn a blank. When the date came there were no grounds on which Barnes needed to intervene either on the question of collusion or adultery, so he could do nothing with an entirely clear conscience, but Mrs Simpson had to remain in uncertainty almost until the last moment.

The question of any government involvement in intervention remains one of the most obscure aspects of the crisis. In itself, intervention was a topic of great sensitivity and is discussed relatively little in even private accounts. Most strikingly of all, Walter Monckton does not mention it in his narrative at all, even though he saw the risk as a major consideration for the King. If Wilson had judged that national security demanded that Mrs Simpson's divorce be blocked and initiated Stephenson's actions, it is not surprising that no evidence should have remained. It would have laid the government open to the charge of manipulating the judicial process in a matter that was already immensely sensitive.

CHAPTER 22

PLENTY OF PEOPLE READY TO KNOCK HER ON THE HEAD

*I told her that most people in England disliked her very much because
the Duke had married her and given up his throne, but if she made
him and kept him happy, all that would change, but that if he
were unhappy nothing would be too bad for her.*
WALTER MONCKTON TO THE DUCHESS OF WINDSOR,
WRITTEN VERSION[1]

*…plenty of people would be ready to knock her on the head if after all this she
failed to make her husband happy, and he (M.) would be glad to do so also.*[2]
WALTER MONCKTON TO THE DUCHESS OF WINDSOR,
AS TOLD TO WINDHAM BALDWIN

NOT THE LEAST of the sacrifices that Mrs Simpson had had to make in order to keep her hold over Edward was to restrain her sense of humour. She is often described as witty, but almost no specimens of her wit have been handed down, so it is likely that it was her penchant for funny remarks rather than their quality that struck people. By contrast,

Edward appears to have been entirely humourless. Just before her flight to France, dogged by stress and fear, she had confessed to the Channons that 'she had not dared be funny for three years'.[3] The remark gives a telling indication of the emotional cost of self-control that had been accumulating long before the crisis broke. It was a small consolation to her claustrophobic exile on the Riviera that she could resume the wise-cracking which had so appealed to people during her early days in London. She could even indulge it at the expense of the Duke of Windsor. On Christmas Day she was invited to lunch by Somerset Maugham at his home on the Côte d'Azur, the Villa Mauresque. Her fellow guests included, to his horror, Bob Boothby, who was staying with his parents in Monaco. The party played bridge after lunch and Mrs Simpson was partnered with Maugham against Boothby and another guest. Maugham so badly overbid his first hand that he felt he had to apologise for his poor play. As he put down his cards, leaving Mrs Simpson with the hopeless task of trying to fulfil the impossibly demanding contract with which he had lumbered her, he confessed how few decent cards he had held: 'I'm afraid I am not a very good partner. I've only got a couple of Kings.' The temptation was too great for Mrs Simpson who cracked: 'What's the use of them? They only abdicate.'[4] Even Maugham, who seems to have invited Boothby and Mrs Simpson out of a spirit of perversity, bridled at this and stuttered, 'I d-d-don't think that's in v-v-very good t-t-taste.'

Mrs Simpson's growing bitterness and contempt was not only directed at the Duke of Windsor. Baldwin, the government and the rest of the royal family all came under her lash. A sense that the Duke was being ineffectual in defending his interests in saving what he could from the wealth and privilege that he had foregone was combined with a hypersensitive propensity to detect slights and hostility. A week after the abdication the police detectives who had remained to protect her were able to earn their keep by giving advance warning that she was already thinking of causing trouble in Britain if she was left feeling hard done by:

> If they don't get you this thing I will return to England and fight it out
> to the bitter end. The Coronation will be a flop compared with the story

that I shall tell the British Press. I will publish it in every paper in the
World so the whole World shall know my story. Your mother is even per-
secuting me now ... On the front page of every paper is a black bordered
notice stating that she has never seen or spoken to me during the past
12 months. I know it is true, but she need not persecute me. She could
have helped you so much; you, the only son that matters.[5]

It is not certain what Mrs Simpson wanted the Duke of Windsor to obtain:
possibly the title of Royal Highness for her, possibly the Civil List pension,
but whatever it was, it is unlikely that she got it. The royal family was not
inclined to be supportive. The letters that Mrs Simpson sent the Duke
during their separation betray frustration, resentment and bitterness at
her treatment.

The question of her reputation lay at the heart of the bitterness towards
the royal family and British politicians that gnawed at Mrs Simpson in the
months before the wedding. She knew that Queen Mary's public statement
was tantamount to an announcement that she was not considered to be
fit for the Queen to have contact with. She understood that the refusal to
accept her as Queen or even the morganatic wife to the King sprang from
the feeling that she was unworthy as a person. She pressured the Duke to
obtain as much recognition as possible from his family for her. She wanted
the new King to do his best 'to prove to the world that we still have a position'.[6] From the start, she knew that the title of Royal Highness would
be a particularly important symbol, although she was doubtful that she
would be granted it.[7] She believed that George VI's mother and wife were
opposed to her having the title and she worked assiduously to poison the
Duke's mind against them.[8] As well as egging the Duke on to protect her,
she began to look for allies in quarters even less reputable than the King's
Party had been recruited from.[9] To counter what she saw as a hostile press,
especially when the moment of the wedding came, she told the Duke to get
Rickatson-Hatt to find a 'good press liaison officer'.[10]

Mrs Simpson was also dogged by fears for her physical safety. She continued to receive abusive mail, which she feared was the precursor to some

attempt to do violence to her. She depended on the presence of the Scotland Yard detectives to protect her, but she did not trust them all.[11] She was too mean to pay for the services of private detectives.[12] Her host in Cannes, Herman Rogers, told her that he slept with a pistol under his pillow, ostensibly to protect her if the need arose, more likely simply to reassure her. Her fears were so extreme that she was easy meat when Kenneth de Courcy arrived at Villa Lou Viei peddling a fantasy of a well-funded 'anti-Simpson organisation' dedicated to her murder, 'Paying well for killing'.[13] In reality, both Mrs Simpson and Wilson were exaggerating wildly in their fears of violence against Mrs Simpson. The 'wave of fury' that Wilson predicted never got further than the tutting exemplified by Nancy Dugdale and children up and down the country singing ditties like the following version of the popular song *Ain't she sweet?*:

> *Walking down the street*
> *Mrs. Simpson, ain't she sweet?*
> *She's been married twice before –*
> *Now she's knocking on Edward's door.*[14]

The first months of exile were miserable for the couple. Both were guests in houses not ideally suited to the purpose. They let out their frustrations in long telephone calls. They spoke almost daily and Mrs Simpson delivered the same litany of complaint as in her letters. She was aggrieved that one of his first visitors was her *bête noire* 'Fruity' Metcalfe, and she nursed the ludicrous notion that the Duke might be unfaithful with his hostess. The Duke was bereft without Mrs Simpson, living in a guest bedroom with practically no possessions of his own. He, in turn, sought release in telephone calls with the new King, whom he nagged about what was happening to him and Mrs Simpson as well as insistently tendering advice on how to reign, as though his brother were merely acting as his regent. George VI's stammer made these conversations an agonising trial and he eventually put an end to them, adding to the Duke's growing list of grievances.

The uncertainty over the divorce put added pressure on Mrs Simpson and, to a lesser extent, the Duke of Windsor, particularly when she was told that the King's Proctor had been formally instructed to investigate the case in late January. It is a constant refrain in her letters from France. Her complaints drip with self-pity. She nagged the Duke of Windsor to make his brother force the process along or at least find out what was going on.[15] She imagined that a sign that the King wanted the divorce to go through would be enough to make the Attorney General back off.[16] It fed her growing dislike of Britain: 'it is a trying time especially with the horror of a hitch in the divorce. England would do anything to me in their smug fashion.'[17]

Mrs Simpson complained about it, but the fear of a successful intervention by the King's Proctor was enough to torpedo a scheme to bring them closer. Both had been finding their first places of exile increasingly claustrophobic, in part because their hosts grew aware of the strain that their celebrated guests brought with them. Mrs Simpson was especially unhappy in the small quarters of the Villa Lou Viei, and found a refuge away from the Riviera, 900 kilometres to the north in the château of an extremely wealthy Franco-American businessman, Charles Bedaux. The Château de Candé at Monts near Tours had added attractions. It offered a more appropriate venue for the planned wedding than a showy villa on the Côte d'Azur. It would also allow Mrs Simpson to be reunited with Slipper, who had had to remain with the Duke of Windsor in Austria, because the Rogers' ferocious Westies would have resented his presence at the Villa Lou Viei. She moved north in early March. The next leg of the plan had been for the Duke of Windsor to move to the Duke of Westminster's house at Saint-Saëns in Normandy, a mere 300 kilometres away. The couple spoke almost daily and they hoped that a line within France would be clearer than the international line between France and Austria. Calls would also be cheaper, although it is unclear whether this burden was falling on the Duke's hosts in Austria.[18] In the event, though, George Allen warned the Duke off living in the same country as Mrs Simpson and he had to settle for another house in Austria.[19] Allen emphasised the symbolic importance of remaining in different countries, but there was an unspoken suggestion that the short distance between Monts and Saint-Saëns would have excited suspicions of clandestine visits. In fact, the fear of the King's Proctor was strong enough to prevent this even being considered. Merely reducing the distance between them would have been comfort enough.

The move to Candé proved a great improvement for Mrs Simpson.[20] The house was more spacious with very large grounds and the Bedaux had moved away, leaving their admirable servants to minister to her. It was a Renaissance house that had been much extended in the nineteenth century and then modernised at vast expense by the Bedaux. It provided the height of luxury for its period. The facilities included sumptuous bathrooms, a modern gymnasium and direct-dial telephones in most rooms. The crowning glory was a Skinner organ, the ultimate in home entertainment then available, imported at vast expense from the US (the manufacturer was a client of Bedaux). One wall of the house had to be removed and then replaced in order to install it. Neither of the Bedaux could play the organ, but its electro-pneumatic mechanism could work like a pianola, automatically controlled by punched paper rolls.

The culmination of Mrs Simpson's move north was to be reunited with Slipper, who arrived in the charge of a Scotland Yard detective. Presumably the intelligence dividends of the mission were felt to be worth deploying a member of Special Branch on a servant's errand. The idyll was doomed to be short and it came to an end when Rickatson-Hatt visited in early April, presumably invited to discuss press coverage. If the surmise that he was MI5's informant is correct, it is almost certain that he would also have gathered intelligence on behalf of the government. On the afternoon of his visit, he played a round of golf on Candé's private course, accompanied by Mrs Simpson and Slipper. They had barely begun when Slipper was found comatose in the bushes. Mrs Simpson thought that he had been bitten by a viper. A vet worked on him through the evening unavailingly and he died that night, the only recorded fatality of the crisis. The Duke and Mrs Simpson were left to mourn the death of the intended 'principal guest at the Wedding'.[21]

Mrs Simpson blamed Baldwin for what she saw as her ill-treatment, even going so far as to label George VI as 'the puppet they [the politicians] have placed on the throne'.[22] It was all part of a seamless conspiracy to force Edward off the throne and then to destroy his memory:

> They had for months an organised campaign to remove you – and how cleverly they worked – so have they one to prove they were right in what they did and the first step is to eliminate you from the minds of the people. I was the convenient tool in their hands to use to get rid of you and how they used it![23]

In reality, the politicians were just glad to have washed their hands of the couple. As Edward's authorised biographer has shown, George VI used ministerial advice as a pretext to follow his own judgement on the questions of whether members of the royal family should attend the wedding and whether the Duchess of Windsor should be allowed the title of Her Royal Highness.[24] The King was especially insistent on the question of the title because he believed that it could only be granted irrevocably.[25] He doubted the marriage would last, creating the horrible vision of the ex-Duchess of Windsor taking the title as alimony into a doubtless unsuitable fourth and subsequent marriages.[26] George VI appears to have been heavily influenced in his efforts to withhold the title by his wife, who was also one of the chief doubters that the marriage would last.[27] The politicians and even the hardline civil servants feared that it would be seen as a spiteful move against the ex-King to withhold the title. Perhaps curiously, they would have found that Churchill agreed with them on this point as he firmly advised against Mrs Simpson becoming a Royal Highness after marrying the Duke of Windsor.[28] Amidst all Churchill's contradictory statements of his view of her, this is perhaps the best clue that he actually held her in low esteem.

Ultimately, the politicians fell in line with George VI's wishes. Simon overcame his initial instinct to apply the ordinary rule that a wife automatically shares her husband's titles and confected an argument that the title of Royal Highness could only be applied within the line of succession. It seems that the matter was only finally settled when George VI wrote directly to Baldwin to break the logjam.[29] The government issued Letters Patent granting the title to the Duke as an exception, after the fact of his abdication, but not to his wife. As with all significant government acts in Britain it was done in the sovereign's name, but for once it was an initiative of the sovereign imposed on reluctant politicians. It is a telling register of the low esteem in which the Duke of Windsor and Mrs Simpson were held that the government accepted not merely the inequity of the move, but, more important, the risk that it would provoke the Duke into some form of misbehaviour. Oceans of ink have been drained criticising the specious injustice, if not downright illegality of this move, but it should be remembered that it arose from the unreflected and informal promise to let the Duke of Windsor keep royal status, which was made in the haste, stress and confusion of the final days of Edward's reign. Unlike the similarly compromised financial arrangements, it could not be revised in private and it might have looked better in the eyes of posterity to live with the full consequences. Once the future George VI had swallowed the precedential camel of allowing Edward to retain royal status, it was perverse to strain at the gnat of allowing his wife to acquire it too. The same legalistic ingenuity that was deployed to allow royal status to only the husband could equally have been used to ensure that the wife would only retain it for the lifetime of the marriage. Sixty years later, Letters Patent were issued stripping the title of Royal Highness from the divorced wives of born royalty and this was applied to both of Elizabeth II's ex-daughters-in-law. The unshakeable resolve of Queens Elizabeth and Mary never to receive the Duchess of Windsor meant that the Duchess of Windsor never became part of the royal family in any meaningful sense.

Even though he had bowed to royal wish, Baldwin was unhappy with this arrangement and shuffled the job of getting it approved by the Dominions onto Chamberlain, who was very soon to succeed him as Prime Minister.[30] Chamberlain grumbled at another example of Baldwin 'shirking' an unpleasant job, but obliged. Perhaps he was less troubled at the thought of delivering so public a snub to the Duchess of Windsor. Unwittingly, the Dominions fell in with royal wishes, notably New Zealand's Prime Minister, who told Baldwin that she could be called 'Her Grace the Duchess of Windsor ... And quite enough too!'[31] Yet again Monckton was used to spread a misleading version of the story that even further exonerated the British government. He was told that the Cabinet left to itself would not have withheld the title, but the Dominions insisted.[32] The King was suitably relieved that Chamberlain's efforts had borne fruit.[33] The Duke of Windsor was predictably furious, railing against what he believed was the breach of a firm promise not to 'make trouble about the title'.[34]

The question of financial provision for the Duke of Windsor had also been left unsettled in the last frantic days before the abdication. The agreement with his brothers only came into play if he did not receive a Civil List pension, so it was inevitable that the question would arise for the government. On this issue, it looked as though Baldwin might face a sterner open political challenge than he had done during the crisis itself. His old and irreconcilable foe David Lloyd George came out publicly in support of the Duke of Windsor's interests. Like Churchill, he had only a tiny parliamentary following, but a great name and immense powers of rhetoric. Unlike Churchill, he had practically no hope of office and thus nothing to lose. He and Churchill had the great tactical strength of sitting on the Parliamentary Civil List Committee, which was the first forum in which the issue would be raised. Lloyd George had avoided the opprobrium garnered by Churchill by supporting Edward before his abdication, partly through the chance of being in the West Indies when the crisis broke. He had scented an opportunity to embarrass the government, rapidly blotting out the bad impression that Edward had made during the visit to Wales the previous year, and had hovered on the verge of intervening, but his children, Megan and Gwilym, who each had political careers of their own, acted as forces for caution. Once Edward had abdicated, Lloyd George had seen the coast clear to cause mischief. He sent the Duke of Windsor a telegram on Christmas Eve, which he copied to the news agencies:

> Best Christmas greetings from an old Minister of the Crown who holds you in as high esteem as ever and regards you with deep and loyal affection, deplores the shabby and stupid treatment accorded to you, resents the mean and unchivalrous attacks upon you and regrets the

loss sustained by the British Empire of a monarch who sympathised
with the lowliest of his subjects.[35]

Thus, Lloyd George launched the legend that Edward had been driven
from his throne because of his social views. Three months later, he followed
this up by lobbying George VI directly in favour of generous financial
treatment for his brother.[36]

Churchill saw an opportunity to needle the government over the Duke
of Windsor's finances, and his personal loyalty dictated that he try to make
sure that his former King was well provided for. He knew from the start,
though, that he was on the back foot and that raising the Duke of Windsor's
finances at the Civil List Committee would be unwise. Baldwin had taken
the precaution of briefing Churchill on the financial affairs of the Duke,
including his private fortune of nearly £1 million and the temporary transfer of the bulk of his wealth into Mrs Simpson's name, and the agreement
with his brothers over Sandringham and Balmoral.[37] Lloyd George knew
none of this when he had spoken to George VI but it is more than likely that
Churchill told him afterwards. This was Churchill's first intimation that the
story the ex-King had told him of impending poverty at Fort Belvedere was
a lie. He also knew how unwise it would be to wash the Duke of Windsor's
financial linen in public. Under the pretext of making sure that Baldwin's
description of the Duke of Windsor's finances was accurate, he prodded
Chamberlain and recruited Lloyd George to the cause.[38] The prospect that
his old foes might unite to embarrass the government was enough to throw
Chamberlain into a fit of near apoplexy, and he fell to ranting against 'these
two pirates' who were 'hunting together' and trying to 'blackmail [George
VI] into a regular swindling arrangement by threats of making trouble in
Committee'.[39] Fisher and Wilson seem to have backed him with direct
pressure applied at court.[40] Their campaign received unexpected fillips at
the Civil List Committee meeting on 7 April 1937, when Attlee raised the
question of the royal family's private finances and Leo Amery spontaneously
spoke in favour of generous financial provision for the Duke of Windsor. This was enough to prompt Chamberlain into going to see the King.

He learned that the Fort Belvedere agreement between the Duke of Windsor and his brothers had been very hastily done, and wanted it to be replaced by a more business-like contract.[41] It took the combined efforts of the Duke of Windsor himself, whom Churchill only told afterwards that he was launching his campaign, and Clive Wigram, Edward VIII's first private secretary who had reappeared in active royal service under George VI, to persuade Churchill to 'cease firing'.[42] Wigram finally resorted to telling Churchill that the Duke of Windsor had lied to his brother about his wealth and backed this by a threat to reveal to Parliament the amount of money the Duke of Windsor had taken abroad with him. The Duke of Windsor was not mentioned at the Civil List Committee and he never received a Civil List pension. Though it was to take many months of agonised and bitter haggling to reach a formal agreement with his brother, the immediate political threat had been defused.

Baldwin's reluctance to take responsibility for withholding royal status from Mrs Simpson did not mean that his view of her had softened at all from his savage judgement at the height of the crisis. He did not hide his low opinion of her and began to speculate that she might not go unpunished. Shortly before he left office, he gave Sir John Reith a long account of the affair over a cosy dinner at Chequers.

> He said Mrs. S, a thorough bad'un all through; he used very strong language about her [the word 'whore' presumably figured]. She had had a tremendous amount of money out of the King. He wondered if Edward would ever find out what a blackguard she was & whether he would shoot her if he did.[43]

Baldwin's comment went well beyond semi-jocular speculation in poor taste. He had already been struck by the contrast between Edward's shining vision of Mrs Simpson and the ugly picture that Downing Street's intelligence sources had fed to him. He knew the ex-King's uncompromising character and, along with many others, doubted his mental stability. When it had seemed as though the intervention of the King's Proctor might prevent him marrying Mrs Simpson, Baldwin had feared these violent traits would lead to suicide. He was now concerned that they would translate into homicidal violence. It was not just Baldwin who entertained fears of what would happen if the Duke of Windsor discovered Mrs Simpson's true nature. Some months later Baldwin told his niece that these were shared by the Duke's family: 'His family are all wondering what will become of him when at last he opens his eyes and sees the sort she really is, Or – will he remain besotted to the end?'[44]

George VI had not merely stepped into his brother's shoes but he had picked up his appointments diary as well. The most significant date had been there for almost a year: 12 May 1937, the day that had originally been fixed for the coronation of Edward VIII, which had seamlessly become the day that George VI was to be crowned. The Duke of Windsor now found himself operating in a timetable he had planned a year before under radically different circumstances. Mrs Simpson's divorce proceedings had been timed to allow time for the decree absolute to be issued before the coronation date and hence to allow him to marry Mrs Simpson before. The timing had been dangerously tight then and was worse after the abdication, above all because the King's Proctor's investigation had pushed up the risk that the marriage might be impossible. In early March, Mrs Simpson had bowed to the inevitable and set a date for the marriage after the coronation.[45] The risk that it might overshadow George VI's ceremony dwindled sharply.

The divorce court finally delivered the decree absolute on 3 May and the Duke of Windsor joined Mrs Simpson at Candé as rapidly as possible. There was no pretence that she was being chaperoned there. It was a slightly more decent interval between divorce and wedding than Edward had originally had in mind. In most other respects, it was a curious ceremony to mark the marriage of a former King of England and Emperor of India. In keeping with French practice, the civil ceremony was performed by the local mayor, but the bottom of the barrel was scraped to find an Anglican clergyman to perform the religious ceremony. Douglas Jardine was a mere provincial curate with no connection to royal circles or personal ties with the couple, who defied his bishop's explicit instructions to officiate.

He later tried to capitalise on his notoriety by opening the 'Cathedral of Windsor' as a wedding venue in Hollywood.[46] He prefigured Squadron-Leader, the Rev. Dennis Barlow, hero of Evelyn Waugh's novel *The Loved One*, who blackmailed the respectable British expatriate community of the Hollywood cricket club into funding his return to Britain by threatening to open for business performing 'non-sectarian' religious services. Candé had a Roman Catholic chapel, but there does not seem to have been any attempt to consecrate the premises for an Anglican service. A reproduction Renaissance chest was adorned to serve as an altar.

Courtiers followed the example of the Duke's brothers and his cousin Louis Mountbatten, who had originally offered to act as best man, and stayed away, and British public servants obeyed rather more direct instructions to do so. The congregation totalled eleven and included the Bedaux, who had been at pains to have the word spread that they were not charging money for the use of the château, as Charles Bedaux feared that this might be taken as a sign that his business was not doing well. No expense was spared on the other aspects of the wedding. The Paris couturier Mainbocher made a wedding gown for the bride in what was to become famous as 'Wallis blue'. Cecil Beaton and Constance Spry, the leaders of London fashion in photography and flower arrangement, were hired to attend to these parts of the day's proceedings. The celebrated organist Marcel Dupré was brought in from Paris, although it is unlikely that anyone involved was aware that the keys of the Skinner organ act merely as on/off switches, so there is no scope for variation or subtlety in fingering them. Any competent organist can achieve the same quality of music. The Duke had some compensation for the expense in the shape of a piece, 'Gloria in Excelsis Deo', that Dupré had written specially, enriching an otherwise mundane programme that concluded with the couple walking out to Vidor's toccata.

Even more curious than the ceremony itself was the message that one of the guests delivered. Walter Monckton was almost the only individual to emerge from the crisis without alienating one side or the other. He had remained a trusted friend to the Duke, but George VI had kept him on as Attorney General to the Duchy of Cornwall – indeed, conferred on him the first knighthood of the new reign – and he acted as intermediary between the Duke and both Buckingham Palace and Downing Street in what was becoming an increasingly fraught relationship. It is a tribute to Monckton's qualities that his relationship with the Duke had not been damaged by two things that he had had to tell him in the first months of his exile: that George VI would no longer speak to him by telephone and, later, that his wife-to-be would not have royal status. The message Monckton brought to the wedding was a private one for the Duchess alone. He asked whether he might have five minutes alone with her. The Duke did not want this, but she insisted on granting Monckton's wish. Even in the decorous, written narrative that Monckton produced, his message was a blunt one: '…most people in England disliked her very much because the Duke had married her and given up his throne, but if she made him and kept him happy, all that would change, but that if he were unhappy nothing would be too bad for her.'[47] This is the version that is usually quoted, but in the course of a far less discreet conversation with Baldwin's son in 1950, he gave another version, in which the menace was quite direct: '…plenty of people would be ready to knock her on the head if after all this she failed to make her husband happy, and he (M.) would be glad to do so also.'[48] In both versions, the Duchess told Monckton that she had already thought about the matter deeply. Over the years, she succeeded in making her husband happy and Monckton never felt the need to carry out his threat. When Maugham had overbid at bridge on Christmas Day at the Villa Mauresque, she had only suffered the consequences for a few minutes, but when Edward had overbid his hand, thinking that his popularity was great enough for him to make Wallis his Queen, she had to cope with the consequences for a lifetime.

AFTERWORD

WILSON'S EFFORTS TO produce a narrative of the crisis that concealed matters that would have embarrassed the government had they come to light, turned out to have been almost entirely unnecessary. The waters of oblivion closed rapidly over the heads of the former King and his new wife. After a flurry of coverage of their wedding, they attracted no more than two or three newspaper stories per month.

Their affairs were still a matter of agonised discussion in the closed worlds of Downing Street and Buckingham Palace, but there was no follow-through for even the muted public controversy at the height of the crisis and its immediate aftermath. The tentative efforts of Churchill and Lloyd George to obtain a Civil List grant were the last hurrah of the King's Party in its largest sense. Stanley Baldwin had succeeded in drawing a line under the whole sorry business, and there was no appetite to look closely at what anyone had done or how.

Discussions between George VI and the government under the new Prime Minister Neville Chamberlain on one side and the Duke of Windsor on the other focused on the two topics that soon became intertwined: the uncompleted agreement with the royal brothers over money and the Duke's desire to return soon to Britain. The Duke also sought some form of recognition by the government and the Court for the Duchess. He displayed the same tactical ineptitude that had marked his handling of the crisis.

His attempt to rebuild a public position through a visit to Nazi Germany together with the Duchess in the autumn of 1937 turned out to be an embarrassment at best, and, at worst, glaring proof of his complete lack of judgement. Chamberlain and Wilson, whose nebulous but enormously powerful role survived into the new premiership and became even stronger, successfully led the fight against the Duke's return.

The disappearance of the Duke and Duchess to the margins of public and political attention was hastened by the worsening diplomatic situation in Europe. After relative calm through 1937, Germany's *Anschluß* with Austria in March 1938 set the continent on track for the Second World War a year and a half later. Contemporaries and later historians were naturally far more interested in how Britain's statesmen had performed when confronted with these tests than on the spectacular, but short-lived and parochial drama of the abdication. Compared to the intense and bitter debate over the parts that Baldwin, Chamberlain and Wilson had played in the appeasement policy towards Hitler and Mussolini, the abdication barely counted. The British government's long-standing reluctance to release any official documents relating to the royal family was further deterrent to discussion.

Perhaps perversely, the fact that the historical verdict on Chamberlain – who died in 1940 – depends so hugely on the verdict on appeasement meant that otherwise well-disposed writers allowed the faintest and most coded of criticism of his performance during the abdication to creep in. This began in 1946 with his first, and de facto, official biographer, Keith Feiling, who hinted at the tension between Chamberlain's pressure for 'some terminus' and Baldwin as the 'Crown's principal and, in this case, best adviser'.[1] Chamberlain's parliamentary private secretary and, eventually, successor as Prime Minister, Alec Douglas-Home, praised Baldwin's sure-footedness, 'discretion, sensitivity and patience' in contrast to Chamberlain's 'restive[ness] with what he judged to be the fumbling indecision by the Prime Minister'.[2] Home was even more forthright to a friendly biographer and labelled Chamberlain's private criticism of aspects of Baldwin's handling of the crisis as simply wrong.[3]

By the time that the Duke of Windsor, egged on by Lord Beaverbrook, set out to present his side of the story, culminating in his memoir *A King's Story* in 1951, the abdication had receded far into the past. The Duke's three principal targets, Baldwin, Archbishop Lang and Geoffrey Dawson of *The Times*, were all dead. Moreover, the actual role of the latter two had been minor, if not downright peripheral, and his version of Baldwin's role was ludicrously garbled, reflecting Beaverbrook's yearning to humiliate posthumously a man who had soundly beaten him in all their political encounters.

Baldwin had savoured the moment of his triumph in the House of Commons on 10 December 1936, but thereafter placed his feet firmly on the ground and minded the fickleness of political opinion. A few days later he was talking to MP Blanche Dugdale, 'quite unmoved by his personal prestige. He says he was on a personal pinnacle before (at the time of the General Strike) and within six weeks all were damning him.'[4] Baldwin never left a written record of the crisis, but he set out what he saw as the key points of the affair to another MP a few weeks later. His own role barely featured. What mattered was that:

> Edward VIII had not the vital gifts which make a King – patience and devotion to duty. It was fortunate for the country that he went when he did; the downfall would have been more catastrophic in later years.[5]

APPENDICES

A. DRAFT OF LETTER OF FORMAL ADVICE TO THE KING

Mr. Baldwin with his humble duty to Your Majesty.

It was with great regret that Mr. Baldwin found it necessary on Tuesday, the 20th October, to communicate to Your Majesty his very real concern at the widespread feelings aroused in all sections of Your Majesty's subjects by Your Majesty's association with Mrs. Ernest Simpson. As an illustration of this attitude Mr. Baldwin left with Your Majesty a number of letters received by him and others and since then many more letters of a similar character have come in. Moreover the legal proceedings instituted on the 27th October by Mrs. Simpson for the divorce of her husband have concentrated the public attention upon the subject and aroused public apprehension to such a degree that Mr. Baldwin feels it necessary to repeat more formally and more emphatically the warning he has already addressed to Your Majesty but to which Your Majesty has hitherto paid but little heed. He feels it his duty as Prime Minister to point out to Your Majesty that the continuance of Your Majesty's association with Mrs. Simpson after these legal proceedings is likely to affect in a manner which cannot be ignored the already very disturbing movement of public opinion. This opinion is now moving rapidly to the conclusion that the dignity and self-respect of the people of this country and of the sister nations are being symbolically affronted and that the conduct of Your Majesty is inconsistent with the whole conception of Kingship and its great tradition. The high expectations which accompanied Your Majesty's succession to the Throne are giving way to doubts as to whether they can conceivably be fulfilled. Unless steps are taken promptly to allay the widespread and growing misgivings among the people, the feelings of respect, esteem and affection which Your Majesty has evoked among them will disappear in a revulsion of so grave and perilous a character as possibly to threaten the stability of the nation and of the Empire. The dangers to the people of this country of such a shock, the disunity and loss of confidence which would ensue at a time when so much of the world is looking to the United Kingdom for guidance and leadership through a sea of troubles cannot but be obvious to Your Majesty.

In Mr. Baldwin's opinion there is but one course which he can advise Your Majesty to take, namely to put an end to Your Majesty's association with Mrs. Simpson. In order to prevent any possible misunderstanding he must add that he would not regard marriage with Mrs. Simpson as a possible solution of Your Majesty's difficulties.[1]

B. DRAFT OF LETTER OF INFORMAL ADVICE TO KING

FISHER'S DRAFT

When Your Majesty was pleased to receive me on October 20th I intimated that the manner of Your Majesty's domestic life was causing me and other Ministers much concern by reason of the feeling to which it was giving rise in the country. Subsequently the divorce proceedings which, in spite of my representations, Your Majesty did not feel disposed to make any attempt to stop, have brought about a situation which threatens not only Your Majesty's own position, but the constitutional stability of the nation.

Your Majesty's Government have information which leaves no doubt that there is throughout the country a growing feeling of discontent and resentment at the example which Your Majesty is setting. They are also aware that, since the divorce proceedings, the ordinary restraint imposed on Your Majesty's subjects has been disregarded, and that Your Majesty's association with the lady in question has continued as before. They think it their duty to inform Your Majesty that already two affidavits have been put in by outside parties requiring the intervention of the King's Proctor.

In these circumstances I have consulted with Ministers and have before me an official communication in which the advice of Your Majesty's Government is formally tendered to the effect that, in view of the grave injury which in their opinion is being inflicted on the people of this country, Your Majesty's association with Mrs. Simpson should be terminated forthwith.

It is hardly necessary for me to point out that the refusal of Your Majesty to follow the requirements of constitutional monarchy and accept this advice can have but one result, namely the resignation of myself and the National Government.

Although in the last resort I have no alternative but to transmit this formal advice to Your Majesty, I have no doubt that, in the event of your giving an undertaking that Mrs. Simpson shall leave the country forthwith, this distasteful matter can be settled in a less formal manner.

I shall be glad to receive Your Majesty's reply as soon as conveniently possible and in the event of Your wishing to discuss the matter I would propose to bring with me the Chancellor of the Exchequer, Lord Halifax (representing the Lord Chancellor), the Lord President of the Council and the Speaker of the House of Commons.[2]

AMENDED BY CHAMBERLAIN

When Your Majesty was pleased to receive me on October 20th I intimated that the manner of Your Majesty's domestic life was causing me and other Ministers much concern by reason of the feeling to which it was giving rise in the country. Subsequently the divorce proceedings which, in reply to my representations, Your Majesty declared yourself unable or indisposed to stop, have brought about a situation which threatens not only Your Majesty's own position, but the constitutional stability of the nation.

Your Majesty's Government have information which leaves no doubt that there is throughout the country a growing feeling of discontent and resentment at the example which Your Majesty is setting. They are also aware that since the divorce proceedings, this feeling has been intensified and fresh apprehensions aroused by the continuance of Your Majesty's association with the lady in question. Further publicity is likely to be involved if, as Your Majesty's Government has been informed, two affidavits by outside parties are being prepared for submission to the Registrar in the proceedings instituted by Mrs. Simpson at Ipswich.

In these circumstances I have consulted with Ministers and have before me an official communication in which the advice of Your Majesty's Government is formally tendered to the effect that, in view of the grave danger to which in their opinion the country is being exposed, Your Majesty's association with Mrs. Simpson should be terminated forthwith.

It is hardly necessary for me to point out that should this advice be tendered and refused by Your Majesty, only one result could follow in accordance with the requirements of constitutional monarchy, namely the resignation of myself and the National Government.

Although in the last resort I should have no alternative but to transmit this formal advice to Your Majesty, I have no doubt that, in the event of my receiving satisfactory assurances of Mrs. Simpson's intention to leave the country forthwith, this distasteful matter could be settled in a less formal manner.

I shall be glad to receive Your Majesty's reply as soon as conveniently possible since I am convinced that there is really no time to be lost if the danger of an explosion is to be averted.[3]

C. HARDINGE'S LETTER TO THE KING, 13 NOVEMBER 1936

SIR,

With my humble duty.

As Your Majesty's Private Secretary, I feel it my duty to bring to your notice the following facts which have come to my knowledge, and which I *know* to be accurate:

(1) The silence of the British Press on the subject of Your Majesty's friendship with Mrs. Simpson is not going to be maintained. It is probably only a matter of days before the outburst begins. Judging by the letters from British subjects living in foreign countries where the Press has been outspoken, the effect will be calamitous.

(2) The Prime Minister and senior members of the Government are meeting to-day to discuss what action should be taken to deal with the serious situation which is developing. As Your Majesty no doubt knows, the resignation of the Government – an eventuality which can by no means be excluded – would result in Your Majesty having to find someone else capable of forming a government which would receive the support of the present House of Commons. I have reason to know that, in view of the feeling prevalent among members of the House of Commons of all parties, this is hardly within the bounds of possibility. The only alternative remaining is a dissolution and a General Election, in which Your Majesty's personal affairs would be the chief issue – and I cannot help feeling that even those who would sympathise with Your Majesty as an individual would deeply resent the damage which would inevitably be done to the Crown, the corner-stone on which the whole Empire rests.

If Your Majesty will permit me to say so, there is only one step which holds out any prospect of avoiding this dangerous situation, and that is for Mrs. Simpson to go abroad *without further delay*, and I would *beg* Your Majesty to give this proposal your earnest consideration before the position has become irretrievable. Owing to the changing attitude of the Press, the matter has become one of great urgency.

I have the honour, etc., etc.,

ALEXANDER HARDINGE.

P.S. – I am by way of going after dinner to-night to High Wycombe to shoot there to-morrow, but the Post Office will have my telephone number, and I am of course entirely at Your Majesty's disposal if there is anything at all that you want.

BIBLIOGRAPHY

PRIVATE OR UNPUBLISHED ACCOUNTS OF THE ABDICATION BY PARTICIPANTS

Beaverbrook, Lord, drafts of narrative, House of Lords Record Office, Beaverbrook papers, BBK 6/G/19

Chamberlain, Neville, diary*, University of Birmingham Special Collections, Neville Chamberlain papers NC 2/23–24

Churchill, Sir Winston, The Abdication of King Edward VIII, Churchill Archives Centre, Cambridge CHAR 2/264

Cooper, Alfred Duff, Diaries, Churchill Archives Centre, Cambridge, the papers of Alfred Duff Cooper (1st Viscount Norwich) DUFC 15

Dugdale, Nancy, Constitutional Crisis (Dugdale diary), Crathorne papers

Goddard, Theodore, Narrative, reproduced in Beaverbrook *The Abdication of King Edward VIII*

Monckton, Walter, Narrative, Balliol College, Oxford, Dep Monckton Trustees C22

Peacock, Sir Edward, Sir Edward Peacock notes, Balliol College, Oxford, Dep Monckton Trustees C22

Wilson, Sir Horace, King Edward VIII: Notes by Sir Horace Wilson, at 10 Downing Street and drafts, National Archives PREM 1/466

---

* Entries 26 October to 11 December all about crisis

Windsor, Duke of, draft memoirs, House of Lords Record Office, Beaver-brook papers, BBK 6/G/23, BBK 6/G/24 and BBK 6/G/27

UNPUBLISHED DIARIES

Hardinge, Helen, The hon. Lady Murray papers
MacDonald, James Ramsay, The National Archives PRO 30/69
Norman, Montagu, Bank of England Archives ADM 34/30
Reith, Sir John, BBC Written Archives, Caversham

GOVERNMENT ARCHIVES

National Archive, NA
National Archives of Australia, NAA

OTHER UNPUBLISHED MATERIAL AND ARCHIVES

Baldwin, Stanley, papers, University Library, Cambridge, 176–8 L3 'The Royal Box'
Baldwin, Windham, papers, University Library, Cambridge
Beaverbrook, Lord, papers (BBK), House of Lords Record Office
Chamberlain, Neville, papers, University of Birmingham Special Collections, Neville Chamberlain papers (NC)
de Courcy, Kenneth, papers, Hoover Institution Archives, University of Stanford (microfilm)
Davidson, J. C. C., papers, House of Lords Record Office (DAV)
Dugdale, Thomas, Crathorne papers
Fielden, Air Vice Marshal Sir Edward, papers, RAF Museum, Hendon
Fisher, Sir Warren, papers
Hesse, Fritz, Nachlaß Hesse (papers), Bundesarchiv, Koblenz

Hoare, Sir Samuel, Templewood papers, University Library, Cambridge

Jones, Thomas, papers, National Library of Wales, Aberystwyth University

Peden, George C., notes of interviews, Bodleian Oxford Library, Special Collections

Rickatson-Hatt, Bernard, papers, Thomson Reuters Archive

Vansittart, Sir Robert, papers, Churchill Archive Centre, Cambridge (VNST)

PUBLISHED COLLECTIONS OF DOCUMENTS

Bloch, Michael (ed.), *Wallis & Edward: Letters 1931–1937* (London: Weidenfeld & Nicolson, 1986).

Cameron, Norman and Stevens, R. H. (translator) *Hitler's Table Talk* (London: Weidenfeld & Nicolson, 1953).

Davenport-Hines, Richard & Sisman, Adam (eds.), *One Hundred Letters from Hugh Trevor-Roper* (Oxford and New York: Oxford University Press, 2014).

Gilbert, Martin (ed.), *The Churchill Documents, Volume 13: The Coming of War 1936–1939* (London: William Heinemann, 1982).

Jones, Thomas, *A Diary With Letters 1931–1950* (Oxford and New York: Oxford University Press, 1954).

Lowndes, Susan (ed.), Belloc Lowndes, Marie, *Diaries and Letters of Marie Belloc Lowndes 1911–1947* (London: Chatto & Windus, 1971).

Nicolson, Harold, *Diaries and Letters 1930–39* (London: Collins, 1966).

Rhodes James, Robert (ed.), *Memoirs of a Conservative: J. C. C. Davidson Memoirs and Papers 1910–37* (London: Weidenfeld & Nicolson, 1969).

Self, Robert (ed.), *The Neville Chamberlain Diary Letters*, Volume IV (references given as Chamberlain to Ida or Hilda respectively) (Burlington: Ashgate, 2005).

Smith, Amanda (ed.), *Hostage to Fortune: The Letters of Joseph P. Kennedy* (New York: Viking, 2001).

Williamson, Philip & Baldwin, Edward, *Baldwin Papers: A Conservative Statesman, 1908–1947* (Cambridge: Cambridge University Press, 2004).

Documents on German Foreign Policy Series C IV (DGFP), H.M.S.O. 1957–83

PUBLISHED DIARIES

Amery, Leo; Barnes, John & Nicolson, David (eds), *The Empire at Bay: The Leo Amery Diaries 1929–1945* (London: Hutchinson, 1988).

Brooks, Collin; Crowson, N. J. (ed.), *Fleet Street, Press Barons and Politics: The Journals of Collin Brooks, 1932–1940* (Cambridge: Cambridge University Press, 1998).

Bruce Lockhart, Robert; Young, Kenneth (ed.), *The Diaries of Sir Robert Bruce Lockhart 1915–1938* (London: Macmillan, 1973).

Channon, Chips; Rhodes James, Robert (ed.), *'Chips': The Diaries of Sir Henry Channon* (London: Weidenfeld & Nicolson, 2004).

Colville, John, *The Fringes of Power: Downing Street Diaries 1939–1955*, Revised edition (London: Weidenfeld & Nicolson, 2004).

Cooper, Duff; Norwich, John Julius (ed.), *The Duff Cooper Diaries* (London: Weidenfeld & Nicolson, 2005).

Crawford, Earl of; Vincent, John (ed.), *The Crawford Papers: The Journals of David Lindsay, Twenty-Seventh Earl of Crawford and Tenth Earl of Balcarres 1871–1940 During the Years 1892–1940* (Manchester: Manchester University Press, 1984).

Dugdale, Blanche; Rose, N. A. (ed.), *Baffy: The Diaries of Blanche Dugdale 1936–1947* (London: Valentine Mitchell, 1073).

Jones, Thomas; Middlemas, Keith (ed.), *Whitehall Diary Volume II 1926/1930* (London: Oxford University Press, 1969).

Lascelles, Alan; Hart-Davis, Duff (ed.), *In Royal Service* (London: Hamish Hamilton, 1989).

Lascelles, Alan; Hart-Davis, Duff (ed.), *King's Counsellor* (London: Weidenfeld & Nicolson, 2006).

Maisky, Ivan; Gorodetsky, Gabriel (ed.), *The Maisky Diaries: Red Ambassador to the Court of St. James's 1932–1943* (Yale: Yale University Press, 2015).

Reith, Sir John; Stuart, Charles (ed.), *The Reith Diaries* (London: William Collins, 1975).

Stevenson, Frances; Taylor, A. J. P (ed.), *Lloyd George: A Diary by Frances Stevenson* (London: Hutchinson, 1971).

Streat, Raymond; Dupree, Margaret (ed.), *Lancashire and Whitehall: The Diary of Sir Raymond Streat* (Manchester: Manchester University Press, 1987).

Sylvester, A. J.; Cross, Colin (ed.), *Life with Lloyd George: The Diary of A J Sylvester 1931–45* (London: Macmillan, 1975).

MEMOIRS

Attlee, C. R., *As It Happened* (Odhams, n.d.)

Avon, Earl of, *The Eden Memoirs: Facing the Dictators* (London: Cassell, 1962).

Baillie, Hugh, *High Tension: The recollections of Hugh Baillie* (London: Laurie, 1960).

Beaverbrook, Lord & Taylor, A. J. P. (ed.), *The Abdication of King Edward VIII* (New York: Atheneum, 1965).

Boothby, Bob, *Recollections of a Rebel* (London: Hutchinson, 1978).

Butler, Lord, *The Art of the Possible* (London: Hamish Hamilton, 1971).

Citrine, Lord, *Men and Work* (London: Hutchinson, 1964).

Cooper, Duff, *Old Men Forget* (London: Rupert Hart-Davis, 1955).

Coote, Colin R., *Editorial* (London: Eyre & Spottiswoode, 1965).

Hardinge, Helen, *Loyal to Three Kings* (London: William Kimber, 1967).

Hesse, Fritz, *Das Spiel um Deutschland* (Munich: Paul List, 1953).

Home, Lord, *The Way the Wind Blows* (London: William Collins, 1976).

MacDonald, Malcolm, *People & Places* (London: Collins, 1969).

Macmillan, Harold, *Winds of Change 1914–1939* (London: Macmillan, 1966).

Massey, Vincent, *What's Past Is Prologue: The Memoirs of the Rt. Hon. Vincent Massey* (London: Macmillan, 1963).

Reith, J. C. W., *Into the Wind* (London: Hodder & Stoughton, 1949).

Schmidt, Paul, *Statist auf Diplomatischer Bühne 1923-45* (Bonn: Athenäum, 1949).

Shaughnessy, Alfred, *Both Ends of the Candle* (London: Peter Owen, 1978).

Sitwell, Osbert, *Rat Week* (London: Michael Joseph, 1986).

Stuart, Viscount, *Within the Fringe* (London: The Bodley Head, 1967).

Templewood, Viscount (Sir Samuel Hoare), *Nine Troubled Years* (London: Collins, 1954).

Ustinov, Peter, *Dear Me* (London: William Heinemann, 1977).

Windsor, Duchess of, *The Heart Has Its Reasons* (London: Michael Joseph, 1956).

Windsor, Duke of, *A King's Story: The Memoirs of H.R.H. The Duke of Windsor* (London: Cassell, 1951).

Woolton, Earl of, *Memoirs* (London: Cassell, 1959).

WORKS BY CONTEMPORARIES*

Baldwin, Windham, *My Father: The True Story* (London: Allen & Unwin, 1956).

Birkenhead, Lord, *Walter Monckton* (London: Weidenfeld & Nicolson, 1969).

Boca, Geoffrey, *She Might Have Been Queen* (London: Express Books, 1955).

Bryan III, J. & Murphy, Charles J. V., *The Windsor Story* (London: Granada, 1979).

Colvin, Ian, *Vansittart in Office* (London: Gollancz, 1965).

Feiling, Keith, *Life of Neville Chamberlain* (London: Macmillan, 1946).

Gourlay, Logan (ed.), *The Beaverbrook I Knew* (London: Quartet, 1984).

Martin, Kingsley, *The Crown and the Establishment* (London: Hutchinson, 1962).

Paterson, Michael, *Personal Accounts of Sir Winston Churchill* (Exeter: David Charles, 2006).

Rhodes James, Robert, *Victor Cazalet* (London: Hamish Hamilton, 1976).

---

* Or drawn essentially from contemporary sources

Roskill, Stephen, *Hankey: Man of Secrets Volume III 1931–63* (London: William Collins, 1974).

Stirling, Alfred, *Lord Bruce: The London Years* (Stroud: Hawthorn, 1974).

Young, G. M., *Stanley Baldwin* (London: Rupert Hart-Davis, 1952).

SECONDARY WORKS

Andrew, Christopher, *Defence of the Realm: The Authorized History of MI5* (London: Allen Lane, 2009).

Beaken, Robert, *Cosmo Lang: Archbishop in War and Crisis* (London: I.B. Tauris, 2012).

Bloch, Michael, *Operation Willi* (London: Weidenfeld & Nicolson, 1984).

Bloch, Michael, *The Secret File on the Duke of Windsor* (London: Bantam, 1988).

Bloch, Michael, *The Reign & Abdication of Edward VIII* (London: Bantam, 1990).

Bloch, Michael, *Ribbentrop* (London: Bantam, 1994).

Bloch, Michael, *The Duchess of Windsor* (London: Weidenfeld & Nicolson, 1996).

Bourne, Richard, *Lords of Fleet Street: The Harmsworth Dynasty* (London: Unwin Hyman, 1990).

Bradford, Sarah, *George VI* (London: Weidenfeld & Nicolson, 1989).

Brendon, *Our Own Dear Queen* (London: Secker & Warburg, 1986).

Bullock, Alan, *The Life and Times of Ernest Bevin Vol. 1* (London: Heinemann, 1969).

Campbell, John, *Lloyd George: The Goat in the Wilderness* (London: Jonathan Cape, 1977).

Chisholm, Anne & Davie, Michael, *Lord Beaverbrook: A Life* (New York: Knopf, 1992).

Day, Peter, *The Bedbug* (London: Biteback Publishing, 2014).

Donaldson, Frances, *Edward VIII* (London: Weidenfeld & Nicolson, 1974).

Donaldson, Frances, *A Twentieth Century Life* (London: Weidenfeld & Nicolson, 1992).

Dorril, Steven, *MI6: Inside the Covert World of Her Majesty's Secret Intelligence Service* (London: Fourth Estate, 1998).

Farman, Christopher, *The General Strike: May 1926* (London: Panther, 1974).

Gilbert, Martin, *Prophet of Truth: Winston S. Churchill 1922–1939* (London: William Heinemann, 1976).

Graves, Robert & Hodge, Alan, *The Long Weekend* (London: Hutchinson, 1940).

Greig, Geordie, *Louis and the Prince* (London: Hodder & Stoughton, 1999).

Griffiths, Richard, *Fellow Travellers of the Right: British Enthusiasts for Nazi Germany 1933–39* (London: Constable & Robinson, 1980).

Harris, Kenneth, *Attlee* (London: Weidenfeld & Nicolson, 1982).

Hennessy, Elizabeth, *A Domestic History of the Bank of England 1930–1960* (Cambridge: Cambridge University Press, 1992).

Higham, Charles, *Mrs. Simpson: Secret Lives of the Duchess of Windsor* (London: Sidgwick & Jackson, 1988).

Jago, Michael, *Clement Attlee: The Inevitable Prime Minister* (London: Biteback Publishing, 2014).

Jeffrey, Keith, *MI6: The History of the Secret Intelligence Service 1909–1949* (London: Bloomsbury, 2010).

Jenkins, Roy, *Churchill* (London: Macmillan, 2001).

Kershaw, Ian, *Making Friends with Hitler: Lord Londonderry and Britain's Road to War* (London: Allen Lane, 2004).

Lesley, Cole, *The Life of Noël Coward* (London: Jonathan Cape, 1976). Page reference to 1978 Penguin paperback edition.

Middlemas, Keith & Barnes, John, *Baldwin* (London: Weidenfeld & Nicolson, 1969).

Montgomery Hyde, H., *Baldwin: The Unexpected Prime Minister* (London: Hart-Davis MacGibbon, 1973).

Murphy, Philip, *Alan Lennox-Boyd: A Biography* (London: I.B. Tauris, 1999).

O'Halpin, Eunan, *Head of the Civil Service: A Study of Sir Warren Fisher* (Abingdon-on-Thames: Routledge, 1989).

Padfield, Peter, *Hess, Hitler and Churchill: The Real Turning Point of the Second World War – A Secret History* (London: Icon, 2013).

Parker, R. A. C., *Churchill and Appeasement* (London: Macmillan, 2000).

Perkins, Anne, *A Very British Strike: 3 May–12 May 1926* (London: Macmillan, 2006).

Public Record Office, *The Security Service 1908–1945: The Official History* (Public Record Office, 1999).

Pugh, Martin, *Hurrah for the Blackshirts* (London: Pimlico, 2006).

Ramsden, John, *The Age of Balfour and Baldwin 1902–1940* (London: Longman, 1978).

Rhodes-James, Robert, *A Spirit Undaunted: The Political Role of George VI* (London: Little, Brown, 1998).

Rose, Andrew, *The Prince, The Princess and the Perfect Murder* (London: Coronet, 2013).

Rose, Kenneth, *King George V* (London: Weidenfeld & Nicolson, 1983).

Searle, G. D., *Corruption in British Politics, 1895–1930* (Oxford: Clarendon Press, 1987).

Sebba, Anne, *That Woman* (London: Weidenfeld & Nicolson, 2011). Page references to 2012 Phoenix paperback edition.

Shawcross, William, *Queen Elizabeth: The Queen Mother: The Official Biography* (London: Macmillan, 2009).

Stewart, Graham, *Burying Caesar: Churchill, Chamberlain and the Battle for the Tory Party* (London: Weidenfeld & Nicolson, 1999).

Taylor, A. J. P., *Beaverbrook* (London: Hamish Hamilton, 1972).

Taylor, S. J., *The Great Outsiders: Northcliffe, Rothermere and the Daily Mail* (London: Weidenfeld & Nicolson, 1996).

Thornton, Michael, *Royal Feud* (London: Michael Joseph, 1985).

Thorpe, D. R., *Alec Douglas-Home* (London: Sinclair-Stevenson, 1997).

Toye, Richard, *Lloyd George & Churchill: Rivals for Greatness* (London: Macmillan, 2007).

Vickers, Hugo, *Behind Closed Doors* (London: Hutchinson, 2011).

Vickers, Hugo, *Elizabeth: The Queen Mother* (London: Hutchinson, 2005).

Wheeler Bennett, John W., *King George VI: His Life and Reign* (London: Macmillan, 1958).

Williams, Susan, *The People's King* (London: Allen Lane, 2003).

Ziegler, Philip, *King Edward VIII* (London: Collins, 1990).

Ziegler, Philip, *Mountbatten* (London: Collins, 1985).

ARTICLES

Entwistle, John, http://www.thebaron.info/archives/ultra-british-editor-who-loved-america-took-royal-bribes Accessed 22 June 2016.

White, R. & Yorath, J., 'The Crystal Palace – Demise', The White Files – Architecture. Retrieved 15 June 2010. (Quotations from Yorath's original *Radio Times* article.)

ENDNOTES

Unless otherwise stated, dates are 1936. See bibliography for further details of authorities cited. Authors' names have been omitted for *A King's Story* (Duke of Windsor) and *The Heart Has Its Reasons* (Duchess of Windsor).

NOTES TO PROLOGUE (PP XIII–XXII)

1. Dugdale diary
2. Nicolson diaries, 10 December
3. Boca, *She Might Have Been Queen*, p. 115 quoting Duff Cooper
4. Dugdale diary
5. Templewood, *Nine Troubled Years*, p. 221
6. Channon diaries, 10 December
7. Nicolson diaries, 10 December
8. Hansard, 10 December
9. Dugdale diary
10. Nicolson diaries, 10 December
11. Hansard, 10 December
12. Jones, *A Diary with Letters*, p. 293
13. Amery diaries, 10 December; Nicolson diaries, 10 December
14. Chamberlain diary, 6 December
15. The National Archives [hereafter NA], CAB 23/68
16. Templewood, *Nine Troubled Years*, p. 221
17. Nicolson diaries, 10 December
18. Chamberlain to Hilda, 13 December
19. Chamberlain to Ida, 8 December
20. Nicolson diaries, 10 December
21. Channon diaries, 10 December
22. Amery diary quoted in Gilbert, *Winston S. Churchill*, Vol. V, p. 827
23. Duff Cooper diaries
24. Bruce Lockhart diaries, 10 December

25. NA CAB 1/466; NA CAB 23/68
26. Duff Cooper diaries
27. Duff Cooper review of G. M. Young's *Baldwin* in *Daily Mail*, 14 November 1952

NOTES TO CHAPTER 1 (PP 3–18)

1. Middlemas & Barnes, *Baldwin*, p. 976; Windham Baldwin papers 3/3/14; extracts from Lord Hinchingbrooke's diary, 26 February 1937
2. Ziegler, *King Edward VIII*, Chapters 2 & 3; Frances Donaldson, *Edward VIII*, Chapters 1 & 2
3. Frances Stevenson diary, 16 March 1920, 18 June 1921, 23 May 1934
4. Rose, *The Prince, The Princess and the Perfect Murder*, Chapter 18
5. Mrs Simpson to Duke of Windsor, 7 April 1937
6. Ziegler, *King Edward VIII*, p. 231
7. Vickers, *Behind Closed Doors*, p. 280
8. Roskill, *Hankey: Man of Secrets*, Vol. III, p. 218
9. *The Maisky Diaries*, 15 November 1934, pp 16–17
10. *The Times*, 12 June 1935
11. *A King's Story*, p. 254
12. DGFP Series C, Vol. IV, p. 331
13. *The Times*, 13 June 1935
14. NA CAB 23/82, Meeting of 19 June 1935
15. Ziegler, *King Edward VIII*, p. 209
16. Templewood papers, IX/7, Abdication notes
17. Vansittart papers, VNST 2/27, Vansittart to Wigram, 7 November 1935
18. Lascelles, *King's Counsellor*, p. 104
19. Lascelles, *King's Counsellor*, p. 104
20. Ziegler, *King Edward VIII*, pp 183–5
21. Lascelles, *King's Counsellor*, p. 105
22. NA PREM 1/466
23. Reith diaries, 21 January
24. Attlee, *As It Happened*, p. 102
25. NA PREM 1/466
26. NA MEPO 10/35
27. Chamberlain to Hilda, 13 December
28. NA MEPO 10/35, undated report, ERNEST SIMPSON
29. *Oxford Dictionary of National Biography*, entry for Nancy Cunard, accessed 4 April 2016
30. Windham Baldwin papers, 11/1/1, Monica Baldwin, 'An Unpublished Page of English History'

NOTES TO CHAPTER 2 (PP 19–31)

1. Jones diary, 26 April 1926
2. O'Halpin, *Head of the Civil Service*, Chapter 1
3. NA T199/50b, Treasury Minute, 15 September 1915

4. O'Halpin, *Head of the Civil Service*, pp 8f
5. BBK G/6/9, Fisher to Lord Chamberlain, 18 July 1922
6. NA T160/639, 'Treasury Control', Fisher to Chancellor of the Exchequer and Prime Minister, 6 March 1923
7. Woolton memoirs, p. 139
8. O'Halpin, *Head of the Civil Service*, pp 142–7
9. NA PREM 1/53, Stamfordham to Waterhouse, 26 February and 3 March 1926
10. Streat diary, 16 February 1933
11. Thomas Jones papers, P3/68, notes of conversation with Sir Horace Wilson, 16 July 1942
12. Reith diaries, 2 March 1934, p. 117
13. Bullock, *The Life and Times of Ernest Bevin*, Vol. 1, p. 334
14. George Peden, notes of interview with Sir Thomas and Lady Padmore, 15 March 1975
15. Streat diary, 26 July 1935
16. Lord Donoghue, email to author, 14 February 2006
17. Jones, *A Diary with Letters*, p. 186

NOTES TO CHAPTER 3 (PP 33–59)

1. NA PREM 1/466
2. Roskill, *Hankey: Man of Secrets*, Vol. III, p. 215
3. Duff Cooper diaries, 20 January
4. Jones, *A Diary with Letters*, p. 163
5. NAA M104, Bruce memorandum, 15 November
6. Reith diaries, 21 January, p. 185
7. Duff Cooper diaries, 20 January
8. Ziegler, *King Edward VIII*, pp 249–50, *A King's Story* pp 274–5
9. *The Times*, 3 February
10. *Oxford Dictionary of National Biography*, entries for Albert Baillie and John Dalton, accessed 4 April 2016
11. NA PREM 1/466
12. Lascelles, *King's Counsellor*, pp 107–108
13. Chamberlain diary, first entry, second volume, n.d. but 18–23 November
14. Davidson memorandum, February 1936, quoted in Sebba, *That Woman*, p. 125
15. Channon diaries, 12 June 1935
16. Sitwell, *Rat Week*, p. 35
17. Templewood papers, IX/7 Abdication notes
18. Andrew, *Defence of the Realm*, pp 195–200; Ustinov, *Dear Me*, p. 60
19. *The Heart Has Its Reasons*, pp 234f
20. Ziegler, *Edward VIII*, p. 273
21. Davidson memorandum, February 1936, quoted in Sebba, *That Woman*
22. Reith diaries, 6 March
23. Lascelles, *King's Counsellor*, p. 108
24. NA CAB PREM 1/466
25. Reith diaries, 8 April
26. DGFP Series C, Vol. IV, p. 106
27. Hesse, *Das Spiel um Deutschland*, pp 60f, Bundesarchiv Nachlaß Hesse 1322/1/1

28. Nachlaß Hesse, 1322/4/39
29. Hesse, *Das Spiel um Deutschland*, p. 37
30. Bloch, *Ribbentrop*, p. 129
31. Nuremberg Trials evidence 075-TC, von Ribbentrop to Hitler, 2 January 1938
32. NA PREM 1/466, Ziegler, *King Edward VIII*, p. 273
33. NA PREM 1/466
34. NA PREM 1/466
35. Ziegler, *King Edward VIII*, pp 255f
36. Donaldson, *King Edward VIII*, p. 184
37. Channon diaries, 6 December 1935
38. Lascelles, *King's Counsellor*, p. 138
39. Channon diaries, 6 December 1935, NA PREM 1/466
40. Ziegler, *King Edward VIII*, pp 259ff
41. Greig, *Louis and the Prince*, pp 258-62
42. *The Times*, 3 March
43. Jones, *A Diary with Letters*, p. 189
44. *The Times*, 16 March
45. *The Heart Has Its Reasons*, p. 243
46. Reith diaries, 28 May
47. Nicolson diaries, 28 May, pp 261-2
48. Brooks journal, 22 July
49. NA PREM 1/466
50. Nicolson diaries, 13 July
51. NA PREM 1/466
52. Streat diaries, 13 December
53. DGFP Series C, Vol. IV, p. 980
54. DGFP Series C, Vol. IV, pp 980-81
55. DGFP Series C, Vol. IV, p. 1001
56. NA PREM 1/466
57. Wallis to Ernest Simpson, quoted in Sebba, *That Woman*, p. 141
58. *Aberdeen Evening Express*, 23 September
59. Citrine, *Men and Work*, p. 327
60. Channon diaries, 11 November
61. Brooks journal, 22 October
62. Thornton, *Royal Feud*, p. 75
63. Goddard narrative
64. Bruce Lockhart diaries, 1 September 1928, pp 70-71
65. Beaverbrook (ed. A. J. P. Taylor), *The Abdication of King Edward VIII*, pp 19-20
66. Beaverbrook (ed. A. J. P. Taylor), *The Abdication of King Edward VIII*, p. 30
67. Beaverbrook (ed. A. J. P. Taylor), *The Abdication of King Edward VIII*, p. 30 fn.
68. Mrs Simpson to King, 15 October [misdated as 14 in *Wallis and Edward*]
69. Beaverbrook (ed. A. J. P. Taylor), *The Abdication of King Edward VIII*, p. 30
70. Jones, *A Diary with Letters*, p. 277
71. Chamberlain to Ida, 13 April
72. Ramsden, *The Age of Balfour and Baldwin 1902-1940*, pp 297f and 306-12; Searle, *Corruption in British Politics, 1895-1930*, pp 399-404 and 409ff

NOTES TO CHAPTER 4 (PP 61–70)

1. NA PREM 1/466
2. Jones, *A Diary with Letters*, pp 236–7
3. Baldwin to Brett Young, 31 August, reproduced in Williamson & Baldwin, *Baldwin Papers*, p. 381
4. Crathorne papers, Baldwin to Thomas Dugdale, 11 August; Baldwin to Nancy Dugdale, 25 January 1941
5. Jones, *A Diary with Letters*, pp 266–7
6. Windham Baldwin papers, 3/3/9, note dated 10/5/61
7. Jones, *A Diary with Letters*, p. 266
8. Recollection of Florence Copeland, head cook at Blickling Hall, displayed on National Trust information board
9. Hardinge, 'Before The Abdication' letter to *The Times*, 29 November 1955
10. NA PREM 1/466
11. NA PREM 1/466
12. NA PREM 1/466
13. Chamberlain to Ida, 11 October
14. NA PREM 1/466, NA KV 4/1
15. NA PREM 1/466 Draft
16. NA PREM 1/466
17. Dugdale diary
18. NA KV 4/1
19. Andrew, *Defence of the Realm: The Authorized History of MI5*, pp 125f; Perkins, *A Very British Strike: 3 May–12 May 1926*, Chapter 3

NOTES TO CHAPTER 5 (PP 73–86)

1. NA PREM 1/466
2. Sitwell, *Rat Week*, p. 30
3. NA PREM 1/446, Constitutional Crisis: Attitude of the British Press
4. Chamberlain diary, 25 October
5. Chamberlain to Hilda, 17 October
6. Chamberlain to Ida, 24 October
7. Chamberlain diary, 25 October
8. Hardinge, *Loyal to Three Kings*, pp 117–18
9. Chamberlain to Hilda, 17 October
10. Chamberlain to Hilda, 4 April; Chamberlain to Ida, 13 April
11. Citrine, *Men and Work*, p. 326
12. Schmidt, *Statist auf Diplomatischer Bühne, 1923–45*, p. 376
13. NA PREM 1/466
14. NA PREM 1/466
15. NA CAB 23/68 meeting of 27 November
16. NA PREM 1/466
17. PREM NA PREM 1/466
18. Hardinge, *Loyal to Three Kings*, p. 119

19. Hardinge, *Loyal to Three Kings*, p. 119
20. Chamberlain diary, 25 October
21. Goddard narrative
22. NA PREM 1/466
23. Monckton narrative
24. NA CAB 127/372, Bridges to Lascelles, 17 December 1945
25. Goddard narrative
26. Chamberlain diary, 26 October
27. Chamberlain diary, 26 October
28. Vickers, *Behind Closed Doors*, p. 13
29. NA PREM 1/466
30. Chamberlain diary, 26 October
31. Chamberlain diary, 26 October
32. Chamberlain diary, 26 October
33. Chamberlain diary, 26 October

NOTES TO CHAPTER 6 (PP 87–109)

1. Jones, *A Diary with Letters*, p. 280; NA PREM 1/466
2. Channon diaries, 11 November. The headline is almost certainly apocryphal; very few US tabloid readers would have known that Wolsey was the architect of Henry VIII's divorce
3. NA MacDonald diary, 29 October
4. Helen Hardinge diary, 1 November
5. Chamberlain diary, 4 November
6. Chamberlain diary, 4 November
7. Chamberlain diary, 4 November
8. Chamberlain diary, 2 November
9. NA PREM 1/466
10. NA PREM 1/466
11. NA PREM 1/449, Note by Attorney General, 4 November
12. NAA M104, Bruce memorandum, 15 November
13. Somervell journal, quoted in Montgomery-Hyde, *Baldwin: The Unexpected Prime Minister*, p. 567
14. NA PREM 1/449, Memorandum by Parliamentary Counsel, 4 November
15. NA PREM 1/449, Gwyer memorandum, 5 November
16. Middlemas and Barnes, *Baldwin*, p. 987
17. Chamberlain diary, 4 November
18. Chamberlain diary, 4 November
19. Chamberlain to Hilda, 14 November
20. Chamberlain to Hilda, 4 April; Chamberlain to Ida, 13 April
21. Chamberlain diary, 25 November; NA PREM 1/463, Fisher to Chamberlain, 7 November
22. Chamberlain diary, 25 November
23. Chamberlain diary, 4 November
24. NA PREM 1/466
25. NA PREM 1/466
26. Chamberlain diary, 4 November
27. Helen Hardinge diary, 6 November

28. NA PREM 1/463, Fisher to Chamberlain, 7 November; Hardinge *Loyal to Three Kings*, p. 131
29. Hardinge, *Loyal to Three Kings*, p. 131
30. NA TS 22/1/1, Mainwaring to King's Proctor, 20 October; Thomson to Barnes, 6 November
31. Hardinge, *Loyal to Three Kings*, p. 131
32. Hardinge, *Loyal to Three Kings*, p. 131
33. NA PREM 1/463, Fisher to Chamberlain. Drafts also NA PREM 1/463 given in full as Appendices A and B
34. Davidson, *Memoirs of a Conservative*, p. 417
35. NA PREM 1/463
36. NA PREM 1/463, Chamberlain handwritten amendments to draft letter
37. Chamberlain diary, first entry, second volume, n.d. but 18–23 November
38. NA PREM 1/466
39. Stanley Baldwin papers, add. papers, Lucy Baldwin memorandum, 17 November
40. NAA M104, Bruce memorandum, 15 November
41. Hardinge, *Loyal to Three Kings*, p. 132
42. Lascelles to Helen Hardinge, 1964, private collection
43. Hardinge, *Loyal to Three Kings*, p. 133. Given in full as Appendix C
44. Hardinge, *Loyal to Three Kings*, p. 134
45. Hardinge, *Loyal to Three Kings*, pp 14–15
46. Helen Hardinge diary, 13 November
47. NA PREM 1/466
48. Davidson, *Memoirs of a Conservative*, p. 415
49. Stanley Baldwin papers, add. papers, Lucy Baldwin memorandum, 17 November
50. Hardinge letter to *The Times*, 29 November 1955
51. NA PREM 1/466
52. NA PREM 1/466
53. Chamberlain diary, first entry, second volume, n.d. but 18–23 November
54. Chamberlain diary, first entry, second volume, n.d. but 18–23 November
55. NA MacDonald diary, 13 November
56. NA PREM 1/466
57. NA PREM 1/466
58. Reith diaries, 9 February 1940
59. Monckton narrative
60. Chamberlain diary, first entry, second volume, n.d. but 18–23 November

NOTES TO CHAPTER 7 (PP 111–22)

1. *A King's Story*, p. 328
2. Bryan & Murphy, *The Windsor Story*, p. 217
3. *A King's Story*, pp 327f
4. Bryan & Murphy, *The Windsor Story*, pp 217f
5. Monckton narrative
6. BBK G/6/27
7. BBK G/6/4, telegram, Monckton to Beaverbrook, 16 November
8. Beaverbrook (ed. A. J. P. Taylor), *The Abdication of King Edward VIII*, p. 37
9. Duff Cooper diaries; Beaverbrook (ed. A. J. P. Taylor), *The Abdication of King Edward VIII*, p. 37

10. Hardinge, *Loyal to Three Kings*, p. 138; PREM 1/466
11. King's account of the audience, *A King's Story*, pp 331–3, Baldwin's NA CAB 23/86
12. Chamberlain diary, first entry, second volume, n.d. but 18–23 November
13. BBK G/6/27, draft memoirs
14. NA PREM 1/466
15. Duff Cooper diaries
16. Dugdale diary
17. Stanley Baldwin papers, add. papers, Lucy Baldwin memorandum, 17 November
18. Chamberlain diary, first entry, second volume, n.d. but 18–23 November
19. Stanley Baldwin papers, add. papers, Lucy Baldwin memorandum, 17 November
20. Templewood papers, IX/7 Abdication notes
21. Duff Cooper diaries
22. Monckton, additional note, 13 August 1940
23. BBK G/6/27
24. Shawcross, *Queen Mother*, p. 372 fn.
25. Channon diaries, 1 August 1938
26. Channon diaries, 1 August 1938
27. *The Times*, 29 April
28. Margesson, quoted in Middlemas & Barnes, *Baldwin*, p. 996
29. Duff Cooper diaries
30. Chamberlain diary, first entry, second volume, n.d. but 18–23 November
31. Chamberlain diary, first entry, second volume, n.d. but 18–23 November
32. Chamberlain diary
33. NA PREM 1/466
34. Chamberlain diary, 25 November
35. Chamberlain to Ida, 8 December

NOTES TO CHAPTER 8 (PP 123–40)

1. Duff Cooper diaries
2. Nicolson diaries, 28 October, p. 276; Bruce Lockhart diaries, 13 November, p. 357; Chamberlain diary, 25 October
3. Bloch (ed.), *Wallis and Edward*, p. 253
4. Beaverbrook (ed. A. J. P. Taylor), *The Abdication of King Edward VIII*, p. 55
5. *The Heart Has Its Reasons*, p. 269
6. *A King's Story*, p. 342
7. NA PREM CAB 301/101, Grant memorandum, 8 December
8. Dugdale diary, Sitwell, *Rat Week*, pp 35–6
9. NAA M104, Bruce memorandum, 15 November
10. MacDonald diary, 21 November
11. Jones, *A Diary with Letters*, p. 288
12. Windham Baldwin papers, 11/1/1 Monica Baldwin, 'An Unpublished Page of English History'
13. *The Heart Has Its Reasons*, p. 269; *A King's Story*, p. 342
14. *A King's Story*, p. 342
15. NA CAB 23/68
16. NA CAB 23/68
17. Graves & Hodges, *The Long Weekend*, p. 361; Williams, *The People's King*, passim

18. *A King's Story*, p. 346
19. Beaverbrook (ed. A. J. P. Taylor), *The Abdication of King Edward VIII*, p. 51
20. Beaverbrook (ed. A. J. P. Taylor), *The Abdication of King Edward VIII*, p. 54
21. Sebba, *That Woman*, p. 184
22. Churchill to Clementine, 27 November, quoted in Gilbert (ed.), *Prophet of Truth: Winston S. Churchill 1922–1939*
23. NA PREM 1/466
24. *Sunday Times*, 26 April 1964
25. Butler, *The Art of the Possible*, pp 88f
26. Dugdale diary
27. Colville diary, 10 May 1940
28. Lascelles, *King's Counsellor*, p. 270
29. Mrs Simpson to Bessie Merryman, 4 May
30. Churchill memorandum, CHAR 2/264
31. Lascelles, *King's Counsellor*, p. 414
32. Hardinge, *Loyal to Three Kings*, p. 102
33. Lesley, *The Life of Noël Coward*, p. 210 of Penguin 1978 paperback
34. Nicolson diaries 7 December
35. Dugdale diary
36. Beaverbrook (ed. A. J. P. Taylor), *The Abdication Of King Edward VIII*, p. 65
37. Amery diaries, 4 December
38. Amery diaries, 4 December
39. Channon diaries, 22 November
40. Dugdale diary
41. Davidson, *Memoirs of a Conservative*, pp 414–15
42. Dugdale diary
43. Chamberlain diary, 25 November
44. Chamberlain diary, 25 November
45. Chamberlain diary, 26 November
46. Dugdale diary
47. Jones, *A Diary with Letters*, p. 288
48. Chamberlain diary, 2 December
49. Citrine, *Men and Work*, pp 327f
50. Attlee, *As It Happened*, p. 103
51. Harris, *Attlee*, p. 165

NOTES TO CHAPTER 9 (PP 141–51)

1. NA CAB 23/68
2. Duff Cooper diaries
3. Dugdale diary
4. NA CAB 23/68
5. Duff Cooper diaries
6. NA CAB 23/68
7. NA CAB 23/68
8. Lord Zetland to Lord Linlithgow, 27 November, reproduced in Gilbert, Martin (ed.), *The Churchill Documents, Volume 13: The Coming of War 1936–1939*

9. NA CAB 23/68
10. Nicolson diary
11. Channon diaries, 28 November
12. Channon diaries, 30 November
13. Beaverbrook (ed. A. J. P. Taylor), *The Abdication of King Edward VIII*, pp 57f
14. Duff Cooper diaries
15. Colville diaries, p. 667; Boca, *She Might Have Been Queen*, pp 90–92
16. Channon diaries, 3 December
17. *A King's Story*, p. 347; NA CAB 301/101
18. Channon diaries, 27 November
19. *The Heart Has Its Reasons*, p. 271
20. John Entwistle, http://www.thebaron.info/archives/ultra-british-editor-who-loved-america-took-royal-bribes
21. *The Heart Has Its Reasons*, p. 272; *A King's Story*, pp 356–7
22. Bryan & Murphy, *The Windsor Story*, p. 245
23. BBK G/6/29, Brownlow memorandum, 'The Beaverbrook Assignment, Additional Marginal Notes', n.d.
24. Channon diaries, 1 December
25. Channon diaries, 1 December
26. White, R. & Yorath, J., 'The Crystal Palace – Demise'. The White Files – Architecture, Retrieved 15 June 2010. (Quotations from Yorath's original *Radio Times* article.)
27. Michael Paterson, *Personal Accounts of Sir Winston Churchill*, p. 203

NOTES TO CHAPTER 10 (PP 155–63)

1. Chamberlain diary, 30 November
2. Beaverbrook (ed. A. J. P. Taylor), *The Abdication of King Edward VIII*, p. 66
3. Channon diaries, 30 November
4. Beaverbrook (ed. A. J. P. Taylor), *The Abdication of King Edward VIII*, p. 70
5. *History of The Times*, p. 1033
6. BBK G/6/19
7. *A King's Story*, p. 354
8. *A King's Story*, p. 354
9. *A King's Story*, p. 354
10. Beaverbrook (ed. A. J. P. Taylor), *The Abdication of King Edward VIII*, p. 80
11. Beaverbrook to Murphy, 3 September 1949, BBK G/6/23
12. *A King's Story*, p. 372 fn.
13. Baldwin to Selwyn Lloyd, 20 October 1947, quoted in Thorpe, *Alec Douglas-Home*, p. 67
14. NAA CP 4/10, Dominions Secretary to High Commissioner in Australia, 3 December
15. NA CAB 21/4100/2, from High Commissioner, Canberra, 2 December
16. Reith diaries, 16 April 1937, NA CAB 23/68
17. Chamberlain diary, 2 December
18. BBK G/6/12, Monckton to Duke of Windsor, 22 August 1949
19. Chamberlain diary, 2 December
20. NA CAB 23/68, Chamberlain diary, 2 December
21. NA CAB 23/68

2. Dugdale diary
3. CHAR 2/264, Memorandum, The Abdication of Edward VIII
4. CHAR 2/264, Memorandum, The Abdication of Edward VIII
5. Chamberlain diary, 4 December
6. CHAR 2/264, Memorandum, The Abdication of Edward VIII
7. CHAR 2/264, Memorandum, The Abdication of Edward VIII
8. CHAR 2/264, Memorandum, The Abdication of Edward VIII
9. BBK G/6/23
10. CHAR 2/264, Memorandum, The Abdication of Edward VIII
11. BBK G/6/23
12. BBK G/6/23
13. BBK G/6/23
14. CHAR 2/264, Memorandum, The Abdication of Edward VIII
15. CHAR 2/264, Memorandum, The Abdication of Edward VIII
16. Monckton narrative
17. Beaverbrook (ed. A. J. P. Taylor), *The Abdication of King Edward VIII*, p. 77
18. Beaverbrook (ed. A. J. P. Taylor), *The Abdication of King Edward VIII*, p. 76
19. BBK G/6/19
20. Channon diaries, 4 December, p. 92
21. BBK G/6/19
22. NA PREM 1/466
23. Duff Cooper diaries
24. NA CAB 23/68
25. BBK G/6/41, Duff Cooper review of Baldwin biography in *Daily Mail*, 14 November 1952 (quoted)
26. NA CAB 23/68, Duff Cooper diaries
27. Churchill papers 2/264, Churchill to Baldwin, 5 December
28. BBK G/6/23, BBK G/6/24
29. Beaverbrook (ed. A. J. P. Taylor), *The Abdication of King Edward VIII*, p. 78 fn. 1
30. Beaverbrook (ed. A. J. P. Taylor), *The Abdication of King Edward VIII*, pp 81–2
31. BBK G/6/19
32. BBK G/6/19
33. Beaverbrook (ed. A. J. P. Taylor), *The Abdication of King Edward VIII*, p. 105
34. BBK G/6/23, Beaverbrook to Murphy, 3 August 1949
35. Jenkins, *Churchill*, p. 500
36. BBK G/6/16, Churchill to King, evening 5 December
37. Churchill papers, 2/264, Churchill to Edward VIII, 7 December

NOTES TO CHAPTER 14 (PP 219–29)

1. BBK G/6/23
2. Sebba, *That Woman*, pp 150f
3. NAA M104, Bruce memorandum, 15 November
4. Somervell journal quoted in Montgomery-Hyde, *Baldwin: The Unexpected Prime Minister*, p. 567
5. MacDonald diary, 13 November

6. NAA M104, Bruce memorandum, 15 November
7. NA PREM 1/466
8. Chamberlain diary, 2 December
9. Stanley Baldwin papers, Simon to Baldwin, 3 December
10. NA CAB 23/68
11. NA CAB 23/68
12. G. M. Young, *Stanley Baldwin*, p. 240
13. BBK G/6/12, Monckton to Duke of Windsor, 22 August 1949
14. BBK G/6/24
15. BBK G/6/24
16. Dugdale diary
17. NA PREM 1/466
18. Dugdale diary
19. Monckton narrative
20. NA CAB 23/68
21. NA CAB 23/68
22. *A King's Story*, p. 390
23. Chamberlain diary, 5 December

NOTES TO CHAPTER 15 (PP 231–8)

1. Ziegler, *Edward VIII*, p. 315
2. Fielden papers, Fielden to Duke of Windsor, 10 August 1937
3. CHAR 2/264, Memorandum, The Abdication of Edward VIII
4. NA PREM 1/466
5. NA PREM 1/466, Flory cablegrams
6. Dugdale diary
7. NA PREM 1/466, draft
8. Dugdale diary
9. NA PREM 1/466
10. NA CAB 301/101, Hutchinson to Gardiner, 5 December
11. *A King's Story*, p. 386
12. NA PREM 1/466

NOTES TO CHAPTER 16 (PP 239–52)

1. Chamberlain diary, 5 December
2. NA PREM 1/466 draft
3. Chamberlain diary, 5 December
4. Chamberlain to Ida, 8 December
5. NA PREM 1/466
6. Chamberlain diary, 5 December
7. Chamberlain diary, 5 December
8. NA PREM 1/466
9. NA PREM 1/466
10. NA PREM 1/466

11. Windham Baldwin papers, 3/3/8(iii), notes on lunch with Monckton, 27 August 1950
12. CAB 23/68
13. CAB 23/68
14. Monckton narrative
15. Monckton narrative
16. NA CAB 23/68
17. Windham Baldwin 3/3/8(iii), notes on lunch with Monckton, 27 August 1950
18. Windham Baldwin 3/3/8(iii), notes on lunch with Monckton, 27 August 1950
19. Windham Baldwin 3/3/8(iii), notes on lunch with Monckton, 27 August 1950
20. NA PREM 1/466
21. NA PREM 1/466
22. Duff Cooper diaries
23. NA CAB 23/68
24. Chamberlain diary, 6 December
25. NA CAB 23/68
26. CAB 23/68
27. BBK G/6/19, *A King's Story*, p. 391
28. *A King's Story* pp 389–90, Monckton narrative

NOTES TO CHAPTER 17 (PP 255–70)

1. NA PREM 1/466
2. Channon diaries, 6 December
3. Duff Cooper diaries
4. Chamberlain diary, 7 December
5. Chamberlain diary, 7 December
6. MacDonald diary, 2 December
7. Monckton narrative
8. NA PREM 1/466, Goddard section
9. NA PREM 1/466
10. Peacock narrative
11. Chamberlain diary, 7 December
12. Chamberlain diary, 7 December
13. Chamberlain diary, 7 December
14. NA PREM 1/466, draft, TS 22/1/1, P. H. Edwards to Barnes, 5 December
15. NA PREM 1/449, Gwyer to Wilson, 7 December
16. Memo by Wigram quoted in Ziegler, *Edward VIII*, p. 330
17. NA PREM 1/466
18. NA PREM 1/466
19. *A King's Story*, p. 396
20. BBK G/6/23
21. BBK G/6/2-5, Brownlow memorandum, 'The Beaverbrook Assignment, Additional Marginal Notes'
22. Mrs Simpson to King, 6 December
23. Monckton narrative
24. Monckton narrative, Peacock notes
25. Churchill papers, 2/264, Boothby to Churchill, 11 December; de Courcy papers, memorandum 10 December

26. BBK G/6/13, Megan Lloyd George to David Lloyd George, 14 December
27. Nicolson diaries, 9 December
28. Crathorne papers, 'Kakoo' Rutland to Peggy Wakehurst, n.d.; Blanche Dugdale diaries, 13 December
29. Nicolson to Vita Sackville-West, 9 December, p. 284
30. Dugdale diary
31. Monckton narrative, Peacock narrative
32. Chamberlain diary, 7 December
33. Windham Baldwin papers, 11/1/1, Monica Baldwin, 'An Unpublished Page of English History'
34. Dugdale diary
35. Dugdale diary, Goddard narrative
36. Beaverbrook (ed. A. J. P. Taylor), *The Abdication of King Edward VIII*, p. 81
37. Dugdale diary
38. BBK G/6/30, Brownlow memorandum, 'The Goddard Incident', n.d.
39. Dugdale diary
40. Windham Baldwin papers, 3/3/8(iii), notes on lunch with Monckton, 27 August 1950
41. Bloch, *The Reign and Abdication of Edward VIII*, p. 187 fn.
42. Windham Baldwin papers, 11/1/1, Monica Baldwin, 'An Unpublished Page of English History'
43. Beaverbrook (ed. A. J. P. Taylor), *The Abdication of King Edward VIII*, pp 81–2

NOTES TO CHAPTER 18 (PP 271–81)

1. Reith diaries, 17 April 1937
2. NA PREM 1/466
3. NA PREM 1/466
4. Dugdale diary
5. Stanley Baldwin papers, Simon to Baldwin, 3 December
6. NA CAB 21/4100/2, Simon to Baldwin, 8 December
7. Stanley Baldwin papers, 175, Wilson note, 19 December
8. Monckton papers, Peacock notes
9. Somervell journal quoted in Montgomery-Hyde, *Baldwin: The Unexpected Prime Minister*
10. Stanley Baldwin papers, add. papers, Lucy Baldwin memorandum, 9 December; Monckton papers, Peacock narrative, 8 December
11. Windham Baldwin papers, 11/1/1, Monica Baldwin, 'An Unpublished Page of English History'
12. *A King's Story*, p. 398
13. *A King's Story*, p. 231
14. Monckton papers, Peacock narrative, 8 December
15. Stanley Baldwin papers, add. papers, Lucy Baldwin memorandum, 9 December
16. Windham Baldwin papers, 11/1/1, Monica Baldwin, 'An Unpublished Page of English History'
17. Monckton narrative
18. Peacock narrative
19. Dugdale diary
20. Dugdale diary
21. Dugdale diary
22. NA CAB 23/68, Dugdale diary
23. Monckton narrative
24. Dugdale diary

25. NA CAB 127/157, Dugdale notes
26. Dugdale diary, Monckton narrative
27. Peacock narrative
28. *A King's Story*, p. 400
29. Stanley Baldwin papers, add. papers, Lucy Baldwin memorandum, 9 December
30. Chamberlain diary, 8 December
31. Dugdale diary
32. NA CAB 23/68
33. Dugdale diary

NOTES TO CHAPTER 19 (PP 283-97)

1. Windham Baldwin papers, 11/1/1, Monica Baldwin, 'An Unpublished Page of English History'
2. BBK G/6/29, Brownlow memorandum, 'The Goddard Incident'
3. Dugdale diary
4. BBK G/6/29, Brownlow memorandum, 'The Goddard Incident'
5. Chamberlain diary, 8 December
6. NA PREM 1/466
7. NA PREM 1/466
8. NA PREM 1/466
9. Monckton papers, Goddard narrative
10. NA PREM 1/466
11. Chamberlain papers, NC8/22/3, Goddard narrative
12. Goddard narrative
13. NA PREM 1/466
14. NA CAB 23/68
15. NA CAB 23/68
16. Dugdale diary
17. Windham Baldwin papers, 3/3/14, extracts from Lord Hinchinbrooke's diary, 9 December
18. Dugdale diary
19. Dugdale diary
20. NA CAB 127/157, Dugdale memorandum, n.d.
21. NA CAB 23/68
22. NA CAB 23/68
23. NA CAB 23/68
24. Monckton narrative
25. Monckton narrative
26. Lascelles, *King's Counsellor*, p. 177
27. Young, *Stanley Baldwin*, p. 240
28. Murphy, *Alan Lennox-Boyd*, p. 49
29. *The Times*, 7 December
30. Murphy, *Alan Lennox-Boyd*, p. 49; Young, *Stanley Baldwin*, p. 240
31. Padfield, *Hess, Hitler and Churchill*, p. 81
32. Dugdale diary
33. Joseph Kennedy diary, 13 June 1938

34. Joseph Kennedy diary, 14 April 1939 and p. 326 fn.
35. De Courcy papers, memoranda, 10 and 12 March 1951
36. Jeffrey, *MI6*, pp 222f
37. De Courcy papers, memorandum on Kilbritain Newspapers, paper n.d. but post 1957
38. De Courcy papers, memorandum on Kilbritain Newspapers, paper n.d. but post 1957
39. Davenport-Hines & Sisman, *One Hundred Letters from Hugh Trevor-Roper*, pp 264–8, 313; Dorril, *MI6: Inside the Covert World of Her Majesty's Secret Intelligence Service*, p. 506
40. Osbert Sitwell, *Rat Week*, p. 36
41. Peacock narrative
42. Peacock narrative
43. Peacock narrative
44. Peacock narrative
45. Bryan & Murphy, *The Windsor Story*, p. 341
46. Beaverbrook (ed. A. J. P. Taylor), *The Abdication Of King Edward VIII*, p. 93
47. BBK 6/6/29, Additional marginal notes
48. Peacock narrative
49. BBK G/6/29
50. BBK G/6/2-5, notes of conversation with Brownlow
51. *A King's Story*, p. 403
52. Dugdale diary
53. Dugdale diary
54. NA CAB 127/157, Dugdale memorandum, n.d.
55. Reith diaries, 11 December
56. NA PREM 1/466

NOTES TO CHAPTER 20 (PP 299–310)

1. Monckton narrative, author's calculation
2. Hansard, 10 December
3. *A King's Story*, p. 407
4. *A King's Story*, p. 406
5. *A King's Story*, p. 407
6. NA PREM 1/455, undated note on Fort Belvedere paper
7. Monckton narrative
8. NA CAB 21/4100/2, memorandum, 10 December
9. NA CAB 21/4100/2, memorandum, 10 December, manuscript postscript
10. Monckton narrative
11. BBK G/6/23
12. Brooks journal, 10 December
13. Baldwin to Lang, 14 December quoted in Williamson & Baldwin, *Baldwin Papers*, pp 415f
14. *The Times*, 14 December
15. Thomas Jones diary quoted in Williamson & Baldwin, *Baldwin Papers*, p. 388 NA CAB 127/157, Dugdale memorandum, n.d.
16. Ziegler, *Edward VIII*, p. 327
17. Ziegler, *Edward VIII*, p. 326
18. Ziegler, *Edward VIII*, p. 326, author's estimate

19. Peacock narrative
20. George VI abdication narrative quoted in Wheeler-Bennett, *King George VI*, p. 287
21. *A King's Story*, p. 407
22. Boothby papers, Churchill to Boothby, 11 December
23. Alexander to Morshead, 10 March 1942, quoted in Ziegler, *Edward VIII*, p. 327
24. Monckton narrative
25. Ziegler, *Edward VIII*, p. 333
26. *A King's Story*, p. 408
27. Windham Baldwin papers, 3/3/8(iii), notes on lunch with Monckton, 27 August 1950
28. *A King's Story*, p. 412
29. Rhodes-James, *Victor Cazalet*, p. 190
30. Reith diaries, 12 December
31. Templewood, *Nine Troubled Years*, p. 222
32. Boca, *She Might Have Been Queen* p. 140; *The Windsor Story*, p. 287
33. Shaughnessy, *Both Ends of the Candle*, p. 45
34. Shaughnessy, *Both Ends of the Candle*, p. 45
35. Shaughnessy, *Both Ends of the Candle*, p. 45; Templewood papers, IX/7, Howe to C-in-C Portsmouth, 13 December
36. *A King's Story*, p. 409

NOTES TO CHAPTER 21 (PP 311–28)

1. NA PREM 1/452, Wilson to Chamberlain, 10 December
2. Higham, *Mrs Simpson*, p. 191
3. Reith diaries, 10 December
4. Chamberlain diary, 10 December
5. NA PREM 1/460, Wilson to Chamberlain, 10 December
6. Stanley Baldwin papers, 194, Simon memorandum, 6 January 1937
7. Chamberlain diary, 7 December
8. *A King's Story*, p. 373
9. Hesse, *Das Spiel um Deutschland*, p. 81
10. NA WO 339/37027
11. NA WO 339/37027
12. NA WO 339/37027, Rickatson-Hatt to War Office, 24 June and 19 September 1923; Reuters archives, Rickatson-Hatt memorandum, 17 February 1930
13. Bank of England Archive, Montagu Norman diary, 8 April 1941
14. http://www.thebaron.info/archives/ultra-british-editor-who-loved-america-took-royal-bribes
15. Hennessy, *A Domestic History of the Bank of England 1930–1960*, p. 378
16. Reuters archive memo, 26 January 1967, *The Times*, 25 January 1967
17. Nachlaß Fritz Hesse, 1322/4/39, response to criticism in article by G. von Studnitz, Davidson, *Memoirs of a Conservative*, p. 417
18. Jeffrey, *MI6: The History of the Secret Intelligence Service 1909–1949*, p. 317
19. Hesse, *Das Spiel um Deutschland*, p. 82
20. Public Record Office, *The Security Service 1908–1945*, p. 117
21. Andrew, *Defence of the Realm: The Authorized History of MI5*, p. 199
22. Hesse, *Das Spiel um Deutschland*, p. 83; Nachlaß Fritz Hesse, 1322/4/39, response to criticism in article by G. von Studnitz

23. Davidson, *Memoirs of a Conservative*, p. 417
24. DGFP, Series C, Vol. IV, p. 159
25. Public Record Office, *The Security Service 1908–1945*, p. 117, Nuremberg Trials evidence 075-TC, von Ribbentrop to Hitler, 2 January 1938
26. Cameron, *Hitler's Table Talk*, p. 678
27. Schmidt, *Statist auf Diplomatischer Bühne 1923–45*, p. 376
28. Public Record Office, *The Security Service 1908–1945*, p. 117
29. NA PREM 1/460, Wilson to Chamberlain, 11 December
30. NA PREM 1/460, Wilson to Chamberlain, 11 December
31. NA PREM 1/460, Wilson memorandum, 12 December
32. NA PREM 1/460, Wilson memorandum, 11 December
33. Chamberlain to Hilda, 13 December
34. NA TS 22/1/2, statement by Francis Stephenson
35. NA TS 22/1/2
36. Francis Stephenson interview, *Reading Eagle*, 20 March 1937
37. BBK G/6/30, memorandum by Miss O'Callaghan
38. BBK G/6/30, Jenkins to Williams, 20 September 1949
39. Boca, *She Might Have Been Queen*, p. 150
40. *The Times*, law report, 20 March 1937
41. Somervell journal quoted in Montgomery-Hyde, *Baldwin: The Unexpected Prime Minister*, p. 570
42. Somervell journal quoted in Montgomery-Hyde, *Baldwin: The Unexpected Prime Minister*, p. 569
43. NA PREM 1/460, Monckton to Wilson, 2 February 1937
44. NA TS 22/1/2, interview with Mr Cox
45. NA TS 22/1/2, interview with Mr Ernest Simpson
46. Somervell journal quoted in Montgomery-Hyde, *Baldwin: The Unexpected Prime Minister*, p. 570
47. Mrs Simpson to Bessie Merryman, 22 March 1937

NOTES TO CHAPTER 22 (PP 329–42)

1. Monckton narrative
2. Windham Baldwin papers, 11/3/13, note of conversation with Monckton
3. Channon diaries, 27 November
4. Boothby, *Recollections of a Rebel*, p. 197
5. NA MEPO 35/10, Channing (?) to Game, 19 December
6. Mrs Simpson to Duke of Windsor, 12 December
7. Mrs Simpson to Duke of Windsor, 12 December, 14 December
8. Mrs Simpson to Duke of Windsor, 7 February 1937
9. Mrs Simpson to Duke of Windsor, 6 March 1937
10. Duke of Windsor to Mrs Simpson, 2 April
11. NA MEPO 35/10, Channing (?) to Game, 19 December
12. Mrs Simpson to Duke of Windsor, 12 December
13. Mrs Simpson to Duke of Windsor, 6 March 1937
14. Information from Mrs Jackie Holland

15. Mrs Simpson to Duke of Windsor, 6 February 1937, Mrs Simpson to Duke of Windsor, n.d. c. 25 February 1937; Mrs Simpson to Duke of Windsor, 7 February 1937
16. Mrs Simpson to Duke of Windsor, 6 February 1937
17. Mrs Simpson to Bessie Merryman, 21 February 1937
18. Mrs Simpson to Bessie Merryman, 6 March 1937
19. Allen to Mrs Simpson, 8 March 1937
20. Mrs Simpson to Bessie Merryman, 11 March 1937
21. Mrs Simpson to Duke of Windsor, 7 April 1937
22. Mrs Simpson to Duke of Windsor, 3 January 1937
23. Mrs Simpson to Duke of Windsor, 3 January 1937
24. Ziegler, *Edward VIII*, pp 353–9
25. Stanley Baldwin papers, George VI to Baldwin, 4 May 1937
26. Ziegler, *Edward VIII*, pp 358
27. Thornton, *Royal Feud*, p. 147, citing Lady Hardinge, p. 165
28. Churchill papers, Churchill memorandum, 25 April 1937
29. Ziegler, *Edward VIII*, pp 357–60; Stanley Baldwin papers, George VI to Baldwin, 4 May 1937
30. Chamberlain diary, 26 May 1937
31. Baldwin to Selwyn Lloyd, 20 October 1947, quoted in Thorpe, *Alec Douglas-Home*, p. 67
32. Monckton narrative
33. Chamberlain diary, 30 May 1937
34. Bryan & Murphy, *The Windsor Story*, p. 341
35. Quoted in Jones, *A Diary with Letters*, p. 299
36. Frances Stevenson diary, 17 March 1937
37. Spencer Churchill papers, Churchill to Clementine, 25 January 1937, reproduced in *The Churchill Documents*, pp 549f; Churchill to Chamberlain, 24 March 1937
38. Churchill papers, 2/300, Churchill to Chamberlain, 24 March 1937; Churchill to Lloyd George, 25 March 1937, reproduced in *The Churchill Documents*, pp 634–6
39. Chamberlain to Hilda, 10 April; Chamberlain diary, 12 April 1937
40. NA PREM 1/463, Wigram to Chamberlain, 11 April
41. Chamberlain to Hilda, 10 April; Chamberlain diary, 12 April 1937
42. NA PREM 1/463, Wigram to Chamberlain, 11 April and 26 April 1937
43. Reith diaries, 16 April 1937
44. Windham Baldwin papers, 11/1/1, Monica Baldwin, 'An Unpublished Page of English History'
45. Mrs Simpson to Duke of Windsor, 7 March 1937
46. *Sarasota Herald Tribune*, 3 February 1941
47. Monckton narrative
48. Windham Baldwin papers, 11/3/13, note of conversation with Monckton

NOTES TO AFTERWORD (PP 343–5)

1. Feiling, *Neville Chamberlain*, p. 289
2. Home, *The Way the Wind Blows*, p. 51
3. Thorpe, *Alec Douglas-Home*, p. 67
4. Blanche Dugdale diary, 13 December
5. Windham Baldwin papers, 3/3/14, Extracts from Lord Hinchingbrooke's diary, 26 February 1937

NOTES TO APPENDICES (PP 347–51)

1.   NA PREM 1/463
2.   NA PREM 1/463
3.   NA PREM 1/463

INDEX